DICTIONARY OF INTERNATIONAL FINANCE
Second Edition

DICTIONARY OF INTERNATIONAL FINANCE

Second Edition

Julian Walmsley

A WILEY-INTERSCIENCE PUBLICATION

JOHN WILEY & SONS
New York

Published in the U.S.A. by
WILEY-INTERSCIENCE
a Division of John Wiley & Sons, Inc.,
New York

Library of Congress Cataloging-in-Publication Data

Walmsley, Julian.
    Dictionary of international finance.

    "A Wiley-Interscience publication."
    1. International finance–Dictionaries.
2. Finance–Dictionaries. I. Title.
HG151.W34   1985   332'.042'0321   85-12199
ISBN 0-471-83654-0

Printed in Great Britain

To Jane

and

to the memory

of my parents

Foreword

Many changes have taken place in international financial markets since the first edition of this Dictionary in 1979. In particular the growth of financial futures and options markets have spawned many new terms which have been incorporated. In addition, I have taken the opportunity to broaden the coverage of US markets.

Once again I owe an enormous debt to all those, too numerous to name, whose generous help has enabled me to compile the information included here. I must particularly thank my colleagues in the Barclays Group, particularly in the Barclays dealing rooms around the world and in the New York Capital Markets Group for all their help; responsibility for any errors remains my own.

New York
May 1985

A

A1. (1) Rating applied by LLOYDS to ships' seaworthiness; A1 is the top rating. Hence, 'A1 at Lloyds' indicates anything of very high quality or safety. (2) A COMMERCIAL PAPER rating applied by STANDARD & POOR'S. Ratings run from A1,A2,A3 down to D (for an issue either in default or expected to be in default on maturity). Compare MOODY'S.
Bibliography: *Standard & Poor's Rating Guide.* McGraw-Hill, New York, 1979.

AAA. A US BOND rating; the AAA symbol is granted by STANDARD & POOR'S 'only to bonds of the highest quality. The issuers of these bonds... enjoy superior management, have only a moderate amount of debt outstanding, boast a revenue structure that seems more than adequate to meet future spending needs...' Other ratings are AA,A,BBB, ABB,B, CCC,CC,C, D. Bonds below BBB are regarded as speculative; C is reserved for bonds on which no income is paid, and D for bonds in default. The ratings may be further refined by + or − to show relative standing: thus, the full ranking is AAA,AA+,AA,AA− etc. MOODY'S grant parallel ratings.
Bibliography: *Standard & Poor's Rating Guide.* McGraw-Hill, New York, 1979.
F.J. Fabozzi & I.M. Pollack (eds.) *Handbook of Fixed Income Securities.* Dow-Jones Irvin, Homewood, Ill., 1983.

absorption. A term referring to an economy's total demand for internal and external resources. It was introduced by S.S.Alexander in discussing the effects of a devaluation on the trade balance.The BALANCE OF TRADE equalled national income less national absorption.
Bibliography: S.S. Alexander. Effects of devaluation on a trade balance. *IMF Staff Papers,* Washington D.C., 1952.

acceptance. The signing of a BILL OF EXCHANGE or DRAFT (in the US) by the DRAWEE in formal acknowledgement of his obligation to honour the bill. Where the acceptor is a bank, the bill is a 'bank bill' (the US term is BANKER'S ACCEPTANCE) and is more easily discounted (resold).An exporter (or importer) may borrow by arranging for a bank to accept BILLS OF EXCHANGE drawn on them by him. He can then sell the bills, or the bank may do so on his behalf. For the bank's ACCEPTANCE means the buyer of the bills can look to the bank for repayment. For example, an exporter might be due to be paid $1 million in 90 days. He would draw a bill for $1 million on his bank, which would accept it (charging a commission, say ½%, for doing so). The bill is then sold at a DISCOUNT; if the relevant discount rate is 10%, then the value of the bill today is $975,000 (using a 360-day year) which will be paid to the exporter today. On receipt of his $1 million, the exporter is able to repay the bill of exchange (he would of course have to repay this even if he were not paid by his overseas customer). If the exporter has gone bankrupt in the interim, however, the bank remains liable to pay − since it has 'accepted' the liability to repay if the exporter fails to do so. The interest rate payable on an acceptance varies with the standing of the borrower, the nature of the underlying transaction, and also whether the bill is ELIGIBLE for rediscounting with the central bank. Compare BANKERS' ACCEPTANCE, ACCEPTANCE CREDIT, DOCUMENTARY ACCEPTANCE CREDIT.
Bibliography: Gillett Brothers Discount Company. *The Bill on London.* Methuen, London, 1976.
T.Q. Cook & B.J. Summers (eds). *Instruments of the Money Market.* Federal Reserve Bank of Virginia, 1981.
A. Watson. *Finance of International Trade.* Institute of Bankers, London, 1981.

acceptance credit. A credit involving an

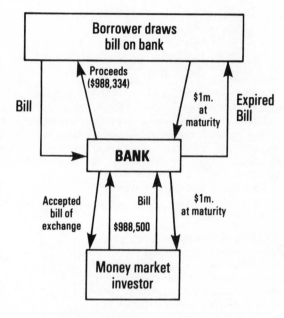

SUMMARY

1. Borrower draws bill on bank which accepts it and buys it for $988,334.
2. Bank sells bill in money market for $988,500.
3. At maturity borrower repays $1m. to investor.

ACCEPTANCE CREDIT

acceptance. (See diagram.) For example, in a 'revolving' acceptance credit, a bank might agree that in the next six months it will accept bills to the total of $500,000, provided it sees evidence of genuine business transactions. If the borrower requires a large sum, the acceptance credit can be SYNDICATED among several banks. Such an acceptance credit facility (involving numerous bills of exchange) should not be confused with a DOCUMENTARY ACCEPTANCE CREDIT, which is a documentary credit involving a single bill of exchange which is then accepted and sold. Compare CLEAN ACCEPTANCE CREDIT.

Bibliography: Gillett Brothers Discount Company. *The Bill on London.* Methuen, London 1976. A. Watson. *Finance of International Trade.* Institute of Bankers, London, 1981.

accepting house.   A member of the London Accepting House Committee. There are 17 such firms, normally regarded as the most prestigious of the merchant banks. The Committee has no written regulations or rules and functions on an informal basis. The principal qualifications for membership are that a house has a first-class reputation, does a meaningful acceptance business, and that its acceptances are discountable at the finest rate.

Bibliography: C.J. Clay & B.S. Wheble. *Modern Merchant Banking.* Woodhead-Faulkner, Cambridge, UK, 1983

acceptor.   The person who accepts a BILL OF EXCHANGE. This is normally the DRAWEE; by accepting it, he is held liable to pay the bill at maturity. Compare ACCEPTANCE.

Bibliography: A. Watson. *Finance of International Trade.* Institute of Bankers, London, 1981.

accommodation paper. Mainly used in the UK, the term refers to a bill to which a person puts his name to oblige another. (The US equivalent is a 'finance' or WORKING CAPITAL ACCEPTANCE.) If B needs money, he draws a bill on A, who accepts it. A's reputation enables the bill to be sold in the market. Effectively, B is borrowing on A's name. When the bill falls due, B pays. Such bills are not normally regarded as first class, since there is no physical collateral. Compare PIG ON PORK.
Bibliography: Gillett Brothers Discount Company.*The Bill on London*. Methuen, London, 1976.

account. A UK Stock Exchange term. The year is divided into twenty-five periods of two or three weeks, called accounts. BARGAINS done on the Stock Exchange must be settled at the end of the account period. If settlement is postponed beyond the account day, CONTANGO is charged.
Bibliography: J. Dundas Hamilton. *Stockbroking Today*. Macmillan Press, London, 1979.

accretion. US term for the addition of principal or interest to a fund over time. It is similar to amortization, but adds economic value instead of reducing it. In a bond portfolio, discount bonds are accreted to PAR while premium bonds are amortized to par. Thus, if I buy a bond, repayable at par in five years' time, and the purchase price is 80, then the accretion will be 4 points per annum on a straight-line basis.

accrued interest. Interest on a financial instrument (such as a bond, or CD) which has accumulated but has not yet been paid. If the instrument is now sold, its price will include an adjustment for accrued interest. Suppose a bond paying interest at $7\frac{1}{8}\%$, due on 31 May and 30 November, is bought for delivery on 10 August (i.e. 71 days into the 183-day period between coupon payments), in an amount of $10 million. Then the accrued interest is given by $10,000,000 × 7.125/100 × 71/183 × 1/2 = $138,217.21
Bibliography: M. Stigum. *Money Market Calcula-*

tions. Dow-Jones Irwin, Homewood, Ill., 1982.
M.S.Dobbs-Higginson. *Investment Manual*. Credit Suisse First Boston, London 1980.
The New 'Beginners Please'. Investors Chronicle, London, 1975.

ACH. *See* AUTOMATED CLEARING HOUSE.

acid test ratio. A measure of a company's financial strength. It is the ratio of a company's 'quick assets' (cash and near-cash assets) to its current liabilities. Sometimes referred to as the 'quick ratio'.
Bibliography: *Standard & Poor's Rating Guide*. McGraw-Hill,New York, 1979.
R. Brealey & S. Myers. *Principles of Corporate Finance*. McGraw-Hill, New York/London, 1984.

action. French term for stock or share.

actual total loss. A marine insurance term. An actual total loss occurs (1) where the subject matter is completely destroyed; (2) where the subject matter insured ceases to be a thing of the kind insured (this is 'loss of specie'); (3) where the assured is irretrievably deprived of the subject matter. UK insurance practice is that a ship is deemed an actual total loss when posted 'missing' at Lloyd's.
Bibliography: V. Dover. *A Handbook to Marine Insurance*. Revised and edited by R.H. Brown. London, Witherby, 1975.

actuals. In the commodity markets, a term for the physical commodity (as distinct from the paper ownership represented by FUTURES).
Bibliography: C.W.J. Granger. *Trading In Commodities*. Woodhead-Faulkner, Cambridge, UK, 1983.

ADB. *see* Asian Development Bank or African Development Bank

Added risk asset. UK term applied in the Bank of England's regulation of the DISCOUNT MARKET. The Bank of England considers cash, and assets with up to three months' maturity to be the most liquid and safest assets. Any other asset has 'added risk'. These assets are weighted according to

their perceived riskiness. Thus a house holding £10 million of fixed rate GILT-EDGED with an added risk weight of two will find that these count as £20 million in its total BOOK.
Bibliography: Prudential arrangements for the discount market. *Bank of England Quarterly Bulletin*. June 1982.

add-on rates.   A US term for interest rates that are added to the principal of the loan, to generate an effective simple interest rate which is higher than the add-on rate, because the add-on rate ignores the fact that repayments are being made. Such rates are used mainly in the consumer installment loan business. Add-on interest is calculated as follows:
Add-on interest = principal of the loan × add-on rate × number of months in the loan/12
Thus the interest on a 12-month loan at 10% on a loan of $1,000 would be reckoned at $100; if monthly repayments are being made the underlying rate is of course higher, since the principal amount declines over time.
Bibliography: J.M. McDonald & J.E. McKinley. *Corporate Banking: A Practical Approach to Lending*. American Bankers' Association, USA, 1981.

ADIBOR.   Abu Dhabi Interbank Offered Rate. *See* LIBOR.

adjustable peg.   Term for an exchange rate regime where a country's exchange rate is 'pegged' (i.e. fixed) in relation to another currency, but where the rate may be changed from time to time. This was effectively the system laid down at BRETTON WOODS. But, depending on the emphasis, rates could be either rigidly fixed or CRAWLING PEGS.
Bibliography: A.D. Crockett. *International Money*. Nelson & Sons, UK, 1977.
N. Carlozzi. Pegs and Floats. *Federal Reserve Bank of Philadelphia Business Review*. May/June 1981.

adjustable rate convertible notes.   A US term for notes bearing a fluctuating rate linked to the issuer's dividend rate, and convertible at maturity into COMMON STOCK of the issuer. The intention was to create an equity-like

instrument which ranked as debt for tax purposes. The US authorities, however, have sought to treat ARCNs as equity.
Bibliography: K.D. Brody *et al*. The Revival of Equity Financing *in* P.H. Darrow & R.A. Mestres (eds). *Creative Financing in the 1980s*. Practising Law Institute, New York, 1983.

adjustable rate preferred stock.   This is a US term for a PREFERENCE SHARE (STOCK) which carries a floating dividend rate, adjusted periodically (usually quarterly) and generally linked to the rate on US Treasury securities. The objective was to create a preferred stock whose price was stable in the SECONDARY MARKET. The ARPs were attractive to US corporate investors as they could exclude 85% of dividends received as taxable income. Compare CONVERTIBLE ADJUSTABLE RATE PREFERRED STOCK.
Bibliography: K.D. Brody *et al*. The Revival of Equity Financing *in* P.H. Darrow & R.H. Mestres (eds). *Creative Financing in the 1980s*. Practising Law Institute, New York, 1983.

adjusted CD rate.   Term sometimes used for an alternative to LIBOR in the pricing of a loan. It means the rate paid on a CD adjusted for reserve costs and FDIC insurance costs, and, like LIBOR, represents an attempt to measure the costs of a bank's funds (*see* CD, FDIC, LIBOR). The calculation would be:

$$\text{adjusted CD rate} = \frac{A}{100 - r} + B$$

where A = CD rate for the maturity in question; B = rate charged by FDIC for insuring such a CD; r = reserve percentage applicable. Thus for a 12% CD, with a 3% reserve percentage, and an FDIC charge of 0.08%, the adjusted CD rate would be 12.45%.
M. Stigum. *Money Market Calculations*. Dow Jones Irwin, Homewood, Ill, 1983.

ADR.   Abbreviation for AMERICAN DEPOSITARY RECEIPT.

ad valorem.   A TARIFF or tax applied as a percentage of the value of a product (as distinct from one applied on the basis of a flat rate – e.g. $10 per ton). From the Latin for 'according to value'.

advance payment bond, letter of credit. A BOND or STANDBY LETTER OF CREDIT protecting a purchaser who makes an advance payment. A typical advance payment bond involves a buyer, a seller, and a bank, which acts as SURETY for the seller. The buyer makes an advance payment to the seller. The latter enters into an advance payment bond, jointly with the bank. If the seller fails to fulfil his obligations, and fails to repay the advance payment, then the seller and the bank become liable under the advance payment bond. It is important to note that some advance payment bonds are of the so-called first demand type, i.e. they fall due for payment on first demand by the purchaser, irrespective of whether the latter has any justification for demanding the money.
Bibliography: Confederation of British Industry. *Performance Bonds and Guarantees*. London, 1978.
D. Sassoon (ed.) *Bidding for Projects Financed by International Lending Agencies*. Gower Press, UK, 1982.

advised line of credit. Term for a credit facility whose terms and conditions are confirmed to the customer by the bank. It may be: (1) Good till cancelled – the bank may terminate the credit at any time, but until that time the borrower may draw at will; (2) annual review – the line is good for one year, during which the beneficiary may draw on it at will; (3) as offered – the bank must be consulted prior to each drawing.
Bibliography: J.M. McDonald & J.E. McKinley. *Corporate Banking: A Practical Approach to Lending*. American Bankers' Association Washington DC, 1981.

advising bank. A term employed in DOCUMENTARY CREDIT business. It denotes the bank which informs the beneficiary of the credit that the credit has been opened. If all documentation is in order, the advising bank will pay the beneficiary and forward the documentation to the ISSUING BANK to obtain reimbursement.
Bibliography: A. Watson. *Finance of International Trade*. Institute of Bankers, London, 1981.
Uniform Customs and Practice for Documentary

Credits. International Chamber of Commerce Brochure no. 290, Paris 1975.

advisory funds. This refers to funds placed with a bank to invest at its own discretion on the customer's behalf. The more normal term is fiduciary funds. The most important centre for this type of business is Switzerland, where in 1980 SF120 billion of fiduciary funds were under management.
Bibliography: M.A. Corti. Switzerland: Banking, Money and Bond Markets *in* A.M. George & I.H. Giddy. *International Finance Handbook*. John Wiley & Sons, New York, 1983.

AfDB *See* AFRICAN DEVELOPMENT BANK.

affreightment. A contract of affreightment is the agreement made by a shipowner to carry goods in consideration of a certain payment, called the FREIGHT.
Bibliography: Mocatta, Mustill & Boyd. *Scrutton on Charterparties and Bills of Lading*. 18th edn, Sweet & Maxwell, London, 1974.
R. Ihre *et al. Shipbroking and Chartering Practice*. Lloyd's of London Press, 1984.

African Development Bank. Formed in 1964, the African Development Bank's role is to provide development capital for Africa. Its headquarters are at Abidjan, Ivory Coast. As of December, 1983 it had 75 members, following a move in 1983 to open membership to include 22 non-African shareholders. Its balance sheet totalled $1.2 billion.
Bibliography: ADB Annual Reports.
C. Peters. Going Global. *Institutional Investor*. New York, May 1984.

after-market. Another term for SECONDARY MARKET. More precisely, in the fixed-interest and Eurobond markets it refers to the period between the issue of the security and the lifting of SYNDICATE RESTRICTIONS.

agency. (1) A US term for the debt of an agency of the US Government. The total outstanding volume in 1982 was over $200 billion, of which the vast bulk were accounted for by the Federal Home Loan Banks, Farm Credit Banks, EXIMBANK and the GOVERN-

MENT NATIONAL MORTGAGE ASSOCIATION.
Bibliography: M. Stigum. Securities of Federal
Government Agencies and Sponsored Corpora-
tions *in* F.J. Fabozzi & I. M. Pollack (eds). *The
Handbook of Fixed Income Securities*. Dow Jones
Irwin, Homewood, Ill., 1983.

(2) A US form of banking operation which
is not empowered to accept deposits from the
public; widely used by foreign banks in the
US market to overcome inter-state banking
restrictions.
Bibliography: Peat, Marwick, Mitchell & Co.
Banking in the United States. New York/London,
1980.

agency bill.   A bill drawn on, and accepted
by, the London branches of banks whose
head offices are located abroad.
Bibliography: Gillett Brothers Discount Company. *The Bill on London*. Methuen, London,
1976.

agent bank.   (1) If a bank is acting for a
foreign bank, for example in collecting
money due on a bill of exchange, it is said to
be acting as an agent bank. (2) In the
EUROCREDIT MARKET and other markets,
the agent bank is one appointed by other
banks in the SYNDICATE to handle the
administration of the loan (e.g. notifying
participants of DRAW-DOWN periods for
which ROLL-OVER loans are drawn, or
changes in the interest rate). The agent is also
often a LEAD BANK or LEAD MANAGER but
the agent function starts with the signing of
the loan when the lead manager function
ends.
Bibliography: P.R. Stansbury. Legal Aspects of
Syndicated Eurocurrency Lending *in* A.M.
George & I.H. Giddy. *International Finance
Handbook*. John Wiley & Sons, New York, 1983.
P.Wood. *Law & Practice of International Finance*.
Sweet & Maxwell, London, 1980.
R.T. Nassberg. Loan Documentation. *The Busi-
ness Lawyer*. New York, April 1981.

agent de change.   French term for STOCK-
BROKER. The 'Compagnie des Agents de
Change' is the official association of stock-
brokers.
Bibliography: F. Aftaion & F. Bompaire. France:

Banking, Money and Bond Markets *in* A.M.
George & I.H. Giddy. *International Finance
Handbook*. J. Wiley & Sons, New York, 1983.

aggregate risk.   A foreign exchange term
covering total EXPOSURE of a bank to a
counterparty for both spot and forward
contracts. Thus, suppose a bank had dealt
with a customer in DM against US$ for $10
million in the six month period, $5 million in
the one year, and $3 million spot, its
aggregate risk with that customer would be
$18 million. Compare MARGINAL RISK.
Bibliography: J.K. Walmsley. *The Foreign Exchange Handbook*. John Wiley & Sons, New York,
1983.

agio.   Term (rarely used) to mean 'differential'.

agreement among managers.   In the EURO-
BOND new issue market it is common for an
issue to be managed by a group of MANA-
GERS. They will agree among themselves as
to their responsibilities and commitments
before entering into the AGREEMENT AMONG
UNDERWRITERS, the SUBSCRIPTION AGREE-
MENT and the SELLING GROUP AGREEMENT.
Bibliography: F.G. Fisher. *International Bonds*.
Euromoney Publications, London 1981.

agreement among underwriters. The legal
document which binds an underwriting group
into a SYNDICATE. Its precise contents vary
widely. In the US, the agreement is usually
between the borrower and all the UNDERWRI-
TERS of an issue and it appoints the MANA-
GERS. In the UK and Eurobond markets, it is
sometimes confined to an agreement between managers (acting as agents for the
borrower) and underwriters.
Bibliography: A.W. van Agtmael. Issuance of
Eurobonds *in* A.M. George & I.H. Giddy. *International Finance Handbook*. J. Wiley & Sons, New
York, 1983.
F.G. Fisher. *International Bonds*. Euromoney
Publications, London, 1981.

agreement corporation.   A US term for a
bank which is organized under Section 25 of
the Federal Reserve Act and which has

agreed with the Federal Reserve to abide by its regulations. It has virtually the same powers and restrictions as an EDGE ACT corporation.
Bibliography: Peat, Marwick & Mitchell. *Banking in the United States*. New York/London 1980.

AIBD. *See* ASSOCIATION OF INTERNATIONAL BOND DEALERS.

AIBD yield. Term for the YIELD on a BOND calculated according to the ASSOCIATION OF INTERNATIONAL BOND DEALERS convention, namely an annual coupon paid on a 30/360 BASIS.

air consignment note/air freight note. See Air waybill

Air Mail Transfer. *See* MAIL TRANSFER.

air waybill. A contract between a shipper and a carrier to transport goods by air is evidenced by an air waybill. It is not normally a negotiable instrument nor a document of title. Hence the goods will be delivered to the named consignee without further formality once customs clearance has been obtained.
Bibliography: A. Watson. *Finance of International Trade*. Institute of Bankers, London, 1981.

AKA. *See* AUSFUHRKREDIT GMBH..

AKV. *See* AUSLANDSKASSENVEREIN.

ALALC. *See* LATIN AMERICAN FREE TRADE AREA.

allonge. A slip of paper attached to a BILL OF EXCHANGE for the purpose of receiving ENDORSEMENTS.

All or None. US securities (and commodities) market term for the requirement that the total amount of a given order be executed at the specific price – no lesser amount will be acceptable.
Bibliography: L.M. Loll & J.G. Buckley. *The Over-the-Counter Securities Markets*. Prentice-Hall, USA, 1981.

R.J. Teweles & E.S. Bradley. *The Stock Market*. John Wiley & Sons, New York, 1982.

allotment. (1) Refers in the Eurobond and US securities markets to the allocation of securities to members of the SYNDICATE involved in the issue.
Bibliography: P. Wood. *Law and Practice of International Finance*. Sweet & Maxwell, London 1980; A.W. van Agtmael. Issuance of Eurobonds in A.M. George & I.H. Giddy. *International Finance Handbook*. John Wiley & Sons, New York, 1983.

(2) UK term for the issue of new shares under a RIGHTS ISSUE to existing shareholders or of GILT-EDGED to applicants for a new issue.
Bibliography: J. Dundas Hamilton. *Stockbroking Today*. Macmillan Press, London 1979.

all risks. In the marine insurance context an 'all risks' clause does *not* insure against all risks. The relevant portion of the INSTITUTE OF LONDON UNDERWRITERS' Institute Cargo Clauses (All risks) clause reads:
'This insurance is against all risks of loss or damage to the subject-matter insured but shall in no case be deemed to extend to cover loss damage or expense proximately caused by delay or inherent vice or nature of the subject-matter insured.'
The clause also excludes strikes, riots, civil commotions, capture, seizure, war, civil war, and piracy, among other perils.
Bibliography: R.J. Lambeth. *Templeman on Marine Insurance*. Macdonald & Evans Ltd, UK, 1981.

alpha. A term of MODERN PORTFOLIO THEORY. The alpha coefficient tries to measure how well a portfolio has performed compared with a risk-free portfolio, after making allowances for how well the other portfolio has performed and the managed portfolio's riskiness (as measured by its BETA). To illustrate, if a managed portfolio A had a rate of return of 15% over a period of time, and another market portfolio B achieved a 10% return, default-free securities yielded 5%, and the beta of portfolio A were 1.2, then alpha would equal $(.15-.05)-1.2(.10-.05)=.04$.

Bibliography: D. Corner & D.G. Mayes (eds). *Modern Portfolio Theory and Financial Institutions.* Macmillan, UK, 1983.
D.E. Logue & R.J. Rogalski. Offshore alphas: should diversification begin at home? *in* P.L.Bernstein (ed.). *International Investing.* Institutional Investor Books, New York, 1983.
W.B. Riley & A.H. Montgomery. *Guide to Computer Assisted Investment Analysis.* McGraw-Hill, New York, 1982.

American Depository Receipt (ADR). A system under which a DEPOSITARY RECEIPT is issued by an American bank to assist trading in a foreign stock or share. The underlying securities are deposited with the bank (or its custodian bank abroad). The US bank then issues an ADR against them. ADRs can be traded on major exchanges or on the OVER-THE-COUNTER market, and they are eligible for deposit or clearing in the DEPOSITORY TRUST COMPANY. In 1983, over $1 billion worth of ADRs were issued (compared with $1.04 billion between 1976-80); and a recent major example of the technique was their use in the simultaneous London/New York issue by British Telecom.
Bibliography: *Depositary Receipts.* Morgan Guaranty Trust Company, New York, 1973.
N. Osborn. The Rise of the International Equity. *Euromoney,* London, May, 1984.
The Stock Exchange Official Year Book. Macmillan, London, 1984.

American option. An OPTION which can be exercised any time before maturity is called an American option to distinguish it from a EUROPEAN OPTION which may be exercised only at its expiry date.
Bibliography: R.M. Bookstaber. *Option Pricing and Strategies in Investing.* Addison-Wesley, Reading, Mass., 1981.

Amortization. Term for the repayment of a loan in periodic instalments; strictly speaking, by the creation of a sinking fund.

Amstel Club. A grouping of finance houses from 15 European countries who make reciprocal arrangements for trade finance. The official name of the institution is Amstel Finance International AG, and its headquarters are in Switzerland.
Bibliography: C.M. Schmitthoff. *The Export Trade.* 7th edn. Stevens & Sons, London 1980.

Andean Group. A group consisting of Bolivia, Colombia, Chile (until 1976), Ecuador, Peru and Venezuela (from 1973). It was founded in 1969 under the Cartagena Agreement to assist economic integration between its members. In 1978, the Group created the Andean Reserve Fund to help regional balance of payments financing. In 1979, the Group created the Andean Parliament, the Andean Court of Justice, and a Council of Foreign Ministers. In 1983 an agreement was signed on environmental protection.
Bibliography: *Economic and Social Progress in Latin America* in *Inter-American Development Bank Annual Report* Washington DC, 1984.

Anleihe. German term for a bond or loan. They include public-sector bonds (Offentliche Anleihen) and industrial companies' bonds (Industrie Anleihen) – the latter being scarce compared to the former.
Bibliography: G. Dufey & E. Krishnan. West Germany: Banking, Money and Bond Markets *in* A.M. George & I.H. Giddy (eds). *International Finance Handbook*, John Wiley, New York, 1983.

Applied proceeds swap. US term for the sale of a block of bonds, proceeds of which are applied to buying another block of bonds.
Bibliography: S. Homer & M.L. Leibowitz. *Inside the Yield Book.* Prentice-Hall, US, 1972.
C. Seix. Bond Swaps *in* F.J. Fabozzi & I.M. Pollack. *The Handbook of Fixed Income Securities.* Dow-Jones Irwin, Homewood, Ill., 1983.

appreciation. A rise in the value of one currency in terms of another; in general, a rise in the value of a thing.

Arab African Bank. Founded in 1964, with headquarters in Cairo. Its members consist of the Central Bank of Egypt (42% shareholding), Ministry of Finance and Oil, Kuwait (42%), Rafidain Bank of Iraq (10%), Central Bank of Algeria (2%), Ministry of Finance, Jordan (1%) and certain others. Its function is to act as a financial and economic link between the Arab and African countries. Compare ARAB BANK FOR ECONOMIC DEVELOPMENT IN AFRICA.

Bibliography: T. Scharf. *Trilateral Cooperation, Vol.I : Arab Development Funds and Banks.* OECD Development Centre Studies, Paris 1978.

Arab Bank for Economic Development in Africa. Founded in 1973 by members of the ARAB LEAGUE (with the exception of Djibouti, Somalia, the Yemen Arab Republic and the Peoples Democratic Republic of the Yemen). Its headquarters are in Khartoum, Sudan. From the start of its operations until the end of 1981, ABEDA had signed 58 loan agreements providing for loans of $399 million to 33 countries.

Bibliography: M. Achilli & M. Khaldi (eds). *The Role of the Arab Development Funds in the World Economy.* Macmillan, London/St. Martin's Press, New York, 1984.

Arab Company for Trading Securities. A Kuwaiti company owned by local investment and commercial banks, the ACTS is responsible for maintaining a secondary market in Kuwaiti securities, CDs, and promissory notes.

Bibliography: L.J. Kemp. *World Money and Securities Markets.* Euromoney Publications, London, 1984.

Arab Fund for Economic and Social Development. Formed in 1968, but started operations in 1973. Its headquarters are in Kuwait. Members include those of the ARAB LEAGUE with the exception of Djibouti and Mauritania. Its functions are to finance joint Arab projects or projects in Arab countries which may be of general Arab interest. From the signing of the first loan agreement in February 1974 until the end of 1981 the Fund committed 75 loans to 15 recipient countries with a total amount of $1.4 billion, as well as 54 grants for a total amount of $20 million.

Bibliography: *Aid from OPEC Countries.* OECD, Paris, 1983.

Arab International Bank. Founded in 1971, with headquarters in Cairo, the AIB's membership includes the Central Bank of Egypt, the Libyan Arab Foreign Bank, the Government of the United Arab Emirates, the Government of Oman and the Government of Qatar. Private individuals hold 4.2% of the capital. Its function is to assist in the financing of development and of foreign trade, particularly the member states and other Arab states.

Bibliography: R. Wilson. *Banking and Finance in the Arab Middle East.* Macmillan, London/St. Martin's, Press, New York, 1983.
T. Scharf. *Trilateral Cooperation, Vol.I: Arab Development Funds and Banks.* OECD Development Centre Studies, Paris, 1978.

Arab Investment Company. Established in 1974 as a joint stock company by Abu Dhabi, Bahrain, Egypt, Kuwait, Qatar, Saudi Arabia and Sudan. Subsequently Iraq, Jordan, Morocco, Syria, Tunisia, Libya, Oman and the Yemen Arab Republic also joined. Headquarters are in Riyadh, Saudi Arabia. Its functions are to promote the investment of Arab capital by undertaking investment projects itself and by operating in the financial markets.

Bibliography: R. Wilson. *Banking and Finance in the Arab Middle East.* Macmillan, London/St Martin's Press, New York, 1983.
T. Scharf. *Trilateral Cooperation, Vol.I: Arab Development Funds and Banks.* OECD Development Centre Special Studies, Paris, 1978.

Arab League. Founded in 1945 with headquarters in Egypt. Its members were Algeria, Bahrain, Djibouti, Egypt, Iraq, Jordan, Kuwait, Lebanon, Libya, Mauritania, Morocco, Oman, Qatar, Saudi Arabia, Somalia, Sudan, Syria, Tunisia, United Arab Emirates, Yemen Arab Republic, Peoples Democratic Republic of the Yemen, and Palestine. Egypt's membership was suspended in 1979. Apart from political activities the League's members have founded a number of joint institutions such as the ARAB BANK FOR ECONOMIC DEVELOPMENT IN AFRICA, the ARAB MONETARY FUND and

Bibliography: *Europa Year Book. Vol.I.* Europa Publications, London, annually.

Arab Monetary Fund. Founded in 1977, with its headquarters in Abu Dhabi, under the auspices of the Council of Arab Economic Unity, the Arab Monetary Fund has 21 Arab member countries, including 'Palestine'. It was conceived as a regional financial institution mainly to help member countries cope with balance-of-payments deficits but also to foster closer monetary cooperation between Arab countries. Loans are intended to finance an overall balance-of-payments deficit and for this purpose a member may automatically draw up to 75% of its capital paid-in in convertible currencies. Larger loans are subject to agreement with the Fund. By the end of 1981 it had made 21 loans, totalling $413 million.
Bibliography: T. Scharf. *Trilateral Cooperation, Vol.I: Arab Development Funds and Banks.* OECD Development Centre Studies, Paris 1978. *Aid from OPEC Countries.* OECD. Paris, 1983.

arbitrage   In general, buying (or borrowing) in one market, selling (or lending) in another.
   (1) In foreign exchange 'space arbitrage' consists of buying in one centre and selling in another. With modern communications, this is now rare, since prices rarely differ by much between centres for long.
   (2) 'Time' or 'maturity' arbitrage, also known as FORWARD-FORWARD, consists of (say) buying a currency forward three months and selling six months. Likewise in money markets a borrowing might be made for three months against a six month lending. Compare MIS-MATCH.
   (3) The term also denotes switching of funds between similar assets (e.g. deposits or Treasury bills) denominated in different currencies. It is COVERED ARBITRAGE if the exchange risk is COVERED by a FORWARD CONTRACT.
Bibliography: J.K. Walmsley. *The Foreign Exchange Handbook.* John Wiley, New York 1983. G. Dufey & I. Giddy. *The International Money Market.* Prentice-Hall, US, 1978.
   (4) Similarly, the term may be applied to switching of funds between assets in one currency – e.g. at times it has been profitable for UK corporations to raise finance by

means of a bill of exchange to on-lend the funds in the wholesale deposit market. Equally, US companies might issue commercial paper to on-lend into the deposit markets. Compare BILL ARBITRAGE.
Bibliography: A note on money market arbitrage. *Bank of England Quarterly Bulletin.* June 1982.
   (5) In fixed-interest markets the term may be used for a SWAP done between two similar issues. The trader anticipates a change in their relative prices. Also termed a SWITCH.
Bibliography: S. Homer & M.L. Leibowitz. *Inside the Yield Book.* Prentice-Hall, USA, 1972.
C. Seix. Bond Swaps *in* F.J. Fabozzi & I.M. Pollack. *The Handbook of Fixed Income Securities.* Dow-Jones Irwin, Homewood, Ill. USA, 1983.
   (6) The term is also used to refer to trading in stocks which are involved in a merger or take-over; it is then usually known as risk arbitrage. A simple example of risk arbitrage is where a stock is purchased at $33 per share when an offer of $35 per share has been announced: the risk here is that for legal or other reasons the offer or takeover may not be consummated, and the price may fall to below $33 per share.
Bibliography: M.A. Weinstein. Arbitrage *in* M.E. Blume & J.P. Friedman. *Encyclopedia of Investments.* Warren, Gorham & Lamont, Boston, 1982.

arbitrageur.   A person systematically involved in arbitrage dealing.

arbitral, arbitration.   Settling a dispute by referring it to a third, independent party. A number of bodies are equipped to provide arbitration facilities for international business disputes, including the Court of Arbitration of the INTERNATIONAL CHAMBER OF COMMERCE, the INTERNATIONAL CENTRE FOR THE SETTLEMENT OF INVESTMENT DISPUTES and in appropriate cases the American Arbitration Association, the British Institute of Arbitrators, etc.
Bibliography: C.M. Schmitthoff. *Export Trade.* (7th edn). London, Stevens & Sons, 1980.
J.D.M. Lew & C. Stanbrook (eds). *International Trade: Law & Practice.* Euromoney Publications, London, 1983.

ARBL. *See* ASSETS REPRICED BEFORE LIABILITIES.

Arcru. A UNIT OF ACCOUNT introduced in November 1974 and based on the movement of 12 Arab currencies against the US dollar. Not widely used.
Bibliography: *Euromoney*, London, July 1975.

Ariel. Acronym of Automated Real-Time Investments Exchange. Conceived by the London Accepting Houses Committee and set up in February 1974, ARIEL is a system for dealing in large blocks of securities. Subscribers enter their buying/selling requirements in the system and they can then be matched up cheaply. After an initially successful launch its business declined (because of the reluctance of dealers to use its impersonal, computerized system) but is now recovering. Compare NASDAQ.
Bibliography: C.J.J. Clay & B.S. Wheble. *Modern Merchant Banking*. 2nd edn. Woodhead-Faulkner, Cambridge, UK, 1983.

around. Foreign exchange term ('around par' is understood). Used in quoting forward PREMIUMS or DISCOUNTS. 'Five-five around' would mean five POINTS on either side of par, i.e. on either side of the present spot rate.

AsDB. *See* ASIAN DEVELOPMENT BANK.

ASEAN. *See* ASSOCIATION OF SOUTH EAST ASIAN NATIONS.

Asialease. The Asian Leasing Association. Founded in 1982, it is a federation of the leasing companies and associations which operate in the Asian market. It has more than 40 members from 10 countries. Compare LEASUROPE.
Bibliography: Y. Miyauchi. A Rising Force in Asia. *The Banker*, London, May 1983.

Asian Clearing Union. A joint arrangement for settling international payments imbalances between Bangladesh, Burma, India, Iran, Nepal, Pakistan, and Sri Lanka. The UNIT OF ACCOUNT is the ASIAN MONETARY UNIT.

Bibliography: *Annual Report on Exchange Arrangements*. International Monetary Fund. Washington DC, annually.

Asian Currency Unit (ACU). In 1968 the Singapore authorities licensed selected banks to establish separate accounting units within the banks to deal in non-resident deposits, i.e. ASIAN DOLLARS. These units were termed Asian Currency Units. Total assets of ACUs at the end of that year were US$30.5 million; by end-December 1980 they had reached US$54 billion.
Bibliography: *Annual Reports of the Monetary Authority of Singapore*.
Y.S. Park. Asian Money Markets *in* A.M. George & I.H. Giddy. *International Finance Handbook*. J. Wiley & Sons, New York, 1983.

Asian Development Bank (ADB). Founded in 1966, the ADB had (as of December 1983) 45 members including the UK, the US, and 12 other European countries in addition to 31 Asian members. Its functions are to help provide development capital for Asia. 1983 loans totalled $1.9 billion. Equity investments were also made. Its headquarters are in Manila, Philippines. (Compare AFRICAN DEVELOPMENT BANK, INTER-AMERICAN DEVELOPMENT BANK, WORLD BANK)
Bibliography: *ADB Annual Reports*.

Asian Dollar Bonds. An extension of the ASIAN DOLLAR MARKET and the EUROBOND market. Singapore is the main centre, with Hong Kong. It began in Singapore in 1972 when the Development Bank of Singapore floated a US$10 million bond. Since then the market has been rather slow to develop.
Bibliography: A.K. Bhattacharya. *The Asian Dollar Market*. Praeger, New York, 1977.
Y.S. Park. Asian Money Markets *in* A.M. George & I.H. Giddy. *International Finance Handbook*. John Wiley & Sons, New York, 1983.

Asian Dollars. By extension from EURODOLLARS, Asian dollars refers to US dollar bank deposits traded outside the US. The term can be loosely used to include other currencies. Much of the market is located in Singapore, but Hong Kong has recently grown in importance. Tokyo is hampered by restrictive controls, although plans have been suggested for INTERNATIONAL BANKING FACILITIES along the lines of the American model.

Bibliography: *Annual Reports of the Monetary Authority of Singapore.*
Y.S. Park. Asian Money Markets *in* A.M. George & I.H. Giddy. *International Finance Handbook.* John Wiley & Sons, New York, 1983.

Asian Monetary Unit.   This unit, with a value equal to that of the SPECIAL DRAWING RIGHT is the accounting unit of the ASIAN CLEARING UNION.

Bibliography: J. Aschheim & Y.S. Park. *Artificial Currency Units: The Formation of Functional Currency Areas.* Princeton Essays in International Finance, No. 114,1976.

asked.   Selling price of a security or currency. The rate at which an inter-bank money market loan is offered.

as-of adjustments.   US term for a correction to a bank's figure for RESERVES. If an error in accounting is discovered, or there was a telecommunications breakdown, a retrospective 'as-of' adjustment is made to the bank's reserve figures.

Bibliography: C.D. Beek. Excess Reserves and Reserve Targeting. *Federal Reserve Bank of New York Quarterly Review,* Autumn 1981.

asset sensitive.   A bank whose ASSETS RE-PRICED BEFORE LIABILITIES figure is positive for a given period is said to be asset sensitive for that period. It is vulnerable to falling rates.

assets repriced before liabilities (ARBL).   A US term for a bank's interest rate sensitivity. A bank with $600 million of assets whose interest rates will change (i.e., reprice) within one year (either by maturing, or because of variable rates) compared with $400 million of liabilities, has an ARBL figure of $200 million and is said to be asset sensitive; a negative ARBL is said to imply liability sensitivity. Asset sensitive banks are vulner-

able if rates fall, liability sensitive banks if rates rise.

Bibliography: B.F. Binder & T.W.F. Linquist. *Asset/Liability and Funds Management at US Commercial Banks.* Bank Administration Institute, Rolling Meadows, Ill., 1982.

Assignment.   In general, the transfer of the rights and duties under a contract to another party, usually in exchange for value received. In the US, assignment of a forward foreign exchange contract may be able to transform it into a capital asset.

Bibliography: H.C. Gutteridge & M. Megrah. *The Law of Bankers' Commercial Credits.* Europa Publications, London 1979.
R.A. Anderson *et al. Business Law.* South-West Publishing Co., Cincinnati, Ohio, 1984.

(2) In OPTIONS markets, the designation of an option writer for fulfillment of his obligation to sell STOCK (if the writer of a CALL option) or to buy stock (if the writer of a PUT option). The writer receives an assignment notice from the OPTIONS CLEARING CORPORATION.

Bibliography: L.G. McMillan. *Options as a Strategic Investment.* New York Institute of Finance, New York, 1980.

Association Cambiste Internationale.   The international society of foreign exchange dealers, consisting of national FOREX CLUBS affiliated on a worldwide basis. The ACI's headquarters are at 16 Boulevard Montmartre, Paris.

Association of International Bond Dealers.   The dealers' professional association, which recommends rules and regulations regarding conditions of dealing, professional examinations and the like. Its headquarters are at Universitatstrasse 105, Zurich, Switzerland.

Bibliography: F.G. Fisher. *International Bonds.* Euromoney Publications, London, 1981.
Rules and Recommendations. AIBD, Zurich.

Association of South-East Asian nations (ASEAN).   The ASEAN was established in 1967 with its headquarters in Indonesia. Its members consist of Brunei, Indonesia,

Malaysia, the Philippines, Singapore and Thailand. It operates preferential tariffs between members, and other measures designed to foster mutual cooperation. The ASEAN-Japan Development Corporation was founded in 1981 and its first project, a gas plant in Singapore, was adopted in 1983.
Bibliography: *ASEAN Newsletter*, monthly, Jakarta, Indonesia; *ASEAN Annual Reports*, Jakarta, Indonesia.

at best. An instruction given to a dealer to purchase or sell currency (or securities) at the best rate he can get.

at or better. An order to deal at a specific rate or better.

at-the-money. Term used in the options markets to denote an option whose STRIKE PRICE is at or near the price of the underlying instrument. For example, suppose the shares of the XYZ Corporation are trading at $4.00. An option to buy the shares at $4.00 would be said to be at-the-money. Compare IN-THE-MONEY, OUT-OF-THE-MONEY.
Bibliography: L.G. McMillan. *Options as a Strategic Investment*. New York Institute of Finance, New York, 1980.
R.M. Bookstaber. *Option Pricing and Strategies in Investing*. Addison-Wesley, USA, 1982.

auction. Generally, a sale of a commodity at which the highest bid is successful. In international finance, the most common instance is the regular auction of TREASURY BILLS in a number of countries, including Australia, Belgium, Canada, France, Germany, Italy, the Netherlands, Spain, Switzerland, the UK and the US. (The UK equivalent is known as the TENDER.) Government bonds are sold in a similar fashion in a number of countries . The technique has also been used in the securities markets.
Bibliography: M. Stigum. *The Money Market*. Dow Jones-Irwin, Homewood, Ill., 1983.
N. Adam. Exxon's Quiet Auction. *Euromoney*, London, December 1982.
Government Debt Management: Debt Instruments and Selling Techniques. OECD, Paris, 1983.

F.G. Fisher. *International Bonds*. Euromoney Publications, London, 1981.

au jour le jour. The rate of money lent from day-to-day on the French money markets; the rate differs according to whether the loan is made against the security of Treasury or private bills. The Banque de France usually stabilizes the rate through the MAISONS DE RÈESCOMPTE (discount houses).
Bibliography: J.K. Walmsley. *The Foreign Exchange Handbook*. John Wiley, New York, 1983.
D. Marteau & E.de la Chaise. *Le marché monétaire et la gestion de trésorerie des banques*. Dunod, Paris, 1981.

Ausfuhrkredit GmbH (AKA). German export credit company formed by a consortium comprising 56 commercial banks to provide medium and long-term export finance. It has three types of loan: A,B, and C. Line A consists of funds pooled by member banks for refinancing supplier credits. Loans are made by AKA direct to the exporter against promissory notes, which are discounted by AKA and then refinanced with member banks. These are usually not more than 10 years and do not involve Government intervention. Line B mainly provides supplier credits to developing and Eastern bloc countries for up to 4 years at 1 ½% over the official Bundesbank discount rate. Line C finances buyer credits at market rates.
Bibliography: *The Export Credit Financing Systems in OECD Member Countries*. OECD. Paris, 1982.
A. Dunn & M. Knight. *Export Finance*. Euromoney Publications, London 1981.

Auslandobligation. German for 'foreign security'. The term is applied in Switzerland to foreign bonds (8 to 15 years maturity) or notes (3 to 8 years). Foreign bonds are normally public issues managed by a consortium of Swiss-based banks, with minimum denominations of SFR5,000, with optional redemption features. Foreign notes are normally private placements handled by a single Swiss bank, with minimum denominations of SFR50,000.
Bibliography: M.S. Dobbs-Higginson. *Investment*

Manual. Credit Suisse First Boston, London, 1980. M.A. Corti. Switzerland: Banking, Money and Bond Markets *in* A.M. George & I.H. Giddy. *International Finance Handbook.* John Wiley & Sons, New York, 1983.

Auslandskassenverein (AKV). The AKV is the central German KASSENVEREIN for handling deliveries of foreign securities. It was founded in 1971 and by 1975 it administered transfers in 12,000 securities yearly from 15 countries as well as 1,200 securities in cooperation with CEDEL of which it is a shareholder.
Bibliography: *Euromoney.* London, January 1977.

autarchy (autarky). Policy of economic self-sufficiency, i.e. of actively discouraging imports.

authorized capital. *See* AUTHORIZED STOCK.

authorized dealer. In foreign exchange, this means banks which are permitted by their regulating body to deal in foreign exchange. Similarly, in stock markets, it refers to institutions permitted by the regulating body to deal in stock or bonds.

authorized stock. US term for the total amount of stock which a company is authorized by its stockholders to issue. The parallel UK term is 'authorized capital'. Compare PAID-UP CAPITAL, ISSUED CAPITAL.

authority to purchase. Term for an alternative to the DOCUMENTARY CREDIT, mainly used for shipments to the Far East. For example, a UK firm, Exporting Co., sells goods to Importing Co. in Singapore. Importing Co. arranges with Singapore Bank Ltd to finance under an authority to purchase. Singapore Bank arrange with London Bank Ltd to act on their behalf in the matter. When the goods are shipped, Exporting Co. Ltd draws a bill on Importing Co. and presents the bill, with the shipping documents, to London Bank Ltd. If the documents are in order London Bank buys the bill from the exporter.

Bibliography: I.H. Giddy & M.A. Ismael. International Trade Financing Techniques *in* A.M. George & I.H. Giddy. *International Finance Handbook.* John Wiley & Sons, New York, 1983.

Automated Clearing House. A US term referring to an organization set up by financial institutions, who agree to send and receive electronic transfers of funds between themselves in settlement of customer transfers. The FEDERAL RESERVE operates a system linking some 10,000 banks and 6,000 corporations. Similar systems operate in a number of countries.
Bibliography: The Federal Reserve and the Payments System. *Federal Reserve Bulletin.* Washington DC, February 1981.
B. Streeter *et al.* Special Report on Automated Clearing Houses. *ABA Banking Journal.* New York, March 1982.

availability clause. *See* CURRENCY AVAILABILITY CLAUSE.

aval. Payment of a BILL OF EXCHANGE or PROMISSORY NOTE may be guaranteed by the signature of a third person appearing on the bill. This is called an aval. It is common in Continental Europe and widely used in FORFAITING. Its use was recognized by the 1930 League of Nations Convention providing a 'Uniform Law on Bills of Exchange and Promissory Notes' (Articles 30-32). It is not generally accepted as part of English law, but is becoming more common.
Bibliography: I. Guild. Forfaiting widens its appeal. *The Banker.* London, April 1984.

average adjuster. In UK marine insurance practice an average adjuster is employed in cases of GENERAL AVERAGE and in the majority of claims relating to HULLS. Usually the adjuster is appointed by the shipowner. In respect of other claims he is appointed by the assured. The average adjuster is not an advocate, but is rather employed to state a claim in accordance with his knowledge of law and practice. In the UK an Association of Average Adjusters was formed in 1876 to ensure uniformity in the preparation and statement of claims.

Bibliography: V. Dover. *A Handbook to Marine Insurance*. Revised and edited by R.H. Brown. Witherby & Co., London, 1975.
Lloyd's Calendar. Lloyd's of London Press, London, annually.

average life.   The average MATURITY of a borrowing after taking into account repayments or sinking fund provisions. For example, suppose a five-year loan of $75 million is repayable in the following amounts: Years 1-2: nil. Year 3:$20 million. Year 4: $20 million. Year 5: $35 million. The average life is the weighted average of the principal repayments,weighted by the number of years. Thus in this case the average life would be calculated as $(1\times0+2\times0+3\times20+4\times20+5\times35)/75=315/75=4.2$.

Bibliography: M.S. Dobbs-Higginson. *Investment Manual*. Credit Suisse First Boston, London, 1980.

average yield.   In the UK this term often refers to the average of all the yields implied by the prices bid for TREASURY BILLS at the Bank of England weekly tender. In the US, the inverse term, 'average issuing price' is normally used. Compare AUCTION.

Bibliography: Allen Harvey & Ross Ltd. *This is Bill-Broking*. London 1975.
T.Q. Cook & B.J. Summers. *Instruments of the Money Market* Federal Reserve Bank of Virginia, USA, 1981.

averaging.   The practice of investing a fixed amount of money in a particular security (or unit/ investment trust/mutual fund) regardless of price. When the market price is high the investor receives proportionately less stock and vice versa. Also known in the US as 'dollar cost averaging'.

B

back. Shortened form of BACKWARDA-
TION.

back freight. Freight payable on goods
back to the port of original shipment when
for some reason they could not be delivered.
Bibliography: Mocatta, Mustill & Boyd. *Scrutton
on Charterparties and Bills of Lading*. 18th edn.
Sweet & Maxwell Ltd, London, 1974.

backspread. An OPTIONS market term for the
sale of a CALL option at one STRIKE PRICE and
the purchase of several calls at a higher strike
price. It is the opposite of a RATIO SPREAD.
The strategy is rational if the investor is
bullish and wishes to buy OUT-OF-THE-
MONEY calls, but also to hedge himself by
selling another call. Suppose XYZ Co. is
selling for 43 and the July 40 call is at 4, with
the July 45 call at 1. Then the investor will
buy two July 45 calls, and sell one July 40.
This will earn him a net of 2. If at expiration
the XYZ stock is selling at 40 or less, all the
calls will expire worthless and the earnings
will be 2. If the stock is at 49 or above, then
the profits on the two 45 calls (4 points or
more on each call) will exceed the loss on the
40 call (8 points or more). On the other hand,
if the stock is at 45 at expiration, the 45 calls
expire worthless and there is a loss of 5 on the
40 calls, for an all-in loss of 3. The investor's
maximum profit comes from a sharp upward
move in the stock, but he is protected against
a sharp drop. His maximum loss comes if
there is no move in the stock.
Bibliography: L.G. McMillan. *Options as a
Strategic Investment*. New York Institute of Finance, New York, 1980.

back-to-back. (1) Operations where a loan
is made in one currency against a loan in
another currency, e.g. a dollar loan in the US
(say by a US insurance company to a UK
insurance company's subsidiary) against a

sterling loan in the UK (by the UK insurance
company to the US insurance company's UK
subsidiary). Such operations do not always
give the right of SET-OFF and so have been
replaced in some cases by a CURRENCY
EXCHANGE OR SWAP.
Bibliography: J.K. Walmsley. *The Foreign Exchange Handbook*. John Wiley & Sons, New York,
1983.
B.Antl(ed.). *Swap Financing Techniques*. Euromoney, London, 1983.

(2) A credit opened by a bank on the
strength of another credit, e.g. if a British
merchant buys cotton in Egypt and sells it to a
Belgian who establishes a credit for payment
to the UK firm, then the firm may be able to
use this as security for opening a credit to
finance payment to the Egyptian.
Bibliography: Gillett Brothers Discount Company. *The Bill on London*. Methuen & Co,
London, 1976.
A. Watson, *Finance of International Trade*. 2nd
edn. Institute of Bankers, London, 1981.

backwardation. (1) Term mainly used in
the commodity markets (and by analogy in
foreign exchange, occasionally) referring to
the amount that the spot price (plus the cost
of storage) exceeds the forward price. For
example, if the price of gold for delivery
today were $350 per ounce, and $325 per
ounce for delivery in three months' time,
there would be said to be backwardation.
Bibliography: C.W.J. Granger (ed.). *Trading in
Commodities*. Woodhead-Faulkner, Cambridge,
UK, 1983.

(2) On the Stock Exchange, backwardation means a percentage charge paid by the
seller for the right to delay delivery. Compare
Contango.
Bibliography: *The New "Beginners Please"*. Investors Chronicle. London, 1975.

(3) Term used occasionally in the Eurobond market to indicate a perverse situation

where a market-maker's bid for a bond is above another market-maker's offer.

balance commerciale. French term for balance of trade in merchandise.

balance des paiements courants. French term for CURRENT ACCOUNT of the balance of payments.

Balance for Official Financing. A UK balance of payments statistic. It consists of the balance on CURRENT ACCOUNT plus the total of investment and other capital flows (whether short- or long-term) plus the balancing item (errors and omissions). It represents the total shortfall (surplus) that the authorities must borrow (invest) and is therefore equal to the change in reserves plus total official borrowing (lending).
Bibliography: *Financial Statistics: Notes and Definitions*. Central Statistical Office, London, annually.

Drawing the line in the balance of payments accounts. *CSO Statistical News*. No. 36, London, 1977.

balance of payments. A systematic record of the economic transactions, during a given period, between the residents of a country and the rest of the world. (see diagram) It covers earnings from flows of real resources, changes in a country's foreign assets and liabilities that arise from economic transactions (thus excluding valuation changes), and unrequited transfers (such as military aid). Strictly, the balance of payments must always balance and it is therefore nonsense to speak of a 'balance of payments deficit'. However, in ordinary usage 'balance of payments' often means either (a) the balance of payments on CURRENT ACCOUNT or (b) the current account plus certain capital movements. The 'basic balance' – including current account plus long-term capital movements – is an example.

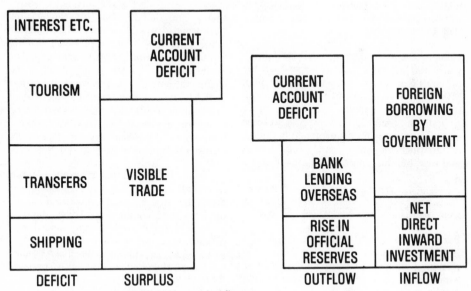

The current account is financed by capital flows

BALANCE OF PAYMENTS OF RURITANIA

Bibliography: M. Levi. *International Finance*. McGraw Hill, New York 1983.
H.G. Grubel. *The International Monetary System*. Penguin Books, London, 1984.

balance of trade.   The value of exports less imports. Usually, the term excludes INVISIBLES in which case it refers to the balance of trade in merchandise. If exports are larger than imports the trade balance is said to be in surplus (or 'active' in French or Continental usage), and the converse case yields a deficit (or 'passive' balance). It may be calculated on a 'balance of payments basis' (exports and imports both F.O.B.) or on a 'customs' or (in the UK) 'Overseas Trade Statistics basis' (exports f.o.b., imports C.I.F.) or in the US on 'f.a.s./f.a.s.' basis. See F.O.B., F.A.S., C.I.F.
Bibliography: As for BALANCE OF PAYMENTS.

balcony group.   A US term for a group of UNDERWRITERS whose commitments are smaller than those of the MAJOR BRACKET underwriters, but larger than those of the sub-major underwriters.
Bibliography: L.M. Loll & J.G. Buckley. *The Over-the-Counter Securities Markets*. Prentice Hall, USA, 1981.

balloon.   A loan repayment scheme under which the last repayment is larger than the previous repayments. For example, a loan of $100 which is repayable over five years, with the following schedule: two years' 'grace period', and then $25, $25 and $50. In some cases, the term is used to refer to a scheme under which the whole loan is repaid at its maturity, but this is more often spoken of as a BULLET.
Bibliography: D. Rao. *Handbook of Business Finance and Capital Sources*. American Management Association, New York, 1982.

Baltic Exchange.   Based in London, the Baltic Exchange has the primary function of matching cargoes to ships and *vice versa*. Thus a shipowner whose ship is empty may approach a member of the Baltic to find a cargo to be carried in her. The Baltic Exchange also handles air charters and the sale and purchase of ships. It also houses the GRAIN AND FEED TRADE ASSOCIATION, the LONDON GRAIN FUTURES MARKET and the Federation of Oils, Seeds and Fats Associations.
Bibliography: W.M. Clarke. *Inside the City*. George Allen & Unwin, London, 1983.
R. Ihre *et al. Shipbroking and Chartering Practice*. Lloyd's of London Press, 1984.

Banco Centroamericano de Integracion Economica.   Founded in 1960, the BCIE's headquarters are at Tegucigalpa, Honduras. Its membership consists of the governments of Costa Rica, El Salvador, Guatemala, Honduras and Nicaragua. Its functions are to finance the economic development and integration of Central America.
Bibliography: *Economic and Social Progress in Latin America*. Inter-American Development Bank Annual Report 1984.

band.   (1) The range within which a currency is permitted to move. Under the BRETTON WOODS system a central bank was under obligation to maintain the rate for its currency within 1% of the currency's PARITY against the dollar. Thus for 1967-71 the sterling parity was $2.40 and the band was the range $2.38-$2.42. Many proposals for reforming the Bretton Woods system hinged on 'wider bands'. Under freely floating exchange rates bands are irrelevant although in the EEC SNAKE by contrast the objective was to maintain bands of 2.25% around parity. Compare EUROPEAN MONETARY SYSTEM.
Bibliography: J.K. Walmsley. *The Foreign Exchange Handbook*. John Wiley & Sons, New York, 1983.

(2) The Bank of England's money market interventions are conducted by means of purchases of BILLS OF EXCHANGE of various maturity bands: Band 1 is 1-14 days, Band 2 is 15-33 days, Band 3 is 34-63 days, and Band 4 is 64-91 days.
Bibliography: The Role of the Bank of England in the Money Market. *Bank of England Quarterly Review*, March 1982.

bank bill.   UK term for a bill of exchange which has been ACCEPTED by a bank and therefore can be sold (discounted) for

a better price. Compare ACCEPTANCE, BANKER'S ACCEPTANCE.
Bibliography: Gillett Brothers Discount Company. *The Bill on London*. Methuen & Co., London, 1976.

banker's acceptance. US and Canadian term for a bill of exchange which has been accepted by a banker. Compare ACCEPTANCE. The market in bankers' acceptances was fairly dormant between 1929 and 1955, until the FEDERAL RESERVE BANKS were authorized to enter the market directly. Since that time the volume outstanding has grown from $640 million to $50 billion by 1980. Around half of the market, historically, involves finance of shipments between third countries, which do not touch US shores, and a strong impetus to growth was provided by the oil crises of the 1970s, since a large part of Japanese oil imports were financed with US$ bankers' acceptances. The Federal Reserve lays down criteria for acceptances' eligibility for purchase in open market operations and for use at the DISCOUNT WINDOW. If a bank sells an ineligible acceptance, it is required to hold reserves against the amount of the acceptance, so that an ineligible acceptance carries a higher cost. In general, (1) acceptances of less than six months' tenor for the financing of (a) export-import, or (b) domestic shipments where documents conveying title are attached at the time of acceptance, and (2) acceptances financing domestic storage of 'readily marketable staples secured by warehouse receipt' are eligible for purchase and discount, and escape reserve requirements.
Bibliography: M. Stigum. *The Money Market*. Dow-Jones Irwin. Homewood, Ill., 1983.
T.Q. Cook & B.J. Summers. *Instruments of the Money Market*. Federal Reserve Bank of Virginia, 1981.

Bankers' Automated Clearing House (BACS). The UK system of ELECTRONIC FUNDS TRANSFER operated by the clearing banks. It handles routine, standard payments pre-submitted by the members of the system. BACS was founded in 1968 and by 1983 600

million items were cleared through the system.
Bibliography: S. Haney. BACS: The world's first EFT system. *The Banker*. London, September 1984.

bankers' draft. A DRAFT payable on demand and drawn by or on behalf of a bank upon itself. A UK resident wishing to pay a US resident might do so by buying a dollar bankers' draft from his bank, and forwarding the draft to the US resident, who would present it to his bank for payment.
Bibliography: Bills of Exchange Act (1882) Amendment Act of 1932.
A. Watson, *Finance of International Trade*, Institute of Bankers, 2nd edn., London, 1981.

banker's lien. *See* LIEN.

banker's payment. An order or draft drawn by one bank in favour of another.

Bank for International Setlements (BIS). A central bank for other central banks. Founded in 1930 to supervise transfers under the Young Plan for restructuring German debt. It now provides the Secretariat for monthly meetings of those European Central Bank Governors who are directors of the BIS. As a result the BIS has often been deeply involved in 'crisis management' in the markets. Compare BASLE AGREEMENT. It also administers the EUROPEAN MONETARY FUND.
Bibliography: J.K. Walmsley. *The Foreign Exchange Handbook*. John Wiley & Sons, New York, 1983.
BIS Annual Reports.

Bank of England, Bank of France, Bank of Italy, Bank of Japan. *See* CENTRAL BANK.

bank rate. Loosely used for the rate at which a CENTRAL BANK is prepared to lend money to its domestic banking system. In the UK the bank rate was used until 1971 when it was replaced by MINIMUM LENDING RATE.
Bibliography: The Role of the Bank of England in the Money Market. *Bank of England Quarterly Bulletin*, March 1982.
E.R. Shaw. *The London Money Market*. Heinemann, London, 1984.

bank release. A document issued by a bank after being paid (or being given an acceptance) on a bill of exchange. The effect of the release is to permit the buyer of the goods involved to take delivery, though the rights of other parties may need to be saisfied before the goods are released for delivery and in any case customs clearance must be arranged in due form.
Bibliography: V. Dover. *A Handbook to Marine Insurance*. Revised and edited R.H. Brown. Witherby & Co, London, 1975.
M. Megrah & F. R. Ryder. *Byles on Bills of Exchange*. 23rd edn., Sweet & Maxwell, London, 1972, p. 129.

Bankwire. A US computer-switched telex system linking banks: its main function is to transmit advice of payments/debits. For example, if Exxon pays Citibank $5 million by debit to its account at Morgan, the latter would make payment by FEDWIRE but would confirm by Bankwire.
Bibliography: The Federal Reserve and the Payments System. *Federal Reserve Bulletin*. Washington DC, February 1981.

Banque Francaise du Commerce Exterieure (BFCE). French quasi-government bank providing export finance at medium or long-term. BFCE endorses medium-term financing provided by the banks, which can then be rediscounted at the Banque de France to relieve the banks of having to finance the lending from their own resources; long-term export credit is financed directly by the BFCE rather than the Banque de France.
Bibliography: *The Export Credit Financing Systems in OECD Member Countries*. OECD, Paris, 1982.

Bardepot. A German regulation, now suspended, requiring that a percentage of German residents' foreign borrowings be deposited in cash at the Bundesbank in a non-interest bearing account, thus reducing the incentive to borrow in an attempt to deter capital inflows.
Bibliography: M. Pelzer & K. Nebendorf. *Banking in Germany*. Fritz Knapp Verlag, 1973.
Annual Reports of the Deutsche Bundesbank. Frankfurt.

bareboat charter. Charter of a ship alone, without a crew. Also known as a DEMISE CHARTER. Distinct from a TIME CHARTER and a VOYAGE CHARTER where the shipowner provides the crew. Under a bareboat charter the charterer provides the crew.
Bibliography: Mocatta, Mustill & Boyd. *Scrutton on Charterparties and Bills of Lading*. 18th edn. Sweet & Maxwell, London, 1974.
M.S.W. Hoyle. *The Law of International Trade*. Laureate Press,London, 1981.

bargain. UK Stock Exchange term for a transaction in a stock or share. Bargains are MARKED and the price at which they are carried out is reported the following day in the press.
Bibliography: J. Dundas Hamilton. *Stockbroking Today*. Macmillan Press, London, 1979.

barter. Exchange of goods or services without the intervention of money. More widespread in international trade since the oil crises of the 1970s and the LDC debt problems of recent years. Barter includes COUNTERTRADING where the exporter is asked to take part-payment in goods, and SWITCH TRADING, a related development. These and other techniques such as PRODUCT PAYBACK and COOPERATION AGREEMENTS are important in trading with certain East European or developing countries.
Bibliography: P.D. Ehrenhaft (ed.). *Countertrade: International Trade Without Cash*. Law & Business/Harcourt Brace Jovanovich, New York, 1983.
P. Verzariu. *Countertrade, Barter and Offsets*. McGraw-Hill, New York, 1984.
R. Birley. Can't pay? Will pay, but in sultanas. *Euromoney*, London, May 1983.
L. Wilt. Why Latin America is Wary of Barter. *Euromoney*, London, January 1984.

base rate. (1) Term used in the UK for the rate used by banks for computing the rate of interest charged to borrowers. Normally, first-class industrial borrowers will pay 1% over base, although in many cases loans will be priced over sterling LIBOR. Compare PRIME RATE.

(2) US and Euromarket term sometimes used for an alternative to PRIME RATE. For example, in the borrowing of $125 million by the Carolina Power & Light Co. in 1981, base

rate was defined as the higher of prime or the three month CD rate adjusted for the cost of reserves. Compare CD; ADJUSTED CD RATE.

basic balance. A term used to describe the sum of the balance of payments CURRENT ACCOUNT plus long-term capital movements. It fell into disrepute in the UK because of the difficulty of deciding what 'long-term' was, and was ultimately repalced by the concept of 'balance for official financing'. In the US the concept is one of several. Compare BALANCE OF PAYMENTS and references cited there.

basis. (1) In the commodity markets, and thus by analogy, the financial FUTURES markets, basis is defined as the arithmetic difference between the CASH price and the futures price. For example, if short-term interest rates are below long-term rates, dealers who own Treasury bonds are earning coupon income which is more than the cost of financing them. Thus they can afford to quote lower prices on deferred sales, so futures prices will be lower than cash prices. This is known as positive basis, and is associated with a POSITIVE YIELD CURVE. Conversely, a NEGATIVE YIELD CURVE is associated with negative basis.

Bibliography: Chicago Board of Trade. *Financial Instruments Markets: Cash-Futures Relationships.* Chicago, USA, n.d.
Chicago Board of Trade. *Understanding the Delivery Process in Financial Futures.* Chicago, n.d.
A.M. Loosigian. *Interest Rate Futures.* Dow-Jones Irwin, Homewood, Ill., 1980.
N.H. Rothstein & J.M. Litle. *The Financial Futures Handbook.* McGraw-Hill, New York, 1984.

(2) The term refers also to interest calculation methods. Thus a bond or loan rate might be quoted on the following different bases:

Actual/365 annual:	annual interest payment, counting the actual days in the loan, using a 365 day year (UK money markets)
Actual/360 annual:	As above using a 360 day year. (US/Euro-money markets. Sometimes refer- red to as 'Euro' or 'CD' basis)
Actual/365 semi-annual:	Semi-annual interest payments, counting actual days, using a 365 day year. (UK gilt-edged US Treasury bonds. Sometimes referred to as 'bond-equivalent basis'.)
Actual/360 semi-annual:	As above using a 360 day year.
360/360 annual:	Calculated using 30 days in each month, rather than the actual days. (Many Continental European bonds, Euro-bonds)
360/360 semi-annual:	As above but semi-annual. (US Federal agencies, municipal bonds, Yankee and corporate bonds)

Bibliography: M. Stigum. *Money Market Calculations.* Dow-Jones Irwin, Homewood, Ill.,1981;
L.J. Kemp. *Guide to World Money and Capital Markets.* McGraw-Hill, UK,1981.

basis points. An American term usually referring to interest rates: 100 basis points equals 1%.

basis risk. Term used in the financial futures markets (and commodity futures markets) to refer to the risk of a change in the BASIS. A hedger might seek to hedge a LONG position in the EUROBOND market by selling US Treasury bond futures (since there are no Eurobond futures). In that case the basis risk is that the cash prices in the Eurobond market might might fall and that the Treasury futures might rise (i.e. cash Treasury prices rise), so that the hedger loses money on both sides of the deal. This would occur if the Eurobond market deteriorated relative to the domestic US bond market.

Bibliography: A.M. Loosigian. *Interest Rate Futures.* Dow-Jones Irwin, Homewood Ill., 1980.
N.H. Rothstein & J.M. Little. *The Handbook of Financial Futures.* Dow-Jones Irwin, Homewood, Ill., 1984.

basket (of currencies). *See* UNIT OF ACCOUNT.

Basle Agreement.   The first version in 1961 was an informal agreement at the central bankers' monthly meeting (Compare BANK FOR INTERNATIONAL SETTLEMENTS) to cooperate in the foreign exchange markets. A facility was agreed in 1966 to offset falls in UK reserves caused by fluctuations in other countries' STERLING BALANCES, another was announced in 1968 at the time of the STERLING GUARANTEE SCHEME. In January 1977, a new Basle facility of $3 billion was announced, again linked to sterling balance withdrawals, accompanied by an offer of foreign currency bonds by the UK government, plus assurances that the sterling balances would not be allowed to rise unduly.
Bibliography: F. Hirsch. *Money International.* Penguin Books, London, 1967.
B. Tew. *The Evolution of the International Monetary System 1945-77.* Hutchinson & Co., London, 1977.
Bank for International Settlement BIS Annual Reports.
Bank of England Quarterly Bulletin, various issues.

Basle Concordat.   Unlike the Basle Agreements, which were generally concerned with shoring up the international financial system, the Basle Concordat was essentially an agreement between the CENTRAL BANKS, within the BIS framework again (*See* BANK FOR INTERNATIONAL SETTLEMENT), on supervisory matters. The first Concordat was adopted in 1975 and laid down certain principles – notably who was to supervise what, and what information should be exchanged between central banks. It broadly laid down that the central banks of the bank's parent country and of the host country in which its branch or subsidiary were located, should share responsibility for supervision. Liquidity was generally to be supervised by the host and solvency by the parent central bank, except for subsidiaries, where the host was to be primarily responsible. The failure of Banco Ambrosiano, and the failure of the Italian and Luxembourg authorities to take responsibility for Ambrosiano's Luxembourg subsidiary, prompted a review of the Concordat in the summer of 1983.
Bibliography: W.P. Cooke. Developments in Cooperation among Bank Supervisory Authorities. *Bank of England Quarterly Bulletin,* June 1981.
R. Dale. Basle Concordat: Lessons from Ambrosiano. *The Banker,* London, September 1983.
G.G. Johnson & R.K. Abrams. *Aspects of the International Banking Safety Net.* Occasional Paper no. 17, IMF, Washington 1983.

BDR.   *See* BEARER DEPOSITORY RECEIPT.

bear.   A person who expects the price of something to fall, e.g. a bear of sterling expects the pound to fall against other currencies. An 'uncovered' bear has contracted to sell something which at the time of the contract he does not actually possess; he hopes that before he has to deliver it, the price will have fallen to enable him to buy more cheaply.

bear covering.   Purchase by bears of the stock, commodity or currency which they have sold.

bearer.   Refers to securities in which the ownership of the security is transferred merely by handing it over as distinct from a security where transfer of ownership has normally to be registered in a central register.
Bibliography: P. Wood. *Law and Practice of International Finance.* Sweet & Maxwell, London, 1980

bearer depositary receipt (BDR).   A DEPOSITARY RECEIPT made out in bearer form. Used to facilitate trading in shares of foreign companies. For example, in the UK, General Motors has issued bearer depositary receipts representing units equivalent to one-twentieth of a fully paid share of General Motors common stock. The BDR permits trading in the UK without the necessity of US paperwork and it permits trading in relatively small amounts.
Bibliography: *Depositary Receipts.* Morgan Guaranty Trust Company, New York, n.d.

The Stock Exchange Official Year Book. Macmillan, London, 1984

bearer deposit note. Canadian term for a bearer, discount instrument evidencing a deposit at a bank (in contrast to an interest-bearing certificate of deposit).

bear raid. Term for a wave of selling a stock, commodity or currency. Usually it implies some concertation between sellers but it is very loosely used.
Bibliography: J. Dundas Hamilton. *Stockbroking Today.* Macmillan Press, London, 1979.

bear spread. An OPTIONS and FINANCIAL FUTURES market term. (1) A bear spread in the options market consists of the purchase of a CALL option at a certain STRIKE PRICE and the sale of a call at a lower strike price. For example, if XYZ Co. stock is trading at 32, the investor would sell, say, the October 30 call, for say, 3; and buy the October 35 call for, say, 1. This earns 2 points. The investor hopes that the stock will fall below 30, in which case both options will be worthless. If the stock rises above 35, the investor protects himself by exercising the 35 call.
Bibliography: L.G. McMillan. *Options as a Strategic Investment.* New York Institute of Finance, New York, 1980.
(2) In the futures markets, a bear spread would usually involve the sale of the nearer month and the purchase of the further month. This will be profitable if rates rise, on the assumption that the nearby month will tend to move faster than the further month. Then the profit on the near sale will more than offset the loss on the further purchase.
Bibliography: N.H. Rothstein & J.M. Little. *The Handbook of Financial Futures.* McGraw-Hill, New York, 1984.

bear squeeze. (1) In general, a situation where BEARS are forced to cover their positions as prices rise; in financial futures and other markets where dealing is largely on MARGIN the bear squeeze is compounded by the fact that MARGIN CALLS increase the financial pressure on the bear.
(2) A tactic often employed by central

banks who know that uncovered bears have sold their currency short. By temporarily bidding up the currency until the time comes for the bears to deliver the currency they had contracted to sell, the central bank can force the bears to take a loss. However, the tactic is by definition a temporary expedient. Compare EUROSTERLING.

Belgo-Luxembourg Economic Union. Belgium and Luxembourg formed a customs and economic union in 1921, eliminating tariff barriers and allowing Belgian currency to circulate freely in Luxembourg.

beneficial owner. The person or institution to whom the benefits of ownership will ultimately accrue. Compare NOMINEE.

Benelux. Abbreviation of Belgium, Netherlands, Luxembourg. Netherlands joined the Belgo-Luxembourg customs union in 1948, and the three countries formed an economic union in 1958; they virtually eliminated tariffs between the countries as well as obstacles to the movement of goods, services and capital – over and above EEC provisions. The Benelux countries also kept their currencies within a narrow range of each other for several years (the 'worm' within the SNAKE).

Berne Union. Founded in 1934, the Berne Union (or The International Union of Credit and Investment Insurers) works for 'the international acceptance of sound principles of export credit and investment insurance'. It comprises 36 members from 29 countries ranging from private organizations to government departments and statutory bodies.
Bibliography: *The Export Credit Financing Systems in OECD Member Countries.* OECD, Paris, 1982.
A. Dunn & M. Knight. *Export Finance.* Euromoney, London, 1982.

best effort. In the US securities market this refers to a new issue which is not underwritten and not purchased as a whole from the issuer but is sold by securities dealers on a

'sell what can be sold' basis. Similarly in the EUROBOND market; and for a syndicated EURO-CREDIT a best-efforts syndication may be done on the basis that the managers do not commit funds in advance, but only if the syndication is successful.
Bibliography: L.S. Goodman. Syndicated Eurolending: Pricing and Practice *in* A.M. George & I.H. Giddy. *International Finance Handbook.* John Wiley & Sons, New York, 1983.

beta.   A term from MODERN PORTFOLIO THEORY. Beta measures the relative volatility, and thus riskiness, of a stock or portfolio relative to the market. For the market as a whole, beta must always be 1; a beta of more than 1 indicates relatively higher volatility than the market.
Bibliography: H. Markowitz. *Portfolio Selection.* John Wiley & Sons, New York, 1959.
W.B. Riley & A.H. Montgomery. *Guide to Computer Assisted Investment Analysis.* McGraw-Hill, New York, 1982.

BF. BFr.   Abbreviation for Belgian franc.

BFCE.   *See* BANQUE FRANÇAISE DU COMMERCE EXTÉRIEURE.

Bibor.   Abbreviation for Bahrain Inter-Bank Offered Rate. *See* LONDON INTER-BANK OFFERED RATE.

bid.   The rate which a bank will pay for a deposit, a security, or a currency. Compare OFFER.

bid bond, letter of credit.   Another term for a TENDER BOND or tender letter of credit: a bid bond is called for by a foreign buyer seeking bids or tenders on a contract who wishes to assure himself that those who tender are financially and technically competent to undertake the contract. In certain cases – notably where the bidder is a US firm, since US banks cannot provide guarantees in the same form as European banks, a STAND-BY LETTER OF CREDIT or 'bid letter of credit' will be used. Compare ADVANCE PAYMENT BOND; MAINTENANCE BOND; PERFORMANCE BOND; RETENTION MONEY BOND.

Bibliography: Confederation of British Industry. *Performance Bonds and Guarantees.* London, 1978.
D. Sassoon (ed.). *Bidding for Projects Financed by International Lending Agencies.* Gower Press, UK, 1982.

big figure.   Foreign exchange dealers' term normally denoting the first three digits of an exchange rate, e.g. $1.82 per L, DM2.02 per $. Dealers might quote dollar/sterling '40-50', leaving the 'big figure' understood, i.e. $1.8240/50. The term is also used in the metals markets. Compare HANDLE.

big ticket.   A LEASING term. It refers to single, large lease transactions.
Bibliography: Recent Developments in Equipment Leasing *Bank of England Quarterly Bulletin, September 1982.*
P.K. Nevitt. *Project Financing.* Euromoney Publications, London, 1983.

bilateral clearing.   A system used in international trade (especially between Eastern Bloc countries and developing countries) in order to economize on the use of scarce foreign exchange. The normal system is to route all payments through the central bank rather than via foreign trade banks or their equivalent, and in the strictest variant, the two countries are required exactly to balance their mutual trade each year. A variation permits the accumulation of credits by one partner. A further relaxation permits the debtor country to settle the balance in a specified currency (usually convertible). Clearing accounts can lead to a SWITCH TRANSACTION if clearing account imbalances can be used in third countries. Compare BARTER, CLEARING ACCOUNT, COMPENSATION TRADING, SWITCH TRADING.
Bibliography: P.D. Ehrenhaft. *Countertrade: International Trade Without Cash.* Law & Business/Harcourt Brace Jovanovich, New York, 1983.
P. Verzariu. *Countertrade, Barter and Offsets.* McGraw-Hill, New York, 1984.

bilateral net credit limits.   A US term referring to payments systems. A bank receiving payments from another bank on the CLEARING HOUSE INTERBANK PAYMENTS SYSTEM, which it must then pay away to customers, faces the risk that the incoming payment from the other bank may not be received, although it has paid the money away to the customer. It might set a bilateral net credit limit on the amount of money it was willing to receive from the other bank for onward payment to third parties.

Bibliography: D.B. Humphrey. Reducing Interbank Risk on Large Dollar Payment Networks. *Journal of Cash Management*. Atlanta, Ga, September 1984.

bilateral trade agreement. An agreement between two countries aimed at regulating their mutual trade, normally to expand it or prevent unfair competition.

Bibliography: *Annual Report on Exchange Arrangements*. International Monetary Fund, Washington DC, annually.
P. Verzariu. *Countertrade, Barter and Offsets*. McGraw-Hill, New York, 1984.

bill arbitrage. A UK term for a situation where a company funds itself by drawing and discounting a BILL OF EXCHANGE and the redepositing the proceeds in the wholesale deposit market: this can occur when the Bank of England's operations in the money market create a shortage of bills, reducing their rate relative to the deposit market.

Bibliography: A note on money market arbitrage. *Bank of England Quarterly Bulletin*. June 1982.

bill broker. A British term for DISCOUNT HOUSES arising from the fact that in the early 19th century most British banks lent via BILLS OF EXCHANGE. Bill brokers acted as intermediaries by placing bills held by banks which were overlent with banks which had surplus funds. Later the brokers began to buy and sell on their own account, so that the term became something of a misnomer.

Bibliography: E.R. Shaw. *The London Money Market*. 3rd edn. Heinemann, London 1983.
J.S.G. Wilson. Recent Changes in London's Money Market Arrangements. *Banca Nazionale del Lavoro Quarterly Review*. March 1983.

billion. Now usually 1,000 million; past European usage was that 1 billion=1,000,000 million.

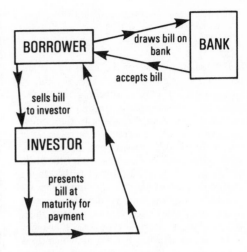

SUMMARY
1. Borrower draws bill on bank which accepts it.
2. Borrower sells bill to investor.
3. At maturity investor is repaid by borrower.

BILL OF EXCHANGE

bill of exchange. A basic instrument of international trade finance. (See diagram.) It is defined in the UK's Bills of Exchange Act of 1882 as: 'an unconditional order in writing, addressed by one person to another, signed by the person giving it, requiring the person to whom it is addressed to pay on demand or at a fixed or determinable future time a sum certaim in money to or to the order of a specified person or to bearer.' If the person to whom the bill is addressed (the DRAWEE) is prepared to pay the bill, he signifies his ACCEPTANCE by writing his signature on the face of the bill. If the drawee/acceptor of the bill is a bank, the bill then becomes a 'bank bill' and is more easily sold (discounted); therefore a number of banks have specialized in this line of business. *See* ACCEPTANCE, ACCEPTING HOUSE, BANKERS' ACCEPTANCE, BILL BROKERS, DISCOUNT HOUSE, DOCUMENTARY CREDIT.

Bibliography: Gillett Brothers Discount Company. *The Bill on London*. Methuen & Co., London, 1976.

A. Watson. *Finance of International Trade.* Institute of Bankers, London, 1981.
1882 Bills of Exchange Act.

bill of lading. One of the most important documents used in foreign trade, the bill of lading (or B/L) is (i) the receipt given by the shipping company to the shipper for goods accepted for carriage; (ii) title to the goods; (iii) evidence of a contract of carriage. It is not a negotiable instrument in the UK although in the US it may be under the Bills of Lading Act 1916. It is said to be 'foul', 'dirty', or 'claused' if the shipping company indicates on it that there is something wrong (e.g. 'Sacks wet', 'Box 60 missing'). Otherwise it is 'clean'. Various types of B/L are met with: (a) a short form B/L is one which does not carry on it all the conditions of carriage; such a bill may be accepted by banks under the UNIFORM CUSTOMS AND PRACTICE FOR DOCUMENTARY CREDITS unless specifically forbidden. In April 1979 the General Council of British Shipping introduced a Common (i.e. standard) Short Form Bill of Lading. (b) A liner B/L applies to goods shipped on regular line steamers (as opposed to tramp steamers); otherwise it resembles an ordinary B/L. (c) Through B/L refers to a B/L which is issued to cover an entire journey, regardless of the fact that the journey is being made by different modes of transport – e.g. to cover a lorry journey from Turkey to Calais and a ship from Calais to Dover. (d)A container B/L is one covering goods shipped in a container. It may bear some wording such as 'received for shipment one container said to contain machine tools'. (e) A shipped B/L carries on it an indication that the goods concerned have actually been shipped (as distinct from a wording such as 'received for shipment'). (f)A charter-party B/L is one evidencing shipment on a chartered vessel. In this case the shipper's contract is not with the owner of the vessel but with its charterer. Banks will not normally accept such bills for credits unless specifically requested owing to the complexity of the usual charterparty contract. Compare COMBINED TRANSPORT DOCUMENT, COMMON SHORT FORM BILL OF LADING, HAMBURG RULES, THROUGH BILL OF LADING.

Bibliography: Mocatta, Mustill & Boyd. *Scrutton on Charterperties and Bills of Lading.* 18th edn., Sweet & Maxwell, London, 1974.
A. Watson, *Finance of International Trade,* 2nd edn. Institute of Bankers, London, 1981.

bind. (1) In general, the term describes a firm commitment. Thus, an insurance UNDERWRITER will be bound by the terms of the SLIP he has signed. (2) A term relating to international trade negotiations: a country is said to 'bind' a tariff if it commits itself not to increase it. Compare GATT.

Bibliography: A. Shonfield (ed.). *International Economic Relations of the Western World 1959-71.* Royal Institute of International Affairs, London, 1976.

BIS. Abbreviation for BANK FOR INTERNATIONAL SETTLEMENTS.

B/L. Abbreviation for BILL OF LADING.

Black-Scholes Model. One of the first, and most widely used, OPTION pricing models. Essentially, the model states that the option price should be a function of the STRIKING PRICE, the current price of the instrument involved, the current risk-free interest rate, the time remaining to the expiration of the option, and the volatility of the price of the instrument.

Bibliography: L.G. McMillan. *Options as a Strategic Investment.* New York Institute of Finance, New York, 1980.
F. Black & M. Scholes. The Pricing of Options and Corporate Liabilities. *Journal of Political Economy,* May 1973.
D.W. French. Black-Scholes vs. Kassouf Option Pricing. *Journal of Business Finance & Accounting.* Oxford, Autumn 1983.

B/Lading. Abbreviation for BILL OF LADING.

blanc. French term, analogous to the English CLEAN, meaning a money-market operation without underlying documentary security.

Bibliography: D. Marteau & E. de la Chaise. *Le*

marché monétaire et la gestion de trésorerie des banques. Dunod, Paris, 1981.

BLEU. Abbreviation for BELGO-LUXEM-BOURG ECONOMIC UNION.

block. US securities market term for a large amount of stock. The New York Stock Exchange defines it as 'a quantity of stock having a market value of $200,000 or more which is acquired by a member organization on its own behalf and/or from others from one or more buyers or sellers in a single transaction'.
Bibliography: L.M. Loll & J.G. Buckley. *The Over the Counter Markets.* Prentice-Hall, USA, 1981.
R.J. Teweles & E.S. Bradley. *The Stock Market.* John Wiley & Sons, New York, 1982.

block automation system. New York Stock Exchange system for facilitating trading in BLOCKS of stock: orders are entered on a daily basis and matched off against each other.
Bibliography: L.M. Loll & J.G. Buckley. *The Over the Counter Markets.* Prentice-Hall, USA, 1981.
R.J. Teweles & E.S. Bradley. *The Stock Market.* John Wiley & Sons, New York, 1982.

blocked accounts. In general, any account with a bank where payments cannot be made freely. The term refers specifically (1)to a system where payments for imports are credited to an account in the name of the foreign exporter, who is prohibited from drawing on it except for payments within the importing country, (2) to accounts which have been 'frozen' for political reasons e.g. Cuban accounts in the US. During 1939-45, UK payments for imports of war materials were often credited to such accounts, leading to a build-up of STERLING BALANCES. Similar systems are currently in operation in a number of countries, particularly in developing countries.
Bibliography: P. Verzariu. *Countertrade, Barter and Offsets.* McGraw-Hill, New York, 1984.

block (or blanket) policy. A marine insurance policy effected for a particular period to meet special circumstances, such as frequent despatches (each of similar value) made of similar goods.
Bibliography: V. Dover. *A Handbook to Marine Insurance.* Revised and edited R.H. Brown. Witherby & Co., London, 1975.

block positioner. US securities market term for a firm which acquires stock in BLOCKS in order to facilitate the handling of customer orders.
Bibliography: L.M. Loll & J.G. Buckley. *The Over the Counter Markets.* Prentice-Hall, USA, 1981.
R.J. Teweles & E.S. Bradley. *The Stock Market.* John Wiley & Sons, New York, 1982.

blue sky. US term for state laws (as against federal laws) regulating the issue and sale of securities. They contain provisions designed to protect the public from securities frauds.
Bibliography: P. Wood. *Law and Practice of International Finance.* Sweet & Maxwell, London, 1980.

Blumenthal bonds. *See* CARTER BONDS.

Bon du Tresor. French Treasury bill; two classes are available: 'Bons du Tresor en comptes courants', a marketable instrument with maturities ranging from 3 to 18 months, and 'Bons du Tresor sur formules', non-marketable instruments designed for individual investors, with a maturity of five years.
Bibliography: *Government Debt Management: Debt Instruments and Selling Techniques.* OECD, Paris, 1983.
D. Marteau & E. de la Chaise. *Le marché monétaire et la gestion de trésorerie des banques.* Dunod, Paris, 1981.

bond. (1) An interest-bearing certificate of debt – a written contract by the issuer to pay the lender a fixed principal amount at a stated future date and a series of interest payments (usually semi-annually except for EURO-BONDS where it is annually) until the bond matures. In the US, a bond is usually secured, while a debenture is not. In the UK, the reverse applies. *See* ASIAN DOLLAR BOND, CONVERTIBLES, DEBENTURE, EURO-BOND, FLOATING RATE BOND, GILT-EDGED, INCOME BOND, MANAGED BOND, PROPERTY BOND.

Bibliography: D.M. Darst. *The Complete Bond Book.* McGraw-Hill, New York, 1975.
F.J. Fabozzi & I.M.Pollack. *The Handbook of Fixed Income Securities.* Dow-Jones Irwin, Homewood Ill, 1983.
D. O' Shea, *Investing for Beginners.* Financial Times Business Information, London, 1984.
(2) The term is also used to cover an investment package such as a 'managed bond' where a lump-sum investment by an individual is reinvested by the bond's managers, usually in a mix of property, equities, and fixed-interest securities.
Bibliography: D. O'Shea. *Investing for Beginners.* Financial Times Business Information, London, 1984.
(3) Also used to mean a guarantee or indemnity. A PERFORMANCE BOND is a sum of money payable, usually by a bank, if a contract is not performed; goods may be 'bonded' in a customs warehouse until duty is paid on them.
Bibliography: D. Sassoon (ed.). *Bidding for Projects Financed by International Lending Agencies.* Gower Press, UK, 1982;
W.F. von Marshall, Recent Developments in the Field of Standby Letters of Credit, Bank Guarantees and Performance Bonds *in* C.M. Chinkin *et al.* (eds). *Current Problems of International Trade Financing.* Butterworths, UK/Malaya Law Review, 1983.

Bond equivalent yield. Term – generally a US term – for the yield on a DISCOUNT security once it has been converted to a BOND basis for comparison purposes by using the DISCOUNT-TO-YIELD conversion formula. The latter converts to an annual basis. If the bond yield needed is a semi-annual one (as is normal in the US and UK, but not in the EUROBOND market, which is annual) the rate must be converted to semi-annual. This results in two formulas for bond equivalent yield: the first is used if the underlying (discount) security has less than six months to run. The second is used if it has more than six months to run. Thus:
Case I: Less than six months to run

$$d_b = \frac{365d}{360 - dt_{sm}}$$

Case II: More than six months

$$d_b = \frac{-\frac{2t_{sm}}{365} + 2\sqrt{\left[\frac{t_{sm}}{365}\right]^2 - \left[\frac{2t_{sm}}{365} - 1\right]\left[1 - \frac{1}{P}\right]}}{\frac{2t_{sm}}{365} - 1}$$

Where:
P = price (per £1 of nominal amount)
d = rate of discount (decimal – e.g. 8.25% = .0825)
d_b = bond equivalent yield
t_{sm} = days from settlement to maturity
The formula as stated shows the conversion from a 360-day discount security to a 365-day bond yield. (See BASIS for an explanation of 360 versus 365-day yields.) As an example, in Case I, a US$ BANKER'S ACCEPTANCE with 182 days from settlement to maturity, with a discount rate of 8%, yields

$$8.45\% = \frac{365 \times 0.08}{360 - (0.08 \times 182)}$$

In Case II, consider a US dollar Treasury bill with 190 days to run. It is offered at a discount rate of 9.35%. The price is calculated from that discount rate (see DISCOUNT) as $95.0653 per $100 nominal. Then the formula yields

$$9.95\% = \frac{-\frac{2 \times 190}{365} + 2\sqrt{\left(\frac{190}{365}\right)^2 - \left(\frac{2 \times 190}{365} - 1\right)\left(1 - \frac{1}{0.950653}\right)}}{\left(\frac{2 \times 190}{365}\right) - 1}$$

Source: M. Stigum. *Money Market Calculations.* Dow-Jones Irwin, Homewood, Ill., 1981.
B.M. Spence *et al. Standard Securities Calculation Methods.* Securities Industry Association, New York, 1973.
P. Phillips *Inside the Gilt-Edged Market.* Woodhead-Faulkner, Cambridge, UK, 1984.

book. (1) Colloquial term referring to dealers' total activity in their markets. Thus a bank will 'run a book' of say £100 million in foreign exchange; its assets and liabilities in foreign exchange at that time will total $100 million. Similarly a DISCOUNT HOUSE may run a book of GILTS or bills or CDs. To be distinguished from the 'books' (accounts) of the business as a whole.

(2) A transaction may be 'booked'- i.e. bookkeeping entries made in a country outside that where the transaction itself is negotiated. This is often done in order to reduce tax liability or to eliminate reserve requirements.

book-entry security. US term for a security issued, not in the form of a certificate, but as an entry in an account at a bank. Practically all marketable US Treasury securities are now held in book-entry form.
Bibliography: M. E. Bedford. Recent developments in Treasury financing techniques. *Federal Reserve Bank of Kansas City Monthly Review*. July-August 1977.

book-runner. A EUROMARKET term for the bank or securities house which plays a central part in organizing the SYNDICATE which is making the loan or buying the bond issue. The book-runner is responsible for sending telexes, disseminating information to interested banks, and informing both the borrower and management group of daily progress. The role is very visible vis-à-vis the borrower and the market. As such it is generally considered the most desirable syndicate position.
Bibliography: R.P. McDonald. *International Syndicated Loans*. Euromoney Publications, London, 1982.

book value. The value of a set of assets as recorded in a firm's accounts; very often the valuation is the original purchase price, which may often differ substantially from the current value. For example, although UK firms are permitted to revalue certain assets such as buildings in line with current prices, this is not the case in the US.
Bibliography: R. Brealey & S. Myers. *Principles of Corporate Finance*, McGraw-Hill, New York/London, 1984, Coopers & Lybrand. *Manual of Accounting*, Gee & Co., London 1981.

book yield. The yield on a portfolio when it is valued at its BOOK VALUE.

boot. A US term. Boot arises from the receipt of property other than stock or securities in an exchange for stock or securities. If stock is exchanged for stock and securities a portion of the gain may be taxable as boot.
Bibliography: N.J. Letizia & A.J. Taranto. Tax Consequences of Exchange Offers *in* F.J. Fabozzi & I.M. Pollack. *The Handbook of Fixed Income Securities*. Dow-Jones Irwin, Homewood Ill., 1983.

borrow. (1) In general, to acquire the use of funds by promising to repay them. (2) In commodities markets, particularly metals, a buyer of the CASH coupled with a simultaneous forward sale is said to 'borrow' the metal.
Bibliography: R. Gibson-Jarvie. *The London Metal Exchange*. Woodhead-Faulkner, Cambridge, UK/ Nichols Publishing, New York, 1983.

bought deal. A EUROBOND market term (now used in US markets also) for a new bond issue handled on the basis that one, or at most, a small number of MANAGERS buy the entire issue at a firm price, taking the risk that the market will deteriorate before they can dispose of their purchases
Bibliography: F.G. Fisher. *International Bonds*. Euromoney Publications, London 1981.
R.M. Kock. Underwriters need to know where they stand. *Euromoney*, London, May 1983.

Bourse. French (and Continental generally) term for stock exchange. In several countries the foreign exchange FIXING takes place at the Bourse.
Bibliography: L.J. Kemp. *A Guide to World Money and Capital Markets*. McGraw-Hill, UK, 1981.
A.M. George & I.H. Giddy. *International Finance Handbook*. John Wiley & Sons, New York, 1983.

box spread. An options market term. In a box spread, the investor holds the stock, buys a PUT with a low STRIKE PRICE, buys a CALL with a high strike price, and writes two calls with an exercise price in between the other two. This admittedly complex exercise has the merit of 'boxing in' the investor – as long as the stock stays inside a given range he will make money.

Bibliography: R.M. Bookstaber. *Option Pricing and Strategies in Investing.* Addison-Wesley, Reading, Mass., 1981.

bracket. A US term for the groupings determined by UNDERWRITING amounts in a new issue or loan. It is also used in the EUROMARKETS. Banks providing funds for a EUROCREDIT or EUROBOND ISSUE are grouped into 'brackets' in the TOMBSTONES with the LEAD MANAGER on top, followed in order by the CO-MANAGERS, special UNDER-WRITERS (if any), underwriters and other selling group managers. In the past there tended to be SPECIAL BRACKET underwriters and major or minor underwriters. Major underwriters took 1%, minor underwriters 1/2% of a borrowing or issue. In larger SYNDICATES it is now common to split into major (0.6% to 1%), sub-major (0.3% to 0.6%), and minor (0.1% to 0.3%).

Bibliography: M. Mendelson. The Eurobond and Foreign Bond Markets *in* A.M. George & I.H. Giddy. *International Finance Handbook.* John Wiley & Sons, New York, 1983.
F.G. Fisher. *International Bonds.* Euromoney Publications, London 1981.

break. (1) In a EUROCREDIT the break clause is one which passes on to the borrower the risk that certain events may curtail that lender's activity or close the Eurocurrency market. Compare CURRENCY AVAILABILITY CLAUSE, DISASTER CLAUSE.

Bibliography: P. Wood. *Law and Practice of International Finance.* Sweet & Maxwell, London, 1980.
(2) In US securities markets, term used to indicate that syndicate restrictions have been removed from a new issue and that the security is trading or expected to trade at discount from its initial offering price.

break-out. A term from TECHNICAL ANALYSIS. A break-out occurs when the price being charted breaks through a limit set by a previous CHANNEL or when the price moves in such a way as to break away from some pattern being formed, e.g. a DOUBLE TOP.

Bibliography: P.J. Kaufman (ed). *Technical Analysis in Commodities.* John Wiley & Co., New York, 1981.
N.H. Rothstein & J.M. Little (eds). *The Handbook of Financial Futures.* McGraw-Hill, USA, 1984.

Bretton Woods. The site of a 1944 agreement, which founded the INTERNATIONAL MONETARY FUND and WORLD BANK, and laid down the ground rules for the international monetary system. The rules stated that members were to adhere (where possible) to fixed exchange rates, and provided means for financing temporary pressures on currencies. The rules also stated that devaluation should only be resorted to if there were 'fundamental disequilibrium' in the balance of the payments.

Bibliography: F. Hirsch. *Money International.* Penguin Books, London, 1967.
J.K. Walmsley. *The Foreign Exchange Handbook.* John Wiley & Sons, New York, 1983.

broadcast system. A method of syndicating EUROCREDITS. A bank or group of banks receive a MANDATE to provide the funds and then offer participation in the loan, more or less indiscriminately, to other banks, by telex or letter.

Bibliography: F.G. Fisher. *International Bonds.* Euromoney Publications, London, 1981.

broken period. A money market or forward foreign exchange deal which is not for a standard maturity (normally one, two, three or six months and sometimes 12 months) involves a broken period.

Bibliography: J.K. Walmsley. *The Foreign Exchange Handbook.* John Wiley & Sons, New York, 1983.

broker. Generally, an agent acting on behalf of a principal, except in the case of a BILL BROKER. Brokers are found in commodity, money, stock and foreign exchange markets. Compare FOREIGN EXCHANGE BROKER.

Bibliography: *The New 'Beginners Please'.* Investors Chronicle. London, 1975.
J.K. Walmsley. *The Foreign Exchange Handbook.* John Wiley & Sons, New York, 1983.

Gerrard & National Discount Corporation. *The London Discount Market.* London, 1981.

brokerage. Commission charged by a BROKER to clients on whose behalf they have acted.

broker's loan rate. The rate charged by US banks to their STOCK-BROKER customers for lendings against the pledge of US Government securities. Because of the first-class COLLATERAL the loan rate is normally well below PRIME – up to 1 per cent. The loans are normally repayable on demand. Movement in the broker's loan rate is often taken as a signal of forthcoming movements in other lending rates. The best UK parallel might be money lent at CALL to a DISCOUNT HOUSE, although the brokers' loan rate does not change as continuously as the call money rate.
Bibliography: M. Stigum. *The Money Market.* Dow-Jones Irwin, Homewood, Ill., 1983.

Brussels Tariff Nomenclature. *See* CUSTOMS COOPERATION COUNCIL NOMENCLATURE.

BTN. *See* CUSTOMS COOPERATION COUNCIL NOMENCLATURE.

bull. An operator who expects the price of a commodity, stock or currency to rise. Compare BEAR.

bullet. A US and EUROMARKET term for a borrowing which is not to be repaid gradually but in a lump sum at the end of its term. As an example, the Chugoku Electric Power Co. Inc. raised a five-year, $50 million Eurobond in August 1984 with a bullet repayment of the total amount due on 21 August, 1989.
Bibliography: L.S. Goodman. Syndicated Euro-Lending: Pricing and Practice *in* A.M. George & I.H. Giddy (eds). *International Finance Handbook.* John Wiley & Sons, New York, 1983.

bullion. Term for gold in bar form as distinct from gold coins. The London market for gold bullion is one of the most important in the world, along with Zurich and Hong Kong; New York is preeminent in gold futures, but not in physical bullion. Estimates of the change (in metric tons) in net global bullion holdings made by Consolidated Gold Fields Ltd. are as follows:

1973	547	1978	149	1983	297
1974	512	1979	385		
1975	130	1980	268		
1976	50	1981	−56		
1977	206	1982	67		

Bibliography: T. Green. *The New World of Gold.* Walker & Co., New York,1981; *Annual Bullion Review.* S. Montagu & Co., London; *Gold 1984.* Consolidated Gold Fields PLC, London 1984 and annually.

bull spread. In the options market, a bull spread consists of buying a 'call' at a lower 'strike price' and selling a call at a higher strike price. (This is called a VERTICAL bull spread because the calls have the same expiration date but different strike prices. Compare DIAGONAL SPREAD; HORIZONTAL SPREAD.) This type of spread is appropriate if the investor is bullish, but only moderately so.
Bibliography: L.G. McMillan. *Options as a Strategic Investment.* New York Institute of Finance, New York, 1980.

bull straddle. Another term for BULL SPREAD. In the FUTURES markets, a bull straddle means the purchase of the nearer month and the sale of the more distant month. The theory is that if prices rise, the nearby month will rise faster.
Bibliography: N.H. Rothstein & J.M. Little. *The Handbook of Financial Futures.* McGraw-Hill, New York, 1984.

bulldog bond. A bond issued by a foreign borrower in the domestic UK bond market. Differs from a EUROSTERLING bond mainly in the distribution system used, in that a bulldog bond is issued subject to a queue system, while Eurosterling bonds are normally 'notified' to the Bank of England but not subject to a queueing system. In line with domestic stocks, bulldogs normally pay in-

terest semi-annually, while Eurosterling bonds normally pay annually. As an example, in 1984 a bulldog bond of £35 million for 30 years was issued by the Eaton Corporation of the USA, paying 12 ½% semi-annually at an ISSUE PRICE of £97.78 per cent. Compare YANKEE BONDS, SAMURAI BOND.
Bibliography: De Zoete & Bevan. *The Bulldog Market*. London, 1983.

B-Unit. An artificial currency unit introduced by Barclays Bank International in 1974 consisting of US dollars, pounds, French francs, Deutschemarks and Swiss francs in approximately equal weights.
Bibliography: J. Aschheim & Y. S. Park. *Artificial Currency Units: The formation of Functional Currency Areas*. Princeton Essays in International Finance No. 114, 1976.
Currency Cocktails. Barclays Bank International, London, 1974.

burning cost. The ratio of REINSURANCE losses incurred to the CEDING COMPANY'S SUBJECT PREMIUM. From the reinsurance company's viewpoint the burning cost measures its losses in relation to the underlying volume of business of its customer, the ceding company.
Bibliography: R. Kiln. *Reinsurance in Practice*. Witherby, London, 1981.
R.L. Carter. *Reinsurance*. Kluwer, London, 1983.

busted convertible. A US term for a CONVERTIBLE whose convertibility is valueless because the underlying equity is low in price.
Bibliography: M. L. Tennican. *Convertible Debentures and Related Securities*. Harvard University Press, Cambridge, Mass., 1975.
J.C. Ritchie. Convertible Bonds and Warrants *in* F.J. Fabozzi & I.M. Pollack (eds). *The Handbook of Fixed Income Securities*. Dow-Jones Irwin, Homewood, Ill., 1983

butterfly. A spread operation that combines a 'bull spread' and a 'bear spread'. For example, in an option market, a butterfly spread would consist of buying one call at the lowest striking price, selling two calls at the middle striking price, and buying one call at the highest striking price. This strategy is profitable provided the underlying instrument's price does not move much.
Bibliography: L.G. McMillan. *Options as a Strategic Investment*. New York Institute of Finance, New York, 1980.

buy-and-write. An OPTIONS market term. The investor buys the underlying instrument (either a stock, or perhaps a futures contract) and writes a CALL option against it. This strategy is appropriate for an investor with a mildly bullish view. Compare COVERED CALL; SELL-AND-WRITE.
Bibliography: *Options on Comex Gold Futures*. New York Commodity Exchange. New York, n.d.

buy-back. *See* PRODUCT PAYBACK; REPURCHASE AGREEMENT.

buy-in. Term used when a seller of securities fails to make delivery of them within the required time. The buyer may buy them in elsewhere if he gave prior written notice to the seller, and may charge the seller all costs and differences involved. Compare SELL-OUT.
Bibliography: L.M. Loll & J.G. Buckley. *The Over-the Counter Markets*. Prentice-Hall, USA, 1981.
R.J. Teweles & E.S. Bradley. *The Stock Market*. John Wiley & Sons, New York, 1982.
Rules and Regulations of the Stock Exchange. The Stock Exchange, London.
Rules & Recommendations. Association of International Bond Dealers, Zurich.

buyer credit. A form of export finance whereby the exporter is paid promptly by the overseas importer, who obtains the necessary funds by means of a loan from the bank. In practice the payment is frequently made directly by the bank to the exporter.
Bibliography: A. Dunn & M. Knight. *Export Finance*. Euromoney Publications, London, 1982.

C

C$. Canadian dollar.

cable. Foreign exchange dealers' slang for the dollar/sterling spot exchange rate (from cable transfer).

cable transfer. Telegraphic transfer of funds from one centre to another.

CACM. *See* CENTRAL AMERICAN CENTRAL MARKET.

CAF. 'Cout, assurance, frêt.' *See* COST, INSURANCE, FREIGHT.

calendar. Generally refers to a set of forthcoming events. In the securities markets the term is used to refer to the dates of forthcoming new issues. An example is that laid down by the German capital issues sub-committee to regulate the issue of domestic and foreign DM bonds.
Bibliography: Why DM external bonds are not true Eurobonds. *The Banker.* London, October 1978.
G. Dufey & E. Krishnan. West Germany: Banking, Money & Bond Markets *in* A.M. George & I.H. Giddy. *International Finance Handbook.* John Wiley & Sons, New York, 1983.

calendar spread. An OPTIONS market strategy in which a short-term option is sold and a longer-term option is bought, both having the same striking price. Either puts or calls may be used. The strategy can also be referred to as a TIME SPREAD or a HORIZONTAL SPREAD. The theory is that time will erode the value of the near-term option at a faster rate than the far-term option. For example, in January, the investor might sell an April 50 call on XYZ Co. at a price of 5, and buy the July 50 at 8, for a net cost of 3. Suppose in April XYZ Co. is trading at 50; then the April 50 call is worthless, while the July 50 might now be worth 5, and the investor can close the position for a net profit of 2.
Bibliography: L.G. McMillan. *Options as a Strategic Investment.* New York Institute of Finance, New York, 1980.

call. (1) Exercising the right of a corporation to pre-pay its debt and demand surrender of its bonds for redemption, refunding or sinking fund purposes. A call is usually exercised at a pre-set CALL PRICE. Investors tend to dislike calls since they are then faced with the risk that the return earned on the investment they make to replace their bond holding may not be so good. Compare CALL PROTECTION.
Bibliography: M.G. Ferri. Features of Fixed Income Securities in F.J. Fabozzi & I.M. Pollack. *The Handbook of Fixed Income Securities.* Dow-Jones Irwin, Homewood, Ill., 1983.
S. Homer & M. Leibowitz. *Inside the Yield Book.* Prentice-Hall, USA, 1972.
(2) An option contract giving the holder the right to purchase from the writer of the call contract a specified amount of securities or commodities at a specified price; the contract is valid for a predetermined time. As an example, one might in October purchase a January call on 100 XYZ Co. at $5.00. This would mean that one has the right to buy 100 XYZ Co. shares at $5.00 per share in January. Compare PUT.
Bibliography: L.G. McMillan. *Options as a Strategic Investment.* New York Institute of Finance, New York, 1980.
D.M. Fitzgerald. Traded Options: a successful innovation. *The Banker,* London, May 1984.
(3) A 'call' can be made on a company's CALLABLE CAPITAL, to raise more funds. Similarly, on a PARTLY-PAID security, calls will be made at specified dates. Thus, if a GILT-EDGED stock is issued at a nominal price of £100, but only £20 is payable today, with

£40 payable in six months and another £40 payable in a year's time, then it is said that there will be two calls of £40 on the stock – the investor is called on to put up the remaining money.

Bibliography: *The New Beginners Please*. Investor's Chronicle, London, 1975.
P.Phillips. *Inside the Gilt-edged Market*. Woodhead-Faulkner, Cambridge, UK, 1984.

(4) In certain UK commodities markets with fixed periods in which the day's trading is conducted, the term refers to a period in which the price for each futures contract is established – thus one might speak of the opening call or the closing call to refer to the first and last trading sessions of the day.

Bibliography: C.W.J. Granger.(ed.). *Trading in Commodities*. Woodhead-Faulkner, Cambridge, UK, 1983.

(5) A commodities market term for the purchase of a specified commodity at a fixed number of points above or below a specified futures price, with the buyer or seller being allowed a period of time in which to fix the futures price by trading in the market.

(6) Refers to CALL MONEY.

callable capital. UK term for that part of a company's CAPITAL which is not yet PAID-UP and on which the company's directors can call for payments to be made.

Bibliography: The New 'Beginners Please'. *Investors Chronicle*. London, 1975.
J. Dundas Hamilton. *Stockbroking Today*. Macmillan Press, London, 1979.

call money. Money lent on the basis that it is repayable at call (on demand). It represents an important part of British banks' liquid assets, since money lent at call is a RESERVE ASSET if it is lent to discount houses and other institutions carrying on essentially similar business. Similarly, money under such conditions is important in many other markets, such as Germany, France, Japan and the EUROMARKETS. Compare AU JOUR LE JOUR, FED FUNDS, TAGESGELD, UNCONDITIONAL CALL MONEY.

Bibliography: J.K. Walmsley. *The Foreign Exchange Handbook*. John Wiley & Sons, New York, 1983.

D. Marteau & E. de la Chaise. *Le marche monétaire et la gestion de trésorerie des banques*. Dunod, Paris, 1981.
Special Paper no. 91: General Features of the Recent Interest Rate Changes. Bank of Japan Economic Research Department, Tokyo, 1980.
H.D. Deppe. Geldmarkt und Geldmarktkonzepte. *Kredit und Kapital*. Vol. 3. Duncker & Humblot, Berlin.

call price. (1) In the US and EUROBOND markets a bond is often issued by a borrower on the basis that after a certain number of years it can be 'called' for repayment. Thus a bond might be issued for 10 years at a price of 100 on the basis that it could be called in Year 5 at a price, say, of 103; in Year 6 the call price might be 102.5, etc.

Bibliography: M.G. Ferri. Features of Fixed Income Securities *in* F.J. Fabozzi & I.M. Pollack. *The Handbook of Fixed Income Securities*. Dow-Jones Irwin, Homewood, Ill, 1983.

(2) In the options markets, refers to the price of a CALL option.

call protection. Protection of an investor against a CALL on his bonds. The exercise of a call is detrimental to the investor, since it is usually done when interest rates have fallen below the COUPON on the bond. Hence the rate to be earned on new investments to replace the existing bond will probably be below the bond's current yield.

Bibliography: M.G. Ferri. Features of Fixed Income Securities *in* F.J. Fabozzi & I.M. Pollack. *The Handbook of Fixed Income Securities*. Dow-Jones Irwin, Homewood Ill, 1983.

cambiste. French term for foreign exchange dealer. Compare ASSOCIATION CAMBISTE INTERNATIONAL.

C & F. Abbreviation for cost and freight.

C & I. Abbreviation for cost and insurance.

CAP. (1) Abbreviation for the Common Agricultural Policy of the EUROPEAN COMMUNITIES.

(2) Abbreviation for CONVERTIBLE ADJUSTABLE RATE PREFERRED STOCK.

cap. A US term for a limit on the upward movement of an interest rate. Thus a variable-rate mortgage might be taken out at 13%, but with a cap of 18%, so that the rate charged in the life of the mortgage can never exceed 18%. If rates rise above this level, there may be a provision to add the excess interest on at a later date.
Bibliography: S.J. Cosham. Capped prime and Libor-based loans; the comparative costs. *The Banker*, London, February 1983.

capital. (1) Refers to the sum subscribed by the members and long-term creditors of a company for the purposes of the business. It usually consists of loan capital and share capital. The nominal capital of a company may exceed the actual figure if it is not PAID-UP.
Bibliography: *The New 'Beginners Please'*. Investors Chronicle, London, 1975.
(2) Refers in the context of the BALANCE OF PAYMENTS to flows of investment funds rather than goods or services. Thus, where in a given year the US might have had a CURRENT ACCOUNT deficit of $25 billion, capital inflows, in the shape of, for example, investments by foreigners in US government securities and bank deposits might have totalled $40 billion, financing the deficit and, perhaps, an increase in the country's external RESERVES. *See* CAPITAL ACCOUNT.

capital account. In the BALANCE OF PAYMENTS the capital account measures short- and long-term financial movements which may be associated with the purchase of physical assets, stocks and shares, or with the placing of money on a short-term basis.

capital lease. A US accounting term for a LEASE which is substantially equivalent to ownership of the asset and so must be included on a firm's balance sheet. The main criteria are that (a) the lease transfers the ownership of the property to the LESSEE by the end of the lease term; (b) the lease contains a cheap purchase option; (c) the lease term is 75% or more of the estimated economic life of the asset; (d) at the start of the lease the present value of the minimum lease payments is 90% or more of the fair value of the asset, less any tax credits retained by the LESSOR.
Bibliography: *Statement of Financial Accounting Standards no. 13*. Financial Accounting Standards Board, Stamford, Connecticut.

capital risk. In the foreign exchange market, the risk arising because a bank will have to pay out currency to the COUNTERPART in the deal without knowing whether the counterpart is able to meet its side of the bargain. This is known as the capital risk. It was highlighted by the HERSTATT AFFAIR when the closure of Herstatt during banking hours meant some banks found they had paid out Deutschemarks without receiving dollars in exchange, because of the time difference between the two centres. Sometimes referred to as settlement risk. Compare AGGREGATE RISK, CREDIT RISK, DELIVERY RISK, MARGINAL RISK.
Bibliography: J.K. Walmsley. *The Foreign Exchange Handbook*. John Wiley & Sons, New York, 1983.

capped prime. A PRIME rate loan with a 'cap' feature preventing it from rising above a certain level would be referred to as a capped prime loan.
Bibliography: S.J. Cosham. Capped prime and Libor-based loans; the comparative costs. *The Banker*, London, February 1983.

captive finance company. A finance company which is controlled by another company. In the US, generally accepted accounting principles permit a properly constructed finance company, even if 100% owned and controlled by its parent, not to be consolidated for accounting purposes.

captive insurance company. An insurance company which is owned by one or more companies which are not insurance companies and which undertakes some or all of its owners' insurance business. A pure captive exists solely to insure the risks of its parent. A mixed, open market or senior captive insurance company will undertake not only its parents' insurance business but also normal commercial insurance business.

Bibliography: M. Rowland. Crisis in Bermuda. *Institutional Investor*. June 1983.
P.A. Bawcutt. *Captive Insurance Companies*. Thetford Press, UK/Dow-Jones Irwin, Homewood, Ill., 1982.

Caribbean Development Bank (CDB). Founded in 1970, the CDB's members consist of the governments of Antigua, Bahamas, Barbados, Belize, British Virgin Islands, Canada, Cayman Islands, Colombia, Dominica, Grenada, Guyana, Jamaica, Montserrat, St Kitts-Nevis, St Lucia, St Vincent, Trinidad and Tobago, Turks and Caicos Islands, the United Kingdom and Venezuela. Its headquarters are in Barbados. Its purpose is to finance economic development and integration in the Caribbean.

Bibliography: United Nations Industrial Development Organization. *Financial Resources for Industrial Projects in Developing Countries*. United Nations, New York, 1978.
Caribbean Development Bank Annual Reports.

Caricom. The Caribbean Community and Common Market founded in 1973, with headquarters in Guyana, consists of Jamaica, Trinidad and Tobago, Guyana, The Bahamas, Barbados, Belize, St Lucia, Grenada, St Vincent, Dominica, Antigua, St Kitts-Nevis, Anguilla and Montserrat. Associated institutions include the Caribbean Investment Corporation and a Caribbean Monetary Fund. In 1981 the seven Eastern Caribbean islands established the Organization of Eastern Caribbean States within Caricom. On the whole, Caricom has had only limited success.

Bibliography: R. Ramsaran. CARICOM: the integration process in crisis. *Journal of World Trade Law*. London, May/June 1978.
Economic and Social Progress in Latin America in *Inter-American Development Bank Annual Report*, Washington DC, 1984.

carriage paid. *See* FREIGHT PAID.

carry. Term originating from the commodities markets, particularly used in the metals markets. The operation consists of a cash purchase matched by a forward : the operator

'carries' the commodity in his books. (i.e. he BORROWS the metal). If the difference between the forward price and the purchase price today is larger than the storage and other expenses, he earns a positive carry. The term is also applied to the converse operation, whereby the trader sells cash and buys forward. (He LENDS the metal.) For example, if the price of copper on the LONDON METAL EXCHANGE were today: cash buyers, £675 per ton, cash sellers, £677; three month buyers £690, three month sellers £692, then a borrower would seek to do his carry at £17 (£692 less £675) and a lender would offer to lend at a cost to him of £13 (£690 less £677). By analogy the term is used in securities: compare CARRY INCOME.

Bibliography: B. A. Goss & B. S. Yamey (eds). *The Economics of Futures Trading*. Macmillan, London, 1978.
R. Gibson-Jarvie. *The London Metal Exchange*. Woodhead Faulkner, Cambridge, UK/ Nichols Publishing, New York, 1983.

carry income (or loss). A US term referring to the difference between the interest yield of a dealers' portfolio and the cost of the funds which support that portfolio. The UK term is 'running margin'. *See also* TRADING PROFITS.

Bibliography: M. Stigum. *The Money Market*. Dow-Jones Irwin, Homewood Ill, 1983.

Carter bonds. Medium-term foreign currency obligations issued by the US government during 1978-9 as a means of obtaining foreign currency balances. Similar to ROOSA BONDS, Carter bonds were issued in Germany and Switzerland. The need to obtain foreign currency balances arose fron the fact that traditionally the US holds most of its RESERVES in gold and SPECIAL DRAWING RIGHTS rather than foreign currency. The bonds also meant that the US government assumed some of the exchange risk of dollar. devaluation – devaluation would make the Carter bonds more expensive to repay. They also reduced the US reliance on central bank SWAPS.

Bibliography: J.K. Walmsley. *The Foreign Exchange Handbook*. John Wiley & Sons, New York, 1983.

case of need. If an exporter draws a bill on a foreign importer he may give instructions 'Refer to XYZ Co. in case of need'. XYZ Co. (in the importers' country) may be an agent or subsidiary, with full powers to act, or merely a source of advice. If anything goes wrong the bank collecting the bill will contact the case of need.
Bibliography: A. Watson, *Finance of International Trade.* Institute of Bankers, London, 1981.

cash and carry. Commodities markets term for a deal in which a trader buys a 'cash commodity' and simultaneously sells it forward; after expenses, if there is sufficient CARRY, the forward sale will yield enough profit to make the deal worthwhile.
Bibliography: R. Gibson-Jarvie. *The London Metal Exchange.* Woodhead-Faulkner, Cambridge, UK/ Nichols Publishing, New York, 1983.

cash delivery. US securities market term denoting same-day delivery of the securities traded. Cash trades must be settled within 30 minutes if made after 2.00 p.m.
Bibliography: *New York Stock Exchange Constitution & Rules.* Commerce Clearing House, New York, 1976, p. 2621.
A.M. George. The United States Equity Markets in A.M. George & I.H. Giddy. *International Finance Handbook.* John Wiley & Sons, New York, 1983.

Cash Management Bill. Introduced by the US Treasury in 1975, these bills are designed to raise funds quickly for a short period. During the 1975-80 period 38 issues of cash management bills were made, with from two to 167 days' maturity, and an average of 51 days. In 1980, the total sold was $45 billion.
Bibliography: T.Q. Cook & B.J. Summers (eds). *Instruments of the Money Markets.* Federal Reserve Bank of Virginia, 1981.

cash market. A market in which the instrument traded is paid for and delivered immediately, or with only a short delay, as distinct from the futures or options markets where the settlement and delivery are postponed. Thus one might speak of ARBITRAGE between Treasury bond futures and the cash market for Treasury bonds. Compare BASIS.

Bibliography: Chicago Board of Trade. *Financial Instruments Markets: Cash-Futures Relationships.* Chicago, USA, n.d.
A.M. Loosigian. *Interest Rate Futures.* Dow-Jones Irwin, Homewood Ill, 1980.

CATS. *See* CERTIFICATE OF ACCRUAL ON TREASURY SECURITIES.

CBOE. Abbreviation for the CHICAGO BOARD OPTIONS EXCHANGE.

cash ratio. A UK term referring to deposits required by the Bank of England. All UK banks and licensed deposit takers with ELIGIBLE LIABILITIES over £10 million must hold interest-free deposits of ½% of eligible liabilities with the bank.
Bibliography: J.S.G. Wilson. Recent changes in London's Money Market Arrangements. *Banca Nazionale del Lavoro Quarterly Review.* March 1983.

CBOT, CBT. Abbreviation for the CHICAGO BOARD OF TRADE.

CD. *See* CERTIFICATE OF DEPOSIT.

CDR. *See* CONTINENTAL DEPOSITARY RECEIPT.

CEDEL (centrale de Livraison de Valeurs Mobilières). A computerized system for safe custody, delivery and settlement for Eurobonds and related securities. CEDEL was founded in 1970 by a group of international financial institutions. Membership in 1980 was around 1000 institutions and 3,500 issues were being cleared through the system. In 1981 an agreement between CEDEL and SWIFT enabled SWIFT member banks to transmit settlement instructions and receive statements from CEDEL. CEDEL operates from 45A Avenue Monterey, Luxembourg. Compare AUSLANDSKASSENVEREIN, EUROCLEAR, SECURITIES INDUSTRY AUTOMATION CORPORATION, TALISMAN.
Bibliography: *Instructions to Participants.* CEDEL, various dates.
T. Anderson. The Growing War Between Cedel and Euro-clear. *Euromoney,* London, May 1981.

ceding company. A REINSURANCE term: the ceding company is the original insurance company which has accepted the risk and cedes part of that risk to a reinsurer.
Bibliography: R. P. Bellerose. *Reinsurance for the Beginner.* Witherby & Co., London, 1978.
R. Clews (ed.). *A Textbook of Insurance Broking.* Woodhead-Faulkner, Cambridge, UK, 1980.

Central American Bank for Economic Integration. *See* BANCO CENTROAMERICANO DE INTEGRACION ECONOMICA.

Central American Clearing House. Established July 1961 to provide a multilateral mechanism for CLEARING international payments between the Central American central banks. The CACM has been relatively successful at the technical level, despite regional political tension; in 1983 it cleared 76% of regional import payments.
Bibliography: *Economic and Social Progress in Latin America* in *Inter-American Development Bank Annual Report,* Washington DC, 1984.

Central American Common Market. Established in 1960 with headquarters in Guatemala with the intention of encouraging economic integration between its members, namely Costa Rica, Guatemala, El Salvador and Nicaragua (Honduras suspended membership in 1970). Despite political difficulties the CACM has had some successes, notably in its clearing house. Associated with the CACM is the BANCO CENTROAMERICANO DE INTEGRACION ECONOMICA.
Bibliography: *Economic and Social Progress in Latin America* in *Inter-American Development Bank Annual Report,* Washington DC, 1984.

central bank. Term referring to the bank which has responsibility for controlling a country's monetary policy. The duties of a central bank will also generally include the provision of lender of LAST RESORT facilities, the supervision of the domestic banking system, and control of exchange rate policy – although this is often jointly shared with the Treasury or Finance Ministry.
Bibliography: J.K. Walmsley. *The Foreign Ex-*

change Handbook. John Wiley & Sons, New York, 1983.
P. Meek (ed.). *Central Bank Views on Monetary Targeting.* Federal Reserve Bank of New York, 1983.

Central European International Bank. Established by the National Bank of Hungary and six leading Western banks, the CEIB was set up to be the first international joint stock bank in which Western banks held a majority share that was located in a COMECON country.

central rate. In December 1971, the INTERNATIONAL MONETARY FUND announced that its members could maintain temporary central rates which might be established without changing the official PAR VALUE. Central rates lapsed after the JAMAICA AGREEMENT.
Bibliography: *IMF Annual Reports.* Washington DC.
J. Gold. *SDRs, Gold and Currencies: Third Survey of Legal Developments.* International Monetary Fund, Washington DC, 1979.

Centrale de Livraison de Valeurs Mobilières. *See* CEDEL.

certain. French foreign exchange term for INDIRECT QUOTATION.

Certificate of Accrual on Treasury Securities (CATS). A US instrument, created in 1982. Effectively, it is a ZERO COUPON Treasury bond. The exact mechanics are as follows. The investment bank creating the CATS buys Treasury securities and deposits them with a bank or trustee. It then issues receipts against every COUPON and principal repayment the Treasury is scheduled to make. The receipts are then sold for the present value of the payments they evidence. This effectively creates a series of zero-coupon Treasury bonds, maturing on every coupon and principal repayment date. Compare FELINES, TIGRS.
Bibliography: J. Laskey. How coupon stripping became respectable. *Euromoney,* London, December 1982.
T.E. Klaffky & R.W. Kopprasch. *Understanding the Volatility of CATS and Other Zero-Coupon*

Bonds. Salomon Brothers Inc., New York, May 1983.

Certificate of Deposit (CD). A CD is generally a NEGOTIABLE INSTRUMENT in BEARER FORM, although non-negotiable and registered CDs are perfectly possible (and indeed, since the 1983 US tax act, US CDs over one year in maturity must be in registered form). It certifies that a sum of money has been deposited with a bank. The crucial factor which distinguishes it from a bank deposit is that it is generally NEGOTIABLE and so can be re-sold on the SECONDARY MARKET. Thus if an investor believes he can spare some funds for six months he can buy a CD which is due for payment at the end of that time knowing he can re-sell it if he unexpectedly needs the money earlier. The CD market began in 1961 in the US when a true secondary market for the CDs was set up. The market grew explosively after the suspension of REGULATION Q on certain maturities. CDs were introduced in London in 1966 and became an integral part of the Euromarkets in their own right. London CDs are issued in sterling and dollars, and London SPECIAL DRAWING RIGHT CDs have also been issued. The method of issue may be TAP or TRANCHE. A restricted type of yen CD was introduced in Tokyo in May 1979.

Bibliography: T.Q. Cook & B.J. Summers. *Instruments of the Money Market.* Federal Reserve Bank of Richmond, Virginia, 1981.
E. R. Shaw. *The London Money Market.* Heinemann. London, 1981.
J.K. Walmsley. *The Foreign Exchange Handbook.* John Wiley & Sons, New York, 1983.

certified invoice. *See* INVOICE.

CFA franc. *See* COMMUNAUTÉ FRANÇAISE AFRICAINE FRANC.

channel. A term from TECHNICAL ANALYSIS in the FUTURES and commodities markets. Suppose a given instrument – say the gold price – shows a clear upward trend, with each day's low being reached at a higher level. When these are connected over an extended time on a chart, they form a trend line. If the lines connecting the daily lows and those connecting the daily highs are parallel, this implies that the volatility of the markets is not changing and a 'channel' has been created. A BREAK-OUT from a channel is considered a strong technical signal for a major uptrend or downtrend.

Bibliography: E.W. Schwartz. *How to Use Interest Rate Futures Contracts.* Dow-Jones Irwin, Homewood Ill, 1979.
N.H. Rothstein & J.M. Little. *The Financial Futures Handbook.* McGraw-Hill, New York, 1984.

CHAPS. *See* CLEARING HOUSE AUTOMATED PAYMENTS SYSTEM.

charterparty. Agreement whereby the owners of a vessel hire it to another person (the charterer). Usually the charterer uses the vessel to convey a cargo of goods. Such charters may be BAREBOAT or DEMISE – that is, charters of the ship alone, without crew. Or they may be VOYAGE – for a specific voyage – or 'time' – for a specific period. The two latter types of charter usually involve the hire of the ship's crew as well.

Bibliography: Mocatta, Mustill & Boyd. *Scrutton on Charterparties and Bills of Lading.* 18th edn. Sweet & Maxwell, London, 1974.
M.S.W. Hoyle. *The Law of International Trade.* Laureate Press, London, 1981.

charterparty assignment. A contractual arrangement under which the contract between the shipowner and the charterer (specifically, the revenue from the charter) is assigned to a bank. It serves as security for the bank's loan to the shipowner, normally to finance the construction of the ship.

Bibliography: R. Pincus. *Ship's Value.* Gothenburg Maritime Law Association, Sweden, 1975.
P. Wood. *Law and Practice of International Finance.* Sweet & Maxwell, London 1980.
C.T. Grammenos. *Bank Finance for Ship Purchase.* University of Wales Press, 1979.

Chicago Board of Trade (CBT). The CBT was founded in 1848 as a centre for the Chicago grain trade. The first recorded FUTURES contract was traded there in 1851. In addition to commodity futures the CBT is a very important centre for FINANCIAL FUTURES, notably with its Treasury bond contract, which by 1981 had become the most widely traded futures contract in America (13 million CONTRACTS traded).

Bibliography: N.H. Rothstein & J.M. Little. *The Handbook of Financial Futures*. Dow-Jones Irwin, Homewood, Ill., 1984.

Chicago Board Options Exchange. Founded in 1973, the CBOE is an exchange for the trading of LISTED OPTIONS. On the first day of trading the volume of contracts totalled 911; a decade later, the volume of options contracts in 1983 totalled 75.7 million. The CBOE currently offers options contracts on about 150 shares, as well as stock index options (S&P 100, S&P 500) and options on sub-indices.

Bibliography: M.D. Fitzgerald. Traded Options: A Successful Innovation. *The Banker*, London, May 1984.

Chicago Mercantile Exchange. Founded in 1919 as a rival to the CHICAGO BOARD OF TRADE, the CME developed into a significant centre for commodity FUTURES trading; it made a major contribution to international finance in founding, in 1972, the INTERNATIONAL MONETARY MARKET where the first FINANCIAL FUTURES – currency futures – were traded.

Bibliography: N.H. Rothstein & J.M. Little. *The Handbook of Financial Futures*. Dow-Jones Irwin, Homewood, Ill., 1984.

Chips, CHIPS. *See* CLEARING HOUSE INTERBANK PAYMENTS SYSTEM.

CIF. Abbreviation for COST, INSURANCE, FREIGHT.

circle. US securities term for a practice where a customer indicates an interest in buying and an underwriter agrees to sell a stated quantity of a new issue, subject to pricing.

claused bill of exchange. A BILL OF EXCHANGE which bears upon the face of it a clause which may specify the underlying

transaction (e.g. 'exports of machine tools to Brazil per S.S. *Fortress*') or which specifies the rate of exchange to be used (e.g. 'Payable at the current exchange rate for sight drafts on London').

Bibliography: Gillett Brothers Discount Company. *The Bill on London*. Methuen, London, 1976.
A. Watson. *Finance of Foreign Trade*. Institute of Bankers, London, 1981.

claused bill of lading. *See* CLEAN.

clean. (1) Refers to a BILL OF LADING which is not qualified in any way.

Bibliography: Mocatta, Mustill & Boyd. *Scrutton on Charterparties and Bills of Lading*. 18th edn. Sweet & Maxwell, London, 1974.
The Problem of Clean Bills of Lading. International Chamber of Commerce Brochure No. 283. Paris.
C. M. Schmitthoff. When a Claused Bill of Lading is Clean. *Export*. London, January 1979.

(2) Refers to a BILL OF EXCHANGE having no documents accompanying it. Compare CLEAN COLLECTION.

(3) In the UK fixed-interest securities market, 'clean' refers to a price quoted excluding ACCRUED INTEREST.

Bibliography: P. Phillips. *Inside the Gilt-Edged Market*. Woodhead-Faulkner, Cambridge, UK, 1984.

(4) A CLEAN float is one not involving central bank intervention to support the exchange rate.

Bibliography: J.K. Walmsley. *The Foreign Exchange Handbook*. John Wiley & Sons, New York, 1983.

(5) A money market transaction not involving documentary securities is said to be clean.

(6) Clean pot: a POT in which no further securities are available.

clean acceptance. An ACCEPTANCE not involving a DOCUMENTARY LETTER of CREDIT. This would generally be an acceptance drawn under an ACCEPTANCE CREDIT. The difference between a clean acceptance and a documentary one is normally as follows. Under a documentary acceptance, US Exporter Inc. draws a bill on UK Co. Ltd. which is sent, with documents, UK Bank Ltd. After UK Bank accepts the bill, the documents are released to UK Co. Ltd. Under a clean acceptance, UK Co. Ltd draws a bill to finance its imports and UK Bank Ltd. accepts it.

Bibliography: A. Watson. *Finance of International Trade*. Institute of Bankers, London, 1981.

clean collection. This term is defined in the International Chamber of Commerce's UNIFORM RULES FOR COLLECTIONS as a collection of FINANCIAL DOCUMENTS not accompanied by COMMERCIAL DOCUMENTS. For practical purposes the term is identical to CLEAN REMITTANCE.

Bibliography: *Uniform Rules for Collections*. International Chamber of Commerce Brochure no. 322, Paris, 1978.
A. Watson. *Finance of International Trade*. Institute of Bankers, London, 1981.

clean remittance. This term was defined by the INTERNATIONAL CHAMBER OF COMMERCE as covering items 'consisting of one or more bills of exchange, whether accepted or not, promissory notes, cheques, receipts or other similar documents for obtaining the payment of money (there being neither invoices, shipping documents, documents of title, or other similar documents whatsoever attached to the said items)'. In the revised UNIFORM RULES FOR COLLECTIONS the term is replaced by CLEAN COLLECTION.

Bibliography: A. Watson. *Finance of International Trade*. Institute of Bankers, London, 1981.
Uniform Rules for Collections. International Chamber of Commerce Brochure no. 322, 38 Cours Albert 1er, Paris, 1978.

clearing. Generally, relates to the process of setting a number of items against each other and dealing only with the net balance. Specifically:
(1) In the UK, the clearing banks arrange that all cheques drawn on them are presented at the Clearing House (in London, or regional centres) each day. The individual bank then settles the net balance due to the others, thus saving unnecessary transactions.
(2) Similar arrangements operate in the New York Clearing House and this is the ultimate clearing centre for all Eurodollar deals (although dollar clearing arrangements have now been set up in London for smaller customer deals).

Bibliography: *Clearing House Interbank Payments System*. New York Clearing House Association, New York, 1982.

(3) Clearing arrangements in the Eurobond market are operated by privately owned computerized securities clearing houses called CEDEL and EUROCLEAR.

(4) In the FUTURES markets, it is normal for a CLEARING HOUSE to be interposed between participants.

clearing account. Two or more countries may operate a system where foreign trade balances are offset against each other and the difference (if this is permitted) credited to the clearing account or paid in foreign currency. Such systems are usually operated via BILATERAL CLEARING. Multilateral clearing arrangements are much less common – one is operated within COMECON on the basis of TRANSFERABLE ROUBLE. Compare BARTER; BILATERAL CLEARING; COMPENSATION TRADING; SWITCH TRADING.

Bibliography: A. Zwass. *Money, Banking and Credit in the Soviet Union and Eastern Europe*. Macmillan, UK/M.E. Sharpe, New York, 1979.

clearing currencies. Many clearing accounts are denominated in, for example, clearing dollars. If the clearing account is not in balance, clearing dollar credits may be available. Eastern European countries typically sell more than they buy from, for instance, Egypt, India, Tunisia and Morocco, and thus have clearing dollar credits available there which they try to offer to Western exporters in payment. Unless the Western exporter can use these credits himself, he must enter into a SWITCH transaction.

Bibliography: A. Zwass. *Money, Banking and Credit in the Soviet Union and Eastern Europe*. Macmillan, UK/M.E. Sharpe, New York, 1979.

clearing house. (1) A place where cheques and other means of payment are cleared.

Compare AUTOMATED CLEARING HOUSE, CLEARING, CLEARING HOUSE FUNDS, CLEARING HOUSE AUTOMATED PAYMENTS SYSTEM, CLEARING HOUSE INTERBANK PAYMENTS SYSTEM, CEDEL, EUROCLEAR.

(2) In the FUTURES markets it is common practice for the exchange to be organized so that every contract traded on the floor of the exchange is executed with the clearing house as counterparty. Thus if A sells to B in the PITS, at the end of the day the clearing house is interposed so that A sells to the clearing house, which sells to B. This eliminates traders' concern with credit risk. The clearing house on the LONDON INTERNATIONAL FINANCIAL FUTURES EXCHANGE is the INTERNATIONAL COMMODITIES CLEARING HOUSE.
Bibliography: N.H. Rothstein & J.M. Little. *The Handbook of Financial Futures*. Dow-Jones Irwin, Homewood Ill., 1984.
J.K. Walmsley. *The Foreign Exchange Handbook*. John Wiley & Sons, New York, 1983.
M.D. Fitzgerald. *Financial Futures*. Euromoney Publications, London, 1983.

Clearing House Automated Payments System (CHAPS).   The central UK money transfer mechanism for larger payments, CHAPS consists of a network of linked computers operated by the UK clearing banks. Other banks' computers can interface to the system via their own systems or via the SWIFT network.
Bibliography: R. Winder. Will CHAPS End up Chums? *Euromoney*, London, December 1983.

Clearing House Funds.   A US term for funds represented by a cheque which has to be cleared through a CLEARING HOUSE (Compare AUTOMATED CLEARING HOUSE; CLEARING.) Normally in the international context the term refers to funds cleared through the New York Clearing House. Until 1981, Clearing House Funds took 24 hours to clear, after which they became FED FUNDS ; this delay gave rise to the so-called 'Thursday-Friday' technicality which has now disappeared.
Bibliography: *Clearing House Interbank Payments System*. New York Clearing House Association, New York, 1982.

clearing house interbank payments system (CHIPS).   A computerized CLEARING system in New York linking the members of the New York Clearing House, CHIPS handles all New York money transfers between major banks, including EURODOLLAR and foreign exchange settlements. On an average day, CHIPS handles $200 billion in payments.
Bibliography: *Clearing House Interbank Payments System*. New York Clearing House Association, New York, 1982.

clearing member.   A firm which is a member of a CLEARING HOUSE. Typically the term is used to members of a FINANCIAL FUTURES clearing house. Clearing members guarantee performance of their trades with the clearing house, make and take delivery of CONTRACTS and collect or pay VARIATION MARGIN.
Bibliography: N.H. Rothstein & J.M. Little. *The Handbook of Financial Futures*. McGraw-Hill, New York, 1984.

close.   (1) The term refers to the end of the day's trading; 'the closing rate' is that quoted at the end of business hours.
(2) In the foreign exchange market, if a dealer is committed, say, to delivering $10 million on 31 March, the action of buying the $10 million for delivery on that date is described as closing out his commitment or position. Compare OPEN POSITION.

closed-end fund.   US term for an INVESTMENT COMPANY with a fixed number of shares outstanding. The shares represent an interest in the fund's portfolio. New shares may not be issued. Prospective investors must buy from existing holders. Compare OPEN-END FUND. The British equivalent is INVESTMENT TRUST.
Bibliography: W.P. Wade. Bank-Sponsored Collective Investment Funds: An Analysis of Applicable Federal Banking and Securities Laws. *The Business Lawyer*. American Bar Association, January 1980.
T.J. Herzfeld. Closed-End Funds *in* M.E. Blume & J.P. Friedman (eds). *Encyclopedia of Investments*. Warren, Gorham & Lamont, Boston, 1982.

club. (1) A EUROMARKET term for a LOAN SYNDICATION technique. Instead of the traditional system where one bank is designated LEAD BANK and tries to sell the deal to other banks, the club approach is one where a group of banks club together to make a loan without trying for a SELL-DOWN to other banks. The club approach is often used when the deal is to be kept private for some reason, or the borrower is unpopular in the market, or when current market conditions are so difficult that there is the prospect of failing to sell the deal.
Bibliography: L.S. Goodman. Syndicated Euro-Lending: Pricing and Practice *in* A.M. George & I.H. Giddy. *International Finance Handbook*. John Wiley & Sons, New York, 1983.
(2) Refers to a grouping of governments involved in a financial arrangement, often an LDC debt rescheduling. Compare PARIS CLUB.
Bibliography: S. Strange. *International Monetary Relations*. Royal Institute of International Affairs. London, 1976.
B. Nowzad & R.C. Williams. *External Indebtedness of Developing Countries*. Occasional Paper no.3, International Monetary Funds, Washington DC, 1981.

CMEA. Initials of COUNCIL FOR MUTUAL ECONOMIC ASSISTANCE.

CMR. (Convention relative un contrât de transport international de marchandises par route.) The Convention on the Contract for the International Carriage of Goods by Road, the CMR was completed at Geneva in 1956 and achieved the force of international law in 1961. It governs liability and contracts in international road transport.
Bibliography: A. E. Donald. CMR—An outline and its history. *Lloyd's Maritime and Commercial Law Quarterly*. UK, November 1975.
C. M. Schmitthoff. *Export Trade*. Stevens & Sons, London, 1980.

COB. *See* COMMISSION DES OPERATIONS DE BOURSE.

COFACE. *See* COMPAGNIE FRANÇAISE POUR L'ASSURANCE DU COMMERCE EXTERIEURE.

co-financing. Term for financing a country carried out in parallel by institutions such as the WORLD BANK of IMF and commercial banks. It may also cover situatons where commercial lendings are made with CROSS-DEFAULT clauses relating to IMF or World Bank loans. Default on the latter will be taken as default on the commercial loans.
Bibliography: *Co-financing*. World Bank, Washington DC, 1983.
J. Cook. Maintaining the flow of loans: the co-financing alternative. *The Banker*. London, May 1983.
Bibliography: J. Williamson (ed.). *IMF Conditionality*. MIT Press, Cambridge, Mass., 1983.

co-insurance. Joint insurance by several companies of a large risk (as distinct from the practice where one company might insure the risk and then seek REINSURANCE).

co-lead manager. In a loan or BOND issue which is made by a SYNDICATE it is common for one bank or securities house to be designated the LEAD MANAGER, but in some cases the responsibility is shared between one or more co-lead managers.
Bibliography: S.I. Davis. *The Euro-Bank*. Macmillan, London / John Wiley, New York, 1981.
L.S. Goodman. Syndicated Eurolending: Pricing and Practice *in* A.M. George & I.H. Giddy (eds). *International Finance Handbook*. John Wiley & Sons, New York, 1983.

collar. A US term for a bank loan, or other financial instrument, offered on the basis that it has both a floor and a ceiling to its rates. Thus a bank might offer, in exchange for an up-front fee, to lend on the basis that the borrower would never pay more than 14% nore less than 9%.

collared offer. A US term for an offer by a company for the shares of another company, under which an upper and lower limit is set for the number of shares of the offering company that will be exchanged for a share of the target company.
Bibliography: M.A. Weinstein. Arbitrage *in* M.E. Blume & J.P. Friedman (eds). *Encyclopedia of Investments*. Warren, Gorham & Lamont, New York, 1982.

collateral. A US term for assets used to provide security for a loan. Article 9 of the US uniform Commercial Code divides collateral into four main categories: goods, paper (negotiable instruments or documents of title), intangibles, and proceeds. The code defines a 'security interest' as 'an interest in personal property or fixtures which secures payment or performance of an obligation'. Such an interest is created by an agreement between the debtor and the secured party, which is made effective either by the secured party's possession of the collateral or his possession of a paper describing the collateral, signed by the debtor.
Bibliography: *Bankers Desk Reference*, Warren, Gorham & Lamont, New York, 1984.
US Uniform Commercial Code Article 9.

collateralized loan. A US term for a loan granted to a customer upon the pledge of: (1) liquid assets, e.g. registered shares or stock, bonds or (2) illiquid assets (mortgage on a building etc.). If the borrower is unable to repay, the lender sells the collateral.
Bibliography: W. H. Baughn & C. E. Walker (eds). *The Bankers' Handbook*. Dow Jones-Irwin, US, 1978, pp. 622-49.

collateralized mortgage security. A US term for a security which is backed by mortgages. The first steps to this market were taken by the issue of PASS-THROUGH certificates by the GOVERNMENT NATIONAL MORTGAGE ASSOCIATION (GNMA – Ginnie Mae) in 1969; by 1980 the outstanding volume exceeded $100 billion. The GNMA certificates, however, did not guarantee certainty of repayment date, as the underlying mortgages could be prepaid. Accordingly, in 1983 the Federal Home Loan Mortgage Corporation (Freddie Mac) introduced its Collateralized Mortgage Obligation: a debt security, with greater certainty of repayment dates, but with the underlying security of the payment stream of a mortgage pool. Subsequent issues were done for private corporations. The total annual volume of mortgages 'securitized' is now around $90-100 billion.

Bibliography: M.A. Smilow. The Move Toward Mortgage Securitization. *Mortgage Banking*. New York, December 1983.
L. Sandler. The mortgage-backed securities bonanza. *Institutional Investor*. New York, March 1984.

collateral trust bond. US term for BONDS secured by securities which are placed with a trustee by the issuing corporation. For example, a holding company may own no fixed assets, but only securities of other corporations. When issuing a bond, the company will deliver to corporate trustee under a bond INDENTURE the securities pledged.
Bibliography: F.J. Fabozzi & H.C. Sauvain. Corporate Bonds *in* F.J. Fabozzi & I.M. Pollack (eds). *The Handbook of Fixed Income Securities*. Dow-Jones Irwin, Homewood, Ill., 1983.

collecting bank. A term used in COLLECTIONS denoting the bank which collects payment on the bill sent by the REMITTING BANK. An exporter will hand a bill to his bank for collection from an importer in another country. The remitting bank will send the bill to the importer's bank. They will collect the money owing and transfer it to the remitting bank.
Bibliography: A. Watson, *Finance of International Trade,* Institute of Bankers, London, 1981.

collection. An exporter may draw a BILL OF EXCHANGE on his customer abroad and hand over the bill to his bank for collection. Under this method (unlike, for example, a confirmed irrevocable DOCUMENTARY CREDIT) the exporter is solely reliant on the importer's willingness to pay. The bank will charge a fee for trying to collect payment, but is not liable should it fail to do so.
Bibliography: A. Watson. *Finance of International Trade.* Institute of Bankers. London, 1981.
Uniform rules for collections. International Chamber of Commerce Brochure No. 322. Paris, 1978.

co-manager. (1) Lender ranking next to the LEAD MANAGER in a Euroloan. The lead manager will usually run the books of the issue, but co-managers may also be involved in some of the work on the issue; for example, one might be given the task of preparing the PROSPECTUS and another the task of preparing the AGREEMENT AMONG UNDERWRITERS.

Bibliography: S. I. Davis. *The Euro-bank*. Macmillan, London/John Wiley, New York, 1981.
A.W. van Agtmael. Issuance of Eurobonds: Syndication and Underwriting Techniques and Costs *in* A.M. George & I.H. Giddy (eds). *International Finance Handbook*. John Wiley & Sons, New York, 1983.

(2) In the US securities industry the term usually refers to any manager of an issue not running the books of the SYNDICATE.

combined transport document. The development of 'multi-modal' transport has meant that the BILL OF LADING is no longer necessarily a convenient form of documentation. Accordingly, the INTERNATIONAL CHAMBER OF COMMERCE has tried to develope a new, more suitable document. Combined transport is defined as the carriage of goods by at least two different modes of transport from one country to another. The carrier is referred to as the combined transport operator (CTO). By issuing the combined transport document, which may be NEGOTIABLE or non-negotiable, the CTO undertakes to perform or procure performance of the combined transport. As yet the combined transport document is not recognized by international convention, but the CTO and his customer may adopt it by contract.

Bibliography: *Uniform Rules for a Combined Transport Document*. Brochure No. 298. International Chamber of Commerce, Paris, 1975.

Comecon. Abbreviation for COUNCIL FOR MUTUAL ECONOMIC ASSISTANCE.

Comex. *See* COMMODITY EXCHANGE OF NEW YORK.

Comfort. *See* LETTER OF COMFORT.

commercial documents. Term employed in the INTERNATIONAL CHAMBER OF COMMERCE UNIFORM RULES FOR COLLECTIONS to mean 'Invoices, shipping documents, docu-

ments of title or other similar documents, or any other documents whatsoever, not being FINANCIAL DOCUMENTS.'

commercial paper. PROMISSORY NOTES sold by companies or institutions to raise cash for working capital purposes. Much more important in the US and Canada than in the UK because it is 'one-name' paper (only the maker of the note is liable). The BILL OF EXCHANGE is 'two-name' paper (both the drawer – the borrower – and the acceptor are liable). Two-name paper is preferred in the UK market, so that until now commercial paper has not been an important instrument in the UK. Some attempt was made in the early 1970s to introduce EUROCOMMERCIAL PAPER but with only modest success although the growth of the EURONOTE market has begun to change the position. In the US, commercial paper is a major borrowing instrument for first-class borrowers. It does not require registration with the SECURITY EXCHANGE COMMISSION provided its maturity is less than 270 days. A company can sell its commercial paper to dealers, or it may place the paper directly in the hands of investors by using its own network of contacts. The market has been in existence for many years but grew rapidly in 1965 – 70 (from $9.3 billion to $40.9 billion) when its growth was checked by the collapse of the Penn Central Railroad, at a time when the latter had large amounts of commercial paper outstanding. The total now stands at around $240 billion.

Bibliography: T.Q. Cook & B.J. Summers (eds). *Instruments of the Money Market*. Federal Reserve Bank of Richmond, Virginia, 1981.
M. Stigum. *The Money Market*. Dow-Jones Irwin, Homewood, Ill., 1983.

commingling. The mixing together of items which would normally be separate. For example, the US FEDERAL RESERVE prohibits brokers and dealers from commingling their customers' securities with the securities owned by other customers (Regulation T). The US also has a wide variety of commingled funds which are used as investment vehicles.

Bibliography: M.E. Blume & J.P. Friedman. *Encyclopedia of Investments*. Warren Gorham & Lamont, Boston, 1982.

Commission des Operations de Bourse. French government agency responsible for supervising the French stock exchange. It has powers to supervise new LISTINGS of shares, takeover bids, insider trading etc.

Bibliography: *Rapport Annuel de la Commission des Operations de Bourse*. Paris.
B. Jacquillat. Paris Equity Market *in* A.M. George & I.H. Giddy (eds). *International Finance Handbook*. John Wiley & Sons, New York, 1983.

commitment fee. In some circumstances, where a bank has granted a overdraft or term loan which is not being fully used, it may charge a commitment fee (for example, up to 0.5% p.a. on the unused balance). This is because it is committing itself to raise the necessary funds, even if it is inconvenient at the time of asking.

Bibliography: R. C. Merris. Loan Commitments and Facility Fees. *Economic Perspectives*. Federal Reserve Bank of Chicago, March/April 1978.
L.S. Goodman. Syndicated Eurolending: Pricing and Practice *in* A.M. George & I.H. Giddy. *International Finance Handbook*. John Wiley & Sons, New York, 1983.

Commodity Credit Corporation. A US Department of Agriculture agency. Its primary job is to support US farm incomes, but is also involved in financing US agricultural exports.

Bibliography: P. K. Oppenheim. *International Banking*. 4th edn. American Bankers Association, 1983.

Commodity Exchange of New York (COMEX). Founded in 1933, the Comex is an important trading center for metals FUTURES, principally in gold but also including copper, silver, and others. Options on gold futures can also be traded through the Comex. Annual contract value turned over on the Comex in 1982 exceeded $700 billion.

Bibliography: T. Green. *The New World of Gold*. Walker & Co., New York, 1981.
The World's Metals Market. Comex, New York,

n.d; *Options on Comex Gold Futures*. Comex, New York, n.d.

Commodity Futures Trading Commission. An independent US federal agency established by the Commodity Futures Trading Act of 1974 and having exclusive jurisdiction over the US commodities futures markets. It supervises the procedures of the individual exchanges and may take action to ensure that violations are disciplined. It also has power to approve or veto proposed new futures contracts.

Bibliography: CFTC, Annual Reports, Washington, DC.
F.R. Edwards. *The Regulation of Futures and Forward Trading by Depository Institutions: A Legal & Economic Analysis*. John Wiley & Sons, New York, 1981.

Common Short Form Bill of Lading. A BILL OF LADING using the 'short form' concept, i.e. a standard clause referring to detailed conditions of carriage available elsewhere, rather than setting out all the clauses in full in each individual document, and 'common' in the sense that it does not carry printed on the face of it any reference to a named carrier (this is inserted by the shipper or his agent when preparing the bill).

Common Stock. US term for the class of capital of a company that has the right of ownership of the residual value of the assets and income of the corporation after all other claims have been satisfied. The UK equivalent is ordinary shares.

Bibliography: R.J. Teweles & E.S. Bradley.*The Stock Market*. John Wiley, New York, 1982.

Commonwealth Development Corporation. A publicly-owned UK corporation founded by Parliament in 1948. Its task is to invest in development projects in Commonwealth and other developing countries, with the objectives of furthering development and of securing a reasonable return. It operates on broadly commercial lines.

Bibliography: W. Rendell. *History of the Commonwealth Development Corporation*. Heinemann, London, 1976.
CDC Annual Reports.

Communauté Française Africaine Franc. The franc used by the members of the CFA, primarily French-speaking West Africa. The CFA franc has a fixed parity with the French franc. Compare FRANC ZONE.

Bibliography: International Monetary Fund. *Annual Report on Exchange Restrictions.* Washington DC, annually.
J.K. Walmsley. *The Foreign Exchange Handbook.* John Wiley & Sons, New York, 1983.

Compagnie Française pour l'Assurance du Commerce Extérieure (COFACE). COFACE was founded in 1946 to operate the French export credit insurance system. Its capital is held by a number of major nationalized banks, the BANQUE FRANÇAISE DU COMMERCE EXTÉRIEURE, and other institutions. It offers coverage of a range of commercial and political risks, and also foreign exchange risk insurance where forward cover cannot be obtained from the market. Compare EXPORT CREDIT GUARANTEE DEPARTMENT, HERMES.

Bibliography: *The Export Credit Financing Systems in OECD Member Countries.* OECD, Paris, 1982.

compensating balance. A US banking term for a deposit required to be made with a bank in exchange for a loan. Thus a loan of $10 million might be made in exchange for the depositor holding a compensating balance of $1 million with the bank. In general, compensating balance requirements are less frequent than in the past.

Bibliography: R.T. Nassberg. Loan Documentation. *The Business Lawyer.* New York, April 1981.

compensation financing. *See* COMPENSATORY FINANCING.

compensation trading. An arrangement where an exporter agrees to accept part payment in goods from the buyer's country in lieu of cash. He will be involved in disposing of the goods himself or via a firm specialized in BARTER TRADING and he may also have to obtain exchange control permission, since normally central banks specify that payments for exports shall be made in convertible currency. Compare CLEARING, SWITCH TRADING.

Bibliography: P.D. Ehrenhaft (ed.). *Countertrade: International Trade Without Cash.* Law & Business/Harcourt Brace Jovanovich, New York, 1983.
R. Birley. Can't pay? Will pay, but in sultanas. *Euromoney,* London, May 1983.
P. Verzariu. *Countertrade, Barter and Offsets.* McGraw-Hill, New York, 1984.

compensatory financing. Name given to a facility offered by the IMF for short-term loans to compensate for fluctuations in a member country's exports. It is chiefly applicable to countries depending on raw materials exports.

Bibliography: A.W. Hooke. *The International Monetary Fund: its Evolution, Organization and Activities.* IMF Pamphlet no. 37, Washington DC, 1981.
The Financial Structure and Operations of the IMF. *Bank of England Quarterly Bulletin,* December 1983.

compensatory official financing. A term sometimes used to refer to a transaction carried out by an official agency to provide (or absorb) foreign exchange to (or from) a person carrying on another transaction (often referred to as an autonomous or underlying transaction); for example, an importer may need to buy dollars in exchange for sterling – an autonomous transaction. Rather than allow the exchange rate to fall the Bank of England might supply dollars. This would be compensatory official financing.

Bibliography: J.K. Walmsley. *The Foreign Exchange Handbook.* John Wiley & Sons, New York, 1983.

competition and credit control. The new form of UK monetary policy introduced in 1971 to free the financial system from rigid controls on lending and encourage flexibility. *See also* CORSET.

Bibliography: *Bank of England Quarterly Bulletin.* June, September, December 1971, March, September 1973.
E. R. Shaw. *The London Money Market.* Heinemann, London, 1983.

composite. (1) UK term for an insurance

company which transacts a number of types of business (e.g. life assurance and fire, motor and marine insurance).

(2) A composite insurance policy is one subscribed to by more than one company on the same form.
Bibliography: V. Dover. *A Handbook to Marine Insurance*. Revised and edited R.H. Brown. Witherby & Co., London, 1975.

comptant.   French term for spot settlement in foreign exchange. Compare SPOT.
Bibliography: P. Coulbois. *Le Finance Internationale: I. Le Change*. Editions Cujas, Paris, 1979.

Comptroller of the Currency.   US official with important regulatory powers over the banking system. Nationally chartered banks are supervised by the Comptroller, who forwards a report of condition to the Federal Reserve and the Federal Deposit Insurance Corporation. The Comptroller's office is part of the US Treasury.
Bibliography: P.M. Horvitz. Consolidation of the regulatory agency structure: has the time for it come? *Economic Review*, Federal Reserve Bank of Atlanta, Dec. 1982.

concordat.   See BASLE CONCORDAT.

conditional bond.   See SURETY BOND.

conditional bond sales.   See REPURCHASE AGREEMENTS, GEN-SAKI, PENSION.

conditional liquidity.   INTERNATIONAL LIQUIDITY which can only be used on certain conditions, such as borrowings from the INTERNATIONAL MONETARY FUND. Only gold, foreign exchange and the IMF GOLD TRANCHE are truly unconditional liquidity. All other forms, even SPECIAL DRAWING RIGHTS, are subject to some conditionality, although the degree varies according to the asset (or borrowing).
Bibliography: J. Gold. *Conditionality*. IMF Pamphlet no. 31, International Monetary Fund, Washington DC, 1980.
J. Williamson (ed.). *IMF Conditionality*. MIT Press, Cambridge, Mass. 1983.

conditions precedent.   Legal term referring to the conditions which have to be fulfilled before a loan can be drawn, or before some other contract (such as an INTEREST RATE SWAP) can be carried out. The scope of these conditions precedent depends on the circumstances but they will usually include a requirement of satisfactory evidence that all legal matters are in order before the loan is drawn, and will often include further sets of conditions precedent applicable to each DRAW-DOWN or ROLL-OVER.
Bibliography: P. Wood. *Law and Practice of International Finance*. Sweet & Maxwell, London, 1980.
R.T. Nassberg. Loan Documentation. *The Business Lawyer*. New York, April, 1981.

confirmed documentary credit.   Where an importer is financing his trade by DOCUMENTARY CREDIT the exporter has to rely on him and on his bank to remit the funds unless the credit is confirmed. This confirmation is a definite undertaking by the bank in the exporter's country that payment will be made.
Bibliography: *Uniform customs and practice for documentary credits*. International Chamber of Commerce Brochure No. 290. Paris, 1974.
A. Watson, *Finance of International Trade*. Institute of Bankers, London, 1981.

confirming house.   A firm concerned with international trade. A confirming house enters usually into two legal relationships: to its overseas customer who asks it to procure certain goods for him, and to the seller in the home market with whom it places the order. The house's relationship with the overseas customer is normally that of agent and principal, while its relationship with the seller in the home market tends to vary with the circumstances.
Bibliography: A. Watson. *Finance of International Trade*. Institute of Bankers, London, 1981.

consensus.   Export credit term relating to a 1976 'gentlemen's agreement' between OECD members regarding the extent to which export credit may be subsidised. The consensus was renegotiated – with great difficulty – during 1983. It sets different minimum interest rates for exports to relatively rich, intermediate and relatively poor countries; and it permits exporters in high interest rate countries to use LOW INTEREST RATE CURRENCIES under certain conditions.

Bibliography: How the Consensus Survived. *Euromoney*, London, January 1984.
K. Taylor. A Case for Export Credit Subsidies. *The Banker*, London, February 1984.
A. Dunn & Martin Knight. *Export Finance*. Euromoney Publications, London, 1982.

consignment note. A document supplied when goods are dispatched, giving details of the goods, the sender, and the person to whom they are sent. The latter signs it on arrival, providing proof of delivery.
Bibliography: D. J. Hill. *Freight Forwarders*. Stevens & Sons, London, 1972.
A. Watson. *Finance of International Trade*. Institute of Bankers, London, 1981.

consignment terms. Export trading on the basis that goods exported on consignment remain the property of the UK exporter, and are sold for him by an agent.
Bibliography: C.M. Schmitthoff. *Schmitthoff's Export Trade*. 7th edn. Stevens & Sons, London, 1980.

consolidation. (1) In relation to the international monetary system, the term refers to the replacement of national currencies (such as the dollar) held in countries' foreign exchange reserves by a new international monetary asset, usually the SDR.
Bibliography: Group of 30. *Towards a Less Unstable International Monetary System*. New York, 1980.
(2) The combination of several issues of stocks and shares into one uniform security.
See FUNDING, REFINANCING, REFUNDING.

consortium bank. A bank whose shareholders consist of a group of other banks. Usually associated with international banking operations, consortium banks became popular during the 1960s and early 1970s. A number were badly affected by the international crises of the 1970s; and, in addition, it

became evident that there were often conflicts of interest between the consortium bank and its parents. Accordingly, banks of this type are now less common.
Bibliography: S.I. Davis. *The Euro-Bank*. Macmillan, London/John Wiley, New York, 1981.

construction trust. A PROJECT FINANCE technique, particularly used in the US for utilities constructing plant. In a construction trust, the utility agrees to refinance the trust by providing permanent financing on its own balance sheet for the power plant once the facility is operational.
Bibliography: *Standard and Poor's Rating Guide*. McGraw-Hill, New York, 1979.
P.K. Nevitt. *Project Financing*. Euromoney Publications, London 1983.

constructive total loss. This was defined in the UK's 1906 Marine Insurance Act as occurring 'where the subject-matter insured is reasonably abandoned on account of its actual total loss appearing to be unavoidable, or because it could not be preserved from actual total loss without an expenditure which would exceed its value when its value when the expenditure had been incurred'.
Bibliography: UK Marine Insurance Act 1906 Section 60.
R.J. Lambeth. *Templeman on Marine Insurance*. Macdonald & Evans, UK, 1981.

contango. (1) Charge made by a UK stockbroker for carrying over a bargain from one Stock Exchange account to the next.
Bibliography: J. Dundas Hamilton. *Stockbroking Today*. Macmillan, London, 1979.
(2) In commodity markets, contango denotes a situation where the forward price of a commodity is above the present, or cash, price.
Bibliography: R. Gibson-Jarvie. *The London Metal Exchange*. Woodhead-Faulkner, Cambridge, UK/Nichols Publishing Co., New York, 1983.

Continental Depositary Receipt (CDR). A development of the DEPOSITARY RECEIPT; the CDR is issued by several Dutch banks. It is made out in BEARER FORM, thus permitting trade in the US, UK and Japanese registered company shares on the Amsterdam Stock Exchange (which permits only trading in bearer shares). As an example, in 1980 Nippon Chemical Condenser Co. issued four million shares in the form of CDRs of 1,000 shares each, to be listed on the Luxembourg Stock Exchange. Compare AMERICAN DE-POSITARY RECEIPT, INTERNATIONAL DE-POSITARY RECEIPT.

contingent immunization. Term used in BOND portfolio management. IMMUNIZATION of the portfolio against interest rate movements is undertaken in accordance with preset criteria. For example, suppose the portfolio manager sets a minimum target return of 8% per annum on the portfolio, when the immunized return is currently 9%, but he hopes to achieve 11%. He will manage the portfolio actively—i.e. he will not immunize it—but if he has bad luck and it appears that the minimum return of 8% is at risk, he will immunize the portfolio. That is, the immunization is contingent on the need to achieve the preset minimum rate of return.
Bibliography: P.E. Christensen, S.G. Feldstein & F.J. Fabozzi. Bond Portfolio Immunization *in* F.J. Fabozzi & I.M. Pollack (eds). *The Handbook of Fixed Income Securities*. Dow-Jones Irwin, Homewood, Ill., 1983.

contingent liability. A liability which may or may not occur (and whose occurrence is regarded as possible rather than probable). For example, an endorser, on a bill of exchange may be required to pay the bill if the drawer/acceptor defaults. In addition, the term covers liabilities under, amongst other things, PERFORMANCE BONDS, LETTERS OF CREDIT and guarantees.
Bibliography: Coopers & Lybrand. *Manual of Auditing* Gee & Co., London 1981.

contract. (1) In general, any business agreement between two or more parties, usually in writing.
(2) In the FINANCIAL FUTURES markets, and other commodities futures markets it is customary to trade in standardized contracts. Thus the CHICAGO BOARD OF TRADE. Treas-

ury bond contract is for US Treasury bonds with a face value of US$100,000, a coupon of 8%, and a remaining life of 15 years to MATURITY or CALL; other bonds may be delivered, subject to the application of a CONVERSION FACTOR.
Bibliography: N.H. Rothstein & J.M. Little (eds). *The Financial Futures Handbook*. Dow-Jones Irwin, Homewood, Ill., 1984.
Chicago Board of Trade. *Understanding the Delivery Process in Financial Futures*. Chicago, n.d.

contract financing. PROJECT FINANCE involving the use of commercial contracts such as a ship charter or TAKE-OR-PAY CONTRACT as security for the loan.
Bibliography: P.K. Nevitt. *Project Financing*. Euromoney Publications, London, 1983.

convergence. A term from the FUTURES markets to describe the fact that the BASIS – i.e. the difference between the cash price and the futures price – must inevitably shrink to zero as the expiry date of the futures contract approaches. Otherwise it would be possible to buy the cash and sell the futures contract, or vice versa, for a risk-free profit at maturity date.
Bibliography: N.H. Rothstein & J.M. Little. *The Handbook of Financial Futures*. Dow-Jones Irwin, Homewood, Ill., 1984.

conversion. (1) The act of converting, e.g., one security into another (for example, a bond into shares – compare CONVERTIBLE), or one currency into another.
(2) In the options markets, a conversion consists of buying the underlying stock, or commodity, and also buying a put option and selling a call option where both options have the same terms. This position will have a locked-in profit if the total cost of the position is less than the striking price of the options. For example, XYZ Co. stock sells at 55, XYZ January 50 call at 6.5, and XYZ January put at 1. The total cost of this position is 55 for the stock, less 6.5 for the call plus 1 for the put, i.e. 49.5. Since this is less than the 50 strike price, there is a locked in profit of half a point. If at expiration of the options the stock price is above 50, the put will be worthless, the call will be exercised by

its buyer, so that the stock is sold at 50: but its net purchase price was 49.5. On the other hand, if the stock price is below 50 at maturity, the call will be worthless, but the trader will exercise his put option to sell the stock at 50, again netting a half point profit. A REVERSAL will be profitable if the opposite situation occurs – that is, if the total cost of the position is greater than the striking price of the options.

Bibliography: L.G. McMillan. *Options as a Strategic Investment*. New York Institute of Finance, New York, 1980.

conversion factor. A FINANCIAL FUTURES market term. When the CASH instrument delivered in settlement of the futures deal does not match exactly that specified in the CONTRACT, a conversion factor must be applied. For example, the CHICAGO BOARD OF TRADE Treasury BOND contract specifies that the bond to be delivered should have an 8% coupon. If the bond delivered had, for example, an 11.3/4% coupon, then the amount of bonds required would be scaled down by the conversion factor, which in this instance would be 1.3974.

Bibliography: N.H. Rothstein & J.M. Little. *The Financial Futures Handbook*. Dow-Jones Irwin, Homewood, Ill., 1984.
Chicago Board of Trade. *Understanding the Delivery Process in Financial Futures*. Chicago, n.d.
Treasury Bond Futures and Treasury Note Futures Conversion Factors. Financial Publishing Company, Boston, Mass. 1980.

conversion issue. A new issue of bonds timed to correspond with a maturing issue by the same borrower. The offering is normally structured in such a way that investors are given an incentive to exchange or convert the old issue into the new one. Conversion issues are a regular feature of government bond markets; in 1980 the EUROPEAN INVESTMENT BANK pioneered the use of the technique in the EUROBOND market with the issue of a $100 million bond rolling over a previous 1975 issue.

Bibliography: OECD. *Government Debt Management*. Paris, 1983.

F.G. Fisher, *International Bonds*. Euromoney Publications, London, 1981.

conversion premium/discount. The additional cost (premium) or gain (discount), expressed as a percentage, that arises from acquiring shares through buying and converting a CONVERTIBLE bond compared to buying the shares directly at the current market price.

conversion price. The share price at which the principal amount of a convertible bond may be used to acquire shares in or owned by the issuing company.

conversion ratio. The number of shares which may be acquired upon the conversion of a convertible bond. The ratio is calculated as bond principal amount divided by conversion price.

convertible. (1) If a currency can be bought and sold at will in exchange for other currencies (a wider definition would add, 'and for gold') it is said to be convertible. Of the majors, the US and Canadian dollars, sterling, the Swiss franc, Japanese yen and the Deutschemark are, broadly speaking, convertible, while the French and Belgian francs, and Italian lira are subject to varying limits on convertibility.

Bibliography: *IMF Annual Reports on Exchange Restrictions*. Washington DC.
J.K. Walmsley. *The Foreign Exchange Handbook*. John Wiley & Sons, New York, 1983.

(2) A DEBENTURE STOCK or BOND which can be converted into ordinary shares at a stated future date. This option usually enables the issuer of the convertible to pay a lower rate of interest on the bond, since the investor is attracted by the chance of buying the shares at a favourable rate.

Bibliography: M. L. Tennican. *Convertible Debentures and Related Securities*. Harvard University Press, Cambridge, Mass. 1975.
P. Welham. *Investing in Share Options, Warrants & Convertibles*. Woodhead-Faulkner, UK, 1975.
J.C. Ritchie. Convertible Bonds and Warrants *in* F.J. Fabozzi & I.M. Pollack. *The Handbook of*

Fixed Income Securities. Dow-Jones Irwin, Homewood. Ill., 1983.

convertible adjustable rate preferred stock. A US term for ADJUSTABLE RATE PREFERRED STOCK which is modified to allow the investor to convert into COMMON STOCK between the announcement of the dividend rate for the next period, and the start of that period. CAPs also allow the issuer to adjust the relationship between US Treasury yields and the preferred dividend. This enables the issuer to adjust the dividend to discourage conversion by making the CAP more attractive.
Bibliography: K.D. Brody *et al.* The Revival of Equity Financing *in* P.H. Darrow & R.A. Mestres (eds). *Creative Financing in the 1980s.* Practising Law Institute, New York, 1983.

convertible Belgian franc. Trading in the Belgian franc is split into two markets: convertible and financial. The latter market is used for financial operations such as the purchase and sale of shares or bonds or deposits, while the former is largely confined to the making of payments for imports or exports.
Bibliography: IMF. *Annual Report on Exchange Arrangements.* Washington, DC, annually.

convertible exchangeable preferred stock. A US term for a PREFERENCE SHARE (STOCK) which is convertible at the option of the holder into COMMON STOCK of the issuer and exchangeable at the option of the issuer into the issuer's CONVERTIBLE debentures. The CEP is attractive to firms interested in issuing convertible debt but who for RATING purposes prefer equity; and who are not currently paying taxes but expect to do so. For the preference dividend is not tax deductible, while the interest on the convertible debenture is. The ability to switch gives flexibility to manage the tax position. An example would be the January 1983 issue of CEP stock by the Boise Cascade Corporation.
Bibliography: K. D. Brody *et al.* The Revival of Equity Financing *in* P.H. Darrow & R.A. Mestres

(eds). *Creative Financing in the 1980s.* Practising Law Institute, New York, 1983.

convertible floater. A FLOATING RATE NOTE which is convertible into a fixed rate bond if rates fall to a certain level. The aim of this formula is to provide the investor with a certain minimum level of interest rate in exchange for accepting the uncertainty of a floating rate on the note.
Bibliography: G. Ugeux. *Floating Rate Notes.* Euromoney Publications, London, 1981.

convertible revolving credit. A REVOLVING CREDIT which may at the end of its period (or some other agreed time) be converted into a fixed-term loan. Compare 'EVERGREEN CREDIT'.
Bibliography: H. V. Prochnow & H. V. Prochnow Jr (eds). *The Changing World of Banking.* Harper & Row, New York, 1974.
P. H. Hunn. Spotlight on the term loan. *Bankers' Magazine.* Boston, Summer 1976.

cooling period. US term for the period between the filing of a registration statement for a security issue, and the date when the SEC authorizes the securities to be released for sale. During this period a preliminary prospectus or RED HERRING is issued and a DUE DILIGENCE meeting is held.

cooperation agreement. In general, any agreement to cooperate; more specifically, used in international trade to refer to deals where mutual cooperation may (at least in part) substitute for payment in cash. An example is the 1977 deal between Cementation International and Poland for the construction of a complex at Warsaw Airport, involving the employment of Polish construction crews on other Cementation sites overseas.
Bibliography: R. Birley. Can't pay? Will pay, but in sultanas. *Euromoney.* May 1983.
P.D. Ehrenhaft (ed.). *Countertrade: International Trade Without Cash.* Law & Business/Harcourt Brace, New York, 1983.
L. Welt. Why Latin America is wary of barter. *Euromoney,* London, January 1984.

corporate bond equivalent. A US term for the semi-annual equivalent rate of return for a security whose interest payments are not on a semi-annual basis. For example, a discount security with less than six months to run is converted to corporate bond equivalent by using the standard DISCOUNT TO YIELD formula; if the discount security has more than six months to run the formula is more complex; the formulae are laid under BOND EQUIVALENT YIELD.
Bibliography: M. Stigum. *Money Market Calculations.* Dow-Jones Irwin, Homewood, Ill., 1981.

corporate tax equivalent. US term for the rate of return required on a PAR BOND to produce the same after-tax yield to maturity as a given bond. The formula required is:-

$$TEY = \frac{ATY}{1-t}$$

where TEY = Taxable equivalent yield

ATY = After-tax yield

t = tax rate (as a decimal e.g. 48% = 0.48)

Thus, as an example, suppose a US tax-exempt bond yields 4.19%. To an investor with a tax rate of 48%, the taxable equivalent yield is:-

$$TEY = 8.07\% = \frac{4.19}{(1-0.48)}$$

Bibliography: M.L. Leibowitz. Total Aftertax Bond Performance and Yield Measures *in* F.J. Fabozzi & I.M. Pollack (eds). *The Handbook of Fixed Income Securities.* Dow-Jones Irwin, Homewood, Ill., 1983.

correspondent. A bank, securities firm or other financial organization which regularly performs services for another in a place or market to which the other does not have direct access. Thus a British bank may act as a correspondent for an Indian bank which has no UK branch, a New York bank may act as correspondent for an Ohio bank with no New York office, etc.

corset. UK slang term for a scheme of monetary control where in INTEREST-BEARING ELIGIBLE LIABILITIES above a certain specified limit, in relation to a specified base period, attracted a penalty in the form of a non-interest-bearing deposit which had to be placed with the Bank of England. The effect was to discourage banks from bidding for funds.
Bibliography: *Bank of England Quarterly Bulletin.* March 1974.
E.R. Shaw. *The London Money Markets.* Heinemann, London, 1981.

cost and freight. Term indicating that the price of a shipment includes the basic price FREE ON BOARD plus the cost of freight to the destination. It is the same as the COST, INSURANCE AND FREIGHT price minus insurance.
Bibliography: D. M. Sassoon. *C.I.F. and F.O.B. Contracts.* Stevens & Sons, London 1975.
C. M. Schmitthof. *The Export Trade.* 7th edn., Stevens and Sons, London 1980.
Incoterms. International Chamber of Commerce Brochure No. 350. Paris, 1980.

cost and insurance. Term indicating that the price of a shipment includes the basic price FREE ON BOARD plus the cost of insurance in transit but excluding freight.
Bibliography: D. M. Sassoon. *C.I.F. & F.O.B. Contracts.* Stevens & Sons, London, 1975.
C. M. Schmitthof. *The Export Trade.* 7th ed., Stevens & Sons, London, 1980.
Incoterms. International Chamber of Commerce Brochure No. 350. Paris, 1980.

Cost, Insurance, Freight (CIF). A contract made on a CIF basis is one specifying that the price includes the cost of the goods plus that of freight to its destination, and of insuring it en route.
Bibliography: D. M. Sassoon. *C.I.F. & F.O.B. Contracts.* Stevens and Sons, London, 1975.
C. M. Schmitthof. *The Export Trade.* 7th edn., Stevens & Sons, London, 1980.
Incoterms. International Chamber of Commerce Brochure No. 350, Paris, 1980.

Council for Mutual Economic Assistance (CMEA). Founded in 1949, the CMEA (frequently called Comecon) now consists of Bulgaria, Cuba, Czechoslovakia, German

Democratic Republic, Hungary, Mongolia, Poland, Rumania, Vietnam and the USSR. Albania has played no part since 1963 but apparently remains formally a member. Its object is to assist the development of its member states through joint utilisation and co-ordination of efforts. Compare INTERNATIONAL BANK FOR ECONOMIC CO-OPERATION, INTERNATIONAL INVESTMENT BANK, TRANSFERABLE ROUBLE.

Bibliography: A. Zwass. *Money, Banking and Credit in the Soviet Union.* Macmillan, London/ M.E. Sharpe, New York, 1979.
A.I. MacBean & P.N. Snowden. *International Institutions in Trade and Finance.* George Allen & Unwin, London 1981.

counterpart. In foreign exchange, the other party in a deal is called the counterpart- a dealer selling dollars three months forward will seek to find a counterpart who wishes to buy three months forward etc.

countertrade. Another term for BARTER : the exchange of goods without (or in part, without) the intermediation of money. It is difficult to estimate the volume of countertrade, but in the difficult international economic climate of recent years it has certainly increased: current estimates put it at 10 – 30% of world trade.

Bibliography: R.N. Bracher. If countertrade is inevitable, make the best of it. *The Banker,* London, May 1984.
P.D. Ehrenhaft (ed.). *Countertrade: International Trade without Cash.* Law & Business/Harcourt Brace Jovanovich, New York, 1983.

countervailing credit. *See* BACK-TO-BACK LOANS.

countervailing duty. A duty imposed on imported goods which the importing country believes are subsidized by the exporter's goverment. In recent years these have formed an increasingly difficult area of international trade negotiations, and have also complicated the arrangement of international COUNTERTRADE since in such trade the measurement of subsidy is extremely difficult.

Bibliography: *The Tokyo Round of Multilateral Trade Negotiations.* GATT, Geneva, 1979.
P.D. Ehrenhaft (ed.). *Countertrade: International Trade without Cash.* Law & Business/Harcourt Brace Jovanovich, New York, 1983.

country risk. Not a clearly defined term. General usage would probably distinguish it from SOVEREIGN RISK. Country risk would be regarded as the risk attaching to a borrower (regardless of its public/private status) by virtue of its being located in a particular country. This encompasses economic, political and even geographical factors.

Bibliography: S. I. Davis. *The Euro-bank.* Macmillan, London/John Wiley, New York, 1981.
P.J. Nagy (ed.). *Country Risk.* Euromoney Publications, London, 1981.

coupon. A detachable certificate sometimes used for the payment of interest or dividends on bearer securities. (The coupon technique is sometimes applied to repayment of principal – compare SERIAL FRN.) By extension, the term is used to refer to the rate of interest on a security. The coupon is an important determinant of the volatility of a BOND since for a given maturity and initial market yield, the volatility of a bond's price increases for lower coupons. The price of a bond yielding 9%, with 20 years to maturity, with a coupon of 5%, will rise by 24.43% if the yield falls by 2%. But a similar two-year bond, currently yielding 9%, having a 10% coupon, will improve by only 20.91% if the yield falls by 2%.

Bibliography: P. Phillips. *Inside the Gilt-edged Market.* Wooodhead-Faulkner, Cambridge, UK, 1984.
F.J. Fabozzi. Bond Yield Measures and Price Volatility Properties *in* F.J. Fabozzi & I.M. Pollack (eds). *The Handbook of Fixed Income Securities.* Dow-Jones Irwin, Homewood, Ill., USA, 1983.

coupon issues. US term generally applied to obligations of the US Government which bear a specified rate of interest or COUPON as distinct from, for example, Treasury bills, where the investors' yield comes from the discount at which he purchases the bill.

Coupon issues include TREASURY NOTES and TREASURY BONDS.

coupon stripping. Term for an operation whereby a firm (usually a US investment bank) buys securities (usually US Treasury BONDS), deposits them with a trustee, and then issues receipts against every payment of interest (COUPON) and principal that are due under the security. The receipts are then sold for the present value of the payment. The purpose of the exercise is to create a ZERO COUPON security whose underlying credit risk is the original securities – i.e. (usually) the US government.
Bibliography: J. Laskey. How stripping became respectable. *Euromoney*. London, December 1982.

court. French for 'short': 'une position courte'='a short position'.
Bibliography: P. Coulbois. *Le Finance Internationale. I. Le Change.* Editions Cujas, Paris, 1979.

courtier. French term for BROKER : on the foreign exchange market there are about 20 firms of courtiers. It is not compulsory for their services to be used. On the French domestic money market there are about 30 courtiers.
Bibliography: P. Coulbois. *Le Finance Internationale. I. Le Change.* Editions Cujas, Paris, 1979. D. Marteau & E. de la Chaise. *Le marche monetaire et la gestion de tresorerie des banques.* Dunod, Paris, 1981.

covenant. A clause in a loan agreement providing that the borrower will do (or not do) certain things, in order to protect the position of the lender. 'The great trilogy of covenants in unsecured international lending comprises the negative pledge, the pari passu clause and the information covenant' (Wood). The information covenant is that whereby the borrower covenants to provide relevant financial and other information to the lenders; NEGATIVE PLEDGE and PARI PASSU covenants protect the lender's security.
Bibliography: P. Wood. *Law and Practice of*

International Finance. Sweet & Maxwell, London 1980.
J.A. Donaldson & T.H. Donaldson. *The Medium-Term Loan Market.* Macmillan, London 1982.

cover. (1) To take out a forward foreign exchange contract. Compare FORWARD CONTRACT.
(2) To close out a SHORT POSITION by buying the currency or securities which have been sold.
(3) To insure.
(4) Refers to DIVIDEND COVER.

covered arbitrage. ARBITRAGE between financial instruments denominated in different currencies, using forward cover to eliminate exchange risk. For example, suppose the spot dollar-sterling exchange rate is £1=$1.50, and the one year forward rate is $1=$1.5750- i.e. the annual cost of forward cover is 5%. Suppose a UK Treasury bill yields 7% and a US Treasury bill yields 11%. Then a US investor will buy spot sterling, simultaneously selling it forward for a yield of 5%, and invest in a UK Treasury bill, earning 7%, for a total yield of 12% compared with 11% available directly.
Bibliography: J.K. Walmsley. *The Foreign Exchange Handbook.* John Wiley & Sons, New York, 1983.

covered call. An OPTIONS market term for a CALL which is written by an investor holding the underlying instrument. Thus an owner of 100 XYZ Co. shares, which are currently selling at $4.80 per share, might sell a July $5.00 call option on 100 shares, earning say $50. If the share price rises to over $5.00 and the buyer exercises the call, the writer of the option is protected by actually owning the underlying shares. The protection is not absolute, since the writer of the option will still lose money if the share price falls below $4.30 (i.e. below the original price adjusted for earnings from writing the option).
Bibliography: L.G. McMillan. *Options as a Strategic Investment.* New York Institute of Finance, New York, 1980.

covered margin. The interest-rate margin

between two instruments denominated in different currencies, after taking account of the cost of forward cover.

Bibliography: J. J. van Belle. The covered margin indicator of speculative activity. *South African Journal of Economics.* March 1977.
J.K.Walmsley. *The Foreign Exchange Handbook.* John Wiley & Sons. New York, 1983.

covered option writer. A person who writes an OPTION which is protected by a corresponding position in the underlying instrument is said to be a covered option writer. Thus an owner of 100 XYZ Co. shares, which are currently selling at $4.80 per share, might sell a July $5.00 call option on 100 shares, earning say $50. If the share price rises to over $5.00 and the buyer exercises the call, the writer of the option is protected by actually owning the underlying shares. The protection is not absolute, since the writer of the option will still lose money if the share price falls below $4.30 (i.e. below the original price adjusted for earnings from writing the option).

Bibliography: L.G. McMillan. *Options as a Strategic Investment.* New York Institute of Finance, New York, 1980.

crawling peg. A method of exchange rate adjustment; the rate is fixed (or pegged) but adjusted at certain intervals in line with certain chosen indicators – such as inflation in the case of Brazil – so that it 'crawls' up or down. Sometimes known as 'gliding' or 'sliding' parity.

Bibliography: P. B. Kenen. *Floats, Glides and Indicators.* Princeton University Reprints in International Finance, No. 18.
N. Carlozzi. Pegs and Floats. *Federal Reserve Bank of Philadelphia Business Review.* May/June 1981.

crédit de mobilisation de créances commerciales. French term for short-term bank lendings in the form of discounted bills of exchange backed by underlying trade debt.

Bibliography: J. Ferroniere & E. de Chillaz. *Les Operations de Banque.* 6th edn. Dalloz, Paris, 1980.

Creditexport. A non-profit-making consortium of Belgian commercial banks and other public and private financial institutions to fund medium- and long-term export credit. The rates charged are linked to medium and long term domestic market rates. Its rates are below market rates but normally above the CONSENSUS guidelines.

Bibliography: *The Export Credit Financing Systems in OECD Member Countries.* OECD, Paris, 1982.

crédit mixte. An export credit term for the integration of an export credit package with development aid funds. While commendable in principle, credit mixte has in practice been used in a number of cases to provide a concealed subsidy to export credit. Compare CONSENSUS, LOW INTEREST RATE CURRENCY.

Bibliography: K. Taylor. A Case for Export Credit Subsidies. *The Banker.* London, February 1984.
A. Dunn & M. Knight. *Export Finance.* Euromoney Publications, London, 1981.

credit rating. In general, this term refers to the quality of a borrower's reputation. More specifically, it is used to refer to a systematic evaluation of a borrower's financial condition by an agency which specializes in this function. The two best-known bond rating agencies are the US firms of MOODY's and STANDARD & POOR's.

Bibliography: *Standard & Poor's Ratings Guide.* McGraw-Hill, New York, 1979.

credit risk. In general, the risk that a debtor will not repay. In foreign exchange, the risk that the COUNTERPART in the deal does not have the currency he is promising to deliver to you. Also called 'capital risk', 'settlement risk' or CUSTOMER RISK. Compare DELIVERY RISK.

Bibliography: J.K. Walmsley. *The Foreign Exchange Handbook.* John Wiley & Sons, New York, 1983.

credit spread. An OPTIONS MARKET term for SPREAD which earns an immediate income. Suppose XYZ Co. stock is selling for 43 and the July 40 call is at 4, with the July 45 call at 1. An investor who establishes a

BACKSPREAD by selling one July 40 call and buying two July 45 calls will earn an immediate income of 2: this would be a credit spread. Compare DEBIT SPREAD.

Bibliography: L.G. McMillan. *Options as a Strategic Investment*. New York Institute of Finance, New York, 1980.

cross-border lease. A LEASE where the lessor and lessee are from different countries. Such leases are appropriate in certain cases because of tax benefits, or as a means to reduce political risks.

Bibliography: G. Reiners. Leasing in an International Context *in* A.M. George & I.H. Giddy. *International Finance Handbook*. John Wiley, New York, 1983.
P.K. Nevitt. *Project Financing*. Euromoney Publications, London, 1983.

cross-currency exposure. A term in INTERNATIONAL MONEY MANAGEMENT denoting a situation where a company's debt servicing requirements in a currency are not covered by its revenue-generating capabilities in that currency.

Bibliography: J.A. Donaldson. *Corporate Currency Risk*. Financial Times, London, 1980.

cross-default clause. A clause in a loan agreement specifying that default on any other loans to the borrower shall be regarded as default on this one. A sample cross-default clause might provide that an event of default occurs if 'any other borrowings of the borrower become due and payable prior to their scheduled maturity as a result of a default thereunder or any such borrowings or interest thereon are not paid when due or any guarantee given by the borrower of any borrowing is not honoured when due and called upon'.

Bibliography: P. Wood. *Law & Practice of International Finance*. Sweet & Maxwell, London, 1980.
W.C.F. Kurz. New Form in the Loan Agreement. *Euromoney*, London, February 1981.
R.T. Nassberg. Loan Documentation. *The Business Lawyer*. New York, April 1981.
J.A. Donaldson & T.H. Donaldson. *The Medium-Term Loan Market*. Macmillan, London, 1982.

cross-hedge. A term from the futures markets for a HEDGE carried out by using one instrument as a proxy for another. For example, a trader holding a US corporate bond might wish to hedge himself against a rise in interest rates. However, in the absence of a financial futures contract on the specific corporate bond he is holding, he would have to hedge by using a futures contract on another instrument – most probably on US Treasury bonds. This would be called a cross-hedge. In general a cross hedge occurs when the hedged and hedging instruments differ with respect to risk level, coupon, or maturity. A cross hedge also occurs if the time span covered by the instrument being hedged differs from that covered by the instrument deliverable against the futures contract. Thus a 90-day borrowing to be contracted in three months' time might be hedged in the futures market by a 90-day Treasury bill contract. But because the delivery date on the futures contract might be, say, 80 days hence, not 90, the hedge is not perfect, but is a cross-hedge.

Bibliography: N.H. Rothstein & J.M. Little (eds). *The Handbook of Financial Futures*. Dow-Jones Irwin, Homewood, Ill., 1984.

cross-over. A term of TECHNICAL ANALYSIS referring to the point at which two different chart lines cross. For example, a cross-over would occur when a three-day moving average line rose above a ten-day moving average, and would normally be a 'buy' signal.

Bibliography: F.H. Hochheimer. Channels and Cross-overs *in* P.J. Kaufman (ed.). *Technical Analysis in Commodities*. John Wiley & Sons, New York, 1980.

cross-rate. The exchange rate between currencies A and C which is derived from the rate between A and B, and the rate between B and C. Thus if $1=DM2.50 and $1=yen 250, the cross-rate between the Deutschemark and the yen is DM1=yen 100.

crowding-out. Term denoting public sector borrowing so large that the private sector is starved of funds. The argument runs: 'the public sector is insensitive to the cost of funds, and has unimpeachable creditworthiness, so can easily borrow when the private sector may not be able to afford to'. But the public sector may equally be sensitive to the political cost of driving up interest rates, and its expenditure may assist private sector financing by improving corporate cash flows.

Bibliography: C.A.E. Goodhart. *Monetary Theory and Practice*. Macmillan, 1984.
O. Eckstein. *The DRI Model of the US Economy*. McGraw-Hill, New York, 1983.

cum coupon. International bond market term for dealings in a bond where the buyer acquires the right to receive the next due interest payment. Compare EX-COUPON, CUM-DIVIDEND.

Bibliography: AIBD. *Rules and Recommendations*.

cum-dividend. A UK Stock Exchange term, meaning that the buyer of a stock has the right to receive the next interest or dividend payment on the stock. The list of stockholders to whom interest is due has to be drawn up some time before the payment is made. If the stock is sold after the list is drawn up, then it is sold EX-DIVIDEND.

Bibliography: J. Dundas Hamilton. *Stockbroking Today*. Macmillan, London, 1979.

cumulative preferred. A stock or share which has the provision that if one or more dividends are omitted, the omitted dividends will be paid before any dividend is paid on any stock or share which does not rank ahead of the preferred stock or share.

Bibliography: *The New 'Beginners Please'*. Investors Chronicle. London, 1975.

Curacao Depositary Receipts. Forerunners of CONTINENTAL DEPOSITARY RECEIPTS.

currency availability clause. A EUROMARKET clause providing that banks may switch their lending to a different currency if the original currency is no longer available.

Bibliography: P. Wood. *Law and Practice of International Finance*. Sweet & Maxwell, London, 1980.

A.M. George & I.H. Giddy. *International Finance Handbook*. John Wiley & Sons, New York, 1983.

currency cocktail. Colloquial term for a UNIT OF ACCOUNT based on a number of currencies, such as the ARCRU, EURCO or ECU.

Bibliography: J.K. Walmsley. *The Foreign Exchange Handbook*. John Wiley & Sons, New York, 1983.

currency exchange or **swap.** A term referring to a longer term exchange of currency between two companies (often in different countries). For example, a UK company may arrange to provide a US company with sterling in exchange for dollars from the US company. The transaction is reversed at maturity by what is in effect a forward exchange contract. Because of its simplicity the currency swap has tended to be more popular than the BACK-TO-BACK loan.

Bibliography: J.K. Walmsley. *The Foreign Exchange Handbook*. John Wiley & Sons, New York, 1983.
B.Antl (ed.). *Swap Financing Techniques*. Euromoney, London, 1983.

currency flow. *See* TOTAL CURRENCY FLOW.

currency option. (1) An OPTION to buy or sell a currency. The currency option market has developed rather patchily since the late 1970s but is now widely developed, with many banks offering their corporate customers currency options. For the individual wishing to trade options it is necessary to use the Philadelphia or Chicago exchanges. Although expensive relative to forward cover, options offer the benefit of potentially unlimited profits coupled with limited risk.

Bibliography: S. Mazloumian. Market Developments. *The Treasurer*. London, November 1984.

(2) Can be used to refer to the choice of borrowing currency in a MULTI-CURRENCY LOAN.

currency swap. *See* CURRENCY EXCHANGE OR SWAP; SWAP; FORWARD CONTRACT.

current account. The net balance of a country's international payments arising from exports and imports of goods and services, together with unilateral transfers (e.g. gifts, emigrants' remittances). Excludes capital flows.
Bibliography: M. Levi. *International Finance.* McGraw-Hill, New York, 1983.
H.G. Grubel. *The International Monetary System.* Penguin Books, London 1984.

current yield. *See* INTEREST YIELD.

cushion bond. Term occasionally applied to a high COUPON bond which is selling at a price above its CALL PRICE. In this situation the investor faces a potential capital loss if the bond is called for repayment. This risk decreases as interest rates rise and the bond's price falls towards its call price: hence the bond's price will fall more slowly than other bonds without this special feature.
Bibliography: D.M. Darst. *The Complete Bond Book.* McGraw-Hill, New York, 1975.
M.S. Dobbs-Higginson. *Investment Manual.* Credit Suisse First Boston, London, 1980.

cusip number system. An American standard alphanumeric system for identifying security issues.
Bibliography: L.M. Loll & J.G. Buckley. *The Over-the-Counter Securities Markets.* Prentice-Hall, NJ. 1981.

customer risk. *See* CREDIT RISK.

Customs Cooperation Council Nomenclature. Formerly known as the Brussels Tariff Nomenclature, the CCCN is an international standard classification of goods for customs tariff. It is divided into 211 sections with 99 chapters and 1098 headings. Each heading consists of a four digit number and has an official description e.g.:-
82.14 Spoons, forks, fish-eaters, butter, knives and similar kitchen or tableware.
This classification system helps identify goods for tariff and statistical purposes.
Bibliography: *Croner's Reference Book for Exporters,* UK, April 1982;
Nomenclature for the Classification of Goods in Customs Tariffs, HMSO, London, 1976.

cycle. (1) In general, refers to the economic cycle of growth and recession.
(2) In FUTURES and OPTIONS markets, refers to the cycle of months for which CONTRACTS are available, e.g. the IMM currency futures dates are March, June, September, December; the options markets have cycles starting in January and February also.
Bibliography: N.H. Rothstein & J.M. Little (eds). *The Handbook of Financial Futures.* McGraw-Hill, New York, 1984.
L.G. McMillan. *Options as a Strategic Investment.* New York Institute of Finance, New York, 1980.
C.W.J. Granger (ed.). *Trading in Commodities.* Woodhead-Faulkner, Cambridge, UK, 1983.

D

DAC. *see* DEVELOPMENT ASSISTANCE COMMITTEE.

Dansk Eksportfinansierungsfond (DEFC). Danish Export Credit Finance Corporation set up in 1975 by the Danish Central Bank (which holds 40% of the capital) and the commercial banking sector. It normally lends for 2–5 years at a preferential rate, but may lend for longer, especially to developing countries. A typical credit with DEFC participation consists of two parts: one financed at a market rate by an outside insitution and one by DEFC at the CONSENSUS rate.
Bibliography: *The Export Credit Financing Systems in OECD Member Countries*. OECD, Paris, 1982.

dawn raid. A UK term for a stock market operation by which a firm seeking to acquire another will bid aggressively for a certain amount of shares before withdrawing. An example was the purchase by De Beers of 25% of Consolidated Gold Fields on 12 February 1980; from a previous close of 525p, de Beers' brokers bid 616p at the start of trading, withdrawing from the market by 10 a.m. when the 25% target was reached. Small shareholders, who had no chance to learn of the raid, were highly critical, and the UK rules were later amended to make a dawn raid more difficult.
Bibliography: G. Cummings. *Investors Guide to the Stock Market*. Financial Times Business Information, London, 1981.

daylight exposure. The term for the total OPEN POSITION permitted to a bank's foreign exchange department during the course of a business day.
Bibliography: J.K. Walmsley. *The Foreign Exchange Handbook*. John Wiley & Sons, New York, 1983.
(2) Term for the total credit exposure an institution has to another institution in the course of any one day – for example, in the CLEARING HOUSE INTER-BANK PAYMENT SYSTEM.
Bibliography: D.B. Humphreys. Reducing Interbank Risk on Large Dollar Payment Networks. *Journal of Cash Management*, Atlanta, USA, September 1984.

day loan. US term for a loan extended to a securities broker/dealer during the course of a day, and expected to be repaid during the course of that day. Its purpose is to finance cash flow mismatches which may occur during the course of a day owing to normal differences in payments timing.

DCE. *See* DOMESTIC CREDIT EXPANSION.

deadweight tonnage. The weight which a ship can carry when loaded down to her load-line level. Compare GROSS REGISTERED TONNAGE.

dealer agreements. US term for contracts between members of the SELLING GROUP and the manager of the SYNDICATE defining terms of the issue and binding members to conform to the requirements of the NASD and the trading restrictions of the SEC. Compare AGREEMENT AMONG MANAGERS, AGREEMENT AMONG UNDERWRITERS.
Bibliography: F.G. Fisher. *International Bonds*. Euromoney Publications, London, 1981.

dealers' loans. *See* BROKERS' LOANS.

debenture. An acknowledgement of indebtedness. Usually given by an incorporated company, but can be given by anyone. (1) In the United Kingdom, it is usually given under seal, and usually accompanied by a charge on the assets of the borrower. It may be unquoted, or quoted and traded on the Stock Exchange. (For example, BULLDOG bonds issued by placing are generally dealt in the debenture market.)

Bibliography: R.R. Pennington. *The Investor and the Law.* McGibbon & Kee, UK, 1968.
de Zoete & Bevan. *The Bulldog Market.* London, 1983.

(2) In the United States, a debenture is generally unsecured.
Bibliography: F.J. Fabozzi & H.C. Sauvain. Corporate Bonds *in* F.J. Fabozzi & I.M. Pollack (eds). *The Handbook of Fixed Income Securities.* Dow-Jones Irwin, Homewood, Ill., 1983.

debt-service ratio. Payments made by a country to service its foreign debt, i.e. interest payments and repayments of PRIN-CIPAL, as a percentage of the country's export earnings. Precise definitions vary. The 'debt' usually includes public-sector debt and publicly guaranteed debt, but also often may include private debt. For a group of 87 non-oil producing developing countries the IMF estimated a debt-service ratio (total medium and long-term debt, including private non-guaranteed debt, as a percentage of exports) of 7% in 1960, 16% in 1970 and 19% in 1980. A common rule of thumb is that a ratio above 20% for any one country is a danger sign, yet some countries have run ratios of 40% without difficulty, because they have been able to roll over borrowing, while others have had to RESCHEDULE with ratios below 20%.
Bibliography: World Bank. *Annual Report* and *World Debt Tables.* Washington DC, annually.
Bank for International Settlements. *Manual on Statistics Compiled by International Organizations on Countries' External Indebtedness.* Basle, Switzerland, March 1979.
B. Nowzad & R.C. Williams. *External Indebtedness of Developing Countries.* IMF, Washington DC, 1981.

Declaration Day. A UK stock market term for the date under which a holder of an OPTION on a stock must either abandon the option or claim his rights under it. Declaration Day is the second last day in the ACCOUNT before the final Account Day on which completion of the option may take place. Thus a Declaration Day on Thursday 5 March would be settled on Monday 16 March.

Bibliography: T.G. Goff. *Theory and Practice of Investment.* Heinemann, London, 1982.

deep discount bond. A bond which is issued at (or currently stands in the market at) a large discount from par: this occurs if the bond bears a low interest rate. For example, if current market rates for 10-year bonds are 15%, and a 10-year bond is issued with a COUPON order to make its YIELD equal 15%. Such an issue may be attractive on tax grounds in certain circumstances, since much of the investor's earnings (and the issuer's costs) come in the form of price appreciation on the bond as it rises to its $100 REDEMPTION PRICE. In addition, from the investor's viewpoint, deep discount bonds have the benefit that they have effective CALL PROTECTION However, there may be tax complications. The ultimate form of deep discount bond is the ZERO COUPON bond.
Bibliography: F.J. Fabozzi. Federal Income Tax Treatment of Fixed Income Securities *in* F.J. Fabozzi & I.M. Pollack (eds). *The Handbook of Fixed Income Securities.* Dow-Jones Irwin, Homewood, Ill., 1983.
S. Homer & M. Leibowitz. *Inside the Yield Book.* Prentice-Hall, NJ. 1972.

default. A borrower who does not repay any amount due under the loan in full and on time is said to be in default. This may include cases where without the consent of creditors, debts are RESCHEDULED or changes are made in the rate of interest payable. Compare NON-PERFORMING LOAN, CROSS-DEFAULT CLAUSE.
Bibliography: P. Wood. *Law & Practice of International Finance.* Sweet & Maxwell, London, 1980.
R.T. Nassberg. Loan Documentation. *The Business Lawyer.* New York, April, 1981.
D. Suratgar (ed.). *Default and Rescheduling.* Euromoney Publications, London, 1984.

defeasance. A US term for the elimination of debt. In its original form (LEGAL DEFEA-SANCE) the term referred to tax-exempt securities. They contained provisions allowing the borrower to be released from his obligations to repay (and from the COVE-NANTS contained in the INDENTURE). This was achieved by placing with a trustee sufficient cash or government securities to generate the cash flow needed to pay all interest and principal when due. In 1982 the technique was applied to a taxable borrowing by Exxon. The corporation removed borrowing from its balance sheet and reported a capital gain (because the debt retired was trading below face value). After a pause owing to uncertainty over accounting treatment the technique revived in 1984.

Bibliography: B. McGoldrick. Why are CFOs so excited about defeasance? *Institutional Investor.* New York, March 1984.
Financial Accounting Standards Board. *Statement of Financial Accounting Standards no.76: Extinguishment of Debt.* Stamford, Conn, 1983.

défection. French term for default.

deferred payment bond. EUROBOND market term for a bond which is issued PARTLY PAID. The first deferred payment bond was the $80 million issue for Alcoa of Australia, of August 1980, with 25% of purchase price payable in September 1980 and the balance in January 1981.

Bibliography: E. Pearlman. The partly paid fiasco. *Institutional Investor*, New York, April 1983.

deficiency guarantee. A guarantee given to a lender but limited in amount to the deficiency suffered by the lender on realization of an asset in the event of the borrower's default. A deficiency guarantee generally covers, in the lender's loss; expenses of resale, lost interest, and the unpaid loan balance. A limited deficiency guarantee might be given: e.g. a 25% deficiency guarantee is a deficiency guarantee with a maximum exposure of 25% o the amount financed. The deficiency guarantee technique is usually used in situations where the underlying asset is marketable (e.g. a ship). It may also be used to cover cost over-runs or revenue deficiencies.

Bibliography: *Standard & Poor's Ratings Guide.* McGraw-Hill, New York, 1979.
P.K. Nevitt. *Project Financing.* 4th edn. Euromoney Publications, London, 1983.

defined assets. Used from 1973-81 for the purposes of the Bank of England's control of the London discount market, defined assets were those defined as public sector assets. UNDEFINED ASSETS were limited to a maximum of 20 times a disount house's capital and reserves. The controls now used are on ADDED RISK ASSETS and NET ADDITIONS.

Bibliography: *Bank of England Quarterly Bulletin.* September 1973.
Prudential arrangements for the discount market. *Bank of England Quarterly Bulletin.* June 1982.

del credere. A del credere commission is an extra commission paid by a principal to an agent when the agent takes the risk that a customer, to whom he has sold goods, is solvent.

delivered at frontier. International trade term meaning that the seller must supply goods which conform with the contract, and at his own risk and expense the seller must put the goods at the disposal of the buyer at the named place of delivery at the frontier at the specified time. The buyer is responsible for complying with import formalities and for duty payment.

Bibliography: *Incoterms.* International Chamber of Commerce Brochure no. 350, Paris, 1980.

delivered duty paid. International trade term meaning that the seller must supply goods in conformity with the contract, and at his own risk and expense the seller must put the goods at the disposal of the buyer, duty paid, and all necessary formalities having been complied with, at the named place of destination.

Bibliography: *Incoterms.* International Chamber of Commerce Brochure no. 350. Paris, 1980.

delivery risk. In foreign exchange, a term sometimes used to denote the risk that a COUNTERPART will not be allowed to complete his side of the deal (e.g. through the imposition of exchange controls), though willing to do so. Compare CAPITAL RISK, TRANSFER RISK.

delta. A term for the relationship between

an option price and the price of the underlying instrument. For example, in the stock market, the delta of an option is the amount by which the option will increase or decrease in price if the underlying stock moves by one point. This is an important piece of information for the option buyer since it tells him how much his option's price will change for a given change in the share price. A CALL option which is deeply IN-THE-MONEY has a delta of nearly 1 (unity); one which is deeply OUT-OF-THE-MONEY has a delta of nearly zero.
Bibliography: L.G. McMillan. *Options as a Strategic Investment.* New York Institute of Finance, 1980.

demain-après. French term meaning TOMORROW-NEXT.

demise charterparty. A CHARTERPARTY under which the charterer leases the ship itself, whereas under a TIME CHARTER or VOYAGE charter the shipowner agrees to provide a service by using his crew to carry goods on his ship on behalf of the charterer. A demise charter tends to be long term (and so better security for the lending banker, providing the charterer is sound). Compare CHARTERPARTY ASSIGNMENT.
Bibliography: Mocatta, Mustill & Boyd. *Scrutton on Charterparties and Bills of Lading.* 18th edn. Sweet & Maxwell, London, 1974.
C.T. Grammenos. *Bank Finance for Ship Purchases.* University of Wales Press, 1979.
M.S.W. Hoyle. *The Law of International Trade.* Laureate Press, London, 1981.

demurrage. A sum agreed by the charterer of a ship to be paid to the shipowner as liquidated damages for delay beyond a stipulated or reasonable time for loading or unloading.
Bibliography: Mocatta, Mustill & Boyd. *Scrutton on Charterparties and Bills of Lading.* 18th edn. Sweet & Maxwell, London, 1974.
M.J. Mustill. *Pseudo-Demurrage and the Arrived Ship.* Scandinavian University Books, Sweden, 1974.

depo. Slang term for deposit.

deport. French foreign exchange term meaning DISCOUNT.
Bibliography: P. Coulbois. *Finance Internationale: 1. Le Change.* Editions Cujas, Paris, 1979.

depositary. *See* AUTHORIZED DEPOSITORY.

depositary receipt. A technique devised to permit trading in security, even though the security does not fulfill the requirements for LISTING on the local stock exchange. They are also used where the underlying security is of high denomination. In the UK, for example, General Motors of the US has issued depositary receipts, in bearer form, entitling the bearer to units representing one-twentieth of a fully paid share of common stock in General Motors Corporation. A security is bought and registered in the name of the depositary bank or company (say) in Amsterdam, which will issue a receipt certifying that the receipt conveys the title to the security deposited with it or held to its order. If the receipt is in BEARER form, it can then be freely bought and sold, whereas direct dealing in the stock would have needed registration of the new owner's name every time the security changed hands. Variants include AMERICAN DEPOSITARY RECEIPTS, BEARER DEPOSITARY RECEIPTS, CONTINENTAL DEPOSITARY RECEIPTS, EUROPEAN DEPOSITARY RECEIPTS, INTERNATIONAL DEPOSITARY RECEIPTS AND JAPANESE DEPOSITARY RECEIPTS.
Bibliography: *Depositary Receipts.* Morgan Guaranty Trust Company, New York, n.d.
N. Osborn. The Rise of the International Equity. *Euromoney,* London, May 1984.

Depository Trust Company. A central securities certificate depository in New York through which clearing members of the NATIONAL STOCKCLEARING CORPORATION effect security deliveries between each other by computerized bookkeeping entries thereby reducing the physical movement of certificates. In October, 1983 the DTC handled just under 200,000 transactions daily; the value of deliveries handled in the preceding

12 months exceeded $3,000,000,000,000 ($3 trillion).
Bibliography: L.M. Loll & J.G. Buckley. *The Over-the-Counter Securities Markets.* Prentice-Hall, USA, 1981.

depot. Deposit.

depreciation. A fall in the value of a currency in terms of others, or in terms of its purchasing power.
Bibliography: M. R. Schuster. *The Public International Law of Money.* Clarendon Press, Oxford, UK, 1973.
J.K. Walmsley. *The Foreign Exchange Handbook.* John Wiley & Sons, New York, 1983.

designated order. US term for a system under which a BROKER will supply an institutional investor with free research or other services. In return, the investor contacts the managing UNDERWRITER of a new issue that the investor is interested in buying and asks that the broker be included in the SELLING GROUP and credited with the sale of the securities to the institutional investor. The broker then receives the SELLING GROUP SPREAD.
Bibliography: H.S. Gerla. Swimming Against the Deregulatory Tide: Maintaining Fixed Prices in Public Offerings of Securities through the NASD Antidiscounting Rules. *Vanderbilt Law Review,* USA, January 1983.

devaluation. A downward change in the official parity of an exchange rate (often loosely used as a synonym for depreciation). A dollar devaluation of 5% in terms of sterling means that a dollar will buy 5% less sterling.
Bibliography: M. R. Schuster. *The Public International Law of Money.* Clarendon Press, Oxford, 1973.
J.K. Walmsley. *The Foreign Exchange Handbook.* John Wiley & Sons, New York, 1983.

Development Assistance Committee. A committee of the ORGANIZATION FOR ECONOMIC COOPERATION AND DEVELOPMENT whose role is to encourage the flow of funds from member countries to the developing countries.

Bibliography: DAC Annual Reports available from OECD.

Devisen, Devises. Foreign exchange in German, French.

Devisenkassamarkt. German for SPOT EXCHANGE MARKET.

Devisenterminmarkt. German for FORWARD EXCHANGE MARKET.

diagonal spread. An OPTIONS market term. A diagonal spread is one using both different STRIKE PRICES and different expiration dates. For example, selling the April 35 option on XYZ Co. while buying the July 30 option would be a diagonal BULL SPREAD. This strategy would be appropriate if the stock were not expected to advance in price until after April.
Bibliography: L.G. McMillan. *Options as a Strategic Investment.* New York Institute of Finance, New York, 1980.

Dillon Round. The 1960-62 international trade negotiations conducted under the auspices of GATT. Followed in 1964 by the KENNEDY ROUND and in 1973 by the TOKYO ROUND. *See* GATT.
Bibliography: A. Schonfield (ed.). *International Economic Relations of the Western World 1959-71.* Vol. I, Royal Institute of International Affairs, London, 1976.

dingo. Australian term for a bond created by STRIPPING the COUPONS from a Government bond. It is an acronym for Discounted Investment in Negotiable Government Obligations and is derived from its US counterparts, notably CATS and FELINES.
Bibliography: Dingos are Australian Cats. *The Banker,* London, September 1984.

direct quotation. Quotation of fixed units of foreign currency in variable amounts of domestic currency. For example in the UK, if I quote $1=£0.53 this would be direct; £1=$1.95 would be indirect. Compare INDIRECT QUOTATION.

dirty.   (1) In foreign exchange a DIRTY float means one in which the value of the currency is controlled by the authorities rather than the market. Most floats are fairly dirty, if only because central banks intervene 'to maintain orderly market conditions'.

(2) Refers to a BILL OF LADING which is qualified as to the condition of the goods to which it relates.

Bibliography: Mocatta, Mustill & Boyd. *Scrutton on Charterparties and Bills of Lading.* 18th edn. Sweet & Maxwell, London, 1974.

(3) Another term for a UK stock which is CUM-DIVIDEND and is close to the date for payment of interest – i.e. it is very full of interest. Compare CLEAN.

disaster clause.   A EUROCREDIT loan agreement clause containing provisions for repayment of the loan if the Euromarket should disappear. It will also often contain other, less extreme provisions, e.g. repayment or renegotiation if for some reason adequate means do not exist to determine the interest rate applicable, or because the rate is not a true reflection of the banks' costs, or because it the banks' ability to fund the loan is impaired by market circumstances. Compare BREAK CLAUSE.

Bibliography: P. Wood. *Law and Practice of International Finance.* Sweet & Maxwell, London, 1980.

T.H. Donaldson. *Lending in International Commercial Banking.* Macmillan, London, 1979.

disbursements.   (1) In general, the payment of funds. Thus, for example, a development loan to a country might be disbursed in several instalments.

(2) A marine insurance term describing any expense, hence INSURABLE INTEREST outside the ordinary interests of hull and machinery, cargo and freight. Because of the structure of marine insurance premiums, a Disbursements Warranty was introduced in the UK in 1909 limiting the amount of insurance on disbursements in relation to the insurance on the HULL.

Bibliography: V. Dover. *A Handbook to Marine Insurance.* Revised and edited R.H. Brown. Witherby & Co, London, 1975.

discount.   (1) In foreign exchange, the term refers to a situation where a currency can be bought more cheaply for a future date than for immediate delivery. For example, if $1 buys $1.7700 for delivery now, while it buys $1.8170 for delivery 12 months hence, then the dollar is said to be at a discount against sterling. The discount may be quoted as 4.7 cents or 470 points. In European foreign exchange quotations, the existence of a discount is normally signified by the fact that the bank's selling price (quoted first) is below the buying price: thus, 470/480 in the example given. US practice is the reverse, since the market there thinks in terms of the dollar: 470/480 would be referred to as a premium for sterling. Compare 'PREMIUM', 'PAR'.

(2) To discount a future payment means to calculate its present value by using some form of discount rate. Hence a sum of $100 due in two years' time would be worth $82.65 today if the discount rate were 10%. The general formula is

$$PV = \frac{FV}{(1 + r)^n}$$

where PV = present value
FV = future value
n = number of periods
r = discount rate (per period) as a decimal.

Bibliography: M. Stigum. *Money Market Calculations.* Dow-Jones Irwin, Homewood, Ill., 1981.

(3) With reference to a bill of exchange, to discount a bill means to buy it for less than its face value, the difference between the price paid and the face value representing the implied rate of interest receivable by th purchaser, during the period before the bill is repaid.

Bibliography: Gillett Brothers Discount Company. *The Bill on London.* Methuen & Co, London, 1976.

(4) If a stock falls below its face value on the stock exchange it is said to stand at a discount.

(5) In the OPTIONS market, an option is said to be trading at a discount if it is trading for less than its INTRINSIC VALUE.

Bibliography: L.G. McMillan. *Options as a*

Strategic Investment. New York Institute of Finance, New York, 1980.

discount arbitrage. OPTIONS market term for the purchase of a DISCOUNT option and an opposite position in the underlying security. Since the option costs less than its INTRINSIC VALUE, the operation is risk-free.
Bibliography: L.G. McMillan. *Options as a Strategic Investment.* New York Institute of Finance, New York, 1980.

discount house. A financial institution specializing in discounting bills of exchange, Treasury bills, etc. Most commonly found in countries where the financial system was developed under British influence (e.g. Singapore, South Africa). In the UK, discount houses have traditionally played a key role in the London money market, since the Bank of England would lend only to the discount houses. However, various changes are under way which are in the process of altering the houses' position in the system. Compare MAISON DE REESCOMPTE.
Bibliography: Gillett Brothers Discount Company. *The Bill on London.* Methuen & Co, London, 1976.
E.R. Shaw. *The London Money Market.* Heinemann, London, 1984.
J.S.G. Wilson. Recent Changes in London's Money Market Arrangements. *Banca Nazionale del Lavoro Quarterly Review,* March 1983.

discount market. The market for discounting bills; in the UK the term is often used loosely to cover the short-term money market.
Bibliography: The Role of the Bank of England in the Money Market. *Bank of England Quarterly Bulletin,* March 1982.
E.R. Shaw. *The London Money Market.* Heinemann, London, 1984.
J.S.G. Wilson. Recent Changes in London's Money Market Arrangements. *Banca Nazionale del Lavoro Quarterly Review.* March, 1983.

discount rate. (1) The rate at which a future sum of money is discounted in order to find its present value.
(2) Hence, the rate at which a BILL OF EXCHANGE is discounted.

(3) Hence, the rate at which a central bank is prepared to discount certain bills for financial institutions as a means of easing their liquidity, in which case it is commonly called the official discount rate.

discount-to-yield conversion. Interest rates may be quoted on a discount basis or a yield basis. Suppose an investor buys $1 million in bills at a discount rate of 8% (on a 360-day basis) with a 'tenor' discount rate of 8% (on a 360-day basis) with a TENOR of 182 days. The discount amount is calculated at $1,000,000 x 0.08 x 182/360 = $40,444.44. Hence the purchase price of the bills will be $959,555.56. To calculate the yield on this investment we write 360/182 x ($1,000,000 – $959,555.56)/$959,555.56 = 8.34%. In general, to make the discount-to-yield conversion we write

$$i = \frac{360d}{360 - dt}$$

where $d =$ discount rate (as a decimal), $i =$ yield (as a decimal) and $t =$ days to maturity. For a 365-day market, such as the domestic UK sterling market, we would substitute 365 for 360 in both lines of the formula. In a few cases, LIBOR has been fixed in terms of discount-to-yield – e.g. the $50 million one-year facility for Corporacion Venezolana Fomento in 1981. This would normally be done for cosmetic reasons.
Bibliography: M. Stigum. *Money Market Calculations.* Dow-Jones Irwin, Homewood, Ill., 1981.

discount window. US term for assistance to banks provided by the Federal Reserve via its discounting of bills etc. Prior to the 1980 Monetary Control Act, discount window assistance was available only to members of the Federal Reserve system. Non-members did not have to keep reserves and conversely did not receive access to the window. All banking institutions must now keep reserves and consequently have access.
Bibliography: T.Q. Cook & B.J. Summers (eds). *Instruments of the Money Market.* Federal Reserve Bank of Virginia, 1981.
P. Meek. *US Monetary Policy and Financial*

Markets. Federal Reserve Bank of New York, 1982.

discretionary funds. Funds placed with a bank by customers for investment on their behalf by the bank at the bank's discretion. Very important in Switzerland and therefore in the EUROBOND market.
Bibliography: M.A. Corti. Switzerland: Banking, Money and Bond Markets *in* A.M. George & I.H. Giddy. *International Finance Handbook*. John Wiley & Sons, New York, 1983.

disintermediation. Shift of funds away from financial intermediaries (commercial banks, savings banks etc.) into Treasury bills and other securities.
Bibliography: T. Congdon. *Monetary Control in Britain*. Macmillan, London, 1982.
S.K. Cooper & D.R. Fraser. *The Financial Markets*. Addison-Wesley, Reading, Mass., 1982.

divergence indicator. A concept employed by the EUROPEAN MONETARY SYSTEM . The indicator represents an attempt to measure which member currency of the EMS is diverging from its central parity against the EUROPEAN CURRENCY UNIT. The divergence indicator is calculated in terms of change in the currency's present value in terms of ECU from the central parity against the ECU which that country has declared. If the divergence indicator moves beyond a certain level, which varies from currency to currency, and is termed the 'divergence threshold', then there is a 'presumption' that the central bank concerned will take corrective action. The divergence threshold has been set at three-quarters of the currency's permitted margin of fluctuation against the central parity (i.e. 2.25% for all member currencies except Italy, which uses a 6% margin). The threshold is calculated in such a way as to exclude the effect of a currency's weight in the ECU: this is because an important currency, such as the DMark, has a large weight in the ECU. If the DMark rises, then the value of the ECU rises. Accordingly, the apparent rise of the DMark in terms of the ECU is reduced, and if this were not offset then the DMark would benefit from greater freedom of movement than a smaller EMS currency such as the Irish punt. The exact formula used is: $0.75 \times 2.25 \times (1-W)$ where W is the weight of the currency concerned. In the case of the DMark the weight is 0.33, so the divergence threshold becomes 1.13%.
Bibliography: J. Salop. The Divergence Indicator. *IMF Staff Papers*, vol. 28, no. 4, 1981.
J.K. Walmsley. *The Foreign Exchange Handbook*. John Wiley & Sons, New York, 1983.
R. Brealy and S. Myers. *Principles of Corporate Finance*. Hill, US/UK, 1984.

dividend. Profit paid to shareholders by a company. A dividend can only be paid after other creditors (e.g. banks and other 'senior' debt holders) have been paid. Generally, a dividend is not deductible from corporate income for tax purposes. In the US, intercompany dividends have in the past qualified for more attractive treatment in that they were partially excluded from income in the hands of the corporate recipient; hence the attractions of ADJUSTABLE RATE PREFERRED STOCK and the like.
Bibliography: J. Dundas Hamilton. *Stockbroking Today*. Macmillan Press, London 1979.
R. Brealey and S. Myers. *Principles of Corporate Finance*. McGraw-Hill. US/UK, 1984.

dividend cover. The number of times by which a company's available profits after tax cover the dividend payment. If profits are £200 million and the dividend payment costs the firm £200 million than the dividend is twice covered.

division des risques. French term for a limitation on a bank's exposure to any one customer: the limit, in general, is 75% of capital.
Bibliography: J. Ferroniere & E. de Chillaz. *Les Operations de banque*. Dalloz, Paris, 1980.

dock warrant. When goods are imported but immediate delivery is not required, they may be deposited in a warehouse, owned either by the dock authority or by public warehousemen. Dock warrants or warehouse warrants may be issued against the consignment. Where this is prescribed under any statutory authority which operates the particular dock, such warrants are NEGOTIABLE INSTRUMENTS, but in other cases are merely receipts for the goods.

Bibliography: V. Dover. *A Handbook to Marine Insurance.* Revised and edited R.H. Brown. Witherby & Co., London, 1975.
A. Watson, *Finance of International Trade.* Institute of Bankers, London, 1981.

documentary acceptance credit. An ACCEPTANCE CREDIT involving the presentation of commercial documents, as distinct from a CLEAN ACCEPTANCE CREDIT.

Bibliography: A. Watson. *Finance of International Trade.* Institute of Bankers, London, 1981.

documentary collection. This term is de-fined in the UNIFORM RULES FOR COLLECTIONS of the INTERNATIONAL CHAMBER OF COMMERCE as a collection of either (a) FINANCIAL DOCUMENTS accompanied by COMMERCIAL DOCUMENTS, or (b) commercial documents unaccompanied by financial documents. For practical purposes the term is identical to the term DOCUMENTARY REMITTANCE.

Bibliography: A. Watson. *Finance of International Trade.* Institute of Bankers, London, 1981.
Uniform Rules for Collections, International Chamber of Commerce Brochure no. 322, Paris, 1978.

documentary credit. An arrangement (see diagram) where a bank, on behalf of a customer, (a) makes payment to (or to the

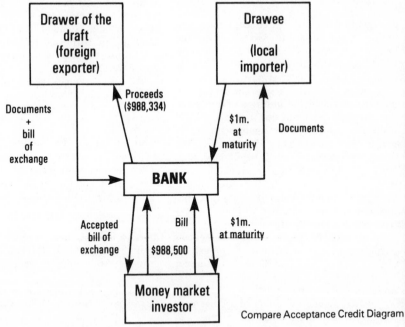

Compare Acceptance Credit Diagram

SUMMARY
1. Exporter sends documents and bill to bank and receives proceeds.
2. Bank sends documents to importer who must pay $1m. at maturity.
3. Bank sells bill to investor for $988,500. Investor receives $1m. at maturity.

DOCUMENTARY CREDIT

order of) a third party (the beneficiary), or is to pay/accept/negotiate 'bills of exchange' (DRAFTS) drawn by the beneficiary; (b) authorizes such payments to be made, or such drafts to be paid/accepted/negotiated by another bank. In all cases the terms and conditions of the credit, in particular as regards the document which the bank must inspect before payment/acceptance/negotiation, must be precisely complied with. The credit itself may be CONFIRMED or UNCONFIRMED, REVOCABLE or IRREVOCABLE. As an example of the system : Exports Ltd ask Import AG to arrange a letter of credit through Import AG's German bank. The German bank will open a letter of credit in favour of Exports Ltd. The German bank will inform a London bank of this. The London bank will advise Exports Ltd that it will pay the relevant amount to Exports Ltd if the right documents are sent to it. Effectively the exporter receives immediate payment while the bank grants the importer credit. Compare ACCEPTANCE CREDIT.

Bibliography: *Uniform Customs & Practice for Documentary Credits.* International Chamber of Commerce Brochure No. 290, Paris, 1974.
Gillett Brothers Discount Company. *The Bill on London.* Methuen & Co, London, 1976.
F.R. Ryder. Challenges to the Use of the Documentary Credit in International Trade Transactions. *Columbia Journal of World Business.* New York, Winter 1981.
B.S. Wheble. Developments Affecting Standby Credits and Documentary Credits: The Forthcoming Revision of the UCP *in* C.M. Chinkin, P.J. Davidson, W.J.M. Ricquier. *Current Problems of International Trade Financing.* Butterworths, London/Malaya Law Review, 1983.

documentary remittance. This term was defined in the Uniform Rules for the Collection of Commercial Paper published by the INTERNATIONAL CHAMBER OF COMMERCE as covering items 'with documents attached to be delivered against payment, acceptance, trust receipt or other letter of commitment, free or on other terms and conditions', in contrast to CLEAN REMITTANCES which do not have such documents attached. In the revised version of these rules, the UNIFORM RULES FOR COLLECTIONS the term is replaced by DOCUMENTARY COLLECTION.

Bibliography: A. Watson. *Finance of International Trade.* Institute of Bankers, London, 1981.

documented discount notes. US term occasionally used for COMMERCIAL PAPER backed by a letter of credit from a bank stating that it will pay off the paper at maturity if the borrower does not. Such paper is often also referred to as LoC (letter of credit) paper.

Bibliography: M. Stigum. *The Money Market.* 2nd edn. Dow-Jones Irwin, Homewood Ill., 1983.

documents against acceptance. An international trade term meaning that a shipper or COLLECTING BANK, may not hand over the documents giving title to the goods until the buyer has ACCEPTED the accompanying bill of exchange. Compare DOCUMENTS AGAINST PAYMENT, TRUST RECEIPT.

Bibliography: A. Watson. *Finance of International Trade.* Institute of Bankers, London, 1981.
C.M. Schmitthoff. *Schmitthoff's Export Trade.* 7th edn. Stevens & Sons, London, 1980.

documents against payment. Means that a shipper or COLLECTING BANK may not hand over the documents giving title to the goods until payment has been made.

Bibliography: A. Watson. *Finance of International Trade.* Institute of Bankers, London, 1981.
C.M. Schmitthoff. *Schmitthoff's Export Trade.* 7th edn. Stevens & Sons, London, 1980.

dollar cost averaging. *See* AVERAGING.

dollar premium. *See* INVESTMENT CURRENCY.

Domestic Credit Expansion (DCE). A measure of the growth of credit in an economy, much favoured by the INTERNATIONAL MONETARY FUND. Essentially DCE consists of money supply growth adjusted for flows across the exchanges. In the UK DCE is, broadly speaking, defined as the growth in STERLING M3 less external and foreign currency finance of the public sector, less increases in overseas sterling deposits, less net increases in banks' foreign currency

liabilities. It is also equal to bank lending to the public and private sectors plus bank lending in sterling overseas (on the grounds that this largely finances UK exports and thus effectively constitutes lending to the UK).
Bibliography: External Flows and Broad Money. *Bank of England Quarterly Bulletin.* September 1969, December 1983.

dossier.   French money market term relating to loans via a PENSION of 'effets prives' (private paper). The borrower will earmark the 'effets prives' that he is using as security for the loan by transferring them in his books to the 'dossier' of the lender: no physical transfer of the securities takes place.
Bibliography: D. Marteau & E. de La Chaise. *Le marché monétaire et la gestion de trésorerie des banques.* Dunod, Paris, 1981.

double.   UK term for an OPTION either to buy or sell, i.e. CALL or PUT, a security or commodity at a specified price. This type of option is useful if one is convinced that the security or commodity is likely to move sharply in price, but one is uncertain of the direction.
Bibliography: C.W.J. Granger (ed.). *Trading in Commodities.* Woodhead-Faulkner, Cambridge, UK, 1983.
L.G. McMillan. *Options as a Strategic Investment.* New York Institute of Finance, New York, 1980.

double bottom.   Term of TECHNICAL ANALYSIS referring to the behaviour of a price on a chart: if the price falls to a new low level, then recovers, falls again to the bottom, and then recovers, it is said to have established a double bottom, which is generally regarded as a signal that the price will now rise.
Bibliography: C.W.J. Granger (ed.). *Trading in Commodities.* Woodhead-Faulkner, UK, 1983.
P.J. Kaufman (ed.). *Technical Analysis in Commodities.* John Wiley & Sons, 1980.

double dip.   A term applied to a LEASE which takes advantage of tax deductions in two countries – for example, a lease written in the UK for a US company where the UK lessor claims UK capital allowances, and the US lessee claims US allowances.

Bibliography: Recent developments in equipment leasing. *Bank of England Quarterly Bulletin.* September 1982.
P.K. Nevitt.   *Project Financing.* Euromoney Publications, London, 1983.

double taxation.   A situation where an income flow is taxed twice; normally the term refers to taxation of the income by two countries.
Bibliography: J.D.R. Adams & J.Whalley. *The International Taxation of Multinational Enterprises.* Institute of Fiscal Studies, UK, 1977. *Double Taxation Relief.* Tolley Publishing Co., London 1979.

double top.   Term in TECHNICAL ANALYSIS ; the opposite of DOUBLE BOTTOM. If a price twice reaches a high point, only to fall back, it is considered to have established a double top, and to be likely to fall.
Bibliography: C.W.J. Granger (ed.). *Trading in Commodities.* Woodhead-Faulkner, Cambridge, UK, 1983.
P.J. Kaufman (ed.). *Technical Analysis in Commodities.* John Wiley & Sons, New York, 1980.

Dow Jones index.   Dow Jones & Co. compiles US stock market indexes for 30 industrial stocks, 20 transportations, 15 utilities, and a composite of all 65.
Bibliography: A.M. George. The United States Equity Markets *in* A.M. George & I.H. Giddy. *International Finance Handbook.* John Wiley & Sons, New York, 1983.

draft.   A BILL OF EXCHANGE drawn by one person on another, by a bank on itself or on another bank. The term is often used in the US to mean a bill of exchange. Compare Banker's Draft.

draw-down.   The act of drawing funds made available under a EUROCREDIT.

drawee.   The person on whom a BILL OF EXCHANGE is drawn: that is, the person who is required by the bill to pay money to the payee, or to his order. The drawee is also the ACCEPTOR.
Bibliography: UK Bill of Exchange Act 1882.
A. Watson. *Finance of International Trade.* Institute of Bankers, London, 1981.

drawer. The person who draws a BILL OF EXCHANGE : i.e. the person who, by means of the bill, is requiring the drawee to pay money to him, or to another person.
Bibliography: UK Bills of Exchange Act 1882. A. Watson. *Finance of International Trade.* Institute of Bankers, London, 1981.

drawn bond. A bond drawn by lottery for repayment in accordance with the terms of issue.

drop lock. Term applied to a hybrid security carrying a floating/fixed rate of interest. When the floating rate of interest falls to a given level, the 'drop lock' converts the security to a fixed rate of interest. For example, in May 1979 Gulf Oil Corporation issued a $250 million 30 year debenture in the US domestic market, paying interest at a specific margin over the 30-year US Treasury bond yield. When that yield falls to 8% or less the Gulf issue will become a fixed rate bond. The term drop lock strictly applies to those issues where the conversion is automatic; because this is not always attractive to the investor (an 'accidental' fall in rates which was purely temporary could trigger the lock) it is more usual to have conversion at the investor's option. The technique has been applied to FLOATING RATE NOTES as well as to bonds.
Bibliography: R. Mitchell. How the drop lock bond fits into place. *Euromoney,* London, June 1979.
M.S. Dobbs-Higginson. *Investment Manual.* Credit Suisse First Boston Ltd., London, 1980.
G. Ugeux. *Floating Rate Notes.* Euromoney Publications, London, 1981.

drop-lock floater. A FLOATING RATE NOTE with a DROP-LOCK feature.

Drysdale. A US securities house which collapsed with heavy losses in the summer of 1982. Its significance lay in the fact that its operations had been in the REPO market; by trading in securities with large amounts of ACCRUED INTEREST it had been able to generate apparent capital. Its collapse prompted a review of methods used to evaluate repo pricing.

Bibliography: M. Stigum. The Money Market. Dow-Jones Irwin, Homewood, Ill., 1983.

D/S. *See* DAYS AFTER SIGHT.

DTC. *See* DEPOSITARY TRUST COMPANY.

dual currency bond. A bond denominated in one currency but with interest payable in another. For example, in 1982 TransAmerica Financial Corporation issued an 8-year note with a coupon of 8.5% payable in Swiss francs, but with the principal amount of SF20 million repayable in US dollars at maturity, at a pre-fixed exchange rate.

dual currency convertible. A DUAL CURRENCY BOND which is CONVERTIBLE. For example, in 1984 Knogo Corporation borrowed SF75 million in bonds whose issue price was SF5,000 and which were denominated as US$2,500; the bonds were convertible into Knogo's US$ denominated shares.

due bill. (1) US term for an instrument evidencing the transfer of rights to any dividend, interest or rights pertaining to securities contracted for.
Bibliography: L.M. Loll & J.G. Buckley. *The Over-the-Counter Securities Markets.* Prentice-Hall, NJ. 1981.
(2) A BILL OF EXCHANGE which is failing due for payment.

due-bill-check. US term for a due bill in the form of a cheque payable on the date of payment of a cash dividend (which prior to such date is considered a due bill for the amount of the dividend).
Bibliography: L.M. Loll & J.G. Buckley. *The Over-the-Counter Securities Markets.* Prentice-Hall, NJ. 1981.

due diligence meeting. US term referring to the meeting of all parties involved in the sale of a security to check the registration statement facts and ensure all members are fully cognizant of the particulars.
Bibliography: L.M. Loll & J.G. Buckley. *The Over-the-Counter Securities Markets.* Prentice-Hall, NJ. 1981.

due from balance. US term for NOSTRO ACCOUNT.

due to balance. US term for VOSTRO ACCOUNT.

dumping. (1) Often used to mean panic selling.

(2) In international trade, the sale of goods at below cost. A major problem in certain areas of international trade.

Bibliography: *Agreement on the Implementation of Article VI* (otherwise known as the Anti-Dumping Code). GATT Secretariat, Geneva, 1967.
P. Lloyd. *Anti-Dumping Actions and the GATT System.* Trade Policy Research Centre, London, 1977.

duration. A measure of the term of a loan or bond. It adjusts the maturity to allow for interest payments. A 10-year bond with a 5% coupon has a different duration than a 10-year bond with a 10% coupon. Specifically, duration is defined as:-

$$\dfrac{\sum\limits_{t=1}^{n}\dfrac{C_t(t)}{(1+r)^t}}{\sum\limits_{t=1}^{n}\dfrac{C_t}{(1+r)^t}}$$

where
C_t = the interest and/or principal in year t

(t) = the length of time to the interest and/or principal payment
n = the length of time to final maturity
r = the yield to maturity
For example, the duration of a \$1,000 bond with a 4% coupon of 10-year maturity currently yielding 8% would be found as below to be 8.12 years approximately.
A similar bond, however, with a coupon of 8%, would have a shorter duration of 7.25 – effectively because the higher coupon means the investor's money is paid back more quickly.

Bibliography: F.K. Reilly & R.S. Sidhu. Duration and Its Properties *in* F.J. Fabozzi & I.M. Pollack. *The Handbook of Fixed Income Securities.* Dow-Jones Irwin, Homewood, Ill., 1983.

dutch auction. A competitive bidding technique sometimes used in US securities markets whereby the lowest price necessary to sell the entire amount of securities offered becomes the price at which all securities are sold.

Bibliography: N. Adam. Exxon's Quiet Auction Brings Uproar to Wall St. *Euromoney*, London, December 1982.
M. Stigum. US Treasury Obligations *in* F.J. Fabozzi & I.M. Pollack (eds). *The Handbook of Fixed Income Securities.* Dow-Jones Irwin, Homewood, Ill., 1983.

Dwt. *See* DEADWEIGHT TONNAGE.

(1) Year	(2) Cash flow	(3) PV of flow at 8%	(4) PV as % of price	(1) x (4)
1	40	37.04	.0506	.0506
2	40	34.29	.0469	.0938
3	40	31.75	.0434	.1302
4	40	29.40	.0402	.1608
5	40	27.22	.0372	.1860
6	40	25.21	.0345	.2070
7	40	23.34	.0319	.2233
8	40	21.61	.0295	.2360
9	40	20.01	.0274	.2466
10	1040	481.73	.6585	6.5850
		731.58	1.0000	8.1193

E

EEC. Abbreviation for EUROPEAN COMMUNITIES.

ECGD. *See* EXPORT CREDIT GUARANTEE DEPARTMENT.

Economic Community of West African States (ECOWAS). Founded in 1975, with its headquarters in Lagos, ECOWAS consists of the following countries: Benin, Burkina Faso, Cape Verde, Gambia, Ghana, Guinea, Guinea-Bissau, Ivory Coast, Liberia, Mali, Mauritania, Niger, Nigeria, Senegal, Sierra Leone, Togo. ECOWAS has set up a development fund with its headquarters in Lomé.
Bibliography: V. Ezenwe. *ECOWAS and the Economic Integration of West Africa.* Macmillan, London/St Martin's Press, New York, 1983.

economic defeasance. A form of DEFEASANCE where the debtor is not legally released from his obligation to repay, but he is unlikely to have to make any further payments. Specifically the term normally refers to an irrevocable placement of cash or government securities in a trust which is used solely to repay the principal and interest on the borrowing. Also referred to as 'insubstance' defeasance. Compare LEGAL DEFEASANCE.
Bibliography: B. McGoldrick. Why are CFOs so excited about defeasance? *Institutional Investor.* New York, March, 1984.
Financial Accounting Standards Board. *Statement of Financial Accounting Standards No.76: Extinguishment of Debt.* Stamford, Conn, 1983.

economic exposure. A term for the impact of exchange rate changes on the discounted cash flows of a company. A corporation owning an asset in, say, Brazil, is exposed to the risk that the Brazilian cruzeiro will depreciate in value, so that the asset is worth less. On the other hand, this exposure is reduced by the fact that the currency's depreciation will probably cause inflation, so that the nominal value of the income from the asset will tend to rise, offsetting the effects of the currency's depreciation. Economic exposure attempts to measure the net effects of these various changes on the economic position of the firm. Compare TRANSACTION EXPOSURE, TRANSLATION EXPOSURE.
Bibliography: J.K. Walmsley. *The Foreign Exchange Handbook.* John Wiley, New York, 1983.
B. Antl (ed.). *Currency Risk.* Euromoney Publications, London, 1981.

Economic Recovery Tax Act. US Tax reform of 1981 which introduced substantial income and corporation tax cuts, together with a switch to Accelerated Cost Recovery System of depreciation which significantly increased the tax benefits of depreciation. Compare TEFRA.
Bibliography: M.E. Holbrook & L.H. MacKirdy. *1982 Depreciation and Investment Manual.* Prentice-Hall, NJ, 1982.

ECOWAS. *See* ECONOMIC COMMUNITY OF WEST AFRICAN STATES.

ECU. Abbreviation for EUROPEAN CURRENCY UNIT.

EDC. *See* EXPORT DEVELOPMENT CORPORATION.

Edge Act. US Act of 1919 (named after Senator Edge), authorizing banking subsidiaries to conduct international banking operations. These companies may operate outside the state in which the parent bank is incorporated.
Bibliography: Peat, Marwick & Mitchell. *Banking in the United States.* New York/London, 1980.

Edge Corporation. A banking corporation in the US formed to carry on international business under the EDGE ACT. There are at present about 60 such corporations.

Bibliography: Peat, Marwick & Mitchell. *Banking in the United States.* New York/London, 1980.

EDR. Abbreviation for EUROPEAN DEPOSITARY RECEIPT.

EEC. *See* EUROPEAN ECONOMIC COMMUNITY.

EEC Unit of Account. The European Economic Community has operated a number of UNITS OF ACCOUNT which have, by and large, been replaced over time with the EUROPEAN CURRENCY UNIT or ECU, which was created at the time of the formation of the EUROPEAN MONETARY SYSTEM to act as a general unit of account for the EEC. Of the various past and present units, the most important aside from the ECU are the 'original' unit, and the EUROPEAN MONETARY UNIT OF ACCOUNT (both now superseded). Agricultural transactions give rise to 'reference rates', GREEN CURRENCIES and MONETARY COMPENSATORY AMOUNTS. (The ECU and other EEC units of account should not be confused with the numerous other units of account used in international security markets and other transactions. See the list in the entry for UNIT OF ACCOUNT.) The original EEC unit of account was defined as equal to one US dollar in 1957, at the time of the EEC's foundation. This implied a gold value of 0.88867088 grams of fine gold. The value of the unit of account (or u.a.) in terms of EEC currencies was calculated by taking the ratio of gold parities. Thus at the time of the UK's entry into the EEC in 1973, $1=u.a. 2.40 (since the nominal gold value of the pound Sterling had not changed since 1967). In March 1975 a new unit was introduced which was the forerunner of the ECU. It was a 'basket' of member currencies: 1 new EUA=Deutschmark 0.828 + French francs 1.15 + $0.0885 + HFL0.286 + Italian lire 109+ FBC 3.66+ DKR0.217+ Irish £0.00759 + Luxembourg franc 0.14. In March, 1979, at the time of the setting-up of the European Monetary System, the basket was renamed the European Currency Unit. The value of this 'basket', in terms of member currencies, is calculated and published daily in the *Financial Times* and elsewhere by the EEC Commission.

Bibliography: *General Report on the Activities of the European Communities.* European Commission, Brussels, annually.

J.K. Walmsley. *The Foreign Exchange Handbook.* John Wiley & Sons, New York, 1983.

effective. A declaration by the SEC of final permission to commence distribution on a new issue of stock of bonds.

effective depreciation. Fall in a country's EFFECTIVE EXCHANGE RATE.

effective exchange rate. An attempt to summarize the effects on a country's trade balance of its currency's changes against other currencies. For example sterling may rise against the $ and fall against the DM. In calculating the effective exchange rate for sterling, the UK Treasury attempts to measure the effect on UK trade arising from these changes, and then calculates what change in the value of sterling (all other currencies unchanged) would have been needed to have the same effect on UK trade. Similar rates are calculated for most major currencies. Compare MERM.

Bibliography: J.K. Walmsley. *The Foreign Exchange Handbook.* John Wiley & Sons, New York, 1983.

J. Artus & A. McGuirk. A Revised Version of the Multilateral Exchange Rate Model. *IMF Staff Papers,* vol.28, no.2, 1981.

effective Fed funds rate. A weighted average of the rates at which different amounts of FEDERAL FUNDS were traded through brokers during the day. It is calculated by the Federal Reserve Bank of New York through its contacts with the market. It is customary for US banks whose accounts are overdrawn because of payments mistakes to be charged at a rate based on the effective Fed funds rate.

effective protection. A concept of international trade theory. Effective protection was originally introduced to show that the real rate of protection afforded a commodity by a tariff depended not only on the nominal tariff rate on that commodity but also on the nominal tariff rates on all commodities used as inputs in its production. Suppose Britain imposes a 10% tariff on flour. Then domestic flour prices (and domestic 'value added') can be up to 10% higher than world prices. But suppose the British flour industry imports all the wheat needed for milling and that there is a 10% tariff also on imported wheat, then the protection given by the 10% flour tariff will be reduced.
Bibliography: D. Greenaway. *International Trade Policy*. Macmillan, London, 1983.

effective yield. Term for the rate of return realized by an investor who buys a security and subsequently sells it. It reflects coupon, interest on interest, principal payments and capital gains or losses in comparison to the original purchase price.
Bibliography: S. Homer & M. L. Leibowitz. *Inside the Yield Book*. Prentice-Hall, NJ, 1972.
M.L. Leibowitz. Total After-Tax Bond Performance and Yield Measures *in* F.J. Fabozzi & I.M. Pollack (eds). *The Handbook of Fixed Income Securities*. Dow-Jones Irwin, Homewood Ill., 1983.

Effektengiro. German term for a security clearing system based on deliveries of securities in the form of book entries rather than physical securities. Compare KASSENVEREIN, CEDEL, STOCK CLEARING CORPORATION.
Bibliography: E. Achterberg & K. Lanz (eds). *Enzyklopadisches Lexikon fur das Geld-, Bank- and Borsenwesen*, F. Knapp Verlag, Frankfurt, 1967.

effets de première/deuxième catégorie. French term for private sector paper which is traded on the domestic money markets; first category paper consists of credits guaranteed by certain specialized credit institutions, certain types of foreign trade finance, and other types of credit listed by the Banque de France as eligible. Such paper commands a finer rate than second category paper.
Bibliography: D. Marteau & E.de la Chaise. *Le marché monétaire et la gestion de trésorerie des banques*. Dunod, Paris, 1981.

EFIC. *See* EXPORT FINANCE & INSURANCE CORPORATION.

EFM. *See* EXPORT-FINANCIERING-MAATS-CHAPPIJ.

EFTA. *See* EUROPEAN FREE TRADE ASSOCIATION.

elasticity. Generally, measures the response of a variable to a (small) given change in another variable (all other things being equal). Perfect elasticity means an infinite response; perfect inelasticity means a nil response. Thus, the *price elasticity* of UK exports is defined as the ratio of the percentage change in their volume to the percentage change in their price. Therefore, a 1% price rise yielding a 2.3% fall in volume would imply an elasticity of -2.3. The *income elasticity* of demand for UK exports would be defined as the ratio of the percentage percentage change in UK export volume, to a small percentage change in the income of the importing country. *Elasticity of substitution* is defined as the percentage rise in sales volume of one commodity in response to a small percentage change in the price of another.
Bibliography: J. Robinson. *Economics of Imperfect Competition*. Macmillan, London, 1936.
R.M. Stern, J. Francis & B. Schumacher. *Price Elasticities in International Trade: An Annotated Bibliography*. Macmillan, London, 1976.

electronic data gathering and retrieval. The SECURITIES AND EXCHANGE COMMISSION system for electronic transmission of 10-K and other corporate information, usually abbreviated EDGAR.
Bibliography: E. Ipsen. The EDGAR Revolution. *Institutional Investor*. New York, September 1984.

electronic funds transfer (EFT). Systems of transferring funds from one account to another by electronic impulses rather than transfer of paper (such as a cheque). Princi-

pal EFT systems include automated teller machines normally activated by entering some form of plastic identification card; AUTOMATED CLEARING HOUSES; point-of sale terminals and facilities for paying bills by telephone.
Bibliography: F.J. Schroeder. *Developments in Consumer Electronic Funds Transfer. Federal Reserve Bulletin*, June 1983.

eligible bills. In the UK this term denotes eligibility for discount at the Bank of England. Broadly this covers BANK BILLS payable in the UK and ACCEPTED by certain UK banks. The US criteria are – in general terms – (1) acceptances of less than six months' tenor for the financing of (a) export-import, or (b) domestic shipments where documents conveying title are attached at the time of acceptance, and (2) acceptances financing domestic storage of readily marketable staples secured by warehouse receipts.
Bibliography: E.R. Shaw. *The London Money Market.* Heinemann, London, 1984.
T.Q. Cook & B.J. Summers (eds). *Instruments of the Money Market.* Federal Reserve Bank of Virginia, 1981.

eligible liabilities. In the UK, this refers to liabilities used in calculating the CASH RATIO. Broadly, eligible liabilities are defined as sterling deposit liabilities (including this with an original maturity of over two years) plus any sterling resources obtained by switching foreign currencies into sterling. Interbank and transit items are, broadly, netted out.
Bibliography: J.S.G. Wilson. Recent changes in London's Money Market Arrangements. *Banca Nazionale del Lavoro Quarterly Review*, March 1983; *Bank of England Quarterly Bulletin*, March 1984.

EMS. *See* EUROPEAN MONETARY SYSTEM.

EMU. (1) Abbreviation for Economic and Monetary Union (of the European Communities).
(2) Abbreviation for EUROPEAN MONETARY UNIT.

encadrement de crédit. French system of credit controls which limit the growth of banks' balance sheets to a certain percentage of the previous year's figure.
Bibliography: D. Marteau & E. de la Chaise. *Le marché monétaire et la gestion de trésorerie des banques.* Dunod, Paris, 1981.

end-end. A foreign exchange/Eurocurrency term relating to VALUE DATES. If the SPOT date is the last possible spot date for the month, then the value date for fixed periods forward is the last day in the month when both dealing centres are open. For example in dealing forward dollar-sterling, if dealing date is Wednesday 24 November, spot date Friday, 26th, London is on holiday Monday 29th and New York on 30th (so the 26th is the last spot date in November) then the value date for one month forward will be the 31 December.
Bibliography: J.K. Walmsley. *The Foreign Exchange Handbook.* John Wiley & Sons, New York, 1983.

endiguer. French term for TO HEDGE.

endorsement. The writing on the back of a bill by which a bill payable to order is transferred from one person to another. The simple signature of a person is valid endorsement.
Bibliography: J. Charlesworth. *Mercantile Law.* Stevens, London, 1984.

endosser. French term for 'to endorse'. Compare ENDORSEMENT.

Equipment Leasing Association. The representative body for equipment leasing companies in the UK. Its headquarters are at 14 Queen Anne's Gate, London, SW1. Compare ASIALEASE; LEASEUROPE.

Equipment Trust Certificate (ETC). A US term for bonds which are secured by specific pieces of equipment (e.g. railroad cars, aeroplanes). As an example of the technique's international use, an issue backed by ETCs was made by American Airlines in the EUROMARKETS for $55 million in 1981.

Bibliography: L.M. Loll & J.G. Buckley. *The Over-the-Counter Securities Markets*. Prentice-Hall, NJ, 1981.

equivalent bond yield. US term for a measurement of the rate of return on a security sold on a discount basis that assumes actual days to maturity and a 365-day year. It is also referred to sometimes as CORPORATE BOND EQUIVALENT. For a discount security with less than six months to run the conversion is made by using the standard DISCOUNT TO-YIELD formula. For a security with more than six months to run (i.e. an intervening COUPON payment) the formula is more complex. Both formulae are laid out under BOND EQUIVALENT YIELD.
Bibliography: M. Stigum. *Money Market Calculations*. Dow-Jones Irwin, Homewood, Ill., 1981. M.L. Leibowitz. Total Aftertax Bond Performance and Yield Measures *in* F.J. Fabozzi & I.M. Pollack (eds). *The Handbook of Fixed Income Securities*. Dow-Jones Irwin, Homewood Ill., 1983.

ERTA. *See* ECONOMIC RECOVERY TAX ACT.

escompte commercial. French term for trade finance by means of a BILL OF EXCHANGE which is then discounted.
Bibliography: J. Ferronniere & E. de Chillaz. *Les Operations de banque*. Dalloz, Paris, 1980.

escrow. A written agreement, for example, deed, bond or other paper, entered into by three parties and deposited for safekeeping with the third party as custodian to be delivered by the latter only when there is fulfillment of some condition. Escrow accounts are frequently used in banking to set aside a sum of money for a specific purpose e.g. loan payment.

étalon de change-or. French term for GOLD-EXCHANGE STANDARD.
Bibliography: P. Coulbois. *Finance internationale. I. Le Change*. Editions Cujas, Paris, 1979.

étalon-or. French term for GOLD STANDARD.

EUA. Abbreviation for the original EEC UNIT OF ACCOUNT.

Eurco. A private (i.e. non-official) UNIT OF ACCOUNT based on member currencies of the European Community; its full name is the European Composite Unit. It was introduced in 1973 in a loan to the EUROPEAN INVESTMENT BANK. A Eurco includes a quantity of each of the European Communities' currencies, in a proportion that roughly reflects the importance of the country. The original formula was 1 Eurco = 0.9 Deutschmark + 1.2 French francs + 0.075 UK£ + 0.005 Irish£ + 80 Italian lire + 4.50 Belgian francs + 0.20 Danish kroner + 0.5 Luxembourg francs. The value of the Eurco is calculated and published daily. Interest is paid in a currency chosen by the borrower, while the lender has the right to choose the currency of repayment. From the lender's viewpoint the Eurco limits exchange risk, compared with near-absolute stability from the EUROPEAN UNIT OF ACCOUNT and the possibility of revaluation profits from the EUROPEAN CURRENCY UNIT. On the whole, the Eurco has had only limited use.
Bibliography: H.C. Donnerstag. The Eurobond market. *Financial Times*. London, 1975, pp. 45-6. J.K. Walmsley. *The Foreign Exchange Handbook*. John Wiley & Sons, New York, 1983.

Eurobill of Exchange. Term occasionally used to denote a BILL OF EXCHANGE drawn and ACCEPTED in the usual way but expressed in foreign currency and accepted as being payable outside the country whose currency is being used. Thus a German firm may wish to finance imports from France and due to a credit squeeze its bank is unable to lend it DM, so the importer draws a bill of exchange in dollars, which a British bank accepts as payable in dollars, in London, to the importer. The bills are negotiable with UK discount houses or other buyers.
Bibliography: L.J. Kemp. *World Money and Securities Markets*. Euromoney Publications, London, 1984.

Eurobond. A 'conventional' Eurobond may generally be defined as a bond issued in a currency other than that of the market (or, more usually, markets) in which it is sold. (Although DM Eurobonds are sold in Germany.) The distinguishing factor is essentially the presence of an INTERNATIONAL SYNDICATE handling the issue. Conventional Eurobonds may be sub-classified into STRAIGHTS and CONVERTIBLES. Other forms of Eurobond include multicurrency issues, where investors are given the option of repayment in one of several currencies, though the issue is denominated in a single currency. Another technique is the use of UNITS OF ACCOUNT of which the most prominent have been the EUROPEAN UNIT OF ACCOUNT, the EUROPEAN CURRENCY UNIT (both the EEC ECU and the private ECU, which is really a multicurrency option), the EURCO the ARCRU, and the SDR. Eurobonds are always available in bearer form. If a borrower is not empowered to issue bearer bonds, arrangements are made with a leading bank to issue BEARER DEPOSITARY RECEIPTS. Interest is paid free of withholding taxes. Clearance and settlement are usually handled through EUROCLEAR or CEDEL.

Bibliography: P. Wood. *Law and Practice of International Finance.* Sweet & Maxwell, London, 1980.
F.G. Fisher. *International Bonds.* Euromoney Publications, London, 1981.
A.W. van Agtmael. Issuance of Eurobonds: Syndication and Underwriting Techniques and Costs *in* A.M. George & I.H. Giddy (eds). *International Finance Handbook.* John Wiley & Sons, New York, 1983.

Euroclear.   A computerized settlement and depositary system for safe custody, delivery of, and payment for Eurobonds. It is owned by 120 banks and securities firms and managed by Morgan Guaranty. Its operations are based in Brussels. By 1982 Euroclear's annual turnover had risen to US$509 billion, with 7,800 securities issues traded by 1,200 participating firms. Compare CEDEL.

Bibliography: Euroclear Annual Reports.
T. Anderson. The Growing War Between Cedel and Euroclear. *Euromoney*, London, May 1981.

Eurocommercial paper (ECP).   COMMER-CIAL PAPER issued in a EUROCURRENCY. Most ECP has been issued in dollar form in London. Such paper is usually issued in denominations of $100,000 upwards, with maturities of 30 to 360 days. Generally speaking, ECP has been little used in London, for the same reasons inhibiting the growth of COMMERCIAL PAPER.

Bibliography: Goldman, Sachs. *Eurocommercial Paper.* Goldman, Sachs International, London, 1971.
E. R. Shaw. *The London Money Market.* Heinemann, London, 1984.

Eurocredit.   Loosely, any lending made using EUROCURRENCY. More specifically, a Eurocredit is usually taken to mean a medium-term bank loan using Eurocurrency. Medium-term is an elastic period which has been as long as 17 years and as short as two years (much depends on usage). Typically, a Eurocredit is at least $500,000. The Swedish government borrowing in 1984 was for $4 billion. Most commonly, the interest rate is fixed by adding a MARGIN or SPREAD to the LONDON INTER-BANK OFFERED RATE for three- or six-month deposits in the currency being used. The banks will borrow (say) six-months' money and charge the rate that they paid, plus the spread. At the end of the six months, new deposits are raised and a new interest rate is fixed in the same way. Because of the size of most credits, it is usual for them to be raised by SYNDICATION. In recent years there has developed a tendency towards hybrid markets combining Eurocredits with securities issues, most notably the emergence of FLOATING-RATE NOTES, REVOLVING UNDERWRITING FACILITIES and EURO-NOTES.

Bibliography: P. Wood. *Law and Practice of International Finance.* Sweet & Maxwell, London, 1980.
S. Davis. *The Euro-Bank.* Macmillan, London/ John Wiley, New York, 1981.
J.K. Walmsley. *The Foreign Exchange Handbook.* John Wiley & Sons, New York, 1983.
A.M. George & I.H. Giddy (eds). *International Finance Handbook.* John Wiley & Sons, New York, 1983.
E.R. Shaw. *The London Money Market.* Heinemann, London, 1983.

Eurocurrency. A currency deposit held outside the country which issued the currency. The deposit may be re-lent to another borrower, either directly, or after conversion into another currency, or after being re-deposited via one or more other banks. It should be noted that all these transactions are carried out by memorandum entries in the domestic country of the Eurocurrency. The dominating currency is the Eurodollar. The market is a telephone and telex one comprising inter-bank dealings (usually short-term) and loans to companies and governments (often medium/long-term). Strictly, it should be called 'offshore-currency' since there is also an Asian market. Compare ASIAN DOLLAR.
Bibliography: P. Wood. *Law and Practice of International Finance.* Sweet & Maxwell, London, 1980.
S. Davis. *The Euro-Bank.* Macmillan, London/John Wiley, New York, 1981.
J.K. Walmsley. *The Foreign Exchange Handbook.* John Wiley & Sons, New York, 1983.
A.M. George & I.H. Giddy (eds). *International Finance Handbook.* John Wiley & Sons, New York, 1983.
E.R. Shaw. *The London Money Market.* Heinemann, London, 1984.
See also BIS Annual Reports.

Eurodollar. A dollar deposit held outside the US. The term is sometimes misleadingly used to cover all Eurocurrencies. The minimum deal in the London inter-bank market is usually $500,000 or $1 million (compared to London $ CDS which can be dealt in down to $25,000). Eurodollars were first used in the 1950s when certain Iron Curtain countries acquired dollar balances but feared they might be 'frozen' if left in the US. They therefore lent them to European banks who in turn, lent them to customers. By 1963, the net size of the market (including other currencies) was estimated at $7 billion. The corresponding figure for 1970 was $65 billion and for 1980, $755 billion. Much of the initial growth was due to the US REGULATION Q and other exchange controls. However, confusion has been caused by linking the size of the market to the US balance of payments. In fact the *stock* of Eurobanks' dollar liabilities and assets may be influenced by transfers into/out of non-Eurodollar uses (e.g. into US domestic uses), independently of any *flow* of dollars appearing from any US payments deficit. The classic source on developments in Eurodollar markets is the Annual Report of the Bank for International Settlements.
Bibliography: P. Wood. *Law and Practice of International Finance.* Sweet & Maxwell, London, 1980.
S. Davis. *The Euro-Bank.* Macmillan, London/John Wiley, New York, 1981.
J.K. Walmsley. *The Foreign Exchange Handbook.* John Wiley & Sons, New York, 1983.
A.M. George & I.H. Giddy (eds). *International Finance Handbook.* John Wiley & Sons, New York, 1983.
E.R. Shaw. *The London Money Market.* Heinemann, London, 1984.
See also: Socialist banks and the origins of the Eurocurrency markets. *Moscow Narodny Bank Quarterly Review*, London, Winter 1976.

Euro-equity. Strictly speaking, equity shares denominated in a currency differing from that of the country in which it is traded. Overseas stocks, however, have long been listed in London and elsewhere without attracting the Euroequity label, mainly because of the absence of a truly international SECONDARY MARKET for them. Currently the term tends to be used for a share which is issued internationally. Problems arise in relation to convertibility into the underlying shares/common stock ('flowback'), withholding tax and capital gains.
Bibliography: N. Osborn. The Rise of the International Equity. *Euromoney*, London, May 1984.

Eurofrancs. Swiss (or French or Belgian, depending on context) francs traded on the EUROCURRENCY MARKETS. Swiss francs are the third major Eurocurrency.
Bibliography: BIS Annual Reports.

Euroguilders. Dutch guilders traded in the EUROCURRENCY MARKETS.

Euroguilder notes. Notes denominated in Euroguilders. The market began in 1969. Terms and conditions have varied over time

but currently (1984) the notes have a present maximum life of seven years with a minimum average life of five years; issues are usually for up to DFls 100 million.
Bibliography: H.A. Lund *et al. Private Placements.* Euromoney Publications, London, 1984.

Euromarkets.   A term loosely used to refer to the aggregate of the short-term EUROCURRENCY, medium-term EUROCREDIT and long-term EUROBOND markets.

Euromarks.   Deutschmarks traded in the EUROCURRENCY MARKET. After the dollar, the second most important Eurocurrency, because it is easy to trade internationally in DM, and because of the DM's strength, which has made it an attractive currency in which to hold deposits. In mid-1982 market volume was approximately DM330 bn. Trading is centred in Luxembourg and London, which account for 60% of the market.
Bibliography: The Euro-DM Market. *Deutsche Bundesbank Monthly Report.* January 1983. BIS Annual Reports.

Euro-notes.   Term sometimes used in respect of a syndicated EUROCREDIT where the actual lending takes the form of short term bearer notes which can be re-sold, but the syndicate participants are committed to underwriting the initial purchases of the paper. The technique was developed in 1980 with a $500 million facility for New Zealand and evolved into other forms, notably the REVOLVING UNDERWRITING FACILITY. As an example, the $4 billion facility for the government of Sweden in 1984 included an option whereby Sweden would issue three, six or twelve month notes to be bid for by a TENDER PANEL.
Bibliography: C.R. Dammers. The Internationalization of the World's Money Markets: Some New Products *in* P.H. Darrow & R.A. Mestres (eds). *Creative Financing in the 1980s.* Practising Law Institute, New York, 1983.
C. Grant. The Liquefaction of the Euromarkets. *Euromoney*, London, October 1983.

Europa.   Name sometimes given to a proposed currency unit of the European Common Market after its eventual monetary unification.

European Communities.   The institutions of the EUROPEAN ECONOMIC COMMUNITY were merged in 1967 with those of the European Coal and Steel Community and of the European Atomic Community to form a single grouping usually called the European Communities (although the three communities retain separate legal identities).
Bibliography: Annual Reports of the European Communities, Brussels.

European Composite Unit.   *See* EURCO.

European Currency Band.   *See* SNAKE.

European Currency Unit.   (1) In the EUROPEAN MONETARY SYSTEM the European Currency Unit is defined as DM0.719 + FFR 1.310 + Lit140 + DFL0.256 + FBC 3.71 + Flux 0.14 + £stg. 0.0378 + £Irl. 0.00871 + DKR 0.217 + GDR 1.15. That is to say the ECU consists of the sum of specified quantities of each of the national currencies of the members of the EEC. Accordingly, the value of the ECU fluctuates in terms of third currencies, such as the dollar, as the values of the national currencies fluctuate. Member countries of the EMS (which as of August 1984 included all EEC members with the exception of the UK and Greece) are obliged to declare a 'central parity' for their currency in terms of the ECU. From these central parities the central banks work out implicit CROSS-RATES which are used, together with the permitted fluctuation limits of the EMS, to define a PARITY GRID. The second role of the ECU, in addition to defining central parities, is in the calculation of a DIVERGENCE INDICATOR which is intended to signal to the monetary authorities which currency is diverging from its central rates and putting pressure on other member currencies. The ECU is also used in the day-to-day accounting of the EEC. Since 1980, the ECU has been used also in a growing number of private transactions and there is a well-established ECU deposit market. Syndicated credits –

such as the ECU 200 million credit for Credit National of France in 1981 – have also been introduced, as have ECU bonds.

Bibliography: *Deutsche Bundesbank Monthly Report*. Frankfurt, March 1979.
T. de Vries. On The Meaning and Future of the EMS. *Princeton Essays in International Finance no. 138*. Princeton NJ, September 1980.
J.K. Walmsley. *The Foreign Exchange Handbook*. John Wiley & Sons, New York, 1983.
N. Faith. The ECU: All Things to All Men. *Euromoney*. London, May 1983

(2) The ECU (also known as 'European Monetary Unit') is a private (i.e. non-official) unit of account devised to give a measure of protection to investors/lenders in private international bond issues. It was introduced in 1970. It is effectively an application of the MULTI-CURRENCY OPTION to the repayment clause, rather than a true UNIT OF ACCOUNT. A fixed parity is laid down between the ECU and member currencies of the EEC (e.g. 1 ECU=DM3.2225). The investor can ask for payment of principal and interest in any of the currencies of the ECU. Since the parities are irrevocably fixed, the investor does not lose from devaluations against his domestic currency (if it is included in the ECU) but he can gain from revaluations. Therefore, the ECU is very attractive to lenders, but less so to borrowers, and it has tended to be used only when bonds are otherwise difficult to sell.

Bibliography: J. Aschheim & Y. S. Park. *Artificial Currency Units: The Formation of Functionary Currency Areas*. Princeton Essays in International Finance No. 114, 1976.

European Depositary Receipt.   A DEPOSITARY RECEIPT traded in Europe and evidencing ownership of a non-European security. The technique is used to facilitate international trading in a company's shares. As an example, in 1980 Taisho Marine & Fire Insurance issued 30 million shares in the form of EDRs of 10 shares each, to be listed on the Luxembourg Stock Exchange.

European Development Fund.   Fund set up by the EUROPEAN ECONOMIC COMMUNITY to provide aid and concessionary finance to developing countries (principally those which

are Associate Members of the EEC). It will also provide technical assistance. For 1976-9 total EDF loans and grants were set at Ecu 3,076 million (say $1,300m.) and for 1980-4 at Ecu 4,542 million (say $3,000 million).

Bibliography: A.I. MacBean & P.N. Snowden. *International Institutions in Trade and Finance*. George Allen & Unwin, London 1981.
D. Sassoon (ed.). *Bidding for Projects Financed by International Lending Agencies*. Gower Press, UK, 1982; Annual Reports of the EDF, Brussels.

European Economic Community.   Economic grouping of Belgium, France, Germany, Italy, Luxembourg and the Netherlands, founded in 1957, and joined in 1973 by Denmark, Eire, and the UK. Greece became a member in 1981; Spain and Portugal are in the process of negotiating entry. Referred to as the Common Market, EEC, EUROPEAN COMMUNITIES or EC.

Bibliography: Annual Reports of the European Communities, Brussels.
M. Davenport. The Economic Impact of the EEC *in* A. Boltho (ed.). *The European Economy*. Oxford University Press, 1982.

European Free Trade Association (EFTA).   A free trade area set up in 1959 as an alternative to EUROPEAN ECONOMIC COMMUNITY with headquarters in Geneva. Its members included Austria. Denmark, Iceland, Norway, Portugal, Sweden, Switzerland and the UK. The UK and Denmark left in 1972 to join the EUROPEAN COMMUNITIES. Since 1977 the European Communities and EFTA have operated a full customs union. Finland is an associate member of EFTA.

Bibliography: *European Yearbook, Vol. I.* Europa Publications Ltd, London.

European Investment Bank (EIB).   The EIB was founded as part of the EUROPEAN COMMUNITIES in 1958. It is an independent, non-profit making institution with a AAA RATING. It finances projects in the EC and more than 60 associated countries where such projects fit Community objectives. Its major lendings have been for regional development in the EC. It is an active borrower in the international capital markets.

Bibliography: *EIB Annual Reports*, Brussels, annually.

European Monetary Agreement. Successor to the EUROPEAN PAYMENTS UNION this was essentially a multilateral clearing payments system between the members of the European Payments Union, set up after the establishment of CONVERTIBILITY of most European currencies in 1958. Its role diminished over the years and it was finaly wound up in 1972. The operating agent was the BANK FOR INTERNATIONAL SETTLEMENTS.

Bibliography: B. Tew. *International Monetary Co-operation: 1945-70.* Hutchinson, London, 1970.
BIS Annual Reports.

European Monetary Co-operation Fund. Sometimes abbreviated to EMCOF, or to FECOM in French- language contexts. EMCOF was established in April 1973 to take over the financing and settlement of claims by EEC central banks on each other, arising from interventions within the SNAKE. It has taken on similar functions in respect of the EUROPEAN MONETARY SYSTEM. These claims are cleared through EMCOF. Balances are settled there 45 days after the month when intervention occured; settlement can be postponed for three months at the request of a borrower. Interest is payable on the outstanding balances. The amount a central bank may borrow is unlimited in the first instance (known as 'very short-term financing'). However, the three-month renewal facility is limited to the quota laid down in the EEC short-term monetary support arrangements.

Bibliography: J.K. Walmsley. *The Foreign Exchange Handbook.* John Wiley & Sons, New York, 1983.
BIS Annual Reports

European Monetary System. Set up in March 1979, the EMS succeeded the former EEC SNAKE. The main changes consisted of the creation of the EUROPEAN CURRENCY UNIT, and a DIVERGENCE INDICATOR, plus some modifications of the snake credit system. The principal modification consists of the plan whereby EMS member countries deposit 20% of their gold and dollar reserves with the EUROPEAN MONETARY CO-OPERATION FUND in exchange for the issue of European Currency Units. These deposits take the legal form of revolving SWAPS between the EMCOF and the central banks concerned. The EMS includes all EEC members except the UK and Greece.

Bibliography: *Deutsche Bundesbank Monthly Report*, March 1979.
J.K. Walmsley. *The Foreign Exchange Handbook.* John Wiley & Sons, New York, 1983.
H. Ungerer. *The European Monetary System: The Experience*, 1979-82. International Monetary Fund, Washington, DC, 1983.

European Monetary Unit. Another name for EUROPEAN CURRENCY UNIT as applied in bond issues. It is not connected with the EEC's EUROPEAN CURRENCY UNIT, or with the EUROPEAN MONETARY UNIT OF ACCOUNT or with the EUROPEAN UNIT OF ACCOUNT or with the EEC UNIT OF ACCOUNT .

European Monetary Unit of Account (EMUA). The EMUA was used in the book-keeping of the EUROPEAN MONETARY CO-OPERATION FUND. One EMUA was defined as equal to 3.21978 DM, or 48.6572 Belgian francs or 7.57831 Danish kroner or 5.55419 French francs or 3.35507 Dutch guilders. It was designed to guarantee the exchange value of outstanding balances in the Fund. Under the EMS it was replaced by the EUROPEAN CURRENCY UNIT.

Bibliography: *Deutsche Bundesbank Monthly Report*, Frankfurt, January 1976 and March 1979.

European option. An OPTION that can only be exercised at maturity, in contrast to the AMERICAN OPTION which can be exercised at any time prior to maturity.

Bibliography: R.M. Bookstaber. *Option Pricing Strategies in Investing.* Addison-Wesley, USA, 1981.

European Payments Union. A clearing system for settling international payments between 17 European countries, operated be-

tween 1950 and 1958. It was replaced by the EUROPEAN MONETARY AGREEMENT. It was managed by the BANK FOR INTERNATIONAL SETTLEMENTS.
Bibliography: G. L. Rees. *Britain and Post-War European Payments Systems.* University of Wales Press. 1962.

European System of Narrower Exchange Rate Margins. *See* SNAKE.

European unit of account (EUA). (1) A private (i.e. non-official) UNIT OF ACCOUNT used for certain bond issues, and abbreviated EUA. The initial formula defined the EUA as equal to 0.88867088 grams of fine gold (the then gold value of the US dollar) and the EUA was linked to the 17 currencies—REFERENCE CURRENCIES—of members of the EUROPEAN PAYMENTS UNION. The value was to change only if *all* 17 currencies changed their parities and at least *two-thirds* devalued, or at least *two-thirds* revalued. If this happened the EUA changed by the same amount as that currency whose value changed least, provided that the change was in the same direction as that of the majority. This complex formula attempted to maximize the EUA's stability, and as a result the EUA has probably been the most successful 'currency cocktail' for bond issues (since the first issue in 1961, it has been used in more then 65 issues involving over $1,250 million). This is because of its very strong emphasis on stability and because of the degree of flexibility available in the choice of currencies to be included; while it has also been possible to vary the complex clause regarding the two-thirds minimum for triggering changes in the value of the EUA and to vary the number of reference currencies.
Bibliography: *The European Unit of Account.* Kredietbank, Brussels, 1967.
Euromoney. London, January 1976.
   (2) European unit of account is unfortunately also used to refer to EEC UNITS OF ACCOUNT, particularly to the EUROPEAN CURRENCY UNIT The value of this ECU is published daily in the *Financial Times* of London and elsewhere.

Eurosterling. A sterling deposit acquired by a bank outside the UK. Most dealing takes place in Paris or Brussels. The market is highly professional, dealing only in large deposits (normally at least £500,000). The market was restrained until 1979 by the UK EXCHANGE CONTROL system but since then has developed into a sizeable market. Eurosterling deposits rose from £7.7 billion in September 1979 to £11 billion a year later, but since then have not grown rapidly, because of the low cost of dealing directly in London. Compare EUROCURRENCY, EURO-DOLLARS.
Bibliography: International Banking Markets in 1983. *Bank of England Quarterly Bulletin*, London, March 1984.

Euro Treasury warrants. A WARRANT issued in the EUROMARKET entitling the holder to buy US government securities. An example was the issue in August, 1983 of 300,000 warrants by Merrill Lynch entitling the holder to buy $1,000 nominal amount of 10⅜% US Treasury bonds due November 2012, at a purchase price of 91.75% of the nominal amount.

Euro-yen. Japanese yen traded in the EUROMARKETS. The Euro-yen market has been restricted by Japanese controls over the years and totals perhaps $30-40 billion at most, although recent moves towards liberalization may encourage growth.
Bibliography: K. Rafferty. Why Japanese CFOs are cool on the Euro-yen. *Institutional Investor.* New York, October 1984.

Euro-yen bonds. Bonds denominated in Euro-yen, first issued in 1977 by the European Investment Bank. As with the Euro-yen deposit market, the growth of the yen Eurobond market has been restricted by government caution, with only 11 issues being made in the first three years of the market's life, but recent liberalization may encourage more rapid growth. Compare SAMURAI BONDS.
Bibliography: K. Rafferty. Why Japanese CFOs are cool on the Euro-yen. *Institutional Investor.* New York, October 1984.

Even par swap.   US term for the sale of one block of bonds and the simultaneous purchase of the same nominal principal amount of another block of bonds, without regard to the net cash difference.
Bibliography: S. Homer & M. L. Leibowitz. *Inside the Yield Book*. Prentice-Hall, NJ, 1972.

evergreen credit.   A REVOLVING CREDIT without a maturity date, it usually allows for annual renewal; a variant gives the bank the opportunity, once a year, to convert into a term loan.
Bibliography: R. Brealey & S. Myers. *Principles of Corporate Finance*. McGraw-Hill, New York/London, 1984.

Excess of Loss Treaty Reinsurance.   REINSURANCE that indemnifies the CEDING COMPANY for the excess over a stipulated sum on the event of loss. Compare STOP LOSS.
Bibliography: R.L. Carter. *Reinsurance*. Kluwer Publishing, UK, 1983.
C.A. Williams & R.M. Heins. *Risk Management and Insurance*. McGraw-Hill, New York, 1984.

excess reserves.   US term for the amount of reserves held by banks, over and above the amount required by law. Excess reserves have a significant influence on the FED FUNDS rate, since this is the rate banks pay to acquire reserves. In turn, the Fed funds rate is an important barometer of the system's behaviour.
Bibliography: D.C. Beek. Excess Reserves and Reserve Targeting. *Federal Reserve Bank of New York Quarterly Bulletin*, Autumn 1981.

exercise price.   OPTIONS market term for the price at which the option holder may buy or sell the underlying security or commodity, as defined in the terms of his option contract. It is the price at which the CALL holder may exercise his right to buy, or the PUT holder to sell. For listed options, the exercise price is the same as the STRIKE PRICE.
Bibliography: L.G. McMillan. *Options as a Strategic Investment*. New York Institute of Finance, New York, 1980.

exchange control.   A system of controlling inflows and outflows of foreign exchange. Forbidden under the BRETTON WOODS regime, but generally tolerated as regards capital flows. The UK, Germany, Canada, Switzerland and the US do not have formal exchange controls. France, Spain and Italy have very tight controls, as do many other countries.
Bibliography: J.K. Walmsley. *The Foreign Exchange Handbook*. John Wiley & Sons, New York, 1983.
Annual Report on Exchange Arrangements. IMF, Washington, DC.

Exchange Equalization Account (EEA).   Established in 1932 as part of the Treasury, the EEA holds virtually the whole of the UK's operational reserves of gold and foreign exchange. The Bank of England operates as its agent. If foreign currency is sold to the Bank, sterling will be paid out in return. The EEA finances this payment in sterling as part of the normal PUBLIC SECTOR DEFICIT – usually by selling from its holdings of Treasury Bills. The net effect depends on where the foreigner's sterling is placed, but there will usually be an increase in domestic liquidity.
Bibliography: *Bank of England Quarterly Bulletin*, 1963.

exchange for physical.   A FUTURES market term. A buyer of a futures contract may elect to take delivery under the contract, but may take delivery in a form which differs from that provided for in the contract. For example, a silver buyer might have bought 10,000 ounces of silver under futures contracts. The seller of the contracts might tender the delivery standard (bars of 1,000 ounces .999 FINE). Alternatively, the buyer might arrange an exchange for physical with a supplier of silver under which he will sell futures contracts to the supplier in exchange for delivery of metal. In this way he will avoid handling charges imposed by the commodity exchange and may be able to arrange delivery of the metal in a more convenient location. A similar arrangement might take place in financial futures between two parties wishing to arrange settlement of a deal with a cash instrument differing from that provided for under the standard contract.

Bibliography: N.H. Rothstein & J.M. Little. *The Handbook of Financial Futures*. McGraw-Hill, New York, 1984.

Exchange Stabilization Fund. The US equivalent of the EXCHANGE EQUALIZATION ACCOUNT. It is controlled by the US Treasury and managed for the latter by the FEDERAL RESERVE in New York.

ex-coupon. International bond market term for dealings in bonds where the date of delivery of the bond falls after the closing of the register for the purposes of interest payments; i.e. the seller of the bond will receive the interest due on the bond because there was insufficient time to notify the company paying interest that the bond changed hands. Compare CUM-COUPON, EX-DIVIDEND.

Bibliography: *Rules and Recommendations*. AIBD.

ex-dividend. A stock is ex-dividend if a buyer has no right to the next interest or dividend payment which is due. Instead, the seller of the stock receives payment. Compare CUM-DIVIDEND.

Bibliography: J. Dundas Hamilton. *Stockbroking Today*. Macmillan Press, London 1979.

EXIM. *See* EXPORT-IMPORT BANK (US or Japan).

Eximbank. *See* EXPORT-IMPORT BANK (US or Japan).

exotic. Foreign exchange dealers' term for currency in which a large international market does not exist (e.g. Indonesian rupiah, Egyptian pound, etc.).

Export Credit Guarantee Department. A UK government organization which provides insurance against bad debts arising from credit given by exporters, and which gives guarantees on bank loans made to exporters or overseas buyers for this purpose.

Bibliography: *The Export Credit Financing Systems in OECD Member Countries*. Organization for Economic Co-operation & Development, Paris, 1982.
A. Dunn & M. Knight. *Export Finance*. Euromoney Publications, London 1982.

Export Development Corporation (EDC). Canadian goverment export finance and insurance corporation founded in 1969. EDC provides credit insurance on commercial terms and also lends directly to foreign buyers of Canadian goods. It generally finances 60-70% of the total. Its lending is mostly funded by EDC's direct medium and long-term borrowings in the international or domestic markets. It lends in Canadian and other currencies.

Bibliography: *The Export Credit Financing Systems in OECD Member Countries*. Organization for Economic Cooperation and Development, Paris, 1982.

Export Finance & Insurance Corporation (EFIC). Australian goverment body founded in 1975 to provide export credit finance directly or via guarantees, and to provide insurance to exporters against non-payment. Its primary source of funds is the Australian banking system. EFIC does not in general provide foreign currency finance.

Bibliography: *The Export Credit Financing System in OECD Member Countries*. Organization for Economic Cooperation & Development, Paris, 1982.

Export-Financiering-Maatschappij. Dutch export finance company set up by the large commercial banks in 1951. The volume of its business is relatively small, since the bulk of export credit is supplied by the Dutch commercial banks.

Bibliography: *The Export Credit Financing Systems in OECD Member Countries*, Organization for Economic Cooperation & Development, Paris, 1982.

Export-Import Bank of Japan. Japanese export credit financing institute established in 1950 which also administers government loans to developing countries within the framework of the official aid programme. It is financed by capital issued by the government and by borrowing from a Trust Fund Bureau (which itself is financed by post office savings) or by borrowing foreign exchange from commercial banks. It may not borrow from the Bank of Japan.

Bibliography: *The Export Credit Financing Systems in OECD Member Countries.* Organization for Economic Cooperation and Development, Paris, 1982.

Export-Import Bank of the United States (Exim-bank). Founded in 1934, Eximbank is an independent US government agency which refinances export credits granted by commercial banks. The bulk of its financial resources come from the US Treasury. It operates on a self-supporting basis, i.e. it aims to make a profit and has no access to preferential funding. Its annual lending limits are fixed by Congress. Its 1982 loan BOOK totalled $15.8 billion, with insurance liabilities of around $5 billion.

Bibliography: *The Export Credit Financing Systems of OECD Member Countries.* Organization for Economic Cooperation and Development, Paris, 1982.
Eximbank Annual Reports.
A. Dunn & M. Knight. *Export Finance.* Euromoney Publications, London, 1982.
J.J. Hillman. *The Export-Import Bank at Work.* Quorum Books, Westport, Conn./London, 1982.

exposure. (1) A company (or individual) may be said to have exposure in a currency when his assets and liabilities in that currency are not equal in amount, in which case an OPEN POSITION exists; or when the maturity structure of the assets and liabilities differs, in which case there is MISMATCH or a MATURITY GAP. A bank's exposure is generally measured on a LADDER listing the net positions. Various accounting definitions may be used in measuring a firm's exposure. (a) *Net working capital* (or current/non-current): exposure equals current assets in a foreign currency, less current liabilities in the currency. (b) *Net financial method:* the same as (a) but adding long-term debt in the currency to the total current liabilities. (c) *Monetary/*

non-monetary method: monetary assets and liabilities in the foreign currency are valued at present exchange rates while non-monetary items are entered at the relevant historic rates. See also CROSS-CURRENCY EXPOSURE; ECONOMIC EXPOSURE; FASB52; TRANSACTIONS EXPOSURE; TRANSLATION EXPOSURE.

Bibliography: J.A. Donaldson. *Corporate Currency Risk.* Financial Times, London, 1980.
J.K. Walmsley. *The Foreign Exchange Handbook.* John Wiley & Sons, New York, 1983.

(2) A bank may be said to have exposure to a company or country to the extent that it has lent funds to (or engaged in foreign exchange dealing with) or invested in that company or country. Compare LIMIT; SOVEREIGN RISK LIMIT.

Bibliography: P.J. Nagy (ed.). *Country Risk.* Euromoney Publications, London, 1981.

ex-quay. International trade term. The seller must place the goods at the disposal of the buyer at the agreed quay at the agreed time. If the contract is 'ex-quay, duty paid', import duties are paid by the seller; if 'ex-quay, duties on buyer's account', the buyer pays.

Bibliography: *Incoterms.* International Chamber of Commerce Brochure no. 350, Paris, 1980.

ex-ship. International trade term. The seller must place the goods at the disposal of the buyer at the agreed time, on board the vessel at the usual unloading point in the named port. The buyer must pay import duty.

Bibliography: *Incoterms.* International Chamber of Commerce Brochure no. 350, Paris, 1980.

extendable, extendible. A security which gives the investor the option of extending its initial maturity for a given number of years. If the option is not exercised, the bond is repaid at the earlier maturity. Extendables and their opposites, RETRACTABLES, have been common for many years in Canada, and have also been used in the EUROBOND and domestic US securities markets.

Bibliography: M.L. Dobbs-Higginson. *Investment Manual.* Credit Suisse First Boston Ltd, London, 1980.

extended fund facility. The INTERNA-

TIONAL MONETARY FUND is prepared, under certain circumstances, to lend over a three-year period rather than the one-year period which is the normal maximum for a fund STAND-BY. This extended fund facility was set up in 1974.

Bibliography: A.W. Hooke. *The International Monetary Fund: Its Evolution, Organization and Activities*. IMF Pamphlet no. 37, Washington DC, 1981.
The Financial Structure and Operations of the IMF. *Bank of England Quarterly Bulletin*. December 1983.

extension swap.   A SWAP in the bond market aimed at extending the maturity of a portfolio, e.g. selling a two-year note and buying a three-year note.

Bibliography: C. Seix. Bond Swaps *in* F.J. Fabozzi & I.M. Pollack. *The Handbook of Fixed Income Securities*. Dow-Jones Irwin, New York, 1983.

ex-works (also ex-factory, ex-mill, ex-warehouse etc).   International trade term. The seller must place the goods at the buyer's disposal at the agreed time, at the agreed place but the buyer is responsible for the export and import duties, shipping etc.

Bibliography: *Incoterms*. International Chamber of Commerce Brochure no. 350. Paris, 1980.

F

factoring. The purchase of trade debts, usually without recourse (i.e. the buyer of the debt has no recourse to the seller if the seller refuses to pay). With recourse factoring may be used to reduce the cost – at an increased risk – to the customer, or where the trade debtors are unacceptable credit risks. Various international factoring firms handle the purchase of overseas debts.
Bibliography: M. Westlake. *Factoring*. Pitman Publishing, London, 1975.
A. Watson. *The Finance of International Trade*. Institute of Bankers, London, 1981.

facultative reinsurance. This is direct REIN-SURANCE, usually of individual RISKS (falcultative meaning optional). The UNDER-WRITER decides that he does not wish to carry the whole of the risk he originally insured and therefore reinsures all or part of the risk with another firm. A reinsurance on this selective basis is termed 'facultative' in contrast to TREATY REINSURANCE, where all of a certain type of risk is reinsured automatically.
Bibliography: R.L. Carter. *Reinsurance*. Kluwer, London, 1983.
L.A. Williams & R.M. Heins. *Risk management Insurance*, McGraw-Hill, New York, 1984.

Fannie Mae. *See* FEDERAL NATIONAL MORTGAGE ASSOCIATION.

f.a.s.. *See* FREE ALONGSIDE SHIP.

FASB8. Abbreviation for the US *Statement of Financial Accounting Standards No. 8.* FASB8 set standards for foreign currency financial statements incorporated in the financial statements of an enterprise; it was superseded by FASB52.
Bibliography: *Statement of Financial Accounting Standards No. 8.* Financial Accounting Standards Board, Stamford, Conn., 1975.

J.K. Walmsley. *The Foreign Exchange Handbook*. John Wiley & Sons, New York, 1983.

FASB52. Abbreviation for the US *Statement of Financial Accounting Standards No. 52.* FASB52 replaced FASB8 in 1981. Its UK counterpart is the Statement of Standard Accounting Practice No. 20. The main changes it made were to transfer the impact of TRANSLATION EXPOSURE of balance sheet items from income to an equity account in the balance sheet, and to permit borrowing as a form of HEDGING in addition to a FORWARD CONTRACT.
Bibliography: *Statement of Financial Accounting Standards no. 52.* Financial Accounting Standards Board, Stamford, Conn. 1981.
J.K. Walmsley. *The Foreign Exchange Handbook*. John Wiley & Sons, New York, 1983.

fate (inquiry). An inquiry as to the position of a bill of exchange, whether it has been accepted, paid, or what. Short for 'Please advise fate'. Applied by extension to other transactions.

FCIA. *See* FOREIGN CREDIT INSURANCE ASSOCIATION.

FECDBA. *See* FOREIGN EXCHANGE AND CURRENCY DEPOSIT BROKERS' ASSOCIATION.

FECOM. *See* EUROPEAN MONETARY CO-OPERATION FUND.

Fed. Abbeviation for FEDERAL RESERVE SYSTEM of the US; in the domestic context usually refers to its Board of Governors or to the Federal Reserve Bank of New York; in the foreign exchange context it usually refers to the latter.
Bibliography: P. Meek. *US Monetary Policy and the Financial Markets*. Federal Reserve Bank of New York, 1982.

M. Stigum. *The Money Market.* Dow-Jones Irwin, Homewood, Ill., 1983.

Federal Financing Bank (FFB). Set up in 1973, the FFB's objective is to assist in financing US government agencies. It is authorized to acquire any obligation that is issued, sold, or guaranteed by any Federal agency – except those of the Farm Credit System, the Federal Home Loan Banks, the Federal Home Loan Mortgage Corporation, and the FEDERAL NATIONAL MORTGAGE ASSOCIATION. It funds itself by borrowing from the US Treasury. By 1982 its borrowings from the Treasury were over $110 billion.
Bibliography: M. Stigum. Securities of Federal Government Agencies and Sponsored Corporations *in* F.J. Fabozzi & I.M. Pollack. *The Handbook of Fixed Income Securities.* Dow-Jones Irwin, Homewood, Ill., 1983.

Federal Deposit Insurance Corporation (FDIC). The US FDIC was organized in 1933 to protect depositors from bank failures. Membership is compulsory for Federal Reserve member banks; 99% of US bank deposits are insured by the FDIC.
Bibliography: FDIC Annual Reports.

Federal National Mortgage Association. An important US body involved in the housing market. Also known as 'Fannie Mae' from its initials, FNMA. It is a federally chartered and privately owned corporation. (As such it is not a US AGENCY but a federally sponsored body; its debt is not guaranteed by the US government.) However its obligations have traditionally been treated as 'US agency debt' in the marketplace. It is the largest supplier of residential mortgage funds in the US, with a portfolio of over $75 billion in mortgage loans at December 1983. It operates by buying mortgages from local lenders, and is active in facilitating the US SECONDARY MARKET for mortgages. Compare GOVERNMENT NATIONAL MORTGAGE ASSOCIATION; PASS-THROUGH.
Bibliography: Federal National Mortgage Association. *Guide to FNMA Debt Securities.* Washington DC, 1984.

M.A. Smilow. The Move towards Mortgage Securitization. *Mortgage Banking.* New York, December 1983.

Federal Open Market Committee. Key decision-making committee of the FEDERAL RESERVE SYSTEM, which is responsible for setting money supply growth targets. Its membership includes the seven members of the Board of Governors, the President of the New York Federal Reserve Bank, and the presidents of four of the other eleven district banks. It meets monthly and issues directives to the managers of the Federal Reserve System's Open Market Account. The minutes of its meetings are published about a month after the event and indicate the current stance of US monetary policy.
Bibliography: P. Meek. *US Monetary Policy and Financial Markets.* Federal Reserve Bank of New York, 1982;
Federal Reserve Bulletin. Board of Governors of the Federal Reserve, Washington DC, monthly.

Federal Reserve System. The central banking system of the US. Founded in 1913, the system consists of 12 Federal Reserve Banks controlling 12 districts. The system has a board of seven Governors. The board supervises the operations of the reserve banks, and through the FEDERAL OPEN MARKET COMMITTEE it co-ordinates monetary policy. Every US commercial bank must maintain reserves with its local Federal Reserve Bank and must submit to its control on certain matters. In return, the bank may borrow from the Fed (as the system is often called), may transfer funds free of charge on the Fed's wires, and receives various other benefits. Of the various reserve banks, New York is *primus inter pares* since it carries out most of the Federal Open Market Committee's instructions in relation to domestic money markets and it also manages the system's foreign exchange transactions.
Bibliography: *The Federal Reserve System: Purposes & Functions.* Board of Governors of the Federal Reserve, Washington DC, 1974.
Federal Reserve Bank of New York Quarterly Review, New York; *Federal Reserve Monthly Bulletin.* Washington DC.

Fed funds (Federal funds). Term applying to cash balances held by banks with their local Federal Reserve Bank. Their crucial characteristic is that they are immediately available, i.e. not subject to clearing delays. The normal definition of a Fed funds deal is a deal between banks which involves the purchase/sale of deposits of a bank belonging to the FEDERAL RESERVE SYSTEM, for one business day, at a specified rate of interest. (However 'term' Fed funds deals are possible.) Funds are typically traded in $1 million blocks. Three types of transaction are possible: (a) 'straight' deals where the funds are traded overnight on an unsecured basis; (b) the borrower may pledge an asset as collateral; (c) a REPURCHASE AGREEMENT may be made where the borrower sells securities in exchange for Fed funds in order to buy them back next day at a fixed rate. Compare CLEARING HOUSE FUNDS; REPURCHASE AGREEMENTS.

Fed Funds Bill. *See* CASH MANAGEMENT BILL.

Fed funds rate. The rate of interest payable on Fed funds. It is probably the key short-term interest rate in the USA, because it signals the intentions of the authorities. Typically, a rise in the money supply figures will induce the authorities to intervene in the market to 'soak up' money, which will induce a rise in the Fed funds rate. Compare OPEN MARKET OPERATIONS, EFFECTIVE FED FUNDS RATE.
Bibliography: T.Q. Cook & B.J. Summers (eds). *Instruments of the Money Market.* Federal Reserve Bank of Virginia, 1981.
M. Stigum. *The Money Market.* Dow-Jones Irwin, Homewood Ill., 1983.

Fed Wire. A computerized system for transferring payments between branches of the FEDERAL RESERVE. It operates on uniform, nationwide hours – 8 a.m. to 5 p.m., Eastern Standard Time. Volume in 1979 was 35 million transfers, for an amount of $64.2 billion.
Bibliography: R.C. Kimball. Wire Transfer and the Demand for Money. *New England Economic*

Review. Federal Reserve Bank of Boston, March/April 1980.
The Federal Reserve and the Payments System. *Federal Reserve Bulletin*, Washington DC, February 1981.
M. Stigum. *The Money Market.* Dow-Jones Irwin, Homewood Ill., 1983.

felines. Slang, generic term covering the artificially created zero-coupon securities backed by US Treasury securities – so-called because Merrill Lynch's version was called TIGRs (Treasury Investment Growth Receipts), Salomon's CATs (Certificates of Accrual on Treasury Securities), Becker Paribas' COUGARs etc.
Bibliography: J. Laskey. How Stripping Became Respectable. *Euromoney*, December 1982.

FIDIC. Abbreviation for Fédération International des Ingenieurs Consultatifs. *See* INTERNATIONAL FEDERATION OF CONSULTING ENGINEERS.

fiduciary deposits. This refers to funds placed with a bank to invest at its own discretion on the customer's behalf. The most important centre for this type of business is Switzerland, where in 1980 SF120 billion of fiduciary funds were under management.
Bibliography: M.A. Corti. Switzerland: Banking, Money and Bond Markets *in* A.M. George & I.H. Giddy. *International Finance Handbook.* John Wiley & Sons, New York, 1983.

figure. Foreign exchange dealers' slang meaning '00' and denoting an exchange rate level. If the DM is quoted at 2.0300/2.0310 per dollar the rate may be quoted 'figure/ten' (leaving 2.03, understood).

fill or kill. US securities market slang for a request to execute an order immediately at the specified price or cancel it. Also used in UK commodity market.
Bibliography: L.M. Loll & J.G. Buckley. *The Over-the-Counter Securities Markets.* Prentice-Hall, New York, 1981.

final underwriting account. Final list of participating UNDERWRITERS based on written responses to underwriting invitations extended by the syndicate manager, and listed alphabetically within each BRACKET.

finance acceptance, finance bill.   A BILL OF EXCHANGE used not to finance a shipment of goods, but as a lending instrument. Such a bill is not generally ELIGIBLE paper in the UK or US. Compare ACCOMMODATION PAPER.
Bibliography: Gillett Brothers Discount Company. *The Bill on London.* Methuen & Co., London, 1976.
M. Stigum. *The Money Market.* Dow-Jones Irwin, Homewood, Ill., 1983.

finance (financial) lease.   (1) A LEASE where the LESSEE pays the full value of the asset over a specified period (sometimes called the primary or basic period). Finance leases are sometimes called full payout leases.
   (2) The US 1982 tax act, TEFRA permitted a new type of tax-oriented lease which is called a finance lease (*see* TEFRA). It works like a true lease but contains purchase options of 10% or more of the original cost at the conclusion of the lease. Compare LEVER-AGED LEASE; MONEY-OVER-MONEY LEASE, OPERATING LEASE.
Bibliography: A.F. Gargiulo & R.J. Kenard. *Leveraged Leasing.* American Management Association, New York, 1981.
P.K. Nevitt. *Project Financing.* Euromoney Publications, London 1983.

financial documents.   Term employed in the INTERNATIONAL CHAMBER OF COMMERCE document UNIFORM RULES FOR COLLECTIONS to mean 'bills of exchange, promissory notes, cheques, payment receipts or other similar instruments used for obtaining the payment of money'.
Bibliography: Uniform Rules for Collections, International Chamber of Commerce Brochure no. 322, Paris, 1978.

financial futures.   The group of FUTURES markets which trade in financial instruments. The first such futures were introduced by the INTERNATIONAL MONETARY MARKET in 1972, in the shape of foreign currency futures, but the financial futures markets did

not really take off until the introduction by the CHICAGO BOARD OF TRADE OF A GNMA interest rate futures contract in 1975 and the IMM 90-day TREASURY BILL futures contract in 1976.
Bibliography: N.H. Rothstein & J.M. Little. *The Handbook of Financial Futures.* Dow-Jones Irwin, Homewood, Ill., 1983.

financial rand.   Introduced in January 1979 and abolished in 1983, the financial rand market consisted of the proceeds of disinvestment of securities of South African companies, and purchases of rand by foreign investors in plant and equipment.

Financial Times Index.   Index computed by the *Financial Times* to measure UK Stock Exchange prices. The *Financial Times* publishes several indexes in cooperation with the Institute of Actuaries, Faculty of Actuaries and the Stock Exchange: the FT 30-share index (of the 30 leading shares), the Industrial Ordinary shares index, the 500-share index of 500 leading shares, and the All-Share index, together with sub-indexes for different sectors. In addition it produces the FINANCIAL TIMES STOCK EXCHANGE INDEX for use on the I ONDON INTERNATIONAL FINANCIAL FUTURES EXCHANGE.

Financial Times Stock Exchange Index.   An index of UK Stock Exchange prices produced jointly by the Stock Exchange and the *Financial Times* which is continuously updated, minute by minute, to form the basis of futures trading on the LONDON INTERNATIONAL FINANCIAL FUTURES EXCHANGE.

fine.   (1) Refers to a relatively low interest rate, or margin. Thus a loan may be made at the finest rate.
   (2) Refers to purity of precious metals. Thus gold bars may be 99.5% fine (995 parts in 1000 pure).

firm price, quotation.   In general, a 'firm price' is one which the maker is willing to substantiate for an amount considered reasonable in the market in question, be it a foreign exchange, money or securities market. Thus, if a company wishing to deal in foreign currency contacts a bank, or if a bank contacts a FOREIGN EXCHANGE BROKER or a bank overseas, to ask for a rate, the other party may quote its rate 'for information only' or the quotation may be 'firm'. The latter implies that the other party would be prepared to deal at this rate (if a bank) or can find a counterparty prepared to deal (if a broker).

first credit tranche. *See* INTERNATIONAL MONETARY FUND; TRANCHE.

first notice day. Commodities market term for the first day of a delivery period when holders of short commodity position can give notice to holders of long positions that they intend to deliver the commodity. The number of contracts circulated on first notice day is often interpreted as an indicator of future supply-demand conditions.

fiscal agent. Term used in EUROBOND issues. For example, in the case of the £25 million Sterling Foreign Currency Notes issued by Total Oil in 1977, Total Oil entered into a fiscal agency agreement with the Banque de Paris et des Pays-Bas pour le Grand Duche de Luxembourg. The latter, as fiscal agent, received from Total Oil the funds necessary to service the notes (i.e. payments of interest and principal) and it made these funds available to the PAYING AGENTS. The agent will also assist in the delivery of the bonds at the closing, authenticate bonds, and effect the exchange of GLOBAL BONDS for definitive securities when these are ready for distribution. The fiscal agent is solely the agent of the borrower: it is not a TRUSTEE for the bondholders.
Bibliography: F.G. Fisher. *International Bonds.* Euromoney Publications, London 1981.

fix, fixing. In certain Continental centres there is, in addition to normal interbank foreign exchange trading over the telephone, a daily meeting at which rates are 'fixed' officially. These rates can then be used for non-bank purposes, e.g. tourist business. The meeting usually takes place around lunchtime and includes a representative of the central bank. Offers to buy/sell a currency are made and the rate is adjusted to clear the market, or the central bank will intervene to set the rate at a desired level.
Bibliography: J.K. Walmsley. *The Foreign Exchange Handbook.* John Wiley & Sons, New York, 1983.

flat. US securities and Eurobond market term meaning: (1) excluding any accrued interest. Preferred stock, INCOME BONDS and bonds in default are quoted and dealt flat.
Bibliography: S. Homer & M. L. Leibowitz. *Inside the Yield Book.* Prentice-Hall, NJ, 1972.
   (2) Transactions executed for no profit.

flat (rate) yield. *See* INTEREST YIELD.

fleet policies. Marine insurance policies which cover all or many of the vessels operating under one ownership/management (sometimes including chartered vessels).
Bibliography: R.J. Lambeth. *Templeman on Marine Insurance.* Macdonald & Evans, UK, 1981.

flip-flop. Term introduced with the Swedish perpetual FLOATING RATE NOTE in 1984. The investor in the FRN may 'flip' out of the FRN into a four-year bond yielding LIMEAN. He can also 'flop' back from the bond into the perpetual.
Bibliography: C. Grant. Borrower of the Year: The Kingdom of Sweden. *Euromoney*, London, October 1984.

float. (1) An exchange rate can be rigidly fixed in relation to, say, the dollar, or some other NUMERAIRE such as gold or the SPECIAL DRAWING RIGHT. Alternatively, its value may be permitted to vary in line with market forces. In this case it is said to 'float'. The float may be 'clean' (uncontrolled) in which case there is no official INTERVENTION except to smooth the operation of the market, or 'dirty' in which case the float is managed so as to keep the currency in a certain 'target zone'.
Bibliography: J.K. Walmsley. *The Foreign Ex-*

change Handbook. John Wiley & Sons, New York, 1983.

(2) 'Float' can refer to cash in hand or in the course of being transferred between banks. In the latter case, it does not earn interest for its owner but is available for the bank to use. It therefore has a cost in terms of interest foregone to the owner of the money. Elaborate systems have been devised for cutting float time on international transfers, where the delays are greatest, though in France or Italy, for example, float costs can be considerable even on internal transfers. (Compare SWIFT.) Negative float or reverse float can be used to offset this - if a Parisian supplier is paid with a cheque drawn on a Marseilles bank, or a New York supplier via Oregon, suppliers can also be made to wait for payment.

(3) Federal reserve float is an extension of (2). It arises from the US system where cheques sent to Federal Reserve Banks are credited to the depositing bank within two business days. In some cases, the funds are credited before the banks on which the cheques are drawn are debit ed, i.e. the depositing bank gains a balance at the reserve bank (which gives it extra reserves) before the other bank loses reserves. Any hold-up in the collection process can produce a sudden expansion of float and hence of bank reserves.

Bibliography: P. Meek. *US Monetary Policy and Financial Markets.* Federal Reserve Bank of New York, 1982.

(4) US securities market term for the portion of an issue expected to trade actively in the secondary market.

floater. *See* FLOATING-RATE NOTE OR FLOATING-RATE CD.

floating policies. Marine insurance policies issued for a lump sum insured sufficient to cover all the voyages anticipated by the assured over a period (say three months). As each shipment is made the value of the sum insured is reduced accordingly. Because of the danger that this sum could be exhausted unnoticed floating policies were issued off

OPEN COVERS. Recently they have been largely replaced by TIME POLICIES.

Bibliography: R.J. Lambeth. *Templeman on Marine Insurance* Macdonald & Evans, UK, 1981.

floating-rate bond. A BOND on which the interest payable is variable. In the past this has tended to result from the INDEXATION of bonds, but the development of the FLOATING-RATE NOTE and CD has meant wider extension of the concept. Compare VARIABLE-RATE GILT-EDGED.

Bibliography: F.G. Fisher. *International Bonds.* Euromoney Publications, London, 1981.
Government Debt Management: Vol. II. Debt Instruments and Selling Techniques. OECD, Paris, 1983.

floating-rate CD (FRCD). A CD whose COUPON is variable and normally linked to the inter-bank money market rate. London dollar FRCDs tend to be denominated in units of $250,000 and upwards with a coupon of $\frac{1}{4}$% over (usually) six-month LIBOR but other possibilities exist. *See also* VARIABLE-RATE CDS

Bibliography: *Floating-Rate CDs.* Sumitomo Finance International, London, 1981.
T.Q. Cook & B.J. Summers (eds). *Instruments of the Money Markets.* Federal Reserve Bank of Richmond, Virginia, 1981.

floating-rate note (FRN). A blend of the ROLL-OVER credit market with the Eurosecurities market. FRNs have been issued for a wide range of maturities (in some cases without maturity – PERPETUAL FLOATERS) and carry a fixed SPREAD over (usually) six-month LIBOR normally with provision for a minimum interest rate. FRNs are usually SUBORDINATED to the claims of depositors. They are primarily used by banks to raise dollars for their Euromarket operations; they are better than CDS for this because they can be for longer maturities and because they can usually form part of a bank's capitalization with consequent benefit to overall balance-sheet ratios. Non-bank use has been rather patchy.

Bibliography: G. Ugeux. *Floating Rate Notes.* Euromoney Publications, London, 1981.

floating rate serial notes. See SERIAL FLOAT-
ING RATE NOTES.

floating spread. Certain EURO-CREDITS
have been made where the SPREAD over
LIBOR is not fixed in advance, but is agreed
among the lenders at the time of the
'roll-over'. Such loans are said to be made at
a floating spread. For example, in April 1980
the Spanish firm Lignitos de Meirama raised
$40 million for eight years, at ⅞% over Libor
for the first year, but thereafter at the average
spread agreed by the participants.

Flower Bond. US Treasury bond that can
be applied to the payment of Federal estate
taxes at par when held by and included in the
estate of a deceased.

flow of funds. Figures showing the sources
and uses of funds in an economy (or firm).
They measure the changes in LIQUIDITY and
of financial behaviour in different sectors of
the economy.
Bibliography: *An Introduction to Flow-of-Funds
Accounting 1963-76.* Bank of England, 1978.

FNMA. See FEDERAL NATIONAL MORT-
GAGE ASSOCIATION.

f.o.b. See FREE ON BOARD AIRPORT.

following underwriter. See LEAD UNDER-
WRITER.

FOMC. See FEDERAL OPEN MARKET COM-
MITTEE.

fonds de roulement. French term meaning
working capital.

footsie. UK slang for the FTSE or FINAN-
CIAL TIMES STOCK EXCHANGE INDEX used in
futures trading on the LONDON INTERNA-
TIONAL FINANCIAL FUTURES EXCHANGE.

f.o.r. See FREE ON RAIL.

force majeure. Term used in commodity
contracts referring to the cessation of supply
(or purchases) due to events beyond the
control of the contracting party.

foreign bond. A security issued by a bor-
rower in the market and the currency of
another country. Compare EUROBOND,
INTERNATIONAL BOND, SAMURAI BOND,
YANKEE BOND.
Bibliography: F.G. Fisher. *International Bonds.*
Euromoney Publications, London, 1981.

Foreign Credit Insurance Association. A
US company formed by about 50 insurance
companies in 1962. It provides export credit
insurance in association with the EXPORT-
IMPORT BANK.
Bibliography: *The Export Credit Financing Systems of OECD Member Countries.* Organization
for Economic Cooperation and Development.
Paris, 1982.

foreign domicile bill. UK term for a bill of
exchange drawn and accepted outside the
UK.

**Foreign Exchange and Currency Deposit
Brokers' Association.** Professional association of FOREIGN EXCHANGE BROKERS and
foreign currency deposit brokers in London.
Its functions are to provide liaison between
the various houses on matters of common
interest, and to liaise with the Bank of
England and the international banking community.

foreign exchange broker. A firm engaged in
bringing together professional buyers and
sellers of foreign exchange. There are many
hundreds of banks active in the international
foreign exchange market. Hence it is time-
consuming for a bank to shop around for
exchange rate quotations. Firms of foreign
exchange brokers have therefore been set up.
When approached by a bank with an order to
buy or sell, the broker will contact other
banks without indicating on whose behalf it is
acting, and it will endeavour to find a
counterparty. Brokers operate in many other
markets, e.g. commodities and stock markets, and in many countries.
Bibliography: T.M. Campfield & J.G. O'Brien.

Foreign Exchange Trading Practices *in* A.M. George & I.H. Giddy. *International Finance Handbook*. John Wiley & Sons, New York, 1983.

foreign exchange market. The aggregate of all transactions in claims to foreign currency. Participants consist of banks, their customers, FOREIGN EXCHANGE BROKERS and from time to time central banks. In most cases the market is a telephone and telex one, but in France, Germany and certain other centres a formal foreign exchange FIXING takes place daily. *See* FORWARD CONTRACT, INTERVENTION, FORWARD EXCHANGE INTERVENTION, OPTION CONTRACT, SPOT, SPOT/NEXT, TOM/NEXT, EUROCURRENCY.

Bibliography: J.K. Walmsley. *The Foreign Exchange Handbook*. John Wiley & Sons, New York, 1983.
J. Heywood. *Foreign Exchange and the Corporate Treasurer*. Adam & Charles Black, London, 1983.

Forex Club. This was formed in London and other foreign exchange centres to encourage educational and social contacts between foreign exchange dealers under the umbrella of the ASSOCIATION CAMBISTE INTERNATIONALE.

forfaiting. The business of discounting medium-term promissory notes or drafts related to an international trade transaction. Normally there is a series of notes or drafts with the final maturity up to five years. Repayments are semi-annual and discounting is at a fixed rate. Effectively the business is medium-term export FACTORING. The difference is that factoring is sometimes done on the basis that the factor has recourse to the exporter, who therefore remains liable if the importer fails to pay. Forfaiting is without recourse. Most forfaiting business is therefore done on transactions guaranteed by a bank or state-trading agency usually through an AVAL, ensuring that the importer pays. The goods involved are usually capital goods, where payment is made over several years; the market is based mainly in Switzerland and in London, which has supplanted Zurich in recent years. Total annual volume is uncertain, but estimated to be around $4 billion.

Bibliography: *The Forfaiting Manual*. Finanz AG. London, 1977.
I. Guild. Forfaiting widens its appeal. *The Banker*. London, April 1984.
H. Berndt. Zurich looks good to the German Exporter. *Euromoney*, April 1984.

forum shopping. UK term for the ability of a plaintiff to choose in which of several jurisdictions he will bring his case, in order to improve his chances of victory, or to be awarded more compensation.

Bibliography: P. Wood. *Law and Practice of International Finance*. Sweet & Maxwell, London, 1980.

forward contract. A forward foreign exchange contract is a contract between a bank and its customer. Each party agrees to deliver at a specified future time a certain amount in one currency in exchange for a certain amount in another currency at an agreed rate of exchange. A forward contract differs from a foreign exchange FUTURES contract in that the former is negotiated privately while the latter is for standard amounts and is traded on a public exchange. Normally no cash is exchanged at the time the contract is taken out, but both parties commit themselves to a currency exchange on the maturity date at the agreed rate. The delivery date may be specified in the contract (a fixed forward contract) or it may be chosen by the customer between two previously specified future dates - an OPTION FORWARD CONTRACT. The latter covers the common situation where a firm cannot be certain of the precise day it will receive/pay the foreign currency, but knows the period in which it is likely to happen. (Such a contract implies the option of of taking delivery between two dates, but does not give the choice of whether to take up the deal or not. The latter case would be covered by a foreign currency OPTION.) In many countries, EXCHANGE CONTROL permission is required to take out a forward contract. Compare FORWARD MARGIN; FINANCIAL FUTURES.

Bibliography: J.K. Walmsley.*The Foreign Exchange Handbook*. John Wiley & Sons, New York, 1983.

forward cover.   The arrangement of a FOR-
WARD FOREIGN EXCHANGE CONTRACT to
protect a buyer or seller of foreign currency
from unexpected fluctuations in the exchange
rate.

forward exchange intervention.   A central
bank may buy or sell its currency in the
forward market to influence the currency's
behaviour in the SPOT MARKET or to manipulate interest rates via INTEREST PARITIES. It is
then undertaking forward exchange intervention. (Compare INTERVENTION.) Such a
tactic was employed by the Bank of England
from mid-1963 until 1967. When devaluation
took place, the Bank's outstanding forward
commitments were estimated at £2 billion. A
heavy loss was incurred. Forward intervention was then stopped. In recent years,
however, the Bank has occasionally inter-
vened in the EUROSTERLING MARKET in
order to drive up short-term Eurosterling
rates. This discourages speculators from
borrowing sterling in order to sell it. Forward
exchange intervention has also been undertaken by other central banks including the
Bundesbank.
Bibliography: E. B. Chalmers (ed.). Forward
Exchange Intervention. Hutchinson Educational.
London, 1971.
P. Coulbois (ed.). Forward interventions of the
Deutsche Bundesbank, in *Le Change à Terme.*
Université de Paris I, 1972.
J.K. Walmsley. *The Foreign Exchange Handbook.*
John Wiley & Sons, New York, 1983.

forward exchange rate.   The rate at which
currency can be bought/sold today for delivery at some future time. Quoted 'outright'
(e.g. if today is 15 May 1978 and I quote
£1=$1.90 for SPOT I might quote £1=$1.85
for 17 May 1979) or as a FORWARD MARGIN,
in which case I would quote the margin as 5
cents or 500 points.

forward Fed funds.   A market exists in the
US for trading in FED FUNDS for future
delivery; e.g. one might deal on Friday for
funds value Monday. It is rather limited in
size and typically deals for only a few days
forward.

forward-forward.   (1) This refers to a deal
for a future date in an instrument which
matures on a further forward date. The
instrument is normally a deposit or CD and
the object can be to extend the term of the
deal: or it may even out a MIS-MATCH without
upsetting the bank's total 'book'. The formula for calculating a forward-forward interest
rate up to one year is as follows:

$$F = \frac{R_2N_2 - R_1N_1}{(N_2 - N_1)\left(1 + \dfrac{R_1N_1}{100 \times B}\right)}$$

where F = forward rate
N_1 = days in shorter period
R_1 = rate for shorter period
N_2 = days in longer period
R_2 = rate for longer period
B = interest basis (i.e 360 or 365)

(2) In foreign exchange a forward-forward
deal refers to (say) a purchase of three-month
dollars against a sale of six-months dollars.
Bibliography: J.K. Walmsley. *The Foreign Exchange Handbook.* John Wiley & Sons, New York,
1983.

forward intervention.   *See* FORWARD EX-
CHANGE INTERVENTION.

forward margin.   The margin between today's price of a currency, and the price at
some date in the future. The forward price
may be higher than today's, in which case the
currency is at a PREMIUM, or it may be lower,
i.e. at a DISCOUNT. The margin may be
expressed as follows. Suppose today $1.76=
£1 and that the dollar is at a premium of 8
cents or 800 points for delivery in 12 months'
time. Expressing this premium as a percentage of today's rate we find it is around 4.4%.
So, ignoring dealing costs, one could make
4.4% by buying dollars today and selling
them back for delivery in 12 months' time. It
follows that the forward margin is intimately
linked with the interest rates payable on
dollars and pounds sterling. *See* COVERED
MARGIN, EUROSTERLING, FORWARD EX-
CHANGE INTERVENTION, INTEREST, OUT-
RIGHT PARITY.
Bibliography: J.K. Walmsley. *The Foreign Ex-*

change Handbook. John Wiley & Sons, New York, 1983.

forward rate. *See* FORWARD EXCHANGE RATE.

f.o.t. *See* FREE ON TRUCK.

foul. Term applied to a BILL OF LADING which is qualified as to condition.

FPA. *See* FREE OF PARTICULAR AVERAGE.

franchise. Insurance term meaning that if a loss is higher than a stated percentage, the entire loss is paid by the insurance company.

franc zone. The role of the franc zone is of a grouping of currencies which are effectively supported by the financial resources of the Banque de France and which in return for accepting French financial guidance receive certain financial assistance from France. The member countries consist of Benin, Cameroon, Central African Empire, Chad, Comoros, Congo, France, Gabon, Ivory Coast, Mali, Niger, Senegal, Togo and Upper Volta. The main currency is the CFA franc which stands (in West Africa) for Communauté financière africaine and in central Africa for Cooperation financière en Afrique centrale; the CFA franc stands at a fixed parity of CFA1=2 French centimes. The franc zone also incorporates the CFP franc (standing for Comptoirs francais du Pacifique) which is used in New Caledonia, French Polynesia and the Wallis and Futura islands and is maintained at CFP1=5.5 French centimes.
Bibliography: J.K. Walmsley. *The Foreign Exchange Handbook*. John Wiley & Sons, New York, 1983.
A. Liddell. Financial Cooperation in Africa – French Style. *The Banker*, London, February 1982.

franked income. A UK term for income which has already suffered corporation tax in the United Kingdom, i.e. ordinary and preference dividends received from companies in the UK. Within an investment trust, for example, franked income is broadly exempt from corporation tax within the investment trust company.
Bibliography: A.A. Arnaud. *Investment Trusts Explained*. Woodhead-Faulkner, Cambridge, UK, 1983.

FRCD. *See* FLOATING-RATE CD.

free alongside ship (f.a.s.). A term used in foreign trade to mean that a price quoted f.a.s. includes the carriage of the goods only as far as the dock beside the vessel by which they are to be transported.
Bibliography: C.M. Schmitthof. *The Export Trade*. 7th edn, Stevens & Sons, London, 1980.
Incoterms. International Chamber of Commerce Brochure no. 350. Paris, 1980.

free carrier. An international trade term. It effectively means the same as FREE ON BOARD, except that the seller fulfils his obligations when he delivers the goods into the custody of the carrier at the named point.
Bibliography: *Incoterms* International Chamber of Commerce Brochure no. 350, Paris 1980.

free of particular average. A marine insurance term meaning that the insurer is not liable for (i.e. is free of) partial loss of the cargo, other than GENERAL AVERAGE. The term is most commonly met with in the Institute Cargo Clauses (ICC) laid down by the INSTITUTE OF LONDON UNDERWRITERS. The only difference between the ICC (FPA) and the ICC (WA) – with average – is that when partial loss is caused by heavy weather and the vessel has not been stranded, sunk or burnt during the voyage, the FPA clause means that the insurer is free of liability whereas he would be liable under the 'with average' clause.
Bibliography: R.H. Brown. *Dictionary of Marine Insurance Terms*. Witherby & Co., London 1975.
V. Dover. *A Handbook to Marine Insurance*. Revised and edited R.H. Brown. Witherby & Co., London, 1975.

free on board. The f.a.s. cost plus the cost of loading on to the vessel.
Bibliography: D.M. Sassoon. *C.I.F. and F.O.B. Contracts*. Stevens & Sons, London, 1975.

C.M. Schmitthof. *The Export Trade.* 7th edn. Stevens & Sons, London, 1980.
Incoterms. International Chamber of Commerce Brochure no. 350. Paris, 1980.

free on board airport. An international trade term derived from FREE ON BOARD but not, in relation to air transportation, to be taken literally; rather it should be taken as announcing that the next word designates the place at which the seller's responsibility terminates. F.o.b. airport means that the seller must place the goods in the hands of the air carrier or on his agent at the named airport of departure.
Bibliography: *Incoterms.* International Chamber of Commerce Brochure no. 350. Paris, 1980.

free on rail. The cost of the goods plus carriage to the specified rail terminal plus the cost of loading on to the rail trucks.
Bibliography: C.M. Schmitthof. *The Export Trade.* 7th edn. Stevens & Sons, London, 1980. *Incoterms.* International Chamber of Commerce Brochure no. 350, Paris, 1980.

free on truck. International trade term sometimes used instead of FREE ON RAIL.
Bibliography: *Incoterms.* International Chamber of Commerce Brochure no. 350, Paris, 1980.

free reserves. Total reserves held by a bank less the reserves required by the authorities. In the US and Germany, for example, the level of free reserves is frquently regarded as an important indicator (directly or indirectly) of the potential for expanding bank credit.
Bibliography: D.C. Beek. Excess Reserves and Reserve Targeting. *Federal Reserve Bank of New York Quarterly Bulletin,* Autumn 1981.

freeze. Colloquial term for the act of preventing the withdrawal of funds from a bank account. The freeze in 1979 of Iranian assets in the US is the best-known recent example. In some ways fortunately, the applicability of the freeze to EURODOLLAR transactions – which are operationally CLEARED through the US – was never fully tested in the courts. Compare SET-OFF.
Bibliography: P. Wood. *Law and Practice of*

International Finance. Sweet & Maxwell, London, 1980.

freight. In ordinary language, freight means the cargo carried by a ship (or other mode of transport); by extension, it denotes the charge made by the freight-carrier for transporting it. Specific types of freight include: (a) common law freight; (b) advance freight; (c) freight payable ship lost or not lost; (d) anticipated freight; (e) time chartered freight; (f) BACK FREIGHT.
Bibliography: V. Dover. *A Handbook to Marine Insurance.* Revised and edited R.H. Brown. Witherby & Co, London, 1975. R. Colinvaux. *Carver's Carriage by Sea.* Vol. 2. 12th edn. Stevens & Sons, London, 1971, pp. 946-1017.

freight forwarder. The intermediary between the consignor (or consignee) of a shipment, and the transport carries, customs authorities, and other third parties with whom the consignor would otherwise have to deal.
Bibliography: D.J. Hill. *Freight Forwarders.* Stevens & Sons, London, 1972.
A. Murr. *Export/Import Traffic Management and Forwarding.* Cornell Maritime Press, USA, 1979.

freight paid to (named destination). International trade term referring to road, rail and inland waterways. The seller must forward the goods at his own expense to the agreed destination and is responsible for all risks of the goods until they are delivered to the first carrier.
Bibliography: *Incoterms.* International Chamber of Commerce Brochure no. 350, Paris, 1980.

freight release. When goods are shipped with freight payable at their destination, a remittance for the amount of freight due must be made to the shipowner who will either endorse a freight release on the bill of lading or retain the bill and issue a freight release as a separate document.
Bibliography: V. Dover. *A Handbook to Marine Insurance.* Revised and edited R.H. Brown. Witherby & Co, London, 1975.

FRN. *See* FLOATING-RATE NOTE.

front-end fees.   Fees payable at the start of a loan- e.g. MANAGEMENT AND PARTICIPATION FEES. Their importance can be seen from the following example. Consider a loan of $100 million with four CO-LEAD MANAGERS each UNDERWRITING $25 million. The total MANAGEMENT FEE is ½% or, on $100 million, a total of $500,000; and the PRAECIPUUM is ⅛%. The following syndication fee structure is agreed:

Participants providing $10 million: 3/8%
Participants providing $ 5 million: 1/4%
Participants providing $ 2 million: 1/8%
Participants providing $ 1 million: nil.

Suppose now that the deal is syndicated and the SELL-DOWN is $52 million, broken down as follows: two providers of $10 million, three of $5 million, five of $2 million, and seven of $1 million. Then the total management fees paid out to the participants will be $125,000. The four co-lead managers will earn a ⅛% praecipuum, or $125,000, plus ⅜% on their commitment which now totals $48 million – the balance which was not sold down – costing $180,000. These fees account for $430,000 out of the original $500,000. The $70,000 balance is the POOL which results from the smaller participants being paid lesser participation fees. This pool will be shared between the co-lead managers. Hence the four co-lead managers will split fees of $375,000 ($125,000 praecipuum, $180,000 management fees, and $70,000 pool), which as a percentage of their commitment ($48 million) is.78125%. If we now suppose the deal has an AVERAGE LIFE of four years, then the front-end fees enhance the yield of the loan over the average life by just under 20 basis points.
Bibliography: S.I. Davis. *The Euro-bank.* Macmillan, UK/John Wiley, New York, 1981.
J.A. Donaldson & T.H. Donaldson. *The Medium-Term Loan Market.* Macmillan, London, 1982.

front-end finance.   Finance for the initial part of a project or contract. The term is loosely used and can cover several areas, but is most frequently encountered in export finance where it refers to the portion of a loan not covered by export credit insurance. For example, if a foreign buyer is borrowing from a British bank, it may be necessary to provide funds to help the buyer make a down payment. Alternatively, in a project which requires infrastructural investment followed by equipment purchases (e.g. laying if some railway track followed by rolling-stock purchases) separate front-end finance for the infrastructure may be arranged to complement the finance of the equipment exports.
Bibliography: P.K. Nevitt. *Project Financing.* Euromoney Publications, London 1983.

front-end loading.   The term is used to refer to fees etc. which are levied more heavily to begin with and which subsequently taper off. Most commonly it refers to unit trust or life assurance contracts.
Bibliography: *The Unit Trust Yearbook.* Fundex, London, 1978.

FTSE.   Abbreviation for the FINANCIAL TIMES STOCK EXCHANGE INDEX.

fuel trust.   A US PROJECT FINANCING technique. A trust formed for the purpose of acquiring fuel for a utility. Fuel trusts are generally supported by a TAKE-OR-PAY contract from the utility which will use the fuel. Fuel trust financing is generally in the form of COMMERCIAL PAPER which will generally be RATED equal to that of the utility.
Bibliography: *Standard & Poor's Ratings Guide.* McGraw-Hill, New York, 1979.
P.K. Nevitt. *Project Financing.* Euromoney Publications, London, 1983.

full pay-out lease.   *See* FINANCE LEASE.

fully invested.   The term refers to a portfolio that has no assets in the form of cash or cash equivalent.

fully modified pass-through.   *See* PASS-THROUGH.

funding.   The term refers to the substitution of longer-term for short-term debt. In the case of the international financial system, the term has been used to refer to the consolidation of external balances- such as the STERL-

ING BALANCES and their substitution for some form of agreed reserve asset such as SPECIAL DRAWING RIGHTS.
Bibliography: C.F. Bergsten. *The Dilemmas of the Dollar.* New York University Press, 1976.

fungible.   This term denotes a thing which is capable of being satisfactorily replaced by another thing answering to the same definition. For ordinary purposes a £1 note is fungible since I may replace it with any other £1 note; although if it were a rare specimen (e.g. misprinted) and I collected rare £1 notes it would not be. Fungibility also applies to securities, which are normally substitutable for similar securities (and although OPTIONS are not fungible, TRADED OPTIONS are). CEDEL operates two types of clearing account, depending on whether the participant requires CEDEL to communicate certificate numbers (non-fungible account) or not (fungible account).
Bibliography: *Instructions to the Participants.* CEDEL, May 1977.
C.T. Crawford. The fallacy of the fungible. *Euromoney*, London, November 1979.
F.G. Fisher. *International Bonds.* Euromoney Publications, London 1981.

futures.   Term referring to deals in a commodity (or financial instrument) which are made today for settlement at some future date. An organized futures market requires some kind of standard contract, a clearing house through which payments are made and which normally requires a MARGIN from participants as a check on their solvency, and finally a commodity which is traded by a reasonably wide range of people. The chief centre of futures trading is the US. Commodities and instruments traded include apples, live hogs, pork bellies, frozen orange juice, copper, silver and gold. Financial instrument futures include US TREASURY BILLS and bonds, CERTIFICATES OF DEPOSIT, and EURO-DOLLAR deposits, together with stock index futures. The main centres are the CHICAGO BOARD OF TRADE and the CHICAGO MERCANTILE EXCHANGE which includes the INTERNATIONAL MONETARY MARKET. In London futures are traded on the LONDON METAL EXCHANGE, the BALTIC EXCHANGE and the LONDON INTERNATIONAL FINANCIAL FUTURES EXCHANGE. The list of commodities includes metals, rubber, cocoa, coffee, sugar, grain and soyabean oil. Financial instruments traded include a sterling interest rate contract, GILT-EDGED, Eurodollar deposits, foreign currencies and a Stock Exchange index. Compare LONDON GRAIN FUTURES MARKET; UNITED TERMINAL SUGAR MARKET ASSOCIATION.
Bibliography: N.H. Rothstein & J.M. Little. *The Handbook of Financial Futures.* McGraw-Hill, New York, 1984.
J.K. Walmsley. *The Foreign Exchange Handbook.* John Wiley & Sons, New York, 1983.
C.W.J. Granger (ed.). *Trading in Commodities.* Woodhead-Faulkner, Cambridge, UK, 1983.

futures commission merchant.   US term for intermediaries between the traders in the FUTURES market PITS and their customers. Also known as commission houses. The futures commission merchants (FCMs) are members of the exchanges who act as agents for their customers. They take the order and arrange for its execution; in addition, they guarantee the contracts to the CLEARING HOUSE, make and take delivery of contracts, collect and pay MARGIN, and provide accounting services to the customer.
Bibliography: N.H. Rothstein & J.M. Little. *The Handbook of Financial Futures.* McGraw-Hill, New York, 1984.

FX.   Abbreviation for foreign exchange.

G

GAB. *See* GENERAL ARRANGEMENTS TO BORROW.

GAFTA. *See* GRAIN AND FEED ASSOCIATION.

gap. US term for MIS-MATCH – the difference between maturities of assets and liabilities in a money market operation, or purchases and sales of currency in foreign exchange.
Bibliography: B.F. Binder & T.W.F. Lindquist. *Asset/Liability and Funds Management at US Commercial Banks.* Bank Administration Institute, Rolling Meadows, Ill., 1982.
J.K. Walmsley. *The Foreign Exchange Handbook.* John Wiley & Sons, New York, 1983.

garage. Term referring to the transfer of assets or liabilities to a centre which has little connection wih the underlying transaction- usually in order to shift profits into a low-tax area.

GATT. *See* GENERAL AGREEMENT ON TARIFFS AND TRADE.

GDP. *See* GROSS DOMESTIC PRODUCT.

gearing. UK term for the relationship between equity capital and fixed interest capital. The American term is LEVERAGE. After deducting interest on a debt, profits are available for dividends on the equity. Thus the effect of high gearing is to make it more uncertain that dividends can be paid, but if the debt is financing profitable business, dividends can grow more than proportionately.
Bibliography: A.J. Merrett & A. Sykes. *The Finance and Analysis of Capital Projects.* 2nd edn, Longman, London, 1973.
A.A. Arnaud. *Investment Trusts Explained.* Woodhead-Faulkner, Cambridge, UK, 1983.

General Agreement on Tariffs and Trade (GATT). An international agreement made in 1947 in order to set up an international trade organization. In the event the ITO was never created. The Secretariat of the GATT has been responsible for organizing a number of 'rounds' of international trade negotiations (the Dillon Round of 1962, the Kennedy Round of 1967 and the Tokyo Round of 1973-79), which aimed at reducing tariff and other obstacles to international trade. As the length of the Tokyo Round indicates, increasingly difficult international trade conditions in the 1970s have tended to reduce the influence of the GATT, but it continues to play an important role at a technical level.
Bibliography: *GATT Annual Report,* Geneva, Switzerland.
K.W. Dam. *The GATT – Law and International Economic Organization.* University of Chicago Press, 1970.
A.I. MacBean & P.N. Snowden. *International Institutions in Trade and Finance.* George Allen & Unwin, London, 1981.

general arrangements to borrow (GAB). An agreement negotiated in 1962,where the GROUP OF 10 agreed to provide special credits to the IMF in their own currency, provided (a) such credits were collectively agreed by the group; (b) the credits were for financing drawings by other Group of 10 countries. Effectively, the GAB was designed to cope with the fact that the IMF did not have the resources to aid the pound and the dollar simultaneously, without adding to the IMF's decision-taking powers. In the most recent review, the GAB were expanded to include Switzerland and, with Saudi Arabia as an associated, now total SDR 17 billion.
Bibliography: S. Strange. *International Monetary Relations 1959-71.* Royal Institute of International Affairs, London, 1976.
The Financial Structure and Operations of the

International Monetary Fund. *Bank of England Quarterly Bulletin*, December 1983.

general average loss. This is defined in the UK's 1906 Marine Insurance Act as follows: 1. A general average loss is a loss caused by or directly consequential on a general average act... 2. There is a general average act where any extraordinary sacrifice or expenditure is voluntarily and reasonably made or incurred in time of peril for the purpose of preserving the property imperiled in the common adventure. 3. Where there is a general average loss, the party on whom it falls is entitled, subject to the conditions imposed by maritime law, to a rateable contribution from the other parties interested, and such contribution is called a general average contribution.

An example might be if my machinery were jettisoned to save a ship during a storm, thus saving yours: I would be entitled to claim a general average contribution from you.
Bibliography:
V. Dover. *A Handbook to Marine Insurance*. Revised and edited R.H. Brown. Witherby & Co. London, 1975.

generalized scheme of preferences (GSP). A system of tariff reductions on manufactured goods and quota increases designed for the benefit of less developed countries. The GSP began to be implemented in the late 1960s and is now operational in the US, EEC and other major trading nations, although the use of restrictive quotas and escape clauses has meant that the full impact of the scheme has been considerably blunted.
Bibliography: L.N. Rangajaran. *Commodity Conflict*. Croom Helm, London, 1978.
A.I. MacBean & P.N. Snowden. *International Institutions in Trade and Finance*. George Allen & Unwin, London, 1981.

gen-saki. A Japanese short-term money market, the gen-saki market is often referred to as the market for conditional bond sales. It is a market in which securities companies sell (buy) bonds, usually for two or three months, while simultaneously including an agreement to repurchase (re-sell) them. Bank debentures and local municipal bonds are mainly used. The significance of the market is that it has been one of the less controlled money markets in Japan. Also, unlike the call money market, the gen-saki market is open to corporations. It constitutes 10-15% of the total short-term money market in Japan.
Bibliography: J.K. Walmsley. *The Foreign Exchange Handbook*. John Wiley & Sons, New York, 1983.
Nomura Securities Co. Ltd. *Gen-saki: An Alternative Way of Cash Management*. London, September 1981.

germinal franc. *See* GOLD FRANC.

gilt-edged securities. (1) UK term for government stocks. Because the risk of government default is considered remote, such stock is said to be 'gilt-edged'. The term is sometimes extended to stocks issued by other bodies under Government guarantee (e.g. local authority bonds, nationalized industry stocks). However, defaults on these stocks have been known, and in such cases the guarantee's protection of the investor's money does not extend to payment *on time,* so that 'gilt-edged' should not strictly be applied to such stocks. Compare TAP; TREASURY BILL; VARIABLE-RATE BILLS.
Bibliography: P. Phillips. *Inside the Gilt-Edged Market*. Woodhead Faulkner, Cambridge, 1984.

(2) A parallel US usage refers to bonds of AAA or comparable standing.

Ginnie Mae. Slang for GNMA: the US GOVERNMENT NATIONAL MORTGAGE ASSOCIATION.

give-up. US term meaning: (1) Reduction in yield resulting from sale of bonds at one yield and the purchase of an equivalent amount of bonds at a lower yield.
Bibliography: S. Homer & M. L. Leibowitz. *Inside the Yield Book*. Prentice-Hall, NJ, 1972.

(2) Notification by a broker on the New York Stock Exchange of a bond buyer's identity to the seller so delivery can be effected.
Bibliography: L.M. Loll & J.B. Buckley. *The*

Over-the-Counter Securities Markets. Prentice-Hall, NJ 1981.

gliding parity. *See* CRAWLING PEG.

global bond. A EUROBOND issue normally results in the printing of a number of pieces of paper showing the debt incurred by the issuer to the bondholder. A global bond is usually issued on a temporary basis with a face value equal to the aggregate amount of the borrowing, until such time as the individual bonds are printed. The use of a global bond helps in the LOCK-UP process whereby Eurobonds are kept out of the US market until they are SEASONED.
Bibliography: F.G. Fisher. *International Bonds.* Euromoney Publications, London, 1981.

GNMA. *See* GOVERNMENT NATIONAL MORTGAGE ASSOCIATION.

GNP. Abbreviation for Gross National Product.

go-around. US term for the process by which the FEDERAL RESERVE seeks offers from the PRIMARY DEALERS in the government securities markets for REPURCHASES or 'reverse repurchases'. The go-around is usually conducted between around 11-11.30 a.m. and the results announced to the market shortly thereafter. The outcome is often read as a signal of the Fed's short-term monetary policy objectives.
Bibliography: M. Stigum. *The Money Market.* Dow-Jones Irwin, Homewood, Ill., 1983.
P. Meek. *US Monetary Policy and Financial Markets.* Federal Reserve Bank of New York, 1982.

gold bullion. Term for gold in ingot form, as distinct from coins or jewellery. Bullion is available in many shapes and sizes ranging from 10 tola bars (3.75 ounces) to 400-ounce bars. The standard traded in the London gold market is a bar of 350-430 ounces of 995 FINE gold, bearing the stamp of an approved assayer. The COMEX standard is a 100-ounce bar of 995 fine gold.

Bibliography: T. Green. *The New World of Gold Today.* Walker & Co., New York, 1981.
Annual Bullion Review. S. Montagu & Co., London.

gold bullion standard. In 1925 the UK returned to the GOLD STANDARD in the form of a bullion standard: notes were not convertible into gold coin, but could be exchanged for bullion. The standard was abandoned in 1931.
Bibliography: B. Tew. *International Monetary Co-operation 1945-70.* Hutchinson, London, 1970.

gold certificate. In the US all officially-owned gold is the nominal property of the US Treasury. In order to use the funds tied up in its gold reserve the Treasury 'monetizes' its gold by issuing gold certificates to a Federal Reserve Bank in exchange for a dollar balance at that bank. The Federal Reserve Banks in turn, use the gold certificates to settle indebtedness between themselves (Compare INTERDISTRICT SETTLEMENT FUND), and also as collateral against their issue of bank-notes.
Bibliography: *The Federal Reserve System: Purposes and Functions.* Board of Governors of the Federal Reserve System, Washington DC, 1974.

gold clause. A clause in a financial agreement linking a monetary payment to the value of gold. A more precise term would be gold value clause. These clauses raise a number of serious legal difficulties and they have been made illegal in a number of countries (although not, apparently, in the UK). Compare GOLD FRANC; NOMINALISM; REVALORIZATION.
Bibliography: F.A. Mann. *The Legal Aspect of Money.* Clarendon Press, Oxford, 1971.
J. Gold. *SDRs, Gold and Currencies: Fourth Survey of New Legal Developments.* IMF Pamphlet no. 33, Washington DC, 1980.

gold exchange standard. A modified form of the GOLD STANDARD under which gold may not be bought by domestic residents at a fixed price – as under the GOLD STANDARD or GOLD BULLION STANDARDS - nor is it the main element of a country's international reserves;

instead these were held in foreign currency deposits or financial instruments, which relied on the fact that the dollar was nominally convertible into gold until 1971.

Bibliography: F. Hirsch. *Money International.* Penguin Books, London, 1967.

B. Tew, *International Monetary Co-operation, 1945-70.* Hutchinson, London, 1970.

J. Gold. *SDRs, Gold and Currencies: Third Survey of New Legal Developments.* IMF Pamphlet no. 26, Washington DC, 1979.

gold franc. Various gold francs are in use. For example, the BANK FOR INTERNATIONAL SETTLEMENTS keeps its balance sheet in terms of Swiss gold francs. Various international conventions use different gold francs; two of the most common are the so-called Latin Union franc (or GERMINAL FRANC), (originally defined as equivalent to 10/31 of a gramme of gold 0.900 FINE) used in telecommunications and postal conventions, and the Poincaré franc (defined originally as 65.5 milligrams of gold 0.900 fine) which is used in conventions relating to pollution and shipping liabilities. The value of these two units is now fixed in terms of SDRs as there is no official gold price. Compare GOLD CLAUSE.

Bibliography: M.L. Bristow. Gold franc – replacement of unit of account. *Lloyd's Maritime and Commercial Law Quarterly.* UK, February 1978.

J. Gold. *SDRs, Gold and Currencies: Fourth Survey of Legal Developments.* IMF Pamphlet no. 33, Washington DC, 1980.

gold market. Like the FOREIGN EXCHANGE MARKET this is world-wide, but it is more constrained by physical influences (the cost of digging it out of the ground, 'good delivery' standards, proximity to smuggling routes etc.) Its operations are complicated by the fact that demand is often influenced by disturbances like civil war or political upheaval, while the supply is dominated by South Africa and the USSR (and, more recently, by stocks held by the US and IMF). The major centres of the market are London, New York, Hong Kong and Zurich. However, the twice-daily London fixing at Rothschilds'

offices is still the key price-setting mechanism.

Bibliography: T. Green. *The New World of Gold Today.* Walker & Co., New York, 1981.

Annual Bullion Review. S. Montagu & Co, London.

Gold. Consolidated Gold Fields, London, annually.

gold pool. The arrangement made in 1961 where the then EEC, the US, the UK and Switzerland formed buying and selling syndicates managed by the Bank of England to deal in the gold market with the objective of stabilizing the price. In 1968 the gold pool was unable to supply enough gold to hold the price steady and a TWO-TIER GOLD MARKET was instituted.

Bibliography: F. Hirsch. *Money International.* Penguin Books, London, 1967.

S. Strange. *International Monetary Relations 1959-71.* Royal Institute of International Affairs. London, 1976.

gold standard. In theory the gold standard is a system where the price of gold is kept fixed in terms of national currency, so that an increased supply of gold does not lower the price of gold, but drives up all other prices instead. Therefore, a balance of payments surplus (implying a rise in gold reserves) drives up domestic prices, until inflation reduces the balance of payments surplus, and a payments deficit leads to a shortage of gold and domestic deflation until equilibrium is restored. It is doubtful whether the gold standard ever worked in the manner generally believed. It was succeeded, so far as the UK is concerned, by the gold bullion standard and the GOLD EXCHANGE STANDARD. The latter was finally abandoned in 1931.

Bibliography: B. Tew. *International Monetary Co-operation 1945-70.* Hutchinson, London, 1970.

F. Hirsch. *Money International.* Penguin Books, London, 1967.

gold tranche. *See* INTERNATIONAL MONETARY FUND; TRANCHE.

good till cancelled. An order to buy or sell a security or commodity which remains in effect until it is either executed or cancelled.

Bibliography: L.M. Loll & J.G. Buckley. *The Over-the-Counter Securities Markets. Prentice Hall, NJ, 1981.*

Government broker. In the UK, the firm of Mullens & Co. have traditionally acted on behalf of the authorities in the market for GILT-EDGED and the senior partner of the firm is known as the Government broker, although changing arrangements in the market will alter this role.

Government National Mortgage Association. A US government-owned entity established in 1968 to take over some of the functions of the FEDERAL NATIONAL MORTGAGE ASSOCIATION. Its obligations (backed by a pool of mortgages) are widely traded and often referred to as Ginnie Maes (from GNMA). As a government-owned agency its paper -unlike that of the Federal National Mortgage Association-bears a government guarantee.
Bibliography: T.Q. Cook & B.J. Summers (eds). *Instruments of the Money Market.* Federal Reserve Bank of Richmond, Virginia, 1981.
D. Senft. Pass-Through Securities *in* F.J. Fabozzi & I.M.Pollack (eds). *The Handbook of Fixed Income Securities.* Dow-Jones Irwin, Homewood, Ill. 1983.
M.A. Smilow. The Move towards Mortgage Securitization. *Mortgage Banker,* New York, December 1983.

Government securities dealers. A US term for a group of firms, including a few large banks with their own dealer departments as well as non-bank dealers, which operates principally in New York. These firms typically finance large inventories of Government stocks via borrowing from banks and corporations.
Bibliography: T.Q. Cook & B.J. Summers (eds). *Instruments of the Money Market.* Federal Reserve Bank of Richmond, Virginia, 1981.
P. Meek. *US Monetary Policy and Financial Markets.* Federal Reserve Bank of New York, 1982.

grace period. The period allowed in a loan schedule during which repayments of loan principal need not be made. For example, a seven-year loan which has a three-year grace period would have to be repaid during the last four years of its life.

Grain and Feed Trade Association (of the UK). Founded in 1973 by an amalgamation between the London Corn Trade Association and the London Cattle Food Trade Asso010n. Its members consist of manufacturers (flour millers etc.), shippers, and brokers who can intermediate between shippers and manufacturers. It supervises the LONDON GRAIN FUTURES MARKET.
Bibliography: *GAFTA Today.* Grain and Feed Trade Association, London, n.d.

green currency. A notional currency used in the Common Agricultural Policy (CAP) of the EUROPEAN COMMUNITIES. The CAP aims to keep agricultural prices at the same level throughout the EEC to ensure a unified market. Because there are different domestic currencies in different member countries, exchange rate changes have to be offset in order to achieve this objective. The prices are fixed in EEC UNITS OF ACCOUNT and the equivalent in members' currencies is calculated by applying the rate of exchange between the unit of account and the domestic currency. This rate is known as the 'green rate' or 'reference rate', or the value of the 'green currency'. The difference between the green rate and the actual market rate is compensated for by MONETARY COMPENSATORY AMOUNTS.
Bibliography: R.W. Irving & H.A. Fearn. *Green Money and the Common Agricultural Policy.* Centre for European Agricultural Studies, Wye College, Ashford, Kent, UK.
Annual Reports of the European Communities.
J.K. Walmsley. *The Foreign Exchange Handbook.* John Wiley & Sons, New York, 1983.

green shoe provision. US term for an UNDERWRITING technique. Underwriters of a new issue may, anticipating customer cancellations, seek to sell more than the amount of securities offered. In order to do so while reducing their risk, they may obtain from the issuer a 'green shoe' provision – an over-allotment option. Then if the cancell-

ations do not occur, the underwriters can buy more securities from the issuer. Reputedly so-called because the technique was first used in an issue by the Green Shoe Company.
Bibliography: K.D. Brody *et al*. The Revival of Equity Financing *in* R.H. Darrow & R.H. Mestres (eds).
Creative Financing in the 1980s. Practising Law Institute, New York, 1983.

grey market. EUROBOND market term for the practice of trading in bonds before the final ALLOTMENTS of the bond have been made and the issue formally released into the SECONDARY MARKET. Compare WHEN ISSUED.
Bibliography: T. Anderson. How the Grey Market became Respectable. *Euromoney,* London, May 1982.

gross domestic product. Total value of a country's output, income or expenditure produced within the country's physical borders.
Bibliography: Central Statistical Office. *The National Accounts: A Short Guide*. HMSO, London 1981.
P. A. Samuelson. *Economics*. McGraw-Hill, New York, 1983.

gross loan. Under the terms of a gross loan, the borrower pays withholding tax to his tax authorities, while paying lenders the gross amount of the interest due. At the same time, the lender is able to claim compensation from its tax authority for the withholding tax paid. For example in 1980 Finasa went to the syndicated credit market for $200 million on the basis that it would pay Mexican withholding tax but lenders would receive credit for the withholding tax paid. Compare TAX SPARING.

gross national product. Gross domestic product plus 'factor income from abroad'– income earned from investment or work abroad.
Bibliography: Central Statistical Office. *The National Accounts: A Short Guide*. HMSO, London 1981.
P.A. Samuelson. *Economics*. McGraw-Hill, New York, 1983.

gross redemption yield. *See* GROSS YIELD TO REDEMPTION.

gross registered tonnage. The tonnage of a ship as registered; it is calculated not on weight but by cubic capacity (100 cu. ft.= 1 registered ton). *See* NET REGISTERED TONNAGE.

gross spread. US securities market term for the dollar difference between the price which the issuing company receives for its securities and the price which the public pays for those securities. The sum of the SELLING CONCESSION, MANAGEMENT FEE and the UNDERWRITING FEE equals the gross spread.
Bibliography: F.G. Fisher. *International Bonds*. Euromoney Publications, London, 1981.

gross yield. Rate of return on a security before tax. If the stock has no redemption date, it is identical to the FLAT YIELD.
Bibliography: P.Phillips.*Inside the Gilt-edged Market*. Woodhead-Faulkner,Cambridge, 1984.

gross yield to redemption. UK term for the INTEREST YIELD on a security plus the annual capital gain if the security is held to REDEMPTION. Tax on income or capital gain is ignored. The formula is laid out under REDEMPTION YIELD. The formula states that the price equals the value at redemption, plus the value of future interest payments, all discounted semi-annually at half the gross yield to redemption (to take account of the payment of interest twice yearly).
Bibliography: P. Phillips. *Inside the Gilt-edged Market*. Woodhead-Faulkner, Cambridge, UK, 1984.

grossed-up net redemption yield. UK term for the NET REDEMPTION YIELD on a security, divided by the proportion of marginal income retained by the investor after tax. The concept's function is to establish a basis of comparison between different investments. Thus if I hold a stock giving me a 6.5% net redemption yield, and my marginal tax rate is 35%, the grossed-up net redemption yield is 10% and this tells me that if I were to switch into a security with no capital gain on redemption I would need an INTEREST YIELD of 10% to match my present return.

Bibliography: P. Phillips. *Inside the Gilt-edged Market*. Woodhead-Faulkner, Cambridge, UK, 1984.

Group of 10. The major industrial countries involved in the GLOBAL ARRANGEMENTS TO BORROW and other financial arrangements. Inevitably, there are really 11, since Switzerland is an informal member of the group. The members are: US, Canada, Japan, Sweden, UK, Germany, France, Italy, Belgium and the Netherlands.

Bibliography: *IMF Annual Report*, Washington DC, 1983.

Group of 24. The countries chosen by the GROUP OF 77 to discuss international monetary affairs in the context of the 1971-5 debate on international monetary reform.

Group of 77. This group has grown to over 120 members. It consists of developing countries and was formed during the UNCTAD negotiations to provide a coherent developing country view.

group sale. US securities market term for a sale of securities shared pro rata by every member of the selling syndicate (as opposed to a designated sale where only certain members participate).

GSP. *See* GENERALIZED SCHEME OF PREFERENCES.

GTC. *See* GOOD TILL CANCELLED.

H

Hague Rules. The International Convention for the unification of Certain Rules of Law relating to Bills of Lading (1924). Now amended to Hague-Visby Rules. They were embodied into UK law by the Carriage of Goods by Sea Acts 1924 and 1971. Compare HAMBURG RULES.
Bibliography: A. Diamond. The Hague-Visby rules. *Lloyd's Maritime and Commercial Law Quarterly*. UK, May 1978;
C.M. Schmitthoff. *Export Trade*. Stevens & Sons, London 1980.
W.E. Astle. *The Hamburg Rules*. Fairplay Publications, London 1981.

Hague-Visby Rules. *See* HAGUE RULES.

haircut finance. US term for a borrowing made against securities as collateral, up to e.g. 80% of the value of the securities. So-called because the 20% is 'trimmed off the top'.
Bibliography: M. Stigum. *The Money Market*. Dow-Jones Irwin, Homewood, Ill., 1983.

half-life. US term for time that must elapse until half the principal amount of a block of bonds has been redeemed (via sinking fund or other process).

Hamburg Rules. The United Nations Convention on the Carriage of Goods by Sea, 1978. Modified rules on carriage of goods by sea and included uniform limits on the liability of carriage in respect of loss or damage to goods.
Bibliography: W.E. Astle. *The Hamburg Rules*. Fairplay Publications, London 1981.
C.M. Schmitthoff. New Rules Relating to Bills of Lading. *Export*. London, May 1978.

handle. US securities market term. The whole-dollar price of a bid or offer is referred to as the handle. For example, if a security is quoted 101-10 bid and 101-11 offer, 101 is the handle. Traders will often quote omitting the handle. Compare BIG FIGURE.

hard currency. A currency whose value is expected to remain stable or increase in terms of other currencies; alternatively, a freely convertible currency may be referred to as 'hard'.
Bibliography: B. Brown. *Money Hard and Soft*. Macmillan, London, 1978.

head and shoulders. Term of TECHNICAL ANALYSIS referring to a situation where a commodity or financial instrument's price has formed an initial peak, followed by a higher peak, and then a lower one. It is usually taken to mean that the price will now fall.
Bibliography: C.W.J. Granger (ed.). *Trading in Commodities*. Woodhead-Faulkner, Cambridge, UK, 1983.
P.J. Kaufman (ed.). *Technical Analysis in Commodities*. John Wiley & Sons, New York, 1980.

hedge clause. US term for a disclaimer that disavows legal responsibility for the accuracy of information from outside sources, e.g. in a market newsletter or PLACEMENT MEMORANDUM.

hedge ratio. (1) Another term for the DELTA – the ratio of the movement in an option's price to the underlying instrument's price.
Bibliography: L.G. McMillan. *Options as a Strategic Investment*. New York Institute of Finance, 1980.
(2) In the futures markets it is sometimes necessary to carry out a WEIGHTED HEDGE because the instrument being hedged does not exactly match the FINANCIAL FUTURE being used to make the hedge. E.g. one might be hedging a position in a one-year CD with the 90-day CD contract, in which case

one would need to hedge with four times the nominal amount of the CD futures: the hedge ratio would be four to one.

Bibliography: J.K. Walmsley. *The Foreign Exchange Handbook.* John Wiley & Sons, New York, 1983.

N.H. Rothstein & J.M. Little. *The Handbook of Financial Futures.* McGraw-Hill, New York, 1984.

hedging. This term means matching a holding of physical stocks of a commodity with an equal and opposite position in the futures markets. By extension, it can be applied to forward cover in foreign exchange or to the matching of assets/liabilities by currencies. A simple hedge might involve a cocoa manufacturer who requires (is short of) 100 tons of cocoa for the next month's production. This short position could be matched by buying 100 tons for delivery next month. Thus the purchase price for the cocoa is fixed, and pricing and production can be planned accordingly.

Bibliography: C.W.J. Granger (ed.). *Trading in Commodities.* Woodhead-Faulkner, Cambridge UK, 1983.

N.H. Rothstein & J.M. Little. *The Financial Futures Handbook.* McGraw-Hill, New York, 1984.

'hell-or-high-water' contract. *See* "TAKE-OR-PAY" CONTRACT.

Hermes Kreditversicherungs-AG. Hermes is a private West German company which is entrusted together with TREUARBEIT with the management of the official export credit insurance scheme. It insures political, commercial and some foreign exchange risks. Its permitted business volume is controlled by Parliament.

Bibliography: *The Export Credit Financing Systems in OECD Countries.* Organization for Economic Cooperation and Development, Paris, 1982.

Herstatt. The ID Herstatt Bank collapsed in June 1974 as the result of very large foreign exchange losses. The Bundesbank closed the bank during New York trading hours. Thus banks found they had delivered foreign currency to Herstatt, but had not received the corresponding dollar payment to close the deal. This caused problems, and the Herstatt collapse led to a general strengthening of controls on dealing imposed by central banks and commercial bank managements. Compare CAPITAL RISK; DELIVERY RISK.

high-powered money. The sum of cash (i.e. notes and coin) in circulation plus required reserves held by commercial banks at the central bank, also known as the MONETARY BASE. Control of high-powered money can be a means of controlling the money supply. Compare MONETARY BASE.

Bibliography: C.A.E. Goodhart. *Monetary Theory and Practice.* Macmillan, London, 1984.

Bank for International Settlements (ed.) *The Monetary Base Approach to Monetary Control.* Basle, Switzerland, 1980.

HKIBOR. *See* HONG KONG INTER-BANK OFFERED RATE.

Hong Kong inter-bank offered rate. The Hong Kong equivalent of LIBOR – the rate at which deposits are offered to prime banks in Hong Kong. See also ADIBOR, MIBOR, KIBOR, SIBOR.

honour policies. Insurance policies which have no legal status. Such policies are issued where the assured has an INSURABLE INTEREST but this interest is difficult to define.

Bibliography: V. Dover. *A Handbook to Marine Insurance.* Revised and edited R.H. Brown. Witherby & Co., London, 1975.

horizontal spread. An OPTIONS market strategy which involves buying one option while selling another option on the same stock, with a different expiration date, but with the same STRIKING price. For example, the investor could establish a spread on IBM by buying in September a January 45 call for 5 and simultaneously writing an October 45 call for 3. If the price remains steady then the October call will expire worthless, and the investor will retain the premium of 3; then the January call can be sold: it will sell for less since its TIME VALUE will have deteriorated, but relatively slowly to begin with, so that in October the January option might still be selling for, say, 4. In this case the investor would have realized a net profit of 2: the initial October premium of 3, less the purchase price of the January call of 5, plus the resale price of the January call of 4.

Bibliography: L.G. McMillan. *Options as a Strategic Investment.* New York Institute of Finance, New York, 1980.

hot money. Short-term international capital movements, motivated by interest rate differentials or revaluation hopes/devaluation fears.

hots. Treasury bills in the UK are said to be 'hot' on the day they are issued with their full term run (hot off the press).

housepaper. A commercial bill of exchange drawn and accepted by companies in the same group, e.g. drawn by a subsidiary and accepted by its parent company.

Bibliography: Gillett Brothers Discount Company, *The Bill on London.* Methuen & Co., London, 1976.

hull. A marine insurance term for the basic body of a ship (as distinct from its machinery or cargo).

Bibliography: V. Dover. *A Handbook to Marine Insurance.* Revised and edited R. H. Brown. Witherby & Co., London, 1975.

hyperinflation. A situation occuring when the rate of increase in prices becomes very rapid and self-sustaining. The point at which inflation passes into hyperinflation is open to dispute and is ultimately determined by empirical definition; the classic article by Cagan defines it as starting in the month when the rise in prices exceeds 50% and ending the month before it drops below 50% and stays below it for at least 12 months.

Bibliography: P. Cagan. The monetary dynamics of hyperinflation *in* M. Friedman (ed.). *Studies in the Quantity Theory of Money.* University of Chicago Press, 1956.

hypothecation. (1) In general, the term refers to the act of taking a charge over property, where neither ownership nor possession pass to the creditor.

(2) The term is mostly used to refer to the hypothecation of maritime property (ship, cargo, FREIGHT).

Bibliography: H. C. Gutteridge & M. Megrah. *The Law of Bankers' Commercial Credits.* Europa Publications, London 1979.

I

IADB *See* INTER-AMERICAN DEVELOPMENT BANK.

IBEC. *See* INTERNATIONAL BANK FOR ECONOMIC CO-OPERATION.

IBELs. *See* INTEREST-BEARING ELIGIBLE LIABILITIES.

IBRD. Initials of the 'International Bank for Reconstruction and Development' now known as the WORLD BANK.

ICSID. *See* INTERNATIONAL CENTRE FOR THE SETTLEMENT OF INVESTMENT DISPUTES.

IET. Abbreviation for INTEREST EQUALIZATION TAX.

ILU. *See* INSTITUTE OF LONDON UNDERWRITERS.

IMF. *See* INTERNATIONAL MONETARY FUND.

IMM. *See* INTERNATIONAL MONETARY MARKET: INTERNATIONAL MONEY MANAGEMENT.

immunization. A BOND market term for a technique which aims to insulate bond portfolios from interest rate risk over a defined time-horizon. By targeting the DURATION of the portfolio, income effects and capital gain effects of interest rate changes are made to offset each other.
Bibliography: P.E. Christensen, S.G. Feldstein, & F.J. Fabozzi. Bond Portfolio Immunization *in* F.J. Fabozzi & I.M. Pollack (eds). *The Handbook of Fixed Income Securities*. Dow-Jones Irwin, Homewood, Ill., 1983.

implied repo rate. A FUTURES market term.

The implied REPO rate measures the time value of money for the period between the CASH and futures market settlement dates. For example, a trader has the choice of buying an ounce of gold for cash today at $350, or of buying an ounce for delivery in a year's time at $385. Then the implied repo rate is 10%, since this is the annual financing cost that makes him indifferent between the two choices.
Bibliography: N.H. Rothstein & J.M. Little. *The Handbook of Financial Futures*. McGraw-Hill, New York, 1984.

incertain. French foreign exchange term for DIRECT QUOTATION.

inchoate. A BILL OF EXCHANGE which has not yet been fully completed – e.g. the date or amount have not yet been filled in – is referred to as inchoate.
Bibliography: A. Watson. *Finance of International Trade*. Institute of Bankers, London, 1981.

income bonds. US term for bonds which are guaranteed as to principal but which have interest payments as a contingent obligation, which are required only if earned and then assented to by the board of directors. Failure to pay interest does not constitute default. Income bonds trade FLAT.
Bibliography: F.J. Fabozzi & H.C. Sauvain. Corporate Bonds *in* F.J. Fabozzi & I.M. Pollack (eds). *The Handbook of Fixed Income Securities*. Dow-Jones Irwin, Homewood Ill., 1983.

income yield. UK term for the return during the next 12 months in interest payments on a security. Defined as the COUPON, divided by the price. The price includes accrued interest – excluding accrued interest gives us the INTEREST YIELD – and the yield takes no account of tax or of capital gain on redemption. (Compare GROSS YIELD TO REDEMP-

TION; NET YIELD TO REDEMPTION; YIELD TO CALL; YIELD TO REDEMPTION).
Bibliography: D. O'Shea. *Investing for Beginners*. Financial Times Business Information, London, 1984.

incoterms. A brochure issued by the INTERNATIONAL CHAMBER OF COMMERCE defining contract terms in international trade.
Bibliography: *Incoterms* International Chamber of Commerce Brochure no. 350, Paris 1980.

inconvertibility. *See* CONVERTIBLE

indenture. The contract that specifies legal obligations of the issuer of a security with respect to the securities, and the duties and responsibilities of the trustee.
Bibliography: F.J. Fabozzi & H.C. Sauvain. Corporate Bonds *in* F.J. Fabozzi & I.M. Pollack (eds). *The Handbook of Fixed Income Securities*. Dow-Jones Irwin, Homewood Ill., 1983.
F.G. Fisher. *International Bonds*. Euromoney Publications, London, 1982.

indexation. *See* INDEX-LINKING; REVALORIZATION.

index-linking. The process of linking wages, prices, interest rates or loan values to an index, usually of prices, though in the case of pensions the chosen index may be wages or earnings. It has been very extensively applied in Brazil, and partially used in Finland, the UK, the US, France, Belgium and several other countries. The usual objection to it is that it institutionalizes inflation; also it is no more equitable than inflation unless it is applied universally to all stocks and flows of money. Other forms of indexation have also been seen, e.g. the gold-indexed bond issued by Refinemet in 1981, the issue of $25 million silver indexed bonds by Sunshine Mining Co. in 1980, and the earlier issue by the Mexican government of bonds linked to the price of oil.
Bibliography: OECD *Government Debt Management* Paris, 1983.
F.G. Fisher. *International Bonds*. Euromoney Publications, London, 1981.

indicator. (1) Any number or statistic giving information about the state of the economy, e.g. the UK and US governments publish an index of 'leading indicators' which are intended to provide advance information about economic activity.

(2) In the UK BULLDOG BOND market, the term indicator is used to refer to the underlying GILT-EDGED stock used as the basis for pricing the bond. For example, the October 1982 £75 million issue for the EUROPEAN INVESTMENT BANK was priced to yield 1% over the average GROSS REDEMPTION YIELD of its indicators, the 11.5% Treasuries 2001/04, the 12.5% Treasuries 2003/05 and 11.75% Treasuries 2003/07.
Bibliography: de Zoete & Bevan. *The Bulldog Bond Market*. London, 1983.

indirect help. If there is a shortage of money in the UK DISCOUNT MARKET, the Bank of England, acting through its bill-broker, buys Treasury bills from the banks for cash; the latter then lends the money to the discount houses, or else buy Treasury bills from the houses. This is known as 'indirect help'.
Bibliography: E.R. Shaw. *The London Money Market*. Heinemann, London, 1983.

indirect quotation. Quotation of fixed units of domestic currency in variable units of foreign currency (e.g. in the UK L1=$y). Compare DIRECT QUOTATION.

indorsement. *See* ENDORSEMENT.

Industrial Revenue Bonds (IRB). A US term for bonds issued by a municipality to finance a project (especially one being leased to a private corporation) that has some community value, such as pollution control, recreation facilities or transportation. The bond is secured by the corporation's credit, and the corporation takes the responsibility of paying the interest on the bond. IRBs are tax-exempt in that holders are allowed to ignore income for US income tax purposes. The borrower may still deduct interest for tax

purposes. Corporate IRBs outstanding in 1983 totalled $66 billion.
Bibliography: *Fundamentals of Municipal Bonds*. Public Securities Association, New York, 1981.

Industrie Clearing. German term for the inter-company money market that has existed for many years whereby major corporations lent directly to each other. Now becoming more integrated into the money markets generally.
Bibliography: G. Dufey & E. Krishnan. West Germany: Banking, Money and Bond Markets *in* A.M. George & I.H. Giddy. *International Finance Handbook*. John Wiley & Sons, New York, 1983.
Economists Advisory Group. *The British and German Banking System: a Comparative Study*. Anglo-German Foundation, London, 1981.

ineligible bills. In the UK, bills which are not eligible for rediscount at the Bank of England. A parallel term is used in the US ACCEPTANCE market, where a bank which sells an ineligible bill is required to hold RESERVES against it.
Bibliography: E.R. Shaw. *The London Money Market*. Heinemann, London 1984.
T.Q. Cook & B.J. Summers (eds). *Instruments of the Money Market* Federal Reserve Bank of Virginia, 1981.

initial margin. A FUTURES market term for the MARGIN which must be deposited when entering into a contract. For example, a trader buying one contract for TREASURY BONDS on the Chicago market might be required to deposit $2,000 initial margin (rather than the full purchase price)
Bibliography: N.H. Rothstein & J.M. Little. *The Handbook of Financial Futures*.McGraw-Hill, New York, 1984.

initial public offering. US term for the public issue of shares (or debt) by a previously unquoted company. These have been particularly important for new high-technology companies.
Bibliography: K.D. Brody *et al*. The Revival of Equity Finance *in* P.H. Darrow & R.A. Mestres (eds). *Creative Financing in the 1980s*. Practising Law Institute, New York, 1983.
P.A. Bernard. Common Stock – New Issues *in*

M.E. Blume & J.P. Friedman. *Encyclopaedia of Investments*. Warren, Gorham & Lamont, New York, 1982.

Instinet. A US computerized system for trading stocks. Instinet handles computer based (rather than telephone/telex) trading in 3,500 stocks in the US and hopes to expand overseas.
Bibliography: R. Winder. The Final Days of the Trading Floor. *Euromoney*, London, October 1984.

Institute of London Underwriters (ILU). An association of marine insurance companies in London, the ILU is an important forum for the discussion of marine insurance problems on the national or international plane. Standard marine insurance clauses issued under its authority are known as 'Institute' clauses. In alliance with LLOYD'S and Liverpool underwriters, the ILU maintains certain specialist sub-committees, of which perhaps the most important is the JOINT HULL COMMITTEE.
Bibliography: H.C. Cockerell. *Lloyd's of London: A Portrait*. Woodhead-Faulkner, Cambridge, UK/ Dow-Jones Irwin, Homewood, Ill., 1984.

institutional pot. US term for that percentage (often 20%) of an offering of a security which is set aside by the managers for large institutional orders.
Bibliography: L.M. Loll & J.G. Buckley. *The Over-the-Counter Securities Markets*. Prentice-Hall, NJ, 1981.

insurable interest. So far as concerns marine insurance, the UK Marine Insurance Act of 1906 states '(1)...every person has an insurable interest who is interested in a marine adventure.

(2) In particular, a person is interested in a marine adventure where he stands in any legal or equitable relation to the adventure or to any insurable property at risk therein, in consequence of which he may benefit by the safety or due arrival of insurable property, or may be prejudiced by its loss, or damage thereto, or by the detention thereof, or may incur liability in respect thereof.'

Bibliography: R.J. Lambeth *Templeman on Marine Insurance*. Macdonald & Evans, UK, 1981.

Inter-American Development Bank (IADB). Formed in 1959, the IADB had 41 members at the end of 1977, including Japan and 14 European countries. Its headquarters are in Washington D.C. Its functions are to provide funds for the development of Central and Latin America. Compare AFRICAN DEVELOPMENT BANK, ASIAN DEVELOPMENT BANK, WORLD BANK.

Bibliography: J. White. *Regional Development Banks*. Praeger, New York, 1972.
IADB Annual Reports, Washington DC,.
D. Sassoon (ed.). *Bidding for Projects Financed by International Lending Agencies*. Gower Press, UK, 1982.

Inter-Arab Investment Guarantee Corporation (IAIGC) Founded in 1972 with headquarters in Kuwait, the IAIGC's objectives are to promote the transfer of capital within the Arab region, in particular by providing insurance coverage for investments with substantial Arab equity against losses resulting from non-commercial risks. Members holding 5% include Algeria, Egypt, Iraq, Jordan, Lebanon, Mauritania, Morocco, Qatar, Sudan, Syria, Tunisia, United Arab Emirates and Yemen Arab Republic. Kuwait and Libya hold 10%. Saudi Arabia joined in 1977.

Bibliography: T. Scharf. *Trilateral Cooperation, Vol. I: Arab Development Funds and Banks*. OECD Development Centre Studies, OECD, Paris, 1978.

inter-bank. Usually refers to a market (such as that for foreign exchange or wholesale money) which is confined to the banks: it is said to be an inter-bank market. The most important internationally of these are in foreign exchange and in EURODOLLARS, the latter running to an estimated volume of $1,000 billion by 1983. The inter-bank market plays an essential part in transmitting local pressures in one area of the market (be it foreign exchange or Eurodollar) into a wider framework capable of easing the pressure. Conversely, any sudden shrinkage of the market makes the international financial structure more vulnerable, as was seen after the collapse of Bank Herstatt in 1974 and the Mexican and other LDC debt crises of 1982-4.

Bibliography: *The International Interbank Market*. BIS Economic Papers no.8, Bank for International Settlements, Basle, July 1983.
G.G. Johnson & R.K. Abrams. *Aspects of the International Banking Safety Net*. IMF Occasional Paper no. 17, Washington DC, 1983.
J.K. Walmsley. Eurocurrency Dealing *in* A.M. George & I.H. Giddy. *International Finance Handbook*. John Wiley & Sons, New York, 1983.
N. Osborn. The Surprising Strength of the Interbank Market. *Institutional Investor*, New York, July 1983.

inter-company market. The market for borrowing and lending of funds between non-banking companies, without the intervention of banks. In the UK this market has had a rather sporadic existence in the shadow of official discouragement; its main periods of activity have been during credit squeezes. The inter-company market as such is not well-developed in the UK or US, though it is of some long standing in Germany under the name of INDUSTRIE CLEARING.

Bibliography: E.R. Shaw. *The London Money Market*. Heinemann, London, 1983.

Interdistrict Settlement Fund. In the US the 12 FEDERAL RESERVE BANKS maintain a GOLD CERTIFICATE fund called the Interdistrict Settlement Fund. It is used to settle the daily balances owed by the district Federal Reserve Banks to each other. The fund settles amounts due by increasing or decreasing the gold certificate balances held by each Reserve Bank.

Bibliography: *The Federal Reserve System: Purposes and Functions*. Board of Governors of the Federal Reserve System, Washington DC, 1974.

interest equalization tax. The IET was a tax on foreign borrowing imposed by the US in 1963. It contributed greatly to the growth of the EUROMARKETS along with REGULATION Q. It was reduced to zero in 1974 and subsequently lapsed.

Bibliography: F.G. Fisher. *International Bonds.* Euromoney Publications, London, 1981.

interest parity. The interest parity theory states that if there are two countries with a financial instrument which is identical in risk and maturity (e.g. UK and US three-month Treasury bills) then if there is a difference in the interest rate on the instrument, that difference will tend to be reflected in the PREMIUM or DISCOUNT for the relevant forward exchange rate. The interest parity theory is controversial in academic circles. Clearly it cannot be exact because of dealing costs, and because there is only one forward rate while there are a number of comparable financial instruments which may be affected by different factors - Eurocurrency deposits, local authority deposits, Treasury bills etc. Also in a crisis the forward margin might determine the rate of interest rather than the other way around.

Bibliography: J.K. Walmsley. *The Foreign Exchange Handbook.* John Wiley & Sons, New York, 1983.

interest period. A ROLL-OVER credit may be made available to a borrower on the understanding that he may choose to borrow for periods varying typically between one month and 12 months. Such a period is known as an interest period (because the rate of interest payable depends on the period).
Bibliography: P. Wood. *Law and Practice of International Finance.* Sweet & Maxwell, London, 1980.

interest rate swap. A technique developed in 1981/2, the interest rate swap consists of an agreement to exchange interest payments (see diagram). Its original rationale was to allow weaker borrowers, who had difficulty in accessing the BOND markets, to take on the interest obligations of first-class bond issuers,

XYZ Corp. has favourable access to the bond market but does not need fixed rate money. So it raises money on (say) a seven year bond at 11.5%. Then it executes a swap with a bank, who pay it 11.75%. In exchange, XYZ pays Libor. Net cost to XYZ is 6 month Libor less ¼%.

ABC Corp. does not have favourable access to the bond market and would have to pay 13% to access the market. It borrows floating rate money at 6 month Libor plus ½% and executes a swap with the bank. It pays 12% and receives Libor. Net cost to ABC is 12.5%.

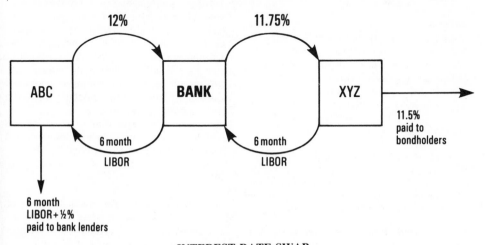

INTEREST RATE SWAP

in exchange for paying them LIBOR. They thus achieved cheaper access to the long term markets, while the first-class borrower paid some rate below Libor for his funding (rather than Libor plus some interest rate spread, as would be normal). The technique has since found widespread applications in many other fields, unconnected with the bond market.

Bibliography: J.K. Walmsley. Understanding Interest Rate Swaps. *The Banker's Magazine*. New York, July/August 1984.
Swaps: The Way to Any Market. *Euromoney*. London, November, 1983.

interest yield. UK term for the annual return in interest or dividend payments on £1 invested. It is defined as the nominal rate of interest or dividend, divided by the price (the latter being adjusted to exclude accrued interest or dividend on the stock). Compare GROSS REDEMPTION YIELD; INCOME YIELD; YIELD.

Bibliography: D. O'Shea. *Investment for Beginners*. Financial Times Business Information, London, 1984.

interest yield equivalent. US term for a measurement of the rate of return on a security sold on a discount basis, that assumes actual days to maturity and a 360-day year. The formula is laid out under DISCOUNT-TO-YIELD.

intermediation. Term for the process whereby a financial institution interposes its name and trustworthiness between a lender and a borrower. For example, instead of my buying a company's security I may prefer to deposit funds with a bank - reducing my risk - which in turn will invest the funds in the security. UNIT TRUSTS are also undertaking intermediation in a similar fashion. DISINTERMEDIATION takes place when relative interest rates make this process unattractive.

Bibliography: C.A.E. Goodhart. *Monetary Theory and Practice*. Macmillan, London, 1984.
S.K. Cooper & D.R. Fraser. *The Financial Markets* Addison-Wesley, Reading, Mass. 1982.

International Bank for Economic Co-operation. Located in Moscow, founded in 1964, IBEC is principally concerned with the organization and execution of payments in TRANSFERABLE ROUBLES between members of COMECON although membership is open to non-Comecon countries. Compare INTERNATIONAL INVESTMENT BANK.

Bibliography: A. Zwass. *Money Banking and Credit in the Soviet Union and Eastern Europe*. Macmillan, UK/M.E. Sharpe, USA, 1979.
A.I. MacBean & P.N. Snowden. *International Institutions in Trade and Finance*. George Allen & Unwin, London 1981.

International Bank for Reconstruction and Development. *See* WORLD BANK.

international banking facility. Set up in 1981, the IBFs permitted EURODOLLAR-style international banking in the United States. Banks were allowed to open separate sets of accounts for deposit business of an international kind: these deposits were exempt from reserve requirements.

Bibliography: J. K. Walmsley. International Banking Facilities – we have lift-off. *The Banker*, London, February 1982.
M. Stigum. *The Money Market*. Dow-Jones Irwin, Homewood, Ill., 1983.

international bonds. A bond issued outside the country of the borrower. International bonds may be divided into EUROBONDS and FOREIGN BONDS. A dollar bond issued in New York by the Norwegian government using a domestic American SYNDICATE would be a traditional or foreign bond (Compare YANKEE BOND). A Eurobond in contrast is usually placed simultaneously with institutions in several countries, none of whose currencies is the currency of issue. Thus, a dollar bond issue by the Norwegian government placed in Frankfurt, London and Zurich in a single placing via an international syndicate would be a Eurobond.

Bibliography: F.G. Fisher. *International Bonds*. Euromoney Publications, London, 1981.

International Centre for the Settlement of Investment Disputes (ICSID). Because of its reputation for impartiality, the WORLD BANK was sometimes approached to mediate between foreign investors and governments. It was therefore decided to set up a separate centre for settling such disputes. The ICSID was created by a 1966 treaty. It is located in the World Bank's headquarters, although it is a legally independent body. A relatively small number of cases have been submitted to ICSID but it has provided a useful option to investors and governments seeking an independent forum for settling disputes.

Bibliography: *The World Bank, IDA & IFC Policies & Operations.* World Bank, Washington DC, 1969.
ICSID Annual Reports.

International Chamber of Commerce. Established in Paris in 1919 this body has 7,500 members in 80 countries (companies, industrial associations, banking bodies and chambers of commerce). It provides an Arbitration Court for settling international business disputes, and is also responsible through its Banking Commission for the UNIFORM CUSTOMS AND PRACTICE FOR DOCUMENTARY CREDITS, UNIFORM RULES ON COLLECTIONS, UNIFORM RULES FOR CONTRACT GUARANTEES, UNIFORM RULES FOR A COMBINED TRANSPORT DOCUMENT and INCOTERMS, a standardized set of international trade terms. Its address is 38 Cours Albert 1er, 75008 Paris.

Bibliography: ICC Annual Reports and Publications.
ICC Arbitration. ICC Brochure no. 301, ICC, Paris 1977.

International Commodities Clearing House. A London company which operates a CLEARING SYSTEM for contracts traded between members of the LONDON INTERNATIONAL FINANCIAL FUTURES EXCHANGE and London commodity markets (cocoa, coffee, rubber, soyabeans, sugar, vegatable oil and wool), as well as for the Sydney Futures Exchange, the Australian Options Market and the Hong Kong Commodity Exchange, and through reciprocal arrangements, in Paris. Formerly it was known as the London Produce Clearing House. It is now owned by the major British clearing banks and Standard Chartered Bank Ltd. Compare FU-

TURES; LONDON COMMODITY EXCHANGE; UNITED TERMINAL SUGAR MARKET ASSOCIATION.

Bibliography: C.W.J. Granger (ed.). *Trading in Commodities.* Woodhead-Faulkner, Cambridge UK, 1983.

international depositary receipts (IDRs). A variation of DEPOSITARY RECEIPTS. IDRs were developed in the early 1970s to help internatonal trading of stocks and shares. The underlying securities are deposited with a bank, or with the bank's custodian in the country of origin. The bank then issues an IDR against them. IDRs are used for transactions outside the US; inside the US, AMERICAN DEPOSITARY RECEIPTS are used. Settlements can be made through EUROCLEAR.

Bibliography: *Depositary Receipts.* Morgan Guaranty Trust Company, New York, n.d.
The Stock Exchange Official Yearbook, Macmillan, London, 1984.

International Development Association. An affiliate of the WORLD BANK founded in 1960, the IDA lends funds to developing countries on noncommercial terms (for example, loans have been made interest-free over a 50-year term). Although legally and financially independent its staff is shared with the World Bank. Its funds are provided by subscriptions from the richer member governments.

Bibliography: *IDA in Retrospect: the First Two Decades of the IDA.* Oxford University Press, 1982.
IDA Annual Reports.

International Federation of Consulting Engineers. An international body (often referred to as FIDIC from its French initials) which has drawn up standard Conditions of for Works of Civil Engineering Construction which are widely used in international PROJECT FINANCE.

Bibliography: D. Sassoon. *Bidding for Projects Funded by International Lending Agencies.* Gower Press, UK, 1982.

International Finance Corporation (IFC). An affiliate of the WORLD BANK.

Founded in 1956, IFC's role is to provide equity and loan finance for private enterprises in developing countries. Finance is provided, broadly speaking, on generous terms but at sufficiently commercial rates for IFC to sell its stake to commercial investors once the project is established.

Bibliography: *The World Bank and the International Finance Corporation.* World Bank, Washington DC,1983.
IFC Annual Reports.

international financial unit. Introduced in 1975 by Crédit Lyonnais the IFU is based on a currency basket of 10 currencies, EEC currencies are weighted 58% and 42% outside currencies. It is not widely used.

Bibliography: J. Aschheim & Y.S. Park. *Artificial Currency Units: The Formation of Functional Currency Areas.* Princeton Essays in International Finance, no. 114, 1976.

International Investment Bank. Based in Moscow, the IIB was founded in 1971 with the goal of partially financing projects within COMECON to 'simulate specialization and the Socialist international division of labour'. Compare INTERNATIONAL BANK FOR ECONOMIC CO-OPERATION. By 1983 the Bank had authorized credits for 83 projects, with a total estimated value of nearly 10 billion transferable roubles.

Bibliography: A. Zwass. *Money Banking and Credit in the Soviet Union and Eastern Europe.* Macmillan, UK/M.E. Sharpe, USA 1979.
Europa Yearbook. Europa Publications, London, annually.

international liquidity. LIQUIDITY capable of being transferred between countries. Usually defined to include gold, convertible foreign exchange, reserve position in the IMF and SDRS. The assets included are restricted to those held by the monetary authorities involved. The term 'international money' has sometimes been used to include private, as well as official, holdings of internationally liquid assets. A broader definition of international liquidity might aim to measure a country's ability to finance a payments deficit without resorting to any adjustment mea-

sures. This might include CONDITIONAL LIQUIDITY and longer-term investments.

Bibliography: R.N. Cooper *et al.* (eds). *The International Monetary System under Flexible Exchange Rates.* Ballinger Publishing Co., Mass., 1982.
J. Williamson (ed.). *IMF Conditionality.* MIT Press, Cambridge Mass, 1983.

International Monetary Fund (IMF). Conceived at BRETTON WOODS and set up in 1947, the IMF acts as a guardian of a code of good behaviour in international finance and to provide international liquidity on a short or medium- term basis to monetary authorities facing balance of payments deficits. It seeks to encourage liberalization of exchange rate practices and of international payments, and publishes an annual yearbook listing the main restrictions in force. Its chief role is as a lender. Its resources are quotas subscribed by its members- 25% of the quota is subscribed in gold, the GOLD TRANCHE. The balance is in the member's own currency. The member may virtually automatically borrow from the IMF an amount equal to its gold tranche. A further amount equal to 25% of the quota- the 'first credit tranche' may be borrowed without difficulty. Further tranches are subject to increasingly stringent requirements. Standby arrangements can be made under which a member receives assurance that during a certain period requests for drawings up to a certain limit will be granted. (Compare EXTENDED FUND FACILITY). In 1963 a new facility for COMPENSATORY FINANCING of temporary export shortfalls was set up, and in 1975 it was enlarged.

Bibliography: A.W. Hooke. *The International Monetary Fund: Its Evolution, Organization and Activities.* IMF Pamphlet no. 37, Washington DC, 1981.
A.I. MacBean & P.N. Snowden. *International Institutions in Trade & Finance.* George Allen & Unwin, London, 1981.
The Financial Structure and Operations of the International Monetary Fund. *Bank of England Quarterly Bulletin,* December 1983.
IMF Annual Reports.

International Monetary Market. A component of the CHICAGO MERCANTILE EX-

CHANGE where FUTURES contracts in foreign currency are traded. These are standardized contracts (as distinct from banks' forward dealings where the amount and maturity are individually agreed) and permit individuals to deal in foreign currency for forward delivery. For example, the standard contract for sterling is £25,000, and contracts are for January delivery, February delivery etc. (Delivery date is the third Wednesday of the month.)

Bibliography: N.H. Rothstein & J.M. Little (eds). *The Financial Futures Handbook*. Dow-Jones Irwin, Homewood, Ill., 1984.
J.K. Walmsley. *The Foreign Exchange Handbook*. John Wiley & Sons, New York, 1983.

international money management. Term for the group of techniques used by firms with multinational cash flows to maximize earnings from interest and exchange rate movements while minimizing exposure to risk. Such techniques can include matching of assets and liabilities by currency, use of LEADS AND LAGS, POOLING of receipts and payments, rapid money transfer systems, etc.

Bibliography: P. Muller (ed.). *Treasury Management* Euromoney Publications, London, 1982.
P.J. Beehler. *Contemporary Cash Management*. John Wiley & Sons, New York, 1983.

intervention. A transaction undertaken by an official monetary agency to manipulate the exchange rate for its currency or the level of its foreign exchange resrves is referred to as intervention. Most major central banks intervene in the foreign exchange markets to provide orderly markets. The only institution which reports on these activities regularly is the Federal Reserve Bank of New York in its quarterly review. (Compare FORWARD EXCHANGE INTERVENTION.) An analogous use of the term is often made in relation to domestic money markets. Compare SUPPORT POINT.

Bibliography: H.W. Mayer. *The Anatomy of Official Exchange-Rate Intervention Systems*. Princeton Essays in International Finance no. 104, 1974.
Intervention, Stabilization and Profits. *Bank of England Quarterly Bulletin*, September 1983.

J.K. Walmsley, *The Foreign Exchange Handbook*. John Wiley & Sons, New York, 1983.

in the box. US securities market jargon meaning that a dealer has a wire receipt for securities, indicating that they have been delivered. A hang-over from the days when Treasury securities were physically delivered and stored in a box.

in-the-money. An OPTIONS market term. A CALL option is in-the-money if the price of the underlying instrument is above the STRIKING PRICE of the option – i.e. if the option is exercised its owner will make a profit. Conversely a PUT is in-the-money if the underlying price is below the option's strike price. Compare INTRINSIC VALUE.

Bibliography: L.G. McMillan. *Options as a Strategic Investment*. New York Institute of Finance, New York, 1980.

intrinsic value. OPTIONS market term for an option which is inherently profitable because it is IN-THE-MONEY. The intrinsic value of an in-the-money CALL is the amount by which the price of the underlying instrument exceeds the STRIKING PRICE of the option. Conversely, for a 'put', it is the amount by which the price of the instrument is below the striking price.

Bibliography: L.G. McMillan. *Options as a Strategic Investment*. New York Institute of Finance, New York, 1980.

introduction. UK Stock Exchange term for a LISTING without the issue of shares. A company which has already issued shares and so does not need new capital, may nevertheless want its stock listed on the Stock Exchange, for purposes of publicity, wider markets for its shares, etc. The majority of London quotations for overseas companies, whose shares are normally widely spread in the country of origin, are by means of introductions.

Bibliography: J. Dundas Hamilton. *Stockbroking Today*. Macmillan, London, 1979.

investment companies. A US term for companies whose sole business is to invest in the securities of other companies, for the benefit of shareholders. US investment companies are normally classified into mutual fund, or OPEN-END FUND and CLOSED-END according to whether the number of out-standing shares is variable (open-end) or fixed (closed-end). They are regulated under the Investment Company Act of 1940. The British equivalents of the open-end and closed-end funds are UNIT TRUSTS and INVESTMENT TRUSTS respectively.

Bibliography: J.C. Bogle. Mutual Funds *in* M.E. Blume & J.P. Friedman. *Encyclopaedia of Investments.* Warren, Gorham & Lamont, New York, 1982.

investment currency. British exchange control device abolished in 1979. Effectively this consisted of a limited pool of funds derived from overseas investments. At times of strong demand, the investment currency premium reached effective rates of 50% +.

Bibliography: B.D. Brown. Exchange restrictions: their implications for portfolio management. *Economic Journal.* UK, September 1977.

investment premium. *See* INVESTMENT CURRENCY.

investment trust. A British limited company, whose function is to invest in other companies or fixed assets. Unlike a UNIT TRUST whose capital may vary, the investment trust's share capital is fixed. The American equivalent is a CLOSED-END FUND. At the end of 1982 there were 185 members of the Association of Investment Trust Companies, managing assets of over £5,500 million.

Bibliography: A.A. Arnaud. *Investment Trusts Explained.* Woodhead-Faulkner, Cambridge, UK, 1983.

invisibles. A term for exports and imports of services as distinct from merchandise (visibles). The UK is a substantial net exporter of invisibles through the City of London, while Germany and Japan, for example, are heavy importers. The US net earnings from invisibles in 1982 were the largest in the world ($47 billion), mainly in the form of income from overseas investments, while the UK ($11 billion) and France ($7 billion) were second and third.

Bibliography: *World Trade in Invisibles.* Committee for Invisible Exports, London, 1984.

invoice. A document giving details of potential or actual sale of goods or services. The following types of invoice are commonly met with in international trade: (i) A proforma invoice is one showing the price and payment terms, together with other relevant details, and inviting the buyer to place an order. Such invoices are often needed to enable the buyer to obtain an import licence or permission to buy foreign exchange. (ii) A commercial invoice is a request for payment for goods or services sold and normally includes a description of the goods, price, settlement terms and shipment details. (iii) Consular invoices are required by some countries; these have normally to be obtained by the exporter from the Embassy of the importer's country. They will stamp the invoice, which is often used for determining import duty and generally checking that the transaction is in order. (iv) Legalized invoices are commercial invoices presented to the importer's Embassy in the exporter's country for stamping. (v) Certified invoices are usually commercial invoices carrying special clauses certifying that particular conditions have been complied with.

Bibliography: A. Watson. *Finance of International Trade.* Institute of Bankers, London, 1981.
G. Whitehead. *Elements of Overseas Trade.* Croner Publications, UK, 1977.

inward collection. Term for the collection of payment on a bill from a firm in the country of the bank to whom the bill is sent. E.g. in the UK it would refer to a bill drawn on a UK firm. Compare COLLECTING BANK; OUTWARD COLLECTION.

irrevocable documentary credit. A DOCUMENTARY CREDIT is an instrument by which a bank undertakes to pay a seller for his goods, subject to the conditions prescribed by the credit. An irrevocable credit is one where the bank issuing the credit gives an irrevocable undertaking to pay the seller provided the conditions are met. (If the credit is revocable it can be cancelled at any time without consulting the seller.)

Bibliography: *Uniform Customs & Practice for Documentary Credits.* International Chamber of Commerce Brochure no. 290, Paris, 1974.
A. Watson. *Finance of International Trade.* Institute of Bankers, London, 1981.

Islamic Development Bank. Founded in 1974 and headquartered in Jeddah, the IDB's function is to assist in the financing of the development of countries with substantial Islamic populations. Financial operations began in 1976. It now has 42 members. The Bank adheres to the Koranic principle forbidding usury and does not grant loans for interest. It prefers to take an equity stake in a project, or lend interest-free.

Bibliography: M. Avhilli & M. Khaldi (eds). *The role of the Arab Development Funds in the World Economy.* Macmillan, London/St. Martin's Press, New York, 1984

Islamic dinar. One Islamic dinar is equal to one SPECIAL DRAWING RIGHT. The dinar is used for accounting purposes in certain Islamic financial institutions.

issued capital (stock). The amount of a company's capital which has actually been issued (as against the amount which the company has been authorized by its members to issue). Compare PAID-UP CAPITAL.

issue price. The price at which shares or bonds are sold on issue. Thus a company may issue shares with a nominal value of 25p at an issue price of 40p or a bond which is repayable at £100 may be issued at £98.

Bibliography: J. Dundas Hamilton. *Stockbroking Today.* Macmillan, London, 1979.
F.G. Fisher. *International Bonds.* Euromoney Publications, London 1982.

issuing bank. A term employed with reference to DOCUMENTARY CREDITS. It denotes the bank which issues a documentary credit, on behalf of the buyer, in favour of the beneficiary. The sequence of events is that the buyer, or importer, approaches his bank, asking it to issue the credit. The issuing bank issues a credit in favour of the exporter, who is advised through a bank in his country (the ADVISING BANK).

Bibliography: A. Watson. *Finance of International Trade.* Insitute of Bankers, London, 1981.
Uniform Customs and Practice for Documentary Credits. International Chamber of Commerce Brochure no. 290, Paris 1975.

Istituto Centrale per Credito a Medio Termine. Italian official agency, founded in 1952, which pays interest rebates on or refinances export credits granted by Italian banks. It supports export credits with a term of over 18 months. Its funds are provided by the Italian Treasury and it also has power to borrow from Italian or foreign institutions.

Bibliography: *The Export Credit Financing Systems in OECD Member Countries.* Organization for Economic Cooperation & Development, Paris, 1982.

J

J-curve. A term describing the expected effect of a devaluation on a country's trade balance. Following a devaluation the volume of imports and exports will not change immediately, but it will after a lag. Thus the import bill rises because foreign goods are more expensive and export earnings fall since export prices are lower in foreign currency terms. Therefore the trade balance worsens initially - the downward curve of the j - to be followed (it is hoped) by an upward curve as trade volumes respond.

Bibliography: S. Carse *et al. The Financing Procedures of British Foreign Trade.* Cambridge University Press, UK, 1980.
W.H. Branson. Economic Structure & Policy for External Balance. *IMF Staff Papers.* IMF, Washington, DC, March 1983.

Jamaica Agreement. The 1976 agreement by the Interim Committee of the INTERNATIONAL MONETARY FUND regarding the Second Amendment to the IMF's Articles of agreement. It legalized floating rates, and abolished PAR VALUES, CENTRAL RATES and the OFFICIAL GOLD PRICE.

Bibliography: J. Gold. *SDRs, Gold and Currencies: Third Survey of New Legal Developments.* IMF Pamphlet no. 26, Washington DC, 1979.
G.N. Halm. *Jamaica and the Par Value System.* Princeton Essays in International Finance no. 120, 1977.

Japanese Long-Term Prime Rate (JLTPR). The rate charged by Japanese banks to their most creditworthy customers for loans of over one year. Typically this rate is 2-3% above the short-term prime rate but it varies. The JLTP rate has been used as a pricing alternative in the EUROMARKETS. For example, in 1984 the BANQUE FRANÇAISE DU COMMERCE EXTERIEUR raised Y25billion for 10 years at 0.1% over the JLTP.

Bibliography: D.L. Allen. Japan: Banking, Money & Bond Markets *in* A.M. George & I.H. Giddy. *International Finance Handbook.* John Wiley & Sons, New York, 1983.
D. Curtin. Zen and the Art of Yen Loan Syndication. *Euromoney,* London, December 1982.

jeopardy clause. A clause in a Eurocurrency agreement specifying that if certain events curtail the lender's activity or the operation of the Euromarkets, other designated actions (such as the substitution of another agreed rate of interest, or the repayment to an affected bank of its portion of the loan) will come into effect. Different names are sometimes given to this clause, e.g. DISASTER CLAUSE, BREAK CLAUSE.

Bibliography: T.H. Donaldson. *Lending in International Commercial Banking* Macmillan, London, 1982.
P. Wood. *Law and Practice of International Finance.* Sweet & Maxwell, London, 1980.

JLTP. *See* JAPANESE LONG TERM PRIME RATE.

job. (1) In the London stock market, a person or firm who deals in stock as a principal rather than as a BROKER, is called a jobber. Stock-jobbers used not to be allowed to deal with the public, a function reserved to stockbrokers, although recent changes in the rules have broken down this distinction.

Bibliography: J. Dundas Hamilton. *Stockbroking Today.* Macmillan, London, 1979.

(2) The term may be used by extension in the foreign exchange or Eurocurrency market to refer to a bank dealing on its own behalf with other banks, (although the term is not precise).

Joint Hull Committee. A body jointly maintained by Liverpool underwriters, the INSTITUTE OF LONDON UNDERWRITERS and

LLOYD'S. The Joint Hull Committee is responsible for the Joint Hull Understanding, which is a system for maintaining insurance premiums on vessels in accordance with formulae based mainly on past loss experience.

Bibliography: H.C. Cockrell. *Lloyd's of London: a portrait*. Woodhead-Faulkner, Cambridge UK/ Dow-Jones Irwin, Homewood, Ill., 1984.

Joint Hull Understanding *See* JOINT HULL COMMITTEE.

judgment currency clause. A clause in a EUROCREDIT or Eurobond agreement protecting the lenders against any loss arising from the fact that the loan is made in one currency and judgment given by the courts in another. A typical judgment currency clause might read (in part): 'The borrower agrees to indemnify the banks against any loss incurred as a result of any judgment or order being given or made for the payment of any amount due hereunder and such judgment or order being expressed in a currency other than that in which the payment was due hereunder and as a result of any variation having occured in rates of exchange between the date of any amount becoming due hereunder and the date of actual payment thereof.'

Bibliography: P. Wood. *Law and Practice of International Finance*. Sweet & Maxwell, London, 1980.

P. Stansbury. Legal Aspects of Syndicated Euro-currency Lending *in* A.M. George & I.H. Giddy *International Finance Handbook*. John Wiley & Sons, New York, 1983.

jurisdiction risk. (1) In its broad sense jurisdiction risk can arise in any international transactions. For example, in selling goods to a customer from a small provincial town in an underdeveloped country or in dealing with the government of another country there is an inherent risk that the legal officials in that country may not be impartial.

(2) The term refers to the risk inherent in placing funds in a centre where they will be under the jurisdiction of a foreign legal authority, which might become hostile, or which might apply biased legal procedures. An example is placing Communist funds in dollars. Reluctance to incur the jurisdiction risk of New York led to their being placed in London and to the birth of the EURODOLLAR MARKET. Sometimes referred to as 'sovereign risk'.

Bibliography: P. Wood. *Law and Practice of International Finance*. Sweet & Maxwell, London, 1980.

P. Stansbury. Legal Aspects of Syndicated Euro-currency Lending *in* A.M. George & I.H. Giddy *International Finance Handbook*. John Wiley & Sons, New York, 1983.

(3) Refers to the risk in making a loan subject to the laws of another country. For example, certain Latin American countries have traditionally insisted on the Calvo doctrine. This insists that all disputes concerning the loan are to be decided in the courts of the borrowing state, the laws of the borrowing state are the governing laws, and the foreign lender surrenders all rights under international law.

Bibliography: P. Wood. *Law and Practice of International Finance*. Sweet & Maxwell, London, 1980.

K

kaffirs. UK slang for shares in South African mining companies.

Kassenobligation. German financial instruments sometimes traded on the Euromarkets. They are normally issued in bearer form for a maximum of four years by government agencies or Giro banks in Germany and are quoted on the domestic stock exchanges. Swiss Kassenobligationen are also traded.
Bibliography: G. Dufey & E. Krishnan. West Germany: Banking, Money and Bond Markets *in* A.M. George & I.H. Giddy. *International Finance Handbook*. John Wiley & Sons, New York, 1983.

Kassenverein. German institutions which handle delivery of securities, along with similar institutions called Wertpapiersammelbanken. German stock exchange regulations state that transactions must be completed either by physical delivery of the security at the stock exchange or by deposit at a Kassenverein. Compare AUSLANDSKASSENVEREIN.
Bibliography: *Euromoney*. London, January 1977, p. 113.

KD. Abbreviation for Kuwaiti dinar.

KDCD. *See* KUWAITI DINAR CD.

keepwell. One of the stronger types of LETTERS OF COMFORT where a provision is made by a parent of a borrowing subsidiary in which the parent specifies that its subsidiary will conform to certain requirements (e.g. minimum working capital).
Bibliography: P.K. Nevitt *Project Financing*. Euromoney Publications, London. 1983.

Kennedy Round. A round of tariff negotiations in the early 1960s named after President Kennedy, who was in large part responsible for its success. Compare DILLON ROUND; GATT; TOKYO ROUND.
Bibliography: A. Shonfield (ed.). *International Economic Relations of the Western World 1959-71.* Vol. 1. Oxford University Press, 1976.

kerb dealing. Dealing in commodity markets which takes place after the official market has ended. Originally it took place in the street on the kerb outside the market. It now also refers to telephone trading or other dealing outside the market.
Bibliography: C.W.J. Granger (ed.). *Trading in Commodities*. Woodhead-Faulkner, Cambridge, UK, 1983.
R. Gibson-Jarvie. *The London Metal Exchange.* Woodhead-Faulkner, Cambridge, UK, 1983.

KfW. *See* KREDITANSTALT FUR WIEDERAUFBAU.

KIBOR. Abbreviation for Kuwait Interbank offered rate. Compare LIBOR, SIBOR.

Kontokorrent. German term for overdraft.

Kreditanstalt fur Wiederaufbau (KfW). Set up in 1948 to fianance West German reconstruction, KfW later became involved in export finance and also became the official executive agency for the German capital aid programme to developing countries. Its capital is held by the Federal and provincial governments but its funding is increasingly provided by raisings from the capital market.
Bibliography: *The Export Credit Financing Systems in OECD Member Countries*. Organization for Economic Cooperation and Development, Paris, 1982.

Kuponsteuer. German 25% tax on interest paid on bonds held by non-residents. Originally introduced to curb the inflow of funds into the country, it has been retained as a bargaining chip for negotiation of DOUBLE TAX treaties and the like but plans have recently been announced for its abolition.

Bibliography: G. Dufey & E. Krishnan. West Germany: Banking, Money & Bond Markets *in* A.M. George & I.H. Giddy. *International Finance Handbook*. John Wiley & Sons, New York, 1983.

Kursmakler. German term for official brokers in the stock market. They may only act as intermediaries between banks, though they may deal for their own account if orders cannot otherwise be executed.

Bibliography: G. Dufey & E. Krishnan. West Germany: Banking, Money and Bond Markets *in* A.M. George & I.H. Giddy. *International Finance Handbook*. John Wiley & Sons, New York, 1983.

Kurspflege. German term for operations by the Bundesbank and the banks to stabilize price movements in the German BOND market in order to prevent technical factors from causing abrupt price changes.

Bibliography: G. Dufey & E. Krishnan. West Germany: Banking, Money and Bond Markets *in* A.M. George & I.H. Giddy. *International Finance Handbook*. John Wiley & Sons, New York, 1983.

Kuwait Fund for Arab Economic Development (KFAED). Founded in 1961 by the Kuwait government, the KFAED is perhaps one of the senior and more experienced Arab development finance institutions. Originally its activities were confined to the Arab world but since 1974 its mandate covers all developing countries. Its loan commitments in recent years have been of the order of $300 million per annum.

Bibliography: T. Scharf. *Trilateral Cooperation Vol. I: Arab Development Funds and Banks*. OECD Development Centre Studies, Paris, 1978. *Aid from OPEC countries*. OECD, Paris, 1983

Kuwaiti dinar bonds. BONDS denominated in Kuwaiti dinars were first issued in 1974 by the Republic of the Philippines, Republic of Ireland and the Osterreichische Kontrollbank. One of the largest issues to date is the KD12 million (approx. $40 million) 1978-90 issue by Sonatrach of Algeria. Approximately 40 issues totalling over $1 billion equivalent have been made so far.

Bibliography: *Euromoney*. London, January 1979. M.S. Dobbs-Higginson. *Investment Manual*. Credit Suisse First Boston Ltd, London 1980.

Kuwaiti dinar CDs. CDS denominated in Kuwaiti dinars were first issued in 1977 under the aegis of Kuwait International Investment Co. So far the majority of issues have been on a TRANCHE basis not exceeding three years' maturity.

Bibliography: L.J. Kemp. *World Money and Securities Markets*. Euromoney Publications, London 1984.

L

ladder. Term used in the control of money market and foreign exchange positions. A ladder consists of a listing, day by day, or month by month, of the outstanding MATURITY of money market deposits or forward exchange contracts. It helps banks to control their GAP or MIS-MATCH.
Bibliography: J.K. Walmsley. *The Foreign Exchange Handbook.* John Wiley & Sons, New York, 1983.

LAFTA. *See* LATIN AMERICAN FREE TRADE AREA.

LAIA. *See* LATIN AMERICAN INTEGRATION AREA.

Landeszentralbank. German regional central bank: there is one for each 'Land' or province. They are legally part of the Bundesbank and act for it in the region, in particular by providing local clearing and settlement services.
Bibliography: *The Deutsche Bundesbank: Its Monetary Policy Instruments and Functions.* Deutsche Bundesbank Special Series no. 7, 1982.

last resort. In each domestic money market, if a bank gets into difficulties, it will ultimately rely on the central bank to support it. The central bank is then the lender of last resort. There is no real lender of last resort in the EUROCURRENCY market.
Bibliography: G.G. Johnson & R.K. Abrams. *Aspects of the International Banking Safety Net.* IMF Occasional Paper no. 17, Washington DC, 1983.

Latin American Free Trade Area (LAFTA). (Also known as ALALC from the Spanish.) LAFTA was founded in 1960 and had its headquarters in Uruguay. Its members consisted of Argentina, Bolivia, Brazil, Chile, Columbia, Ecuador, Mexico, Para-guay, Peru, Uruguay and Venezuela. Its objectives included trade liberalization and a system of reciprocal credits between members for financing payments imbalances. In 1980 it was replaced by the LATIN AMERICAN INTEGRATION ASSOCIATION.
Bibliography: *Economic and Social Progress in Latin America* in *Inter-American Development Bank Annual Report*, Washington DC, 1984.

Latin Union franc. *See* GOLD FRANC.

Latin American Integration Association. Founded in 1980 by the Treaty of Montevideo, the LAIA replaced the LATIN AMERICAN FREE TRADE AREA, albeit with the same membership and objectives.
Bibliography: *Economic and Social Progress in Latin America.* in *Inter-American Development Bank Annual Report*, Washington DC, 1984.

laytime. The time allowed a ship to load or unload. If this is exceeded, DEMURRAGE is incurred.
Bibliography: M. Summerskill. *Laytime.* Stevens & Sons, London 1982.

LBO. *See* LEVERAGED BUYOUT.

LDMA. *See* LONDON DISCOUNT MARKET ASSOCIATION.

lead bank or **lead manager.** In the EUROCREDIT MARKET a potential borower will give a bank a MANDATE to arrange the credit. This bank will normally contact a number of other banks with a view to forming a syndicate where it will be the leading bank. Frequently several banks within the syndicate, with some special contribution to make, are designated co-managers, in which case the original bank will be referred to as the lead manager. It is possible for there to be more than one lead manager.

Bibliography: S.I. Davis. *The Euro-bank*. Macmillan, London/John Wiley, New York, 1981.
L.S. Goodman. Syndicated Euro-lending: pricing and practice *in* A.M. George & I.H. Giddy. *International Finance Handbook*. John Wiley & Sons, New York, 1983.

leads and lags. A term referring to changes in the pattern of international payments terms. At any one time a country is extending and receiving trade credit via its exporters and importers. If a devaluation of its currency is feared, its importers with foreign currency obligations may hurry to pay, otherwise their debts will be greater after devaluation, i.e. they 'lead' payments. Conversely, exporters will benefit by not hurrying to convert export receipts in foreign currency - they 'lag' payments.

Bibliography: P. Einzig. *Leads and Lags*. Macmillan, 1968.
S. Grassman. *Exchange Reserves and The Financial Structure of Foreign Trade*. Saxon House, UK, 1973.

lead underwriter An insurance market term for the UNDERWRITER who is the first of a number of underwriters to accept a LINE on a risk. He will play the major role in establishing the terms under which the risk is to be acepted, and an equally important role in subsequent operations.

Bibliography: V. Dover. *A Handbook to Marine Insurance*. Revised and edited R.H. Brown. Witherby & Co, London, 1975.
R. Clews (ed.). *A Textbook of Insurance Broking*. Woodhead-Faulkner, Cambridge, UK, 1980.

lease. A lease is a contract between lessor and lessee for hire of a specific asset. The lessor retains ownership of the asset. The lessee has possession and use of the asset on payment of specified rentals over a period. If the payments over the life of the lease fully cover the value of the asset, the lease is called a FINANCE LEASE or FULL PAY-OUT LEASE. If not, it is called an OPERATING LEASE. An important function of a lease is to maximize tax benefits: the lessor will normally receive some form of tax benefit or investment credit which will allow him to reduce the rental cost to the lessee. Compare DOUBLE-DIP LEASE; LEVERAGE LEASE; WET LEASE.

Bibliography: A.F. Gargiulo & R.J. Kenard. *Leveraged Leasing*. American Management Association, New York, 1981.
F.P. Slattery. Leasing Ventures *in* M.E. Blume & J.P. Friedman (eds). *Encyclopaedia of Investments*. Warren, Gorham & Lamont, New York, 1982.
P.K. Nevitt. *Project Financing*. Euromoney Publications, London 1983.

Leaseurope. The Federation of European Leasing Associations, which represents the interests of the leasing industry and internationally. Its headquarters are at Ave de Tervuren 267, Boite 10, Brussels 1156, Belgium.

left-hand side. Foreign exchange term; the rate at which a bank will offer currency, against e.g. dollars. A currency will be quoted, say DM2.0755-60. 2.0755 is the rate at which the bank will sell DM against dollars, 2.0760 is the rate at which it will buy DM. Thus from its point of view if a deal is done on the left-hand side it sells DM and buys dollars.

legal defeasance. A form of DEFEASANCE under which the borrower is legally released from his obligation to pay his debt. Legal defeasance originated in the US tax-exempt securities market. INDENTURES of tax-exempt securities often had provisions allowing the borrower to be released from his obligation (and from the covenants in the indenture) by placing with a trustee sufficient cash or government securities to pay the interest and principal amount of the borrowing. Compare ECONOMIC DEFEASANCE.

Bibliography: B. McGoldrick. Why are CFOs so excited about defeasance? *Institutional Investor*. New York, March 1984.
Financial Accounting Standards Board. *Statement of Financial Accounting Standards no. 76*. Stamford, Conn., 1983.

legal list. US term for a list of prime investments selected by various states, into which certain institutions and fiduciaries may invest their funds. Compare TRUSTEE STATUS IN THE UK.

Bibliography: L.M. Loll & J.G. Buckley. *The Over-the-Counter Securities Market*. Prentice-Hall, NJ, 1981.

lend. (1) In general, to provide someone with funds on the understanding that it will be repaid, usually with interest.

(2) A CARRY operation in the commodities markets, especially metals. To lend is to sell cash and repurchase forward – i.e. to 'lend' the commodity, and borrow money.

Bibliography: R. Gibson-Jarvie. *The London Metal Exchange*. Woodhead-Faulkner, Cambridge, UK/Nichols Publishing, New York, 1983.

letter of comfort. A written instrument issued by A, where A agrees to make every effort to assure B's compliance with the terms of a contract, but without committing A to perform B's obligation in the event that B is unable to fulfil his obligation. It is usually issued by a parent company on behalf of a subsidiary in another country. It takes many possible forms. From the lender's point of view it is weaker than a guarantee. Compare KEEPWELL, LETTER OF MORAL INTENT.

Bibliography: P.K. Nevitt. *Project Financing*. Euromoney Publications, London, 1983.

letter of credit. A letter authorizing use of credit; as far as the shipment of goods is concerned *See* documentary credit. Compare STANDBY LETTER OF CREDIT.

letter of hypothecation. A letter given by a person pledging goods (or the documents of title). For example, it may be given by him to the banker who has possession of his goods (or documents). The banker hands over the goods so that the former can sell them (or earn revenue from e.g. a ship) and repay his loan; its purpose is to protect the banker's security. It is also used where A creates a charge over his account in favour of a bank, as security for the obligation of B to that bank. Also known as trust letter or TRUST RECEIPT. The term is loosely used and its legal meaning is not precisely clear. Compare HYPOTHECATION.

Bibliography: H.C. Gutteridge & M. Megrah. *The Law of Bankers' Commercial Credits*. Europa Publications, London, 1979.

letter of moral intent. An undertaking by a company which falls short of a legal guarantee. It is usually given by a parent company in respect of a subsidiary. Akin to a LETTER OF COMFORT.

Bibliography: International project finance survey. *The Banker*. London, December 1977, p. 58.

leverage. US term for (1) the proportion of debt to equity in a firm's capitalization. After deducting interest on debt, profits are available for dividends on the equity. Thus the effect of high leverage is to make it more uncertain that dividends can be paid, but if the debt is financing profitable business, dividends may grow more than proportionately. Compare GEARING.

Bibliography: R. Brealey & S. Myers. *Principles of Corporate Finance*. McGraw-Hill, New York/London, 1984.
A.F. Gargiulo & R.J. Kenard. *Leveraged Leasing*. American Management Association, New York, 1981.

(2) Measures a portfolio's exposure to market risk.

leveraged buyout. US term for an operation whereby the managers of a division of a company borrow money to buy the division from its parent; or where the management of a publicly-held company borrow money to buy out the public shareholders and make the company private again.

Bibliography: N. Osborn. Leveraged Buyouts: Too Good to be True? *Euromoney*, London, April 1984.

leverage lease. US term for a LEASE under which the lessor invests only a part of the cost of the asset he is leasing out to the lessee. The balance borrowed from another lender. American rules – as laid down by the Financial Accounting Standards Board – have laid down that if the loan is WITHOUT RECOURSE to the borrower, the lease is a

leveraged lease. In this case the lender's only security will normally be a LIEN on the equipment and the rental payments from the user.
Bibliography: A.F. Gargiulo & R.J. Kenard. *Leveraged Leasing.* American Management Association, New York, 1981.

LIBO, LIBOR. *See* LONDON INTER-BANK OFFERED RATE.

liée. French term for a swap: 'operation liee' = 'swap operation'.
Bibliography: P. Coulbois. *Le Finance Internationale.I.Le Change.* Editions Cujas, Paris, 1979.

lien. A lien is the right to retain the property of another until he has paid his debt to the person holding the property subject to the lien. In the UK lien usually affords the right to retain the property only until the debt is paid. There is no power of sale. However, a banker's lien is regarded as an implied pledge, conferring power of sale in respect of fully negotiable securities.
Bibliography: L.C. Mather. *Securities Acceptable to the Lending Banker.* Waterlow, London, 1973. P. Wood. *Law & Practice of International Finance.* Sweet & Maxwell, London, 1980. W.C.F. Kurz. New Form in the Loan Agreement. *Euromoney*, London, February 1981.

lift a leg. Term sometimes used in foreign exchange, money, futures or commodity markets in respect of an ARBITRAGE or STRADDLE deal. Such deals will usually have more than one 'leg': to lift a leg means to close out part of the deal while leaving some part open. For example, suppose that a trader has borrowed three-month money, hedging his position by buying a three-month futures contract. If he decided to sell the futures contract while leaving the deposit position unchanged, he might be said to lift the futures leg of the deal.

Limean. Term for 'the mean of London inter-bank bid and offer rates'. Compare LIBOR.

limit. (1) The phrase 'limit up' or 'limit down' in commodity markets refers to the maximum price change permitted in one trading session.
(2) In domestic banking, a bank may place a limit on the total it is prepared to lend a customer.
(3) Analogously in international banking, country limits may be fixed. Compare SOVEREIGN RISK LIMIT.
(4) In foreign exchange dealing a bank will set a limit on the amount it is prepared to trade or deposit with another bank.
(5) A central bank will regulate dealings in foreign exchange by means of limits. For example, the Bundesbank sets a limit of 30% of 'liable capital': a bank's open positions (long or short of foreign currency) may not exceed this limit. Similar limits are set in the UK, US and elsewhere.
Bibliography: S.I. Davis. *The Euro-Bank.* Macmillan, London, 1976.
J.K. Walmsley. *The Foreign Exchange Handbook.* John Wiley & Sons, New York, 1983.
D.R. Mandich (ed.). *Foreign Exchange Trading Techniques & Controls.* American Bankers' Association, Washington DC, 1976.

limited recourse finance. Finance arranged on the basis that the lender has RECOURSE to the borrower only in certain circumstances – e.g., it may be agreed that the borrower is not obliged to repay the loan to the extent that a loss results from a certain risk. Such a risk in an oil project might include, for example, the absence of expected reserves of oil. Compare NON-RECOURSE FINANCE.
Bibliography: P. Wood. *Law and Practice of International Finance.* Sweet & Maxwell, London, 1980.
P.K. Nevitt. *Project Financing.* Euromoney Publications, London, 1983.

limit order. Order to buy or sell at a specific price or better.
Bibliography: L.M. Loll & J.G. Buckley. *The Over-The-Counter Securities Markets.* Prentice-Hall, NJ, 1981.
N.H. Rothstein & J.M. Little. *The Handbook of Financial Futures.* McGraw-Hill, New York, 1984.

line. (1) A line of credit refers to an

arrangement where a firm may borrow up to an agreed amount from a bank, subject to availability of funds at the time. (Compare ADVISED LINE OF CREDIT.) By analogy the term may be used to describe country borrowing from the IMF. The term is also applied in export finance, where a line is established to finance purchases of exports. Compare PROJECT LINE.

Bibliography: W.H. Baughn & C.E. Walker. *The Bankers' Handbook*. Dow-Jones Irwin, US, 1978, pp. 613-21.

ECGD Services. Export Credit Guarantee Department, London, 1978.

(2) In the UK, 'line' can refer to large quantity of stock or shares. Compare BLOCK.

(3) A SWAP line is a term often used to refer to the system of bi-lateral standby credit agreements negotiated between central banks. Each agreement provides for an exchange, or swap of currencies to help finance what are considered to be temporary payments imbalances. Technically, the swap is a spot foreign exchange deal combined with a forward deal in the reverse direction. Compare SWAP.

Bibliography: J.K. Walmsley. *The Foreign Exchange Handbook*.
John Wiley & Sons, New York, 1983.

(4) In the UK insurance market, 'line' is used to denote an acceptance of a risk by an underwriter and, where there is more than one underwriter, each underwriter's proportion of the sum assured. The line may be written as a sum of money or as a percentage; today the latter tends to be more common.

Bibliography: V. Dover. *A Handbook to Marine Insurance*. Revised and edited R.H. Brown. Witherby & Co., London, 1975.

line slip. A term used at LLOYD'S. An arrangement whereby a group of UNDER-WRITERS agree that each will accept the same LINE or proportions of a given class of risk, on a regular basis, provided that the business proposed by the broker's SLIP is agreed by one or more of the LEAD UNDERWRITERS.

Bibliography: R. Clews (ed.). *A Textbook of Insurance Broking*. Woodhead-Faulkner, Cambridge, UK, 1980.

liquidity.   Generally, the ease with which an asset can be turned into money. The more quickly an asset can be encashed, and the smaller the risk of loss in so doing, the greater its liquidity. For example, one could arrange assets in an order which might include cash, Treasury bills, government securities, equities, commodities, and property, in descending order of liquidity. In monetary discussions, the term liquidity is often used to refer to the aggregate of money and 'near-money'. Compare INTERNATIONAL LIQUIDITY.

Bibliography: C.A.E. Goodhart. *Money, Information and Uncertainty*. Macmillan, London, 1975.
The Measurement of Liquidity. *Bank of England Quarterly Bulletin*, September 1982.

liquidity balance.   A measure of the US balance of payments now superseded by 'transaction in US official reserve assets and in foreign official assets in the United States', a global measure which has given up any attempt to classify payments transactions.

Bibliography: N.S. Fieleke. *What is the Balance of Payments*. Federal Reserve Bank of Boston Research Department, July 1976.
R.M. Stern *et al*. *The Presentation of the US Balance of Payments: A Symposium*. Princeton Essays in International Finance No. 123, 1977.

LIRC.   *See* LOW INTEREST RATE CURRENCY.

listing.   Refers to the process of public quotation on a stock exchange of a share or bond. The listing of an issue generally helps its marketability and enhances its SECONDARY MARKET. New EUROBONDS are generally listed in Luxembourg or London. It is possible for a firm's shares which have already been issued – e.g. via a PRIVATE PLACEMENT – to be listed at a later date. As an example of the criteria applied to listings, the UK Stock Exchange's requirements are that the initial market value of the securities to be listed should be at least £500,000; applications would not normally be considered for any class of security whose market value is expected to be less than £200,000; at least 25% of any class of issued equity capital or convertible debt is required to be in the hands of the public, though exceptions may be made for large issues. By comparison, the New York Stock Exchange requires – for domestic companies – at least 1 million shares with a market value of $16 million to be publicly held; net tangible assets of the company must be at least $16 million; the most recent year's earnings must be at least $2.5 million.

Bibliography: *Admission of Securities to Listing.* Quotations Department, Stock Exchange, London, 1984.
Price Waterhouse & Co. *World's Major Stock Exchanges Listing Requirements.* UK/USA, 1984.

Lloyd's. The major centre of the world insurance market, the organization of Lloyd's is rather complex. Essentially it consists of a number of SYNDICATES of UNDERWRITERS and NAMES (whose personal liability is unlimited) prepared to UNDER-WRITE almost any type of insurance proposition. Lloyd's also controls Lloyd's Register of Shipping which lays down internationally accepted construction standards for ships, oil rigs and the like. Additionally, it publishes (through Lloyd's of London Press) vast amounts of daily and weekly commercial intelligence.

Bibliography: W.M. Clarke. *Inside the City.* George Allen & Unwin, London 1983.
H.C. Cockerell. *Lloyd's of London: a portrait.* Woodhead-Faulkner, Cambridge UK/Dow-Jones Irwin, Homewood, Ill. 1984.

Lloyd's agents. Appointed by the corporation of LLOYD'S. These agents have the duty of keeping Lloyd's informed of shipping movements and accidents. The agents act in all matters on behalf of and in the interests of the general body of UNDERWRITERS; and, frequently, make payments in respect of claims on Lloyd's.

Bibliography: H.C. Cockerell. *Lloyd's of London: a portrait.* Woodhead-Faulkner, Cambridge UK/ Dow-Jones Irwin, Homewood, Ill., 1984.

Lloyd's Underwriters' Association. Established 1909 to deal with matters generally affecting the business of marine UNDER-WRITERS at LLOYD'S.

Bibliography: V. Dover. *A Handbook to Marine Insurance.* Revised and edited by R.H. Brown. Witherby & Co, London, 1975.

LME. *See* LONDON METAL EXCHANGE.

location clause. In marine insurance, a location clause mau be used to limit the UNDERWRITER'S liability in respect of goods which may have been accumulated in one place, e.g. a pile-up of goods awaiting shipment.

Bibliography: R.J. Lambeth. *Templeman on Marine Insurance.* Macdonald & Evans, UK, 1981.

locked market. A situation where the bid price equals the offer price.

lock-up. (1) Term for a CERTIFICATE OF DEPOSIT issued on the understanding that it will not be traded in the secondary market. Quite often the issuing bank will insist on holding the CD so as to ensure the understanding is honoured. Banks like to see their CDs held firmly, so a lock-up CD is attractive to them, and they may be prepared to bid a slightly better rate on a lock-up.

(2) EUROBOND term for new issue procedures designed to prevent the flow of securities into the United States, or their sale to US persons, during the period of initial distribution. This is relevant in cases where the issue has not been registered with the SECURITIES AND EXCHANGE COMMISSION. The technique involves the use of a GLOBAL BOND.

Bibliography: F.G. Fisher. *International Bonds.* Euromoney Publications London 1982.

loco. Commodities market term meaning 'at'. Thus gold may be traded 'loco London'. From the Latin *locus*= place.

Lombard rate (also **Lombardsatz, Lombardzinfuss**). German term for the rate of interest charged for a loan against the security of pledged paper. Particularly used with reference to the Bundesbank, which normally maintains its Lombard rate at about ½% above its DISCOUNT RATE.

Bibliography: *The Deutsche Bundesbank: Its Monetary Policy Instruments and Functions.* Deutsche Bundesbank Special Series no.7, 1982.

Lomé Convention. An agreement between the EUROPEAN COMMUNITIES and a number of developing countries, giving the latter preferential trading access to the EC and also providing for a commodity stabilization fund, STABEX and transfers of capital and technical assistance.

Bibliography: C.C. Twitchett. Lome II: a new ACP-EEC Agreement. *The World Today,* Royal Institute of International Affairs, London, March 1980.
Annual Report of the EC, Brussels.
Annual Report of the ACP-EEC Council of Ministers, Brussels.

LOMI. Abbreviation for LETTER OF MORAL INTENT.

London Commodity Exchange. A company responsible for the provision of services to the 'soft', i.e. non-metal,commodity markets in London. Its members consist of the market associations of the cocoa, coffee, petroleum, rubber, sugar, soyabean, vegetable oil and wool markets. Compare INTERNATIONAL COMMODITY CLEARING HOUSE, LONDON INTERNATIONAL FINANCIAL FUTURES EXCHANGE.

Bibliography: *London Commodity Exchange,* LCE, London, 1983.

London Discount Market Association. Association grouping together the London DISCOUNT HOUSES. It forms an essential link between the discount market and the Bank of England.

Bibliography: J.S.G. Wilson. Recent Changes in London's Money Market Arrangements. *Banca Nazionale del Lavoro Quarterly Review,* March 1983.

London Grain Futures Market. A market in FUTURES for grain (wheat and barley). It is housed in the BALTIC EXCHANGE under the auspices of the Grain and Feed Trades Association. The standard contract is for 100 tonnes of grain of London Grain Futures Quality Standard.

London International Financial Futures Exchange (LIFFE). In September 1982 the LIFFE began trading in FINANCIAL FUTURES contracts for sterling, Deutschemarks, yen, and Swiss francs against the dollar, 20-year gilt-edged stock, and 3-month time deposits in dollars and sterling. In 1984 a contract based on the Financial Times-Stock Exchange index was introduced.

Bibliography: M.D. Fitzgerald. *Financial Futures.* Euromoney Publications, London, 1983.
M. Blanden. LIFFE looks to the Future. *The Banker,* May 1984.

London Inter-Bank Offered Rate (LIBOR). A key international interest rate, LIBOR is the interest rate at which banks in London are prepared to lend funds to first-class banks. LIBOR is used to determine the interest rate payable on most Eurocredits and is also used in the sterling market. A typical Eurocredit LIBOR clause might define LIBOR as 'the arithmetic mean of the respective rates notified to the AGENT by the REFERENCE BANKS as the rate at which deposits of the relevant amount for a period equal to the relevant INTEREST PERIOD and in the relevant currency were offered to prime banks by the Reference Banks in the London Inter-Bank Eurocurrency Market as at 11.00 am (London time) two business days prior to the date of DRAW-DOWN or renewal for VALUE on such date'. Compare BIBOR, HKIBOR, LUXIBOR, MIBOR, SIBOR, ADIBOR, MULTI-TIER LIBOR.

Bibliography: S.I. Davis. *The Euro-Bank.* Macmillan, London/John Wiley, New York 1981.
J.K. Walmsley. *The Foreign Exchange Handbook,* John Wiley & Sons, New York, 1983.
P. Wood. *Law and Practice of International Finance.* Sweet & Maxwell, London, 1980.

London Metal Exchange (LME). A major world centre of metals trading, the LME trades copper, silver, tin, lead and zinc. It also organizes warehouse facilities for physical storage of metal.

Bibliography: R. Gibson-Jarvie. *The London Metal Exchange*. Woodhead-Faulkner, UK, 1983.

London Sugar Terminal Market. *See* UNITED TERMINAL SUGAR MARKET ASSOCIATION.

long. A term used in commodity, foreign exchange, option and stock markets to denote a net asset position. 'I am long of $5 million' means the speaker's net holding of dollars is $5 million: conversely 'short' denotes a net liability. Also in French: 'une position longue' is a long position.

Loro Account. A banking term used to denote the account of a third party (*loro* = Italian for their). For example, a London bank might pay $1 million to the Bank of America for the credit of the Loro Account of the Dresdner Bank which is held by the Bank of America.

Bibliography: A. Watson. *Finance of International Trade*. Institute of Bankers, London, 1981.

lower floater. *See* SEVEN-DAY PUT BOND

low interest rate currency. A feature of the latest renegotiation of the international export credit CONSENSUS is that exporters may be funded at rates below the Consensus minimum if they borrow in currencies designated as low-interest-rate currencies. Such currencies are designated from time to time by the countries operating the Consensus.
Bibliography: A. Dunn & M. Knight. *Export Finance*. Euromoney, London, 1982.
K. Taylor. A Case for Export Credit Subsidies. *The Banker*, London, February 1984.

Luxibor. Abbreviation for Luxembourg inter-bank offered rate. *See* LIBOR.

M

M0. UK term for a measure of the 'wide MONETARY BASE'. It comprises notes and coin in circulation and at the banks, plus banks' operational balances with the Bank of England.
Bibliography: Changes to monetary aggregates and the analysis of bank lending. *Bank of England Quarterly Bulletin* March, 1984.

M1. Term used in a number of countries to define a narrowly-based monetary aggregate which approximates to cash (i.e. 'transactions balances' used by consumers and businesses). In the UK the definition is notes and coin in circulation plus private sector sterling sight bank deposits. In the US the definition is currency outside the Federal Reserve and the Treasury, travelers checks, demand deposits at commercial banks (other than those due to domestic banks, the US government, and foreign banks and official institutions) plus NEGOTIABLE ORDER OF WITHDRAWAL and automatic transfer service accounts, plus demand deposits at thrift institutions, less cash items in the process of collection and Federal Reserve FLOAT.
Bibliography: Changes to monetary aggregates and the analysis of bank lending. *Bank of England Quarterly Bulletin*, March, 1984.
Federal Reserve Bulletin, Washington, DC, monthly.

M2. A term for a measure of the money supply including 'quasi-cash' balances. In the UK, M2 = M1 less private sector non-retail interest-bearing sterling sight bank deposits plus private sector holdings of retail building society deposits and national savings banks ordinary accounts. In the US, M2 = M1 plus overnight repurchase agreements and overnight Eurodollars held by US residents at foreign brances of US banks, money market deposit accounts, savings and small time deposits.

Bibliography: Changes to monetary aggregates and the analysis of bank lending. *Bank of England Quarterly Bulletin*, March, 1984.
Federal Reserve Bulletin, Washington, DC, monthly.

M3. A term for a wider measure of money supply that includes longer-term bank deposits and other 'savings' instruments. In the UK, sterling M3 = M1 plus private sector holdings of sterling bank CD's and all sterling time deposits. In the US, M3 = M2 plus large denomination time deposits (over $100,000) and term repurchase contracts, term Eurodollar deposits held by US residents at foreign branches of US banks, and funds held in institutional money market funds.
Bibliography: Changes to monetary aggregates and the analysis of bank lending. *Bank of England Quarterly Bulletin*, March, 1984.
Federal Reserve Bulletin, Washington, DC, monthly.

Macaulay duration. The original definition of DURATION – an attempt to adjust the MATURITY of a BOND by the size of its COUPON to provide a better estimate of its true maturity. Macaulay duration discounts the cash flows by the prevailing average yield to maturity; another measure (Fisher-Weil) uses a set of forward rates to do the discounting.
Bibliography: F.K. Reilly & R.S.S. Sidhu. Duration and Its Properties *in* F.J. Fabozzi & I.M. Pollack (eds). *The Handbook of Fixed Income Securities*. Dow-Jones Irwin, Homewood, Ill., 1983.

Madrid inter-bank offered rate (Mibor). The Spanish equivalent of LIBOR. From the market's opening in 1980 to mid-1983 the Mibor market is estimated to have totalled over $8 billion.

Bibliography: N. Bance. Spain's Very Own Euro-market. *Euromoney*. July 1983.

mail transfer.   An airmail request by a bank to its agent in a centre abroad to pay a stated sum of money to a named person in that centre. Except for small sums, the mail transfer has generally been replaced by the TELEGRAPHIC TRANSFER and by SWIFT payments.

maison de réescompte.   French equivalent of British DISCOUNT HOUSES. There are six and they have the monopoly of operations with the Banque de France. They invest in Treasury bills and other assets, financing themselves by short-term borrowing.
Bibliography: D. Marteau & E. de la Chaise. *Le marché monétaire et la gestion de trésorerie des banques*. Dunod, Paris, 1981.

major bracket, underwriter.   *See* BRACKET.

make-up day.   UK banking term for the day of the month on which figures are compiled for reporting to the Bank of England. Usually the third Wednesday of the month.

Makler.   German term for a BROKER in the stock market. The Makler is only allowed to act as an intermediary between traders and may not take a position for his own account unless it is necessary to complete an order.
Bibliography: G.Dufey & E. Krishnan. West Germany: Banking, Money and Bond Markets *in* A.M. George & I.H. Giddy. *International Finance Handbook*. John Wiley & Sons, New York, 1983.

Maloney Act.   US Act passed in 1938 allowing the OVER-THE COUNTER-MARKET to regulate itself, by the creation of the NATIONAL ASSOCIATION OF SECURITIES DEALERS.

managed bond.   UK term for a single-premium life insurance policy whose proceeds are invested in a fund which buys land or buildings, equities, fixed-interest stocks or other assets.
Bibliography: D. O'Shea. *Investing for Beginners*. Financial Times Business Information, London 1984.

management fee.   A fee charged by a bank for managing a credit or bond issue. The system is most widely used in the EUROMARKETS and the US securities market where a typical fee would be 17 ½ – 20% of the GROSS SPREAD. Compare FRONT-END FEES; PRAECIPIUM; PARTICIPATION FEE; POOL; UNDERWRITING FEE.
Bibliography: L.S. Goodman. Syndicated Eurolending: Pricing and Practice *in* A.M. George & I.H. Giddy. *International Finance Handbook*. John Wiley & Sons, New York, 1983.

manager.   In international banking this refers to a bank involved in managing a Euro-credit or an issue of a security. Such a bank may either be the LEAD MANAGER or else a 'co-manager' in which case it will usually receive a smaller fee. The managers are responsible for the terms and conditions of the loan, its documentation etc.
Bibliography: L.S. Goodman. Syndicated Eurolending: Pricing and Practice *in* A.M. George & I.H. Giddy. *International Finance Handbook*. John Wiley & Sons, New York, 1983.

mandate.   In the context of international finance, this term is used when firm instructions are given to a commercial or investment bank to undertake a transaction. For example,a borrower wishing to raise funds in the Euromarket will discuss terms with various banks and, having chosen one as LEAD MANAGER will give it a mandate to arrange the credit on certain terms.
Bibliography: S.I. Davis. *The Euro-bank*. Macmillan, London/John Wiley, New York, 1981.

Mareva injunction.   UK term for an injunction to prevent the defendant in a court case from removing his assets (often a ship) from the jurisdiction of the court.
Bibliography: F. Maisel. The Mareva Injunction: Recent Developments. *Lloyd's Maritime and Commercial Law Quarterly*, vol. I, 1980.

marge à terme.   French foreign exchange term for FORWARD MARGIN.
Bibliography: P. Coulbois. *Finance Internationale: I. Le Change*. Editions Cujas, Paris, 1979.

margin. (1) Refers to the difference between a bank's borrowing and lending rates, e.g. it may borrow at LIBOR, add a margin of 1%, and lend the money to a customer.

(2) Refers to additional security provided to cover a possible fall in the value of the collateral lodged against a loan.

(3) In the commodity and financial futures markets, the term refers to money put up as security that a contract will be fulfilled. It may consist of INITIAL MARGIN or VARIATION MARGIN.

Bibliography: M.D. Fitzgerald. *Financial Futures*. Euromoney Publications London, 1983.

(4) US term for a purchase of stock with borrowed funds; this is referred to as a margin transaction.

Bibliography: J.W. Jenkins. The Use of Margining to Enhance Aftertax Yields *in* F.J. Fabozzi & I.M. Pollack (eds). *The Handbood of Fixed Income Securities*. Dow-Jones Irwin, Homewood, Ill., 1983.

marginal risk. A foreign exchange term relating to FORWARD CONTRACTS. It refers to the risk that a customer goes bankrupt after entering into a forward contract; in that event the bank must CLOSE its commitment in the market, thereby running the risk that the exchange rate has moved unfavourably in the interim. Its risk is confined to the marginal amount of such a movement. For example, consider a bank which has contracted to sell forward £1 million against receipt of $2.0 million, and has already hedged the deal by buying forward at the same rate. Suppose the counterparty now fails, and the bank closes the contract by selling off the sterling which it no longer requires. Say the rate in the market is $1.50. It will now receive only $1.5 million for the sterling for which it earlier paid $2 million. Its loss, however, is less than the full principal amount, being only that due to the change in rates. Compare CAPITAL RISK.

Bibliography: J.K. Walmsley. *The Foreign Exchange Handbook*. John Wiley & Sons, New York, 1983.

margin call. If a commodity market moves against a speculator after he has entered into a futures contract, or a security bought on margin loses its value, the BROKER will probably ask the speculator to provide extra funds with a view to maintaining his margin at the initial level. This is a 'margin call'. Compare INITIAL MARGIN, VARIATION MARGIN.

Bibliography: C.W.J. Granger (ed.). *Trading in Commodities*. Woodhead-Faulkner, Cambridge, UK, 1983.

mark. UK Stock Exchange term. Each BARGAIN is marked as to price and date, for subsequent printing in the Stock Exchange Daily Official List. The purpose is so that the investor can check that his transaction was carried out at a price reasonably near the market level. The total number of marks is usually also used as an indicator of the activity in markets, although it is only an approximate guide, as one mark may represent a bargain in 100 or 100,000 shares.

Bibliography: J. Dundas Hamilton. *Stockbroking Today*. Macmillan Press, London, 1979.

market if touched (MIT). An order on commodity, stock or FUTURES markets. An MIT order becomes a MARKET ORDER when the MIT price is reached. An example of a market-if-touched order is: 'Buy 15 Dec. IMM T-bills at 87.16.' This instructs the floor broker to buy the TREASURY BILL futures at the best possible price when the market reaches 87.16.

Bibliography: N.H. Rothstein & J.M. Little. *The Financial Futures Handbook*. McGraw-Hill, New York, 1984.

market maker. A bank or broker that is prepared to make a TWO-WAY PRICE, (to buy or sell), for a currency or a security on a continuous basis.

market order An order to buy or sell a stock, commodity or financial future at the best possible price and as soon as possible, in contrast to a LIMIT ORDER, which will specify a limit.

marking name. UK Stock Exchange term. A system to help trading in American and

Canadian shares. If an individual buys such a share it is normally registered, not in his name but in the 'marking name' of a London broker, jobber or bank whose name is acceptable to the Stock Exchange as a marking name. Shares in these names can be transferred after endorsement as though they were bearer certificates. The certificate is held by an AUTHORIZED DEPOSITARY on behalf of the owner, and the depositary claims dividends etc. from the 'marking name'.

Bibliography: J. Dundas Hamilton. *Stockbroking Today*. Macmillan, London 1979.
Rules and Regulations of the Stock Exchange. (Rule 141), London, 1978.

MAS. *See* MONETARY AUTHORITY OF SINGAPORE.

masse monétaire. French term for money supply.

matched sales. US term for action by the Federal Reserve to absorb reserves temporarily by selling securities with an agreement to buy them back within a specified period (up to 15 days) at a specified price. Also called reverse repurchase agreements or reverse repos.

Bibliography: M. Stigum. *The Money Market*. Dow-Jones Irwin, Homewood, Ill. 1983.

matching. Refers to the process of equating assets and liabilities, either in terms of currency or in terms of time. For example, one can match a DM asset against a DM liability or one can match a three-months deposit by on-lending it for three months. Compare ASSETS REPRICED BEFORE LIABILITIES; GAP; MIS-MATCH.

Bibliography: S.I. Davis. *The Euro-bank*.Macmillan, London/John Wiley, New York, 1981.
B.F. Binder & T.W.F. Lindquist. *Asset/Liability and Funds Management at US Commercial Banks*. Bank Administration Institute, Rolling Meadow, Ill., 1982.
J.K. Walmsley. *The Foreign Exchange Handbook*. John Wiley & Sons, New York, 1983.

matrix. The CONSENSUS on export credit subsidies has laid down a set of interest rates which varies according to the relative wealth of the country which is borrowing, and the maturity of the deal. The rates are commonly set out in matrix form, and the set of rates as a whole referred to as 'the matrix'.

Bibliography: A. Dunn & M. Knight. *Export Finance*. Euromoney Publications, London, 1982.
K. Taylor. A Case for Export Credit Subsidies. *The Banker*. London, February 1984.

maturity. (1) When an obligation has been entered into for a specified period of time, it is said to have a maturity of that period. For example, if a deposit is placed with a bank for an agreed period of three months it is said to have a maturity of three months. The maturity date of a bond is the final date by which it must be repaid. As a measure of the term of an obligation, maturity ignores the effect of interest rates, which are adjusted for in the concept of DURATION; and it ignores the repayment structure within the life of the deal, which is measured by the concept of AVERAGE LIFE. Compare CALL; MIS-MATCH; REDEMPTION; YIELD TO MATURITY; YIELD CURVE.

(2) Commodity market term for the period within which a futures contract can be settled by delivery of the actual commodity : the period between the first notice day and the last trading day of a commodity futures contract.

maturity gap exposure. A term used in foreign exchange and money markets denoting the risk arising from having an asset and liability of the same size and in the same currency but of different maturity. If a bank sells $1 million spot and buys $1 million three months forward, this leaves it short of dollars now, and long in the future: the risk arises from the possibility of its having to 'close out' the swap before it matures by buying $1 million and selling it forward. A similar risk arises where a bank has made a one-year loan, funded by a three-month deposit: if rates rise, the loan may have to be funded at a loss. Compare ASSETS REPRICED BEFORE LIABILITIES.

Bibliography: J.K. Walmsley. *The Foreign Exchange Handbook*. John Wiley & Sons, New York, 1983.
B.F. Binder & T.W.F. Lindquist. *Asset/Liability and Funds Management at US Commercial Banks*. Bank Administration Institute, Rolling Meadows, Ill., 1982.

MCA.   Abbreviation for MONETARY COMPENSATORY AMOUNT.

Mediocredito Centrale.   *See* ISTITUTO CENTRALE PER IL CREDITO A MEDIO TERMINE.

merchanting.   The process where an operator in country A buys goods in country B and ships them direct from B to C without bringing them to A. Often referred to as third-country trade.

MERM.   Abbreviation for the International Monetary Fund's MULTILATERAL EXCHANGE RATE MODEL.

Mibor.   *See* MADRID INTERBANK OFFERED RATE.

mille.   Latin for thousand: '6 per mille' = '0.6%'.

milliard.   European term for 1,000 million. Now generally superseded by 'billion'.

minimum lending rate (MLR).   In the past, the Bank of England would fix a minimum rate at which it would lend to the DISCOUNT HOUSES. In 1981 this was abolished, to be replaced by a system of various BANDS within which the Bank would lend to the discount houses against bills of differing maturity.
Bibliography: Monetary Control Provisions. *Bank of England Quarterly Bulletin*. September 1981.
E.R. Shaw. *The London Money Market*. Heinemann, London, 1983.
The Role of the Bank of England in the Money Market. *Bank of England Quarterly Bulletin*. March 1982.

minimum rate.   In a FLOATING RATE NOTE issue, it is customary to make a provision that the rate payable on the note can never fall below a certain minimum rate.
Bibliography: G. Ugeux. *Floating Rate Notes*. Euromoney Publications, London, 1981.

minimum yield.   US term referring to the lesser of YIELD-TO-CALL and YIELD-TO-MATURITY.
Bibliography: S. Homer & M. L. Leibowitz. *Inside the Yield Book*. Prentice-Hall, NJ, 1972.

minor bracket, underwriter.   *See* BRACKET.

mis-match.   A situation where assets and liabilities in a foreign currency do not balance; the imbalance may be either in size or maturity. Similarily, in money markets the term is used in a situation where an asset is being funded by a liability of dissimilar maturity, e.g. money is borrowed, repayable in one month, and is deposited for three months, in the belief that when the one-month borrowing matures it can be 'rolled over'.
Bibliography: J.K. Walmsley. *The Foreign Exchange Handbook*. John Wiley & Sons, New York, 1983.

MITI.   Japanese Ministry of International Trade and Industry.

MLR.   Abbreviation for MINIMUM LENDING RATE.

mobilisation.   French term for discounting of paper (with the Banque de France in most circumstances).

modern portfolio theory.   Term for a body of theories about the way in which stock markets work and portfolios should be managed. The most notable concepts are the relationship of risk to reward, and its measurement through BETA, and the 'efficient markets' theory which holds that at any one point in time the market discounts all available known information.
Bibliography: D. Corner & D.G. Mayes (eds). *Modern Portfolio Theory and Financial Institutions*. Macmillan, UK, 1983.
R. Dobbins & S.F. Witt. *Portfolio Theory and*

Investment Management. Martin Robertson, UK, 1983.

momentum model. A theory, much used in TECHNICAL ANALYSIS. Momentum measures the absolute change in price over an interval of time. A 10-day momentum is the net price change over a 10-day period; an n-day momentum can be expressed as $M(n) = P(t) - P(t - n)$.
Bibliography: N. Rothstein & J.M. Little. *The Financial Futures Handbook*. McGraw-Hill, New York, 1984.

monetarist. A person believing that monetary factors have a determining influence on the behaviour of an economy. A central tenet of this approach is frequently a (more or less sophisticated) QUANTITY THEORY of money. Monetarism fell out of favour during Keynes' times and was very largely revived by Professor Milton Friedman of the University of Chicago. Compare M1, M2, M3.
Bibliography: M. Friedman (ed.). *Studies in the Quantity Theory of Money*. Chicago University Press, UK, 1956.
C.A.E. Goodhart. *Monetary Theory and Practice*. Macmillan, London, 1984.
N. Kaldor. *The Scourge of Monetarism*. Oxford University Press, UK, 1982.

Monetary Authority of Singapore (MAS). Fulfilling the functions of a Central Bank of Singapore, MAS effectively supervises much of the ASIAN DOLLAR MARKET.
Bibliography: MAS Annual Reports & Quarterly Review.

monetary base. Generally defined as currency in circulation plus banks' required and excess deposits at the central bank; more precise definitions vary from country to country. The essence of the concept is that it attempts to measure the liabilities of the central bank to the public and the banks, on the grounds that the central bank should be able to control this aggregate more easily than it can control the MONEY SUPPLY.
Bibliography: The Monetary Base – a Statistical Note. *Bank of England Quarterly Bulletin*. March 1981.

Bank for International Settlements (ed.). *The Monetary Base Approach to Monetary Control*. Basle, Switzerland, 1980.
P. Meek (ed.). *Central Bank Views on Monetary Targeting*. Federal Reserve Bank of New York, New York, 1983.

monetary compensatory amounts (MCA). A term used in EEC agricultural finance. EEC agricultural prices are intended to be uniform throughout the Community, and are therefore fixed in EEC UNITS OF ACCOUNT. When a currency is floating, its value – and therefore agricultural prices expressed in it – fluctuate in relation to the unit of account. Monetary compensatory amounts counterbalance the fluctuation. When a currency is revalued, MCAs are charged on imports – otherwise they would be cheaper in the revaluing country – and paid on exports, since otherwise these would be more expensive than in other EEC countries. Vice versa for devaluation.
Bibliography: R.W. Irving & H.A. Fearn. *Green Money and The Common Agricultural Policy*. Centre for European Agricultural Studies, Wye College, Ashford, Kent, UK.

monetize. Term meaning 'to convert assets into money'. For example, an increase in the US Treasury's gold stock is monetized when the Treasury issues GOLD CERTIFICATES to the Federal Reserve in exchange for cash. In effect, the Treasury mortgages its gold to the Federal Reserve, obtaining money in exchange for its gold stock.
Bibliography: *The Federal Reserve System: Purposes and Functions*. Board of Governors of the Federal Resrve, Washington DC, 1974.

money broker. Term for a firm which specializes in introducing banks to each other to take and place deposits with each other. Such firms are active in the domestic money markets of the US, UK, Japan, Germany, France, Italy, Spain and many other countries, and also operate internationally in the EUROMARKETS. They are often allied with, or part of, a firm of FOREIGN EXCHANGE BROKERS.
Bibliography: J.K. Walmsley. Eurocurrency Deal-

ing *in* A.M. George & I.H. Giddy (eds). *International Finance Handbook*. John Wiley & Sons, New York, 1983.

money market deposit account. Introduced in December 1982 the MMDA was effectively the first US retail deposit account free from interest rate controls. As such it represented an important step in the deregulation of the banking industry.
Bibliography: J.A. Talom. Money Market Deposit Accounts, Super-NOWs and Monetary Policy. *Federal Reserve Bank of St, Louis Review,* March 1983.

money market preferred. A US term for a type of share issue. It resembles ADJUSTABLE RATE PREFERRED STOCK and derivatives of the latter. An example is the issue of $500 million money market preferred in 1984 by American Express via Lehman Brothers. Dividends were kept in line with the AA commercial paper rate and set by regular auctions. The benefits of the technique are to provide equity capital to the issuer at money market rates, while the investor (if a US corporation) could exclude 85% of the dividend income from taxable income.

money-over-money lease. Money-over-money leases are structured so that the sum of the lease rental payments plus any additional obligation the lessee has at the end of the lease term will pay off the original cost and give the lessor an interest rate of return in excess of his funding cost. I.e. a money-over-money lease guarantees the lessor a spread over his funding cost. As such, it is generally rather an expensive financing alternative, but sometimes may be the only appropriate alternative.
Bibliography: G. Reiners. Leasing in an International Context *in* A.M. George & I.H. Giddy (eds.). *International Finance Handbook*. John Wiley & Sons, New York, 1983.
F.P. Slattery. Leasing Ventures *in* M.E.Blume & J.P. Friedman. *Encyclopaedia of Investments*. Warren, Gorham & Lamont, New York, 1982.

Moody's. A US firm which provides a system of rating bonds, in grades from Aaa through Baa down to C. Moody's also rates commercial paper. Compare STANDARD & POOR'S.
Bibliography: *Moody's Bond Record*, New York, monthly.

moratorium. An arrangement where a borrower declares inability to repay some or all of his outstanding debts. Compare DEFAULT, RESCHEDULING.

mortgage-backed securities. US term for BONDS which are backed by the COLLATERAL of mortgages – either by mortgages guaranteed by GNMA or similar institutions, or other pools of mortgages. The market in such securities has grown explosively since 1970 and more than 50% of US housing finance is now packaged through this market.
Bibliography: M.A. Smilow. The Move Towards Mortgage Securitization. *Mortgage Banking*. New York, December 1983.
L.C. Brendsel. Freddie Mac's Swap Programs. *Mortgage Banking*. New York, October 1983 .

most favoured nation. A term of international trade. It refers to an agreement by one state to treat another state at least as well as any third state. Thus country A would agree with B that if A made any concessions to C, then B would automatically benefit from the same concession. This protects B's interests since its advantage will not be eroded by a later concession to C. B knows that it will always be treated as well as the most favoured nation. The concept is a key one in international trade negotiations.
Bibliography: A. Shonfield (ed.). *International Economic Relations of the Western World 1959-71.* Royal Institute of International Affairs, London, 1976.
A.I. MacBean & P.N. Snowden. *International Institutions in Trade and Finance*. George Allen & Unwin, London, 1981.

MTN *See* MULTILATERAL TRADE NEGOTIATIONS.

multi-currency loan. A loan in which several currencies are involved. It may be a bond denominated in several currencies whose parities are irrevocably fixed, such as the EUROPEAN CURRENCY UNIT or a bond denominated in one currency and convertible into equities denominated in another; or it may be a bond denominated in a UNIT OF ACCOUNT where the lender is paid as to interest and principal in one or more currencies depending on circumstances or his choice. Or the loan may be provided in the form of a medium-term ROLL-OVER CREDIT with the option of drawing different currencies in successive roll-overs.

Bibliography: F.G. Fisher. *International Bonds.* Euromoney Publications London, 1982.

Multilateral Exchange Rate Model (MERM). A model developed by the INTERNATIONAL MONETARY FUND to measure changes in the EFFECTIVE EXCHANGE RATES of certain countries. Its primary function is to develop sophisticated weights (rather than, e.g. the weights based on bilateral trade used in many indices) for inclusion in the calculation of trade- weighted exchange rates.

Bibliography: J.R. Artus & R.R. Rhomberg. A Multilateral Exchange Rate Model. *IMF Staff Papers,* November 1973.
J. Artus & A. McGuirk. A Revised Version of the Multilateral Exchange Rate Model. *IMF Staff Papers vol. 28, no. 2, 1981.*

multilateral netting. Term often used in INTERNATIONAL MONEY MANAGEMENT. A company with multinational trade flows may be able to net out its credits and debits between subsidiaries or associates in various countries leaving only the balance to be settled, thus reducing its need to acquire foreign currency.

Bibliography: J.K. Walmsley. *The Foreign Exchange Handbook.* John Wiley & Sons, New York, 1983.

multilateral trade negotiations. In general, trade negotiations conducted between many countries. Often used to refer to a 'round' of negotiations begun in Tokyo in 1973 (the 'Tokyo round'). Compare DILLON ROUND, KENNEDY ROUND.

Bibliography: A.I. MacBean & P.N. Snowden. *International Institutions in Trade and Finance.* George Allen & Unwin, London,1981.
GATT Annual Reports.

multiple exchange rates. A number of countries operate systems where different exchange rates are used for different transactions. For instance, there may be one exchange rate for the import of essential raw materials, and a less favourable one for luxuries. The IMF disapproves of multiple exchange rates but has to tolerate them.

Bibliography: *Annual Report on Exchange Arrangements & Exchange Restrictions.* IMF, Washington DC.

multi-tier LIBOR. A situation where LIBOR varies according to the standing of the bank. Normally there is relatively little variation but in difficult conditions a 'second-tier' or 'third-tier' bank will have to pay substantially more than a 'prime' bank for its money.

Bibliography: S.I. Davis. *The Euro-bank.* Macmillan, London/ John Wiley & Sons, New York 1981.
T. Anderson and P. Field. The Tremors that Threaten the Banking System. *Euromoney.* London, October 1982.

municipal bond. A bond issued by a municipality. The term normally refers to US issues. These fall into two classes: general obligation bonds, backed by the 'full faith and credit' (and the taxing power) of the issuer and REVENUE BONDS backed by specific revenues.

Bibliography: *Fundamentals of Municipal Bonds.* Public Securities Association, New York, 1981.

mutual fund. *See* INVESTMENT COMPANY.

N

naked. Refers to the writer of an OPTION who does not hold the underlying stock or commodity against which he is writing a CALL option. A naked writer has a limited profit potential and an unlimited risk (although in practice the risk is limited by the life of the option); but the initial cash cost of the position is small, and in stable markets the strategy will be more profitable than a short sale of the stock or commodity.
Bibliography: L.G. McMillan. *Options as a Strategic Investment*. New York Institute of Finance, New York, 1980.

naked option. An OPTION contract where the writer of the option does not have a position in the underlying stock or commodity which protects him.
Bibliography: L.G. McMillan. *Options as a Strategic Investment*. New York Institute of Finance, New York, 1980.

name. (1) Refers to a member of a Lloyd's insurance syndicate who provides part of its capital, is personally liable for losses and receives part of any profits. Compare LLOYD'S.
Bibliography: H. C. Cockrell. *Lloyd's of London: a portrait*. Woodhead-Faulkner, Cambridge, UK/ Dow Janes Irwin, Homewood, Ill., 1984.
(2) Shorthand in money and foreign exchange markets referring to other participants. For example, 'I can't do the name' means 'I am not permitted to trade with that institution'.
(3) In US securities markets, a STREET NAME is used for easing security transfers.
Bibliography: L. M. Loll & J. G. Buckley. *The Over-the-Counter Securities Markets*. Prentice-Hall, USA, 1981.
(4) MARKING NAME is used similarly in the UK.

NASD. *See* NATIONAL ASSOCIATION OF SECURITIES DEALERS.

NASDAQ. *See* NATIONAL ASSOCIATION OF SECURITIES DEALERS AUTOMATED QUOTATIONS.

National Association of Securities Dealers. US body regulating OVER-THE-COUNTER securities industry practice. Like the UK Stock Exchange it operates primarily by self-regulation rather than law. It regulates trading practices, registration of new issues and the like, as well as administering NASDAQ. Compare SECURITIES & EXCHANGE COMMISSION.
Bibliography: L.M. Loll & J.G. Buckley. *The Over-the-Counter Market*. Prentice-Hall, NJ, 1981.

National Association of Securities Dealers Automated Quotations. A US computerized system providing bid and offer prices on 3,900 unlisted stocks, supplied by nearly 500 firms making markets in these securities. Founded in 1971, by 1983 annual trading volume was 16,000 million shares. The system provides three levels of operation. Level 1 is available to National Association of Securities Dealers members' sales staff. Level 2 is available to retail traders in stocks. Level 3 is available only to MARKET-MAKERS.
Bibliography: L.M. Loll & J.G. Buckley. *The Over-the-Counter Market*. Prentice-Hall, NJ, 1980.
R. Winder. The Final Days of the Trading Floor. *Euromoney*, London, October 1984.

National Securities Clearing Corporation (NSCC). The company which handles STOCK transfer arrangements in the US. The National Securities Clearing Corporation began operations in 1977. Until that time, CLEARING functions had been handled by individual exchanges. The NSCC is jointly owned by the New York and American Stock Exchanges and the NATIONAL ASSOCIATION

OF SECURITIES DEALERS. With the SECUR- ITIES INDUSTRY AUTOMATION CORPORATION as its processing agent, the NSCC nets all trades submitted to it and then determines the balances in securities and cash that must be settled. It then transfers securities held in participants' accounts at the DEPOSITORY TRUST COMPANY, or produces 'balance orders' that ensure the necessary physical transfer of securities between firms.

Bibliography: R.J. Teweles & E.S. Bradley. *The Stock Market.* John Wiley & Sons, New York, 1982.
L.M. Loll & J.G. Buckley. *The Over-The-Counter Securities Markets.* Prentice-Hall, NJ, 1981.

NCM. *See* NEDERLANDSCHE CREDIETVER- ZEKERING MAATSCHAPPIJ.

nearby month. Commodity market term for the FUTURES CONTRACT closest to MATURITY.

Nederlandsche Credietverzekering Maats- chappij. A privately owned Dutch insur- ance company. It reinsures with the state non-commercial risks and certain medium and long- term commercial risks.

Bibliography: *The Export Credit Financing Sys- tems in OECD Member Countries.* Organization for Economic Cooperation and Development, Paris, 1982.

negative carry. A situation where the YIELD on a security is less than the cost of funds borrowed to finance it.

negative float. *See* FLOAT (2).

negative interest. In certain circumstances a depositor may be forced to pay interest rather than receive it. The classic example is Swiss franc deposits. Foreign buyers of Swiss franc deposits have been required by the authorities to pay interest of up to 40% per annum on the deposits.

Bibliography: J.K. Walmsley. *The Foreign Ex- change Handbook.* John Wiley & Sons, New York, 1983.

negative pledge. A clause in a loan agree- ment where the borrower agrees with the lender that it will not create security in favour of a subsequent creditor without the approval of the lender, or without extending the benefit of the security equally to the first creditor. A typical clause in respect of a bond issue might read (in part): 'The company shall not and shall procure that no subsidiary shall create or permit to subsist any mort- gage, lien, pledge or other charge upon any part of their respective undertakings or assets as security for any obligation...without at the same time according to the bondholders a pari passu and rateable interest in the same security...'.

Bibliography: M.W. McDaniel. Are negative pledge clauses in public debt issues obsolete? *The Business Lawyer,* New York, May 1983.
P. Wood. *Law and Practice of International Finance.* Sweet & Maxwell, London, 1980.

negatively sloping yield curve. A YIELD CURVE where interest rates in the shorter dates are above those in the longer. For example, if one week sterling costs 6%, one month 5.5%, and six months 5% the slope is negative. Such a shape is unusual, occurring only when interest rates are expected to fall, though a yield curve may often be negatively sloping along part of its length.

negotiable instrument. A negotiable instru- ment has the following characteristics:
(1) The title to it passes on delivery or delivery and endorsement.
(2) The holder for the time being can sue in his own name.
(3) No notice of assignment need be given to the person liable on the instrument.
(4) A holder in due course takes free from any defect in the title of his predecessors. Examples of negotiable instruments include bills of exchange, cheques, and dividend warrants. Compare NEGOTIATION; BILL OF EXCHANGE.

Bibliography: J.D. McLoughlin. *Introduction to Negotiable Instruments.* Butterworths, London, 1975.
C.M. Schmitthoff & D.A.G. Sarre. *Charlesworth's Mercantile Law.* Stevens & Sons, London, 1984.

negotiable order of withdrawal (NOW). A US term for a device creating an interest bearing current account (checking account) at a bank for non-business depositors, originating in New England. NOW accounts are considered in law as savings accounts but in practice the negotiable order of withdrawal is a cheque.

Bibliography: D.B. Crane & M.J. Riley. *NOW Accounts: Strategies for Financial Institutions.* Lexington Books, US, 1978.
J.A. Tatom. Money Market Deposit Accounts, Super-NOWs and Monetary Policy. *Federal Reserve Bank of St. Louis Review*, March 1983.

negotiation. (1) Generally, the discussions concerning an agreement or contract.

(2) The negotiation of a BILL OF EXCHANGE is defined in the UK Bills of Exchange Act, 1882: (a) A bill is negotiated when it is transferred from one person to another in such a manner as to constitute the transferee the holder of the bill. (b) A bill payable to bearer is negotiated by delivery. (c) A bill payable to order is negotiated by the endorsement of the holder completed by delivery.'

(3) Negotiation is also used to refer to the purchase by a bank of its customer's OUTWARD COLLECTION. The customer – usually an exporter – is thus given finance, and the bank looks to the overseas party for payment. If he does not pay, the bank will normally have RECOURSE to its customer for the funds, although it is also possible for a bill to be negotiated without recourse. The negotiating bank acquires full rights in the bill, whereas if it is merely collecting the bill it has no rights as such – it is merely an agent for its customer. The following table, adapted from Watson's *Finance of International Trade*, compares negotiation and DISCOUNTING:

Discounting	Negotiation
(1) There must be a bill of exchange.	(1) It is possible to negotiate shipping documents.
(2) The bill must be a term bill.	(2) Sight or term bills can be negotiated.
(3) The bill must be accepted.	(3) The bill is unlikely to be accepted.
(4) There needs to be a market for rediscounting.	(4) No market for negotiated paper.

(5) The bill can be held in portfolio or rediscounted.	(5) The bill is sent abroad for payment.
(6) The drawee/acceptor must be known locally.	(6) The drawee/acceptor is a foreign name.
(7) The bill is payable locally.	(7) The bill is payable abroad.

Bibliography: M. Megrath & F. R. Ryder. *Byles on Bills of Exchange.* 23rd edn. Sweet & Maxwell, London, 1972.
A. Watson. *Finance of International Trade.* Institute of Bankers, London, 1981.

net additions. A term used in the control of the UK DISCOUNT MARKET. The Bank of England has laid down a limit for a discount house's total value of assets held plus net additions, which must not exceed 40 times the capital base of the discount house. Net additions are the total of a risk weighting factor multiplied by the value of assets in each of the three classes of ADDED RISK .

Bibliography: Prudential arrangements for the Discount Market. *Bank of England Quarterly Bulletin.* June 1982.
J.S.G. Wilson. Recent Changes in London's Money Market Arrangements. *Banca Nazionale del Lavoro Quarterly Review.* March 1983.

net borrowed reserves. US term indicating a shortage of reserves in the banking system as a whole – NET FREE RESERVES are negative. A net borrowed reserve position indicates that interest rates will probably tighten.

Bibliography: P. Meek. *US Monetary Policy and Financial Markets.* Federal Reserve Bank of New York, 1982.

net free reserves. US term for available RESERVES in the banking system. The exact definitions are: Net free reserves = total reserves – required reserves – adjustment borrowing = non-borrowed reserves – required reserves. A net free reserve position indicates that interest rates will probably tend to ease. Compare NET BORROWED RESERVES.

Bibliography: P. Meek. *US Monetary Policy and Financial Markets.* Federal Reserve Bank of New York, 1982.

net registered tonnage. The gross registered tonnage of a ship (calculated on cubic capacity at 100 cubic feet per ton) less engine room, navigation, light, air, locker room spaces etc. It represents the actual carrying capacity of the ship; port dues and similar charges reflect the net registered tonnage.

net yield to redemption. The GROSS YIELD TO REDEMPTION on a security, adjusted to take account of taxation. *See also* YIELD.
Bibliography: The New 'Beginners Please'. Investors Chronicle, London, 1975.

new money. US term for the amount by which a replacement (REFUNDING) issue of securities exceeds the original issue.

new time bargain. UK Stock Exchange term. The Stock Exchange year is divided into 25 ACCOUNTS. A new time BARGAIN is one made during one account for settlement in the next; usually new time bargains may be done from the Thursday before the Monday on which the next account begins.
Bibliography: J. Dundas Hamilton. *Stockbroking Today*. Macmillan Press, London, 1979.

New York Futures Exchange (NYFE). NYFE opened in 1980. After a shaky start, it began trading stock exchange index FUTURES contracts in 1982; during the first 10 months of 1983, three million index contracts changed hands.
Bibliography: The New York Futures Exchange. *Euromoney Supplement* London January 1984.

New York Insurance Exchange. Set up in 1980, after the passage in 1978 of a law permitting a 'free trade zone' in New York for large (annual premiums over $100,000) commercial insurance contracts. Its chief objective has been to offer a North American alternative to LLOYD'S OF LONDON. Its early development has been relatively slow.
Bibliography: G.E. Rajda. *Principles of Insurance*. Scott, Foresman & Co., New York, 1982.

Nibor. Abbreviation for New York interbank offered rate. Compare LIBOR.

nickel. US term for five basis points (0.05%).

NINOW. Abbreviation for non-interest-bearing negotiable order of withdrawal. *See* NEGOTIABLE ORDER OF WITHDRAWAL.

nominal. Refers to the face value of a bond. For example, a GILT-EDGED security may represent £100 of Government debt to be repaid in five years' time, but may now be bought at a price of £85; i.e. for £85 I receive a piece of paper which states that I will be paid £100 in five years' time. The price is thus £85 per £100 nominal.

nominal effective exchange rate. An EFFECTIVE EXCHANGE RATE which is not adjusted for relative inflation differentials. Compare REAL EFFECTIVE EXCHANGE RATE.
Bibliography: J. Artus & A. McGuirk. A revised version of the multilateral exchange rate model. *IMF Staff Papers*, Washington DC, vol. 28, no 2, 1981.
G. Hacche & J. C. Townend. A Broad Look at Exchange Rate Movements for Eight Currencies. *Bank of England Quarterly Bulletin*, December, 1981.

nominalism. The legal principle that 'a pound is a pound'—a debt of £100 can be settled by tendering an amount specified by the law to be £100. One is not entitled to claim (say) that '£100 when the contract was drawn up was worth one once of gold; therefore I am entitled to payment of an once of gold rather than £100 in notes'. Compare REVALORIZATION.
Bibliography: F.A. Mann. *The Legal Aspect of Money*. Clarendon Press, Oxford, 1982.

nominee name. For convenience or concealment, a stock holding may be registered in the name of a company whose sole function is to hold stocks; this is a nominee company or nominee name.

non-borrowed reserves. US term for total reserves of the banking system, less borrowings from the DISCOUNT WINDOW. Under the operating systems introduced in October

1979, the Federal Reserve made the movement in non-borrowed reserves a central target in its monetary control procedures. Compare NET FREE RESERVES; net borrowed reserves.

Bibliography: P. Meek.*US Monetary Policy and Financial Markets*. Federal Reserve Bank of New York, 1982.

non-callable. US term for a bond which is exempt from redemption for a stated time period.

non-exempt. US term for securities subject to provisions of the Securities Acts of 1933 and 1934.

non-performing loans. US term for loans which are in trouble. Precise definitions vary. A common one would define non-performing loans as those where the lender's management judges that the borrower does not have the ability to meet the original contractual terms of the loan or where payments of interest or principal are overdue by 90 days or more. Compare DEFAULT.

non-proportional reinsurance. A term for REINSURANCE—such as EXCESS OF LOSS REINSURANCE—where the reinsurer's liability is not calculated proportionately to the insurer's.

non-recourse finance. A loan where the lenders look solely to the cash flow generated by the project being financed for repayment. There is no recourse to the sponsor of the project, so that the lenders assume all the commercial and political risks of the project. Pure non-recourse loans are rare (but see FORFAITING). However, certain components of a project are frequently financed on a non-recourse basis. In the financing of the UK's Forties oil field the lenders took the risk that sufficient oil reserves were there to finance repayment. Compare LIMITED RECOURSE FINANCE.

Bibliography: *Standard & Poor's Ratings Guide*. McGraw-Hill, New York, 1979.
P.K. Nevitt. *Project Financing*. Euromoney Publications, London, 1983.

non-refundable. Bonds ineligible, during a stated period, for redemption with funds raised through the sale of an issue having a lower interest cost. Non-refundable bonds are still subject to sinking funds provisions.

Bibliography: F.J. Fabozzi & I.M. Pollack.*The Handbook of Fixed Income Securities*. Dow-Jones Irwin, Homewood,Ill., 1983.

non-resident account. A bank account held by a person who is defined as non-resident for the purposes of exchange control. Compare RESIDENT.

Bibliography: J. Swidrowski. *Exchange and Trade Control*. Gower Press, UK, 1975.
Annual Report on Exchange Restrictions, International Monetary Fund, Washington DC, annually.

non-tariff barriers. These are factors (other than tariffs) inhibiting international trade. They include requiring advance deposits on import payments, customs and administrative procedures (e.g. at one time cars sold in Japan had to be shipped there for testing; if they failed they had to be shipped back and the potential expense deterred importers) and similar practices. The issue has been studied in detail by the Committee on Trade in Industrial Products of GATT.

Bibliography: Director General of GATT. *The Tokyo Round of Multilateral Negotiations.*, GATT, Geneva, April 1979.
GATT Annual Reports.
D. Greenaway. *International Trade Policy*. Macmillan Press, London, 1983.

northbound swap. US foreign exchange market term for a foreign exchange SWAP from US dollars into Canadian dollars – e.g. 'price in northbound threes, please' indicates a request for a quotation for a three-month swap into Canadian dollars. Compare SOUTHBOUND SWAP.

nostro account. If a British bank has an account in Paris with a French bank it will refer to that account as a nostro account. (*Nostro* = 'our' in Italian.) Compare LORO ACCOUNT; VOSTRO ACCOUNT.

Bibliography: A. Watson. *Finance of International Trade*. Institute of Bankers, London, 1981.

J.K. Walmsley. *The Foreign Exchange Handbook.* John Wiley & Sons, New York, 1983.

note. (1) A financial instrument consisting of a promise to pay (i.e. a PROMISSORY NOTE) rather than an order to pay (such as a bill OF EXCHANGE) or certificate of indebtedness (such as a BOND).

(2) If a bill of exchange is dishonoured by non-payment or non-acceptance it may be handed by the holder to a notary to be noted. The notary presents the bill again, and if it is still unpaid, or not accepted, it is noted. The noting consists of the notary's initials, the date, the noting charges, and a mark referring to the notary's register, written on the bill itself. The notary keeps these details and from them draws up the PROTEST if required.
Bibliography: *Thomson's Dictionary of Banking.* Pitman & Co., London, 1974.

NOW account. *See* NEGOTIABLE ORDER OF WITHDRAWAL.

NTB. *See* NON-TARIFF BARRIERS.

numeraire. Term denoting something which is used as a standard of measurement. For example, in an economy containing *n* goods, we may select one good, in terms of which we measure the relative values of the other *n*-1 goods. The good which is used for measuring the value of other goods is frequently defined as the 'money' of that economy. Internationally it is convenient to have a standard of measurement for international transactions. Internationally, the numeraire is frequently taken to be the US dollar, but it may equally well be the SDR or gold or some UNIT OF ACCOUNT.
Bibliography: J. Gold. *SDRs, Gold and Currencies: Fourth Survey of Legal Developments.* IMF Pamphlet no. 33, Washington DC, 1980.

Nybor. Abbreviation for New York Inter-Bank Offered Rate. Compare LIBOR.

O

objective indicators. During the debate on international monetary reform an attempt was made to define objective indicators which would determine when an exchange rate should be changed. Such indicators included changes in reserves, trade balance etc. The attempt did not meet with widespread success.

Bibliography: T. Underwood. *Analysis of Proposals for using Objective Indicators as a Guide to Exchange Rate Changes.* IMF Staff Papers, March 1973.
J.K. Horsefield. *Proposals for Using Objective Indicators as a Guide to Exchange Rate Changes: A Historical Comment.* IMF Staff Papers, November 1973.

OBU. *See* OFF-SHORE BANKING UNIT.

odd lot. A non-standard amount in a securities or foreign exchange transaction. It can be used to refer to a deal for less than the normal minimum.

OECD. Abbreviation for the ORGANIZATION FOR ECONOMIC CO-OPERATION AND DEVELOPMENT.

off. (1) A price quotation is said to be off if it is uncompetitive.
(2) A foreign exchange or money market dealer cancelling a previous bid with a BROKER might do so by saying 'off' – e.g. 'off the three-month guilders, I dealt elsewhere'.

off-balance-sheet finance. Pure NON-RE-COURSE FINANCE is 'off-balance-sheet' in the sense that finance is obtained but the borrower assumes no liability which could affect his balance sheet. A LEASE is also a form of off-balance-sheet finance in that it enables a company to acquire the use of an asset for a period without showing in the balance sheet either the asset or a borrowing to finance it. Compare LIMITED RECOURSE FINANCE.

Bibliography: T.M. Clark. *Leasing.* McGraw-Hill, UK, 1978.
P.K. Nevitt. *Project Financing.* Euromoney Publications, London, 1983.

offer. (1) The price at which a dealer will sell a currency or a security.
(2) The rate at which a bank will lend funds. Compare LONDON INTER-BANK OFFERED RATE.

offer for sale. UK Stock Exchange term for a new issue procedure whereby the STOCK-BROKERS sponsoring the issue offer to purchase the entire issue and then resell the issue to the public. Compare PLACING; INTRODUCTION.

Bibliography: J. Dundas Hamilton. *Stockbroking Today.* Macmillan Press, London, 1979.

offering telex. In the Euromarkets, a telex is often sent out by the MANAGER to banks offering participation in a bond issue or a credit. Compare BROADCAST SYSTEM; EURO-BOND; PROSPECTUS; SPECIAL BRACKET; UNDERWRITER.

Bibliography: L.S. Goodman. Syndicated Euro-currency Lending: Pricing and Practice *in* A.M. George & I.H. Giddy. *International Finance Handbook.* John Wiley & Sons, New York, 1983.

Office National du Ducroire. Official Belgian agency founded in 1939 with the function of providing export credit insurance and guarantees, and export finance. Its funds are provided by the government. It concentrates on insurance rather than direct financing.

Bibliography: *The Export Credit Financing Systems in OECD Member Countries.* Organization for Economic Cooperation and Development, Paris, 1982.

official gold price. This was the price at which the US Treasury was prepared to buy gold – for many years $35 per ounce. It become increasingly nominal and was abolished in 1976.

Bibliography: G.N. Halm. *Jamaica and the Par Value System.* Princeton Essays in International Finance No. 120, 1977.
T. Green. *The New World of Gold.* Walker & Co., New York, 1981.

official settlements balance. A means of measuring the US BALANCE OF PAYMENTS now replaced by 'Transactions in US Official reserve Assets and in Foreign Official Assets in the US'.

Bibliography: N.S. Fieleke. *What is the Balance of Payments?* Federal Reserve Bank of Boston Research Department, July 1976.
R.M. Stern *et al. The Presentation of the US Balance of Payments: A Symposium.* Princeton Essays in International Finance No. 123, 1977.

off-shore. A term describing the operations of a financial institution which, although physically located in a country, has little connection with that country's financial system. An example might be an investment trust with headquarters in the Bahamas whose business consists of receiving US dollar funds from European residents and investing them in New York. In absolute terms the largest off-shore centre is London because of the EUROMARKETS.

Bibliography: The Bahamas: Offshore Haven. *Euromoney*, London, October 1984.
R.C. Effros (ed.). *Emerging Financial Centers: Legal and Institutional Framework.* International Monetary Fund, Washington DC, 1982.

off-shore banking unit. A bank in Bahrain – or any other centre with similar organization – which is not permitted to do business in the domestic market, but only with other OBUs or with foreign institutions. By 1982 assets with Bahraini offshore banking units had reached $59 billion, with 75 OBU's operational, although growth now seems to have slowed somewhat, as the Saudi authorities have moved to tighten controls on off-shore riyal business.

Bibliography: Offshore Banks Hit the Spotlight. *Arab Banking and Finance.* London, July 1983.
OBUs: Beware of the Saudis. *Euromoney,* London, September 1984.

OKB. *See* OSTERREICHISCHE KONTROLL-BANK AG.

Old Lady. Popular term for the Bank of England.

OND. *See* OFFICE NATIONAL DU DUCROIRE

on-demand bond. A BOND, for example a PERFORMANCE BOND, under which the SURETY is obliged to pay to the beneficiary the full amount of the bond immediately upon first demand, *whatever the reason for the demand* (even if frivolous or unfair). Compare TENDER BOND.

Bibliography: Confederation of British Industry. *Performance Bonds and Guarantees.* London, 1978.
D. Sassoon. *Bidding for Projects Financed by International Lending Agencies.* Gower Press, UK, 1982.
W.F. von Marschall. Recent Developments in the Field of Standby Letters of Credit, Bank Guarantees and Performance Bonds *in* C.M. Chinkin *et al* (eds). *Current Problems of International Trade Financing.* Butterworths, UK/Malaya Law Review, 1983.

OPEC. *See* ORGANIZATION OF PETROLEUM EXPORTING COUNTRIES.

open account. A form of export transaction. The exporter forwards the shipping documents to the importer who is therefore able to obtain the goods immediately after they arrive without payment. There is usually an agreement between the two parties as to when the payment is to be made. The system depends on complete trust between the two parties. It is becoming more popular as the amount of trade between foreign subsidiaries of multinationals increases. It is also cheaper than payment by BILL OF EXCHANGE.

Bibliography: C.M. Schmitthoff. *The Export Trade.* 7th edn, Stevens & Sons, London, 1980.
A. Watson. *Finance of International Trade.* Institute of Bankers, London, 1981.

open cover. It is often inconvenient for a shipper to arrange separately for the insurance of individual shipments as isolated transactions; he will arrange a long-term insurance contract (termed 'open cover') against which all shipments can be declared and certificates of insurance issued. An open cover is not an insurance policy as such.
Bibliography: R.J. Lambeth. *Templeman on Marine Insurance.* Macdonald & Evans, UK, 1981.

open end. US term meaning to liquidate all or part of a portfolio and to hold cash or cash equivalents.

open-end fund. US term for a type of INVESTMENT COMPANY that has no fixed number of shares outstanding. It is analogous to the UK UNIT TRUST. The shares represent an interest in the fund's portfolio. New shares in the fund are offered to the public and any investor can sell shares back to the fund at market value. Price is determined by the net asset value, per share, or the underlying portfolio. Compare CLOSED-END FUND; INVESTMENT TRUST.
Bibliography: J.C. Bogle. Mutual funds *in* M.E. Blume & J.P. Friedman. *Encyclopaedia of Investments.* Warren, Gorham & Lamont, New York,1982.

open interest. The number of contracts with an exchange at the close of business each day which are recorded as not having been offset by an opposite trade, or settled by delivery. Open interest counts one side only – that is, an open interest of 5,000 contracts is 5,000 bought positions and 5,000 sold positions. A relatively large open interest tends to indicate commercial hedging, because hedgers are more likely than speculators to hold positions as prices fluctuate. Open interest is frequently watched as a technical indicator of the state of the market. Thus, a rising price trend with a gradual increase in open interest means that new long hedgers or speculators are entering the market. Such a market is technically strong.
Bibliography: N.H. Rothstein & J.M. Little (eds). *The Handbook of Financial Futures.* McGraw-Hill, New York, 1984.

J.K. Walmsley. *The Foreign Exchange Handbook.* John Wiley & Sons, New York, 1983.
C.W.J. Granger (ed.). *Trading in Commodities.* Woodhead-Faulkner, Cambridge, UK, 1983.

open market committee. A key committee of the FEDERAL RESERVE SYSTEM responsible for deciding on policy with regard to US interest rates. Normally referred to as the Federal Open Market Committee. Its minutes are published in the Federal Reserve Monthly Bulletin.
Bibliography: P. Meek. *US Monetary Policy and Financial Markets.* Federal Reserve Bank of New York, 1982.

open market operations. Term for central bank operations in money or securities markets. By buying or selling securities the central bank is in a position to influence interest rates.
Bibliography: E.R. Shaw. *The London Money Market..* Heinemann, London, 1983.
P.Meek. *US Monetary Policy and Financial Markets.* Federal Reserve Bank of New York, 1982.

open outcry. A system of dealing in markets where the dealers shout their bids or offers and the price varies accordingly.
Bibliography: R. Gibson-Jarvie. *The London Metal Exchange.* Woodhead-Faulkner, Cambridge, UK, 1983.
N.H. Rothstein & J.M. Little. *The Handbook of Financial Futures.* McGraw-Hill, New York, 1984.

open position. Foreign exchange term referring to a dealer's aggregate assets and liabilities in a currency. If they do not balance he is said to have an open position (or 'open net position'). For example, if a bank's assets denominated in DM, together with its outstanding forward contracts to receive DM, are greater than its DM liabilities and forward sales of DM, then the bank's open position is LONG of DM. Conversely, if total present and forward liabilities exceed present and forward assets it has an open 'short' position. Compare CLOSE.
Bibliography: J.K. Walmsley. *The Foreign Exchange Handbook.* John Wiley & Sons, New York, 1983.

open repo.   US securities market term for a REPO or repurchase contract which has no fixed maturity date; not particularly common.
Bibliography: M. Stigum. *The Money Market*. Dow-Jones Irwin, Homewood, Ill., 1983.

operating lease.   A LEASE where the payments received under the lease do not necessarily cover the purchase price, and the lessor expects to take the asset back and release it or resell it. By comparison, under a FINANCE LEASE the rental payments normally cover the full purchase price of the asset. Operating leases are often offered by equipment manufacturers rather than finance houses. Compare LEVERAGED LEASE; WET LEASE.
Bibliography: P.K. Nevitt.   *Project Financing*. Euromoney Publications, London, 1983.
A.F. Gargiulo & R.J. Kenard. *Leveraged Leasing*. American Management Association, New York, 1981.

Options Clearing Corporation (OCC).   A corporation formed for the purpose of clearing options by the various options exchanges in the US (including the CHICAGO BOARD OPTIONS EXCHANGE, and the New York, American, Philadelphia and Pacific Stock Exchanges). The OCC is the seller to every option holder and the buyer from every option holder: i.e., it stands between the writers of options and those who buy options, so as to eliminate the credit risk that would otherwise be present.
Bibliography: *Understanding the Risks and Uses of Listed Options*. Options Clearing Corporation, Chicago, 1983.

option contract.   (1) In foreign exchange, a contract to deal in foreign exchange, where the *date* of completion of the deal, but not the existence of the deal, is at the customer's choice within a specified period. He might, for example, sell forward DM with an option to deliver between October 1 and October 31. He is committed to selling forward,but has the option of the date on which he executes.If an exporter wishes to sell forward the proceeds from a delivery, but does not know the exact day on which the funds will arrive, such a contract is convenient.
Bibliography: J.K. Walmsley. *The Foreign Exchange Handbook*. John Wiley & Sons, New York, 1983.
J. Heywood. *Foreign Exchange and the Corporate Treasurer*. Adam & Charles Black, London, 1983.
(2) In a stock exchange or commodity market it is possible to buy an option which gives the choice of dealing in the commodity or shares at a certain price before a certain date. This differs from the foreign exchange option in that the deal itself – rather than its date – is optional. Thus, I might buy an option to buy shares in XYZ Co. at 50, with the option expiring in June. I am not committed to executing the purchase at all, but may choose to do so, or may sell the option, until June. Compare BEAR SPREAD; BOX SPREAD; BULL SPREAD; BUTTERFLY SPREAD; CALL; DIAGONAL SPREAD; HORIZONTAL SPREAD; PUT; SPREAD; VERTICAL SPREAD.
Bibliography: P. Welham. *Investing in Share Options, Warrants & Convertibles*. Woodhead-Faulkner, UK, 1975;
L.G. McMillan. *Options as a Strategic Investment*. New York Institute of Finance, 1980.

options markets   Markets in OPTIONS CONTRACTS have been known for many years, usually in conjunction with stock or commodity markets. However, they have, in general, been traded on a direct, or 'over-the-counter' basis. The main thrust towards the rapid development of options markets came with the development of LISTED OPTIONS which could be traded in a liquid secondary market. The CHICAGO BOARD OPTIONS EXCHANGE and the Philadelphia Stock Exchange were the main forces in developing the market in listed options on stocks, but since the last quarter of 1982 there has been an explosive growth in the number and type of options available, notably on foreign currency and on stock market indices, as well as options on futures contracts.
Bibliography: L.S. Goodman. New Options Markets. *Federal Reserve Bank of New York Quarterly Review*. Autumn, 1983.

L.G. McMillan. *Options as a Strategic Investment.* New York Institute of Finance, New York, 1980.

Organization for Economic Cooperation and Development (OECD). Set up in 1961 as a wider version of the Organization for European Economic Cooperation, which had been founded in 1948 to help coordinate the Marshall Plan aid and subsequently was involved in running the EUROPEAN PAYMENTS UNION. The OECD's main functions are monitoring economic developments – especially balances of payments in its WORKING PARTY 3 – in member countries; acting as a forum in coordinating aid to less developed countries through its DEVELOPMENT ASSISTANCE COMMITTEE and generally assisting economic cooperation. Further information may be obtained from the OECD's Information Department, 2 rue Andre-Pascal, 75775 Paris CEDEX 16, France.

Organization of Arab Petroleum Exporting Countries (OAPEC). Although OPEC is usually regarded as the prime force in determining international oil prices, OAPEC plays an important role in liaising between the Arab oil states and other Arab countries. Its membership is that of OPEC, less Ecuador, Gabon, Indonesia, Iran, Nigeria and Venezuela, plus Bahrain, Egypt and Syria.
Bibliography: L. Turner. *Oil Companies in the International System.* George Allen & Unwin, London 1983.

Organization of Petroleum Exporting Countries (OPEC). Founded in 1960, with headquarters in Vienna, OPEC's primary function is to facilitate the setting of world oil prices. Its members consist of Algeria, Ecuador, Gabon, Indonesia, Iran, Iraq, Kuwait, Libya, Nigeria, Qatar, Saudi Arabia, United Arab Emirates, and Venezuela.
Bibliography: P.R. Odell. *Oil and World Power.* 5th edn, Penguin Books, London, 1979, L. Turner. *Oil Companies in the International System.* George Allen & Unwin, London, 1978.

original issue discount. US term for the DISCOUNT on a newly issued security. Until 1982 there were some tax advantages in issuing a deeply discounted original issue discount security, and in certain circumstances there are other advantages to such a security. The classic OID is now the ZERO COUPON bond.
Bibliography: F.J. Fabozzi. Federal Income Tax Treatment of Fixed Income Securities *in* F.J. Fabozzi & I.M. Pollack (eds). *The Handbook of Fixed Income Securities.* Dow-Jones Irwin, Homewood, Ill., 1983.

Osterreichische Kontrollbank AG. Austrian export credit and insurance body founded in 1946 and owned by 12 Austrian credit institutions.Its resources are provided by borrowing, in particular by large-scale borrowing abroad. By 1980, 70% of its borrowings were in foreign currency.
Bibliography: *The Export Credit Financing Systems in OECD Member Countries.* Organization for Economic Cooperation and Development, Paris, 1982.

OTC. Abbreviation for OVER-THE-COUNTER.

out-of-the-money. Term relating to an OPTION which has NO INTRINSIC VALUE. A CALL option is out-of-the-money if the STRIKING PRICE on the option is above the market price; conversely a PUT option is out-of-the-money if the striking price is below the market price.
Bibliography: L.G. McMillan. *Options as a Strategic Investment.* New York Institute of Finance, 1980.

outright. Term referring to a purchase/sale or FORWARD EXCHANGE without a corresponding transaction SPOT. If I contract to buy dollars three months forward I make an outright forward purchase. If I simultaneously sell the same amount of dollars spot the deal would no longer be outright but would be a SWAP. The outright price is calculated from the spot price (£1 = $1.76 for example) and the FORWARD MARGIN – e.g. 5.2 cents or 520 points PREMIUM. In this case the outright price would be $1.7080.
Bibliography: J.K. Walmsley.*The Foreign Ex-*

change Handbook. John Wiley & Sons, New York, 1983.

outward collection. UK term for the collection of payment on a bill of exchange from a firm abroad. Compare COLLECTING BANK; INWARD COLLECTION.

over-carriage. Carriage of goods, beyond the initially intended destination (usually because they were refused at the destination).
Bibliography: R. Colinvaux. *Carver's 'Carriage of Goods by Sea'*. Stevens, London, 1971, pp. 621-2.

over-the counter (OTC). Term for a market in stocks and bonds which operates outside the stock exchanges. The OTC market is the principal market for US Government bonds. A small OTC market operates in the UK. There is also a substantial over-the-counter market in OPTIONS on foreign currency – competing with the Philadelphia options exchange in the US.
Bibliography: L.M. Loll & J.G. Buckley. *The Over-the-Counter Securities Markets*. Prentice-Hall, NJ., 1981.

Overseas Sterling Area. *See* STERLING AREA.

overshooting. Term for the failure of an exchange rate to find its true level, but to move beyond it, owing to temporary pressures, which then are reversed as the excessive movement of the exchange rate is perceived.
Bibliography: J.A. Frankel & C.A. Rodriguez. Exchange Rate Dynamics and the Overshooting Hypothesis. *IMF Staff Papers*, vol.29, No.1, 1982.

overtrade. A US securities market term for a method by which a discount is sometimes given on a new issue of securities. An institutional investor may be unwilling to pay cash for a new issue. Then the underwriter will take in exchange securities held by the investor. This SWAP is called an overtrade if the old securities are worth less than the new: e.g. if the underwriter sold $100,000 of new securities in exchange for $98,000 worth of the old.
Bibliography: H.S. Gerla. Swimming Against the Deregulatory Tide: Maintaining Fixed Prices in Public Offerings of Securities Through the NASD Antidiscounting Rules. *Vanderbilt Law Review*, US, January 1983.

P

paid-up capital. That part of the subscribed or issued CAPITAL of a company which has actually been paid for by shareholders. If the total capital authorized by the shareholders exceeds the paid-up capital, the remainder is said to be 'uncalled'. If there is no uncalled capital, the company's capital is said to be fully paid.
Bibliography: J. Dundas Hamilton. *Stockbroking Today.* Macmillan, London 1979.

paper. Generic term for Treasury bills, CDs, government and corporate securities etc.

par. (1) Refers to the nominal value of a security. If a share is issued with a face value of £1 and is subsequently traded at that price it is said to stand 'at par'.
Bibliography: L.M. Loll & J.G. Buckley. *The Over-the-Counter Securities Markets.* Prentice-Hall, NJ, 1981.
D. O'Shea. *Investing for Beginners* Financial Times Business Information, London, 1984.
 (2) The official value of a currency is its PAR VALUE.

par bond. Term for a bond selling at par, in line with prevailing new issues or estimated going yield rates.
Bibliography: S. Homer & M.L. Leibowitz. *Inside the Yield Book.* Prentice-Hall, US, 1972.

par value. Term for the official value of a currency. Following the entry into force (in April, 1978) of the Second Amendment to the Articles of Agreement of the INTERNATIONAL MONETARY FUND, par values no longer exist. The Second Amendment provides that, on a vote assented to by 85% of the voting power of the Fund, par values may be reintroduced 'in terms of the SDR, or in terms of such other common denominator as is prescribed by the Fund. The common denominator shall not be gold or a currency'. Compare SDR, Jamaica Agreement, Central Rate.
Bibliography: J. Gold. *SDRs, Gold and Currencies: Fourth Survey of New Legal Developments.* IMF Pamplet no. 33, Washington DC, 1980.

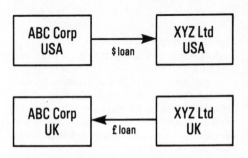

SUMMARY
1. US Corporation makes US$ loan to UK Corporation's US subsidiary.
2. In exchange UK Corporation makes £ loan to US Corporation's UK subsidiary.

PARALLEL LOAN

parallel loan. If ABC Corp. borrows sterling from XYZ Ltd in exchange for lending dollars to XYZ Ltd, the operation is called a parallel loan (see diagram). The technique has advantages in permitting a company with good natural access to one currency, which it does not need, to use that access to obtain another currency which it does need. Compare BACK-TO-BACK; CURRENCY EXCHANGE.
Bibliography: B. Kucinski. Where parallel loans may meet. *Euromoney,* London, January 1984.
B. Antl (ed.). *Swap Financing Techniques* . Euromoney Publications, London, 1983.

parastatal. Term referring to bodies having a quasi-government standing such as nationalised industries, highway authorities etc. It often applies to agencies more than 50% government controlled.

pari passu clause.   A clause in a loan agreement providing that the debt being incurred will rank equally and ratably with all other debts incurred by the borrower. 'The great trilogy of COVENANTS in unsecured international lending comprises the NEGATIVE PLEDGE, the pari passu clause, and the information covenant.' (Wood).
Bibliography: P. Wood. *Law and Practice of International Finance.* Sweet and Maxwell, London, 1980.
W.C.F. Kurz. New Form in the Loan Agreement. *Euromoney,* London, February, 1981.

Paris Club.   An informal grouping of governments which meets on an *ad hoc* basis to seek agreement on measures to be taken when a country is unable to repay its foreign borrowings on time. It began in 1956 with negotiations over Argentina's external debt. By the end of 1980, out of 47 RESCHEDULINGS for 16 countries, 32 had been had under the auspices of the Paris Club.
Bibliography: B. Nowzad & R.C. Williams. *External Indebtedness of Developing Countries.* IMF, Washington DC, 1981.
M.S. Mendelsohn. International debt crisis: the practical lessons of restructuring. *The Banker,* London, July 1983.

parity.   (1) Another term for par value.
(2) Foreign exchange dealers' slang for 'your price is the correct market price'.
(3) In the OPTIONS market, parity describes an IN-THE-MONEY option trading at its INTRINSIC VALUE. That is, it is an option which is trading at parity with the underlying commodity or stock: the investor will be indifferent between buying the stock directly or via an option.
Bibliography: L.G. McMillan. *Options as a Strategic Investment.* New York Institute of Finance, New York, 1980.

parity grid.   A term used in the context of the EEC SNAKE. The grid consists of the upper, central, and lower intervention points

of the snake, as defined by 2 ¼% fluctuation limits around the central rate. The grid lays out the permitted limits of fluctuation between, say, the Deutschemark and the Belgian franc, or between any two other currencies in the European Monetary System.
Bibliography: J.K. Walmsley. *The Foreign Exchange Handbook.* John Wiley & Sons, New York, 1983.

participating preference shares.   Term for stocks or shares where the holder is entitled to a preferential dividend and also in certain circumstances to a further participation in profits.
Bibliography: T.G. Goff. *Theory and Practice of Investment.* Heinemann, London, 1982.
L.M. Loll & J.G. Buckley. *The Over-the-Counter Securities Markets.* Prentice-Hall, NJ, 1981.

participation certificate.   (1) A document evidencing participation in a SYNDICATED domestic credit or EUROCREDIT. In the true participation deal, the lending bank makes the loan and then or later sells a portion of the loan to other banks, giving them a participation certificate, (Alternatively, the bank may act as AGENT BANK in putting together the credit.) The certificate may be in negotiable form so that it can more easily be sold. Compare TRANSFERABLE LOAN INSTRUMENT; SILENT SUBPARTICIPATION.
Bibliography: P. Wood. *Law and Practice of International Finance.* Sweet & Maxwell, London, 1980.
R.T. Nasberg. Loan Documentation. *The Business Lawyer.* New York, April 1981.
(2) US term for a certificate representing a beneficial interest in a pool of federal agency loans or mortgages. It is a formal credit instrument carrying a contractual interest obligation on a specified principal. The investor does not acquire title to the pooled assets, which continue to be held by the agency. Compare PASS-THROUGH.
Bibliography: D. Senft. Pass-Through Securities *in* F.J. Fabozzi & I.M. Pollack (eds). *The Handbook of Fixed Income Securities.* Dow-Jones Irwin, Homewood Ill., 1983.

participation fee. EUROMARKET term for a bank's fee for participating in a loan.
Bibliography: L.S. Goodman. Syndicated Euro-currency Lending: Pricing and Practice *in* A.M. George & I.H. Giddy. *International Finance Handbook*. John Wiley & Sons, New York, 1983.

particular average loss. This is defined in the UK's 1906 Marine Insurance Act as 'a partial loss of the subject matter insured, caused by a peril insured against, and which is not a GENERAL AVERAGE loss'.
Bibliography: Marine Insurance Act 1906, Section 64.
R. J. Lambeth. *Templeman on Marine Insurance.* Macdonald & Evans, UK, 1981.

partly paid. Term for a BOND or STOCK which is issued on the basis that the full purchase price need not be paid at once, but falls due to be payable over a period of time. For many years the UK government has issued GILT-EDGED stock on this basis, in order to smooth the impact on monetary aggregates of particular issues, and the technique has been widely used in the US and EUROBOND markets.
Bibliography: E. Pearlman. The partly paid fiasco. *Institutional Investor.* April, 1983.

pass-through. US term for a mortgage-backed security for which the payments on the underlying mortgages are passed from the mortgagee through the servicing agent to the security holder (see diagram). There may be (1) straight pass-through, whereby the security holder receives payments actually collected by the servicing agent; (2) fully modified pass-through where the security holder is paid whether or not the servicing agent has collected any money. GNMA pass-throughs are fully modified.
Bibliography: D.Senft. Pass-Through Securities *in* F.J. Fabozzi & I.M. Pollack (eds). *The Handbook of Fixed Income Securities.* Dow-Jones Irwin, Homewood Ill., 1983.

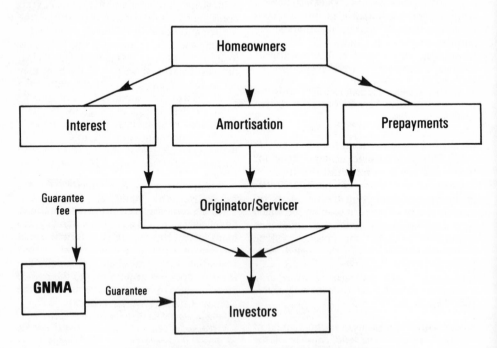

THE PASS-THROUGH PROCESS FOR GNMA'S

pay.   US slang for currency of denomination of a bond; e.g., 'yields rose on the US pay against Canadian pay'.

payables.   Refers to sums of money payable by a company. Compare RECEIVABLES.

pay-down.   US term for the sum by which the principal amount of securities maturing exceeds the amount of new securities being issued to replace them. The opposite of NEW MONEY.

payee.   The person in whose favour a BILL OF EXCHANGE is drawn.

paying agent.   In the process of issuing international securities it becomes necessary to arrange for the payment of cash or cheques to holders of the securities who will be receiving interest or dividends etc. The firm responsible, usually a bank, is known as the paying agent. Holders of the bonds present coupons and bonds to the paying agent in order to receive payments. Compare FISCAL AGENT.
Bibliography: F.G. Fisher. *International Bonds.* Euromoney Publications, London 1982.

payments balance.   *See* BALANCE OF PAYMENTS.

payment guarantee.   A guarantee to the supplier of goods that if he performs his obligations, he will be paid. The guarantee is the reverse, or counterpart, of a PERFORMANCE BOND.
Bibliography: W. von Marschall. Recent Developments in the Field of Standby Letters of Credit, Bank Guarantees and Performance Bonds. *in* C.M. Chinkin, P.J. Davidson & W.J.M. Riguier (eds). *Current Problems of International Trade Financing.* Malaya Law Review/Butterworths, 1983.

pay-up.   US term for the loss of cash resulting from the sale of one block of funds and the purchase of another block at a greater cost. Compare EVEN PAR SWAP.

peg.   A chosen level of an exchange rate. An exchange rate may be pegged above, at or below its PAR VALUE. The peg may be fixed, occasionally adjustable, or regularly altered.
Bibliography: P.B. Kenen. *Floats, Glides and Indicators.* Princeton International Finance Reprints No. 18, n.d.

pension.   French term for a money market borrowing against securities which are held 'in pension' by the lender until repayment.
Bibliography: D. Marteau & E. de la Chaise. *Le marché monétaire et la gestion de trésorerie des Banques.* Dunod, Paris, 1981.

Pensionsgeschaft.   German term (borrowed from the French) for a money market borrowing against securities which are held 'in pension' by the lender until repayment.
Bibliography: Deutsche Bundesbank. *The Deutsche Bundesbank: its monetary policy instruments and functions.* Deutsche Bundesbank Special Series no. 7, 1982.

performance bond guarantee.   An instrument of international trade. If a company is undertaking a contract, it may be asked to give a performance bond for, say, 10% of the value of the contract. If the customer feels that the compay's performance has been unsatisfactory, he will be able to take the bond to the banker providing the bond and demand payment. The bond is issued by the bank on behalf of the company, and therefore increases the bank's potential EXPOSURE to the company. It is important to note that some performance bonds have been required in the form of ON-DEMAND BONDS which present considerable risks in that the bank will be required to pay under the bond on demand, no matter whether there is any justification for the demand.
Bibliography: D. Sassoon (ed.). *Bidding for Projects Financed by International Lending Agencies.* Gower Press, UK, 1982.
W.F. von Marschall. Recent Developments in the Field of Standby Letters of Credit, Bank Guarantees and Performance Bonds *in* C.M. Chinkin *et al.* (eds). *Current Problems of International Trade Financing.* Butterworths UK/ Malaya Law Review, 1983.

performance letter of credit.   A LETTER OF

CREDIT which fulfils the same functions as a PERFORMANCE BOND. Such letters of credit may be opened by American banks in support of American companies' TENDERS for export contracts, as US banks are not permitted to issue performance or analogous bonds.
Bibliography: D. Sassoon(ed.). *Bidding for Projects Financied by International Lending Agencies*. Gower Press, UK, 1982.
W.F. von Marschall. Recent Developments in the Field of Standby Letters of Credit, Bank Guarantees and Performance Bonds *in* C.M. Chinkin *et al.* (eds). *Current Problems of International Trade Financing*. Butterworths, UK/ Malaya Law Review, 1983.

perpetual floater.   A FLOATING-RATE NOTE without any maturity date. The first perpetual floater was introduced for National Westminster Bank in 1984, to be followed by issues of $300 million by Belgium, $750 million by Sweden and $600 million by Denmark.

Pfandbriefe.   Paper issued by German mortgage banks (with an original maturity of up to 30 years) and sometimes traded on the Euromarkets. Secured by lendings of at least equal amount and yielding at least equal interest.

pick-up.   US term for the gain in yield resulting from the sale of one block of bonds and the purchase of another block with a greater yield.
Bibliography: S. Homer & M.L. Leibowitz. *Inside the Yield Book*. Prentice-Hall, NJ, 1972.

pig on pork.   British term for ACCOMMODATION PAPER: a BILL OF EXCHANGE drawn without an underlying transaction to support it.

pink book.   UK slang for the Central Statistical Office's Balance of Payments Yearbook.

pip.   Foreign exchange dealers' term for 0.00001 of a unit, e.g. if the $/Yen rate is quoted 220.20 then a rise of five pips would

yield 220.25. Sometimes used to mean POINT. Compare BIG FIGURE.

pit.   Futures market term for the (generally octagonal) space on the floor of the Exchange where traders gather.

placement memorandum.   A document prepared by the LEAD MANAGER of a SYNDICATE in the EUROCREDIT MARKET or the arranger of a PLACING. The memorandum seeks to give sufficient information to other potential lenders to enable them to decide whether to participate in the credit.
Bibliography: L.S. Goodman. Syndicated Eurocurrency Lending: Pricing and Practice. *in* A.M. George & I.H. Giddy. *International Finance Handbook*. John Wiley & Sons, New York, 1983.

placing.   Term for the process by which a new issue of BONDS or SHARES are sold to a pre-selected group of buyers. A placing may be 'public' or 'private'. Different rules operate in different markets. For example, in the UK, there are no fixed limits; but in the US, sale of a security to more than 35 buyers implies a public offering.
Bibliography: H. Lund *et al. Private Placements*. Euromoney Publications, London, 1984.

placing power.   Term for the ability of a bank or broker to sell securities to investors, i.e. to place the securities. Placing power is an important determinant of a bank's position in a SYNDICATE. Compare PRIVATE PLACEMENT.
Bibliography: S.I. Davis. *The Eurobank*. Macmillan, London/John Wiley, New York, 1981.
Union Bank of Switzerland. *The Underwriting Business in Switzerland*. Zurich, 1979.

plus.   US term for an additional 1/64th on stock quotations. If a security is quoted 98.4+ this means 98 and 4/32 plus 1/64th i.e. 98.140625. .

Poincaré franc.   *See* GOLD FRANC.

point.   (1) Foreign exchange dealers' term for 0.0001 of a unit, e.g. if the £/$ rate is 1.8495 then 1.8494 is one point lower. One point =

10 PIPS although the two terms are often used interchangeably.

(2) BOND market term for $1 per $100 or £1 per £100. For example, if a bond is quoted at $89 ½ per $100 nominal then a fall of one point would imply $88 ½.

pool. In most syndicated loans in the EURO-MARKET the LEAD MANAGERS negotiate with the borrower a 'management fee'. It is usual for the lead managers to cream off from this a PRAECIPUUM and to pay out to individual participants part of the total management fee on a sliding scale. Hence, the more the participants in the final syndicate, the larger the pool of unspent management fees available to be shared by the lead managers. Consider a loan of $100 million with four CO-LEAD MANAGERS each UNDERWRITING $25 million. The total MANAGEMENT FEE is ½% or, on $100 million, a total of $500,000; and the PRAECIPUUM is ⅛%, or $125,000. The following syndication fee structure is agreed: Participants providing $10 million: ⅜%; participants providing $5 million: ¼%; participants providing $2 million: ⅛%; participants providing $1 million: nil. Suppose now that the deal is syndicated and the SELL-DOWN is $52 million, broken down as follows: two providers of $10 million, three of $5 million, five of $2 million, and seven of $1 million. Then the total management fees paid out to the participants will be $125,000. The four co-lead managers will earn a ⅛% praecipuum, or $125,000, plus ⅜% on their commitment which now totals $48 million – the balance which was not sold down – costing $180,000. These fees account for $430,000 out of the original $500,000. The $70,000 balance is the POOL which results from the smaller participants being paid lesser participation fees. This pool will be shared between the co-lead managers, providing an extra 14 basis points in fees. If we suppose the deal has an AVERAGE LIFE of four years, then the effect of the pool is to enhance the lead managers' yield by 3.5 basis points per annum.
Bibliography: S.I. Davis. *The Euro-bank*. Macmillan, UK/John Wiley, New York, 1981.

pooling. The combination of the liquid assets of several companies into one account or one control point in order to optimize their management.
Bibliography: P. Muller (ed.). *Treasury Management*. Euromoney Publications, London, 1982.
P.J. Beehler. *Contemporary Cash Management*. John Wiley & Sons, New York, 1983.

positively sloping yield curve. A YIELD CURVE where interest rates in the shorter periods are below those in the longer. If one week sterling costs 5%, one month 5 ½%, and six months 6%, the yield curve is said to slope positively. This is the normal form. Compare NEGATIVELY SLOPING YIELD CURVE.

pot. US term for the portion of a security issue set aside by the syndicate manager for distribution to dealers or institutions.
Bibliography: L.M. Loll & J.G. Buckley. *The Over-the-Counter Securities Markets*. Prentice-Hall, NJ, 1981.

pot protection. US term for an arrangement ensuring an institution receives a specified amount of stock or bonds from a pot.
Bibliography: L.M. Loll & J.G. Buckley. *The Over-the-Counter Securities Markets*. Prentice-Hall, NJ, 1981.

praecipium, praecipuum. In the EUROMARKET the MANAGER of a credit or bond will negotiate a MANAGEMENT FEE payable by the borrower. From this the manager will deduct a specified amount for itself – the praecipium – before dividing the balance of the fee between the rest of the management group.
Bibliography: L.S. Goodman. Syndicated Eurocurrency Lending: Pricing and Practice. *in* A.M. George & I.H. Giddy. *International Finance Handbook*. John Wiley & Sons, New York, 1983.

preference share (stock). A share of stock which entitles the holder to preferential rights to the dividend over other shareholders. They bear a stated rate of dividend. Cumulative preference shares also carry the right to have any omitted dividend carried over to subsequent years; non-cumulative preference shares are only entitled to a dividend if profits in the current year are sufficient to pay it.

Bibliography: H.C. Sauvain. Preferred Stock *in* F.J. Fabozzi & I.M. Pollack (eds). *The Handbook of Fixed Income Securities*. Dow-Jones Irwin, Homewood, Ill., 1983.
D. O'Shea. *Investing for Beginners* . Financial Times Business Information, London, 1984.

premium. (1) A forward exchange rate standing at a premium over today's rate means that the currency concerned is more expensive in the forward market than now. If the 12 months forward dollar/DMark rate is DM2.7080 per $1 and today's spot rate is DM2.76, then the DMark is at a premium over the dollar for 12 months forward because $1 buys less DMarks 12 months ahead than it does today. The premium is 5.2 pfennigs or 520 points. In European foreign exchange forward quotations the existence of a premium is normally signified by the bank's selling price (quoted first) being above the buying price, thus: 520/510 in the example given. However, in the US, the markets tend to think in terms of the dollar, so the rate just quoted would be referred to as a dollar discount rather than a DMark premium.

Bibliography: J.K. Walmsley. *The Foreign Exchange Handbook*. John Wiley & Sons, New York, 1983.

(2) A bond, or share, is issued at a certain issue price: if the price at which it is traded rises over the issue price it is said to be standing at a premium over the issue price.

(3) The total price of an option contract – INTRINSIC VALUE plus TIME VALUE – is referred to as the premium.

Bibliography: L.G. McMillan. *Options as a Strategic Investment*. New York Institute of Finance, New York, 1980.

premium currency. *See* INVESTMENT CURRENCY.

prepayment fee (penalty). A penalty charged by banks for early repayment of a loan. The justification is that the loan is negotiated for a definite period, and the bank had to raise funds to cover this loan; early

termination means that it now has the problem of finding alternative employment of the funds.

prescription period. The period of time after which holders of a BOND cease to be entitled to principal and interest. The period for interest is normally half that for principal in the UK, usually 5 years and 10 years, or 6 and 12, while in Germany the practice tends to be 10 years for all claims.

Bibliography: P. Wood. *Law and Practice of International Finance*. Sweet & Maxwell, London, 1980.

pre-shipment finance. Finance to cover an exporter's costs prior to despatch of the goods. Most export finance such as DOCUMENTARY or SUPPLIER CREDITS depends on evidence that the goods have been shipped overseas. The exporter has to finance himself until this point. In certain cases however banks may be able to make finance available to cover pre-shipment expenses, and in some countries the export credit agency may also be able to provide assistance.

Bibliography: A. Dunn & M. Knight. *Export Finance*. Euromoney Publications, London, 1982.

price auction. *See* AUCTION.

price-earnings ratio. The ratio of estimated earnings from a company's STOCK to the price paid for it. A high P/E ratio means the market values a company's earnings highly: either because they are expected to continue growing rapidly, or because of other reasons, such as an expected takeover.

Bibliography: R. Brealey & S. Myers. *Principles of Corporate Finance*. McGraw-Hill, New York/London, 1984.

primary commodity. A commodity which has not yet undergone any significant degree of processing. Examples include raw wool, natural rubber, crude oil, iron ore etc.

primary dealer. US term meaning a dealer in US government securities with whom the

Federal Reserve conducts 'open market operations'. When an institution believes it is performing the function of a government securities dealer and is a significant market participant, it may contract the New York Federal Reserve Bank and begin reporting activity and positions informally. After evaluation the Reserve Bank may add the dealer to its list of primary dealers.

Bibliography: P. Meek. *US Monetary Policy and Financial Markets*. Federal Reserve Bank of New York, 1982.

primary market. Term referring to securities markets. The primary market is the market for new security issues; in other words, participants consist of all those to whom newly issued securities are sold. Subsequent transactions in the security are said to take place in the SECONDARY MARKET. Compare AFTER-MARKET; PRIVATE PLACEMENT; SYNDICATE TERMINATION.

Bibliography: *The Underwriting Business in Switzerland*. Union Bank of Switzerland, Zurich, 1979.

F.G. Fisher. *International Bonds* Euromoney Publications, London, 1982.

primary producer. A country producing a PRIMARY COMMODITY.

prime rate. A US term for the rate of interest at which a bank will lend to its most favoured, or 'prime', customers. Compare BASE RATE. In recent years, there is evidence that the prime rate has been becoming a less important indicator of borrowing costs, as banks have moved more and more to 'cost-plus' pricing.

Bibliography: R.W. Hafer. The Prime Rate and the Cost of Funds. *Federal Reserve Bank of St Louis Review*. May, 1983.

M.A. Arak, A.S. Englander & E.M.P. Tang. Credit Cycles and the Pricing of the Prime Rate. *Federal Reserve Bank of New York Quarterly Review*. Summer, 1983.

prime underwriting facility (PUF). A type of REVOLVING UNDERWRITING FACILITY. As an example, in 1984 First Chicago arranged a $270 million PUF for Denmark. The loan was for seven years, but initially it was offered to US regional banks for maturities of one to three years. If First Chicago cannot fully place the loan, it will call on the facility's nine UNDERWRITERS to fund the credit. The cost to Denmark is the underwriter's fee plus the spread over prime of the short term loans, which will vary with the market.

Bibliography: C. Grant. The Liquefaction of the Euromarkets.*Euromoney*, London, October 1983.

principal. (1) The face amount or par value of a debt, excluding interest or premium.

(2) A person employing another to act as agent (and hence by extension a person engaged in the management of a firm's business—usually refers to smaller firms).

(3) A person acting on his own account as a dealer (i.e. not as a BROKER).

principal balance. The outstanding total of a mortgage or other debt excluding interest or premium.

Privatdiskont AG. A German company owned by a consortium of banks whose business it is to make a market in BANKER'S ACCEPTANCES. When buying or selling acceptances in its open market operations the Bundesbank deals exclusively through Privatdiskont.

Bibliography: Deutsche Bundesbank. *The Deutsche Bundesbank: Its Monetary Policy Instruments and Functions*. Deutsche Bundesbank Special Series no. 7, 1982.

Private Export Funding Corporation (PEFCO). A US company owned by the EXPORT-IMPORT BANK and some 60 US commercial banks and industrial corporations. It works with Eximbank by purchasing foreign buyers' medium – and long-term debt obligations, which are unconditionally guaranteed by Eximbank. PEFCO funds itself by public issues of long-term secured notes, unsecured medium-term obligations, short-term notes sales, and by credit lines from the banks and from Eximbank. Its loans outstanding at 31 December 1981 totalled $1.15 billion.

Bibliography: A. Dunn & M. Knight. *Export Finance*. Euromoney Publications, London, 1982. J.J. Hillman. *The Export-Import Bank at Work*. Quorum Books, Westport, Conn. 1982. Export-Import Bank Annual Reports.

private placement.   A method of borrowing by selling BONDS (or other financial instruments such as shares), to a limited group of investors. The disinguishing characteristic of such a sale – or placement – is that no advertising is undertaken to sell the bonds or shares. (Although advertisements may subsequently be published in order to inform investors that a placement has been made.) The American private placement market is the largest in the world and is an extremely significant source of long-term capital up to 30 years. The Swiss market is also a significant international force.
Bibliography: *The Underwriting Business in Switzerland*. Union Bank of Switzerland, Zurich, 1979. H.A. Lund, R.P. Sibert & P.K. Chamberlain (eds.). *Private Placements*. Euromoney Publications, London, 1984.

privilege money.   A facility granted to the British discount houses enabling them to borrow last-minute funds from certain banks in order to balance their books by 3 p.m. daily.

product payback.   A form of trade financing in which an import is financed with some of the exports it helps to produce. For example, the USSR bought materials for gas pipelines from Germany in exchange for natural gas deliveries. Such deals are mostly encountered with COMECON countries but have also been made elsewhere.
Bibliography: I. Outters-Jaeger. *The Development Impact of Barter in Developing Countries*. OECD, Paris, 1979. P. Verzariu. *Countertrade, Barter & Offsets*. McGraw-Hill, New York, 1984.

pro-forma invoice. *See* INVOICE.

project finance.   Strictly, finance satisfying the following conditions: (a) it is used solely for the purchase of machinery, equipment and know-how relating to a specific project; (b) its maturity is related to the ability of the project to generate sufficient cash flow to repay the loan; (c) if the finance is in foreign currency, the project should generate sufficient foreign exchange to cover repayments. However, because project finance is more 'respectable' there has been a tendency, in the Euromarkets at least, to apply the label to any financing for projects without any link between the financing, the project, and repayments.
Bibliography: P.K. Nevitt. *Project Financing*. Euromoney Publications, London, 1983.

project line.   Term for a LINE OF CREDIT made available to finance a particular project; used particularly in export credits financing. Compare PROJECT FINANCE.
Bibliography: P.K. Nevitt. *Project Financing*. Euromoney Publications, London, 1983.

promissory note.   Defined by Section 83 of the UK Bills of Exchange Act as 'an unconditional promise in writing made by one person to another signed by the maker, engaging to pay, on demand or at a fixed or determinable future time, a sum certain in money, to, or to the order of, a specified person or to bearer'.
Bibliography: UK Bills of Exchange Act, 1882.

prompt date.   LONDON METAL EXCHANGE term for the date on which a metal has to be delivered to fulfil the terms of the purchase contract.
Bibliography: R. Gibson-Jarvie. *The London Metal Exchange*. Woodhead-Faulkner, Cambridge, UK, 1983.

property bond.   A UK term for a single-premium life insurance policy whose proceeds are invested in a fund which purchases properties.
Bibliography: D. O'Shea. *Investing for Beginners*. Financial Times Business Information, London, 1984.

proportional reinsurance.   Term referring to REINSURANCE where the premiums and the losses are shared proportionately between the insurer and the reinsurer.

pro-rata sinking fund.   A sinking fund that allocates redemption payments according to a formula established by the issuer. When the issue is CALLED for sinking fund payments each investor loses an equal percentage of his holdings to the issuer.

prospectus.   A statement filed with a Stock Exchange giving all relevant information about a security being issued and about the issuer.Compare OFFERING TELEX.
Bibliography: D. O'Shea. *Investing for Beginners.* Financial Times Business Information, London, 1984.
H.A. Lund *et al. Private Placements.* Euromoney Publications, London 1984.
H.E. Dougall & F.J. Corrigan. *Investments.* Prentice Hall, NJ, 1984.

protect.   US term for a guarantee to a customer to deal at a certain price (the 'protect price') for a security. The customer has the option of dealing or refusing.

protest.   A document drawn up by a notary certifying that a bill of exchange was duly presented for acceptance or payment and that acceptance or payment was refused. Compare NOTE.
Bibliography: A.Watson. *Finance of International Trade.* Institute of Bankers, London, 1981.

PSBR.   Abbreviation for PUBLIC SECTOR BORROWING REQUIREMENT.

public offering.   An offering of BONDS or SHARES to the public is called a public offering; the exact definitions vary from country to country. For example, in the US, private placements may not be sold to more than 35 purchasers. Any sale to a larger number becomes a public offering (with certain exceptions).
Bibliography: H.A. Lund *et al. Private Placements.* Euromoney Publications, London 1984.

public sector.   In the UK this comprises central govenment, local government author-

ities, and public corporations (excluding the Bank of England Banking Department, which is included in the banking sector).

public sector borrowing requirement.   In the UK consists of the PUBLIC SECTOR DEFICIT plus net lending to the private sector and overseas, plus certain other items on the financial accounts. (Net lending to the private sector includes cash expenditure on company securities, e.g. nationalization.) Detailed figures and definitions may be had from the *Financial Statistics* published monthly by HMSO for the Central Statistical Office.

public sector current surplus.   Equals (in the UK) gross trading surplus of public corporations (excluding depreciation and stock appreciation) plus rent and interest, plus income and expenditure taxes plus national insurance contributions, minus current spending on goods and services, subsidies, grants and debt interest. *See Financial Statistics* HMSO, London, monthly.

public sector deficit.   In the UK, equals current surplus plus taxes on capital, minus capital transfers, minus investment in fixed assets or stocks. *See Financial Statistics* published by HMSO for the Central Statistical Office.

purchase fund.   A fund created by a borrower for the purpose of redeeming bonds. Its management is put in the hands of a purchase agent (usually a bank). For example, for the $100 million Eurobond 1977-92 issued by Barclays Overseas Investment Company BV on behalf of Barclays Bank International, the Purchase Agent, Union Bank of Switzerland (Securities) Ltd, was required to buy bonds to the principal amount of $5 million in 1978, $4 million annually in 1979 and 198, and $3 million annually in 1981-84 inclusive; such purchases to be at prices not exceeding the principal amount (i.e. not above 100%).The effect of the latter provision is that if the bonds are trading at a price above par – i.e. over 100 – the purchase fund does not operate. By contrast, a SINKING FUND where bonds are drawn for redemption by lottery, may result in a bond being redeemed at par although its market price is higher.

Bibliography: F.G. Fisher. *International Bonds.* Euromoney Publications, London,1982.

purchasing power parity (PPP).   The purchasing power parity beween two countries is defined as either the ratio of the countries' price levels (absolute PPP) or the product of the exchange rate in a chosen period and the present ratio of the countries' price levels indices based on that period (relative PPP). The so-called PPP theory states that the equilibrium exchange rate tends towards either the absolute or relative PPP. It is extremely uncertain whether or not this proposition holds.

Bibliography: L.H. Officer. The Purchasing Power Parity Theory of Exchange Rates. IMF Staff Papers, US, 1976.

J.K. Walmsley. *The Foreign Exchange Handbook.* John Wiley & Sons, New York, 1983.

purpose clause.   A clause in a EUROMARKET (or other) borrowing which states the purpose for which the borrowing is made. Banks like to have these clauses as they give some reassurance that the proper use of the funds can be supervised. This could be achieved by defining the 'events of default' to include a breach of the purpose clause: in that case the bank could demand its money back.

purpose credit.   US term for credit by banks specifically for the purpose of financing securities subject to the margin requirements of Federal Reserve Regulation T.

Bibliography: SEC Act, Section 221.3(b)(1). Federal Reserve Regulations T & U.

put.   A contract which entitles one party to it, at his option, to sell a specific amount of securities or commodities to the other party, at the price fixed in the contract, during the life of the contract.

Bibliography: The New 'Beginners Please'. *Investors Chronicle,* London, 1975.

L.G. McMillan. *Options as a Strategic Investment.* New York Institute of Finance, New York, 1980.

Q

Q. *See* REGULATION Q.

quantity theory of money. An economic theory relating economic activity and inflation to the supply of money and the speed of its circulation. Compare HIGH-POWERED MONEY; M1; M2; M3; MONETARIST; VELOCITY.
Bibliography: M. Friedman (ed.). *Studies in the Quantity Theory of Money.* Chicago University Press, 1956.
C.A.E. Goodhart. *Monetary Theory and Practice.* Macmillan, London, 1984.

quasi-money. A term referring to assets which have properties resembling those of money in the strict sense (namely notes and coin plus bank deposits payable at sight). Such assets would frequently be classed as including savings deposits, time deposits, certificates of deposit, building society deposits (in the UK), deposits at non-bank thrift institutions (in the US) and the like. Compare M2, M3.
Bibliography: C.A.E. Goodhart. *Monetary Theory and Practice.* Macmillan, London, 1984.
T.D. Simpson & R.D. Porter. Some issues involving the definition and intepretation of Monetary Aggregates *in* Federal Reserve Bank of Boston. *Controlling the Monetary Aggregates.* Boston, Mass, 1980.

Quick ratio. *See* ACIDTEST RATIO.

quota. (1) In international trade the term quota is used to refer to a quantative limit on imports or exports. If the UK only permits the import of 2,000 cars from Czechoslovakia in any one year, for example, there is said to be an import quota on Czechoslovak cars.

(2) In the context of the INTERNATIONAL MONETARY FUND quota refers to a country's subscription to the IMF's resources. Each country, on joining, is obliged to subscribe an amount equal to the quota laid down for it, and until this is done it is unable to use the fund's resources. As and when its quota is increased, further payments must be made. Voting in the fund is weighted according to the size of the members' quotas.
Bibliography: A.W. Hooke. *The International Monetary Fund: its Evolution, Organization and Activities.* IMF Pamphlet no. 37, Washington DC, 1981.
The Financial Structure and Operations of the IMF. *Bank of England Quarterly Bulletin*, December 1983.

quota share treaty. A form of TREATY INSURANCE which provides for a fixed proportion of all the risks of a given class of insurance as a whole to be ceded to the reinsurer, together with the same proportion of the premium (less commission). Compare SURPLUS TREATY, EXCESS OF LOSS REINSURANCE, FALCULTATIVE REINSURANCE.
Bibliography: R.L. Carter. *Reinsurance.* Kluwer, London, 1983.
C.A. Williams & R.M. Heins. *Risk Management & Insurance.* McGraw-Hill, New York, 1984.

quotation. (1) In general, refers to the quotation of an interest rate or price. Thus, in the foreign exchange markets the term refers to the price at which a bank quotes one foreign currency in terms of another; such quotations may be 'for information' only, or they may be 'firm' - the price at which the bank is prepared to deal.

(2) A stock or bond which is formally permitted to be traded on a Stock Exchange is said to be granted a quotation; the term derives from the fact that the price of the security is quoted in the official lists of the Exchange concerned. Compare NASDAQ, OTC, PROSPECTUS.
Bibliography: J. Hamilton Dundas. *Stockbroking Today.* Macmillan, London, 1979.
F.G. Fisher. *International Bonds.* Euromoney Publications, London, 1982.
Admission of Securities to Listing. Quotations Department, Stock Exchange, London, 1984.

R

random walk A theory sometimes applied to stock and exchange markets, random walk is a mathematical term denoting a situation in which an object is seen as taking a series of single steps forward or backward, independently of all past events. The path so traced is described as a random walk, and the random walk hypothesis has been applied to analyses of stock market prices and foreign exchange rates.
Bibliography: B.G. Malkiel. *A Random Walk Down Wall St.* W. W. Norton Co., New York/London, 1981.

ratings. A term derived from the existence of companies in the US whose job it is to evaluate the credit rating of prospective borrowers on the securities markets. Thus a firm may be allotted a triple A rating if it is of unimpeachable creditworthiness. Compare MOODY'S, STANDARD & POOR'S.
Bibliography: *Standard & Poor's Rating Guide.* McGraw-Hill, New York, 1979.

ratio call spread. An OPTIONS market term for a neutral strategy in which one buys a number of calls at a lower STRIKE PRICE and sells more calls at a higher strike. Compare BACKSPREAD.
Bibliography: L.G. McMillan. *Options as a Strategic Investment.* New York Institute of Finance, New York, 1980.

ratio call writing. An OPTIONS market term for a strategy in which one owns a certain number of shares of an underlying stock and sells calls against more shares than one owns. Thus one might own 100 shares in a company and sell options on 200 shares. This strategy will earn larger profits than a NAKED write or a covered write, provided the stock remains relatively unchanged.
Bibliography: L.G. McMillan. *Options as a*

Strategic Investment. New York Institute of Finance, New York, 1980.

ratio strategy. An OPTIONS market strategy in which one holds an unequal number of short options and long options, or long stock. For example, a ratio CALENDAR SPREAD consists usually of selling more near-term options than longer-term options purchased.
Bibliography: L.G. McMillan. *Options as a Strategic Investment.* New York Institute of Finance, New York, 1980.

real effective exchange rate. An EFFECTIVE EXCHANGE RATE which is adjusted for inflation differentials between the country whose exchange rate is being measured, and the other countries making up the group against which the exchange rate is calculated.
Bibliography: J. Artus & A. McGuirk, A Revised Version of the Multilateral Exchange Rate Model. *IMF Staff Papers,* vol. 28, no. 2, 1981.
J.L. Llewellyn & S. Potter. Competitiveness and the current account. in A. Bolthof (ed.). *The European Economy.* Oxford University Press, 1982.

Real Estate Investment Trust. US bodies engaged in the finance of land and property purchases or developments. They grew rapidly in the 1970s but were in some cases overextended when interest rates rose. They remain, however, important investment vehicles.
Bibliography: J.A. Nicholson. Real Estate Investment Trusts *in* M.E. Blume & J.P. Friedman. *Encyclopaedia of Investments* Warren, Gorham & Lamont, NJ, 1982.
H. E. Dougall & F. J. Corrigan. *Investments* Prentice-Hall, NJ, 1984.

realized compound yield to maturity. US term for the return a bond earns over a stated period of time, based on the purchase price and on the assumption that the incoming cash is reinvested at a stated rate. For example, suppose we wish to compute the realised compound yield to maturity on a 12% seven-year bond selling for $100 (at par). The steps to compute the realized compound yield are as follows: (i) Compute the total future sum that will be received from the investment, i.e. the sum of the coupon payments, the interest-on-interest from reinvesting the coupon payments at an assumed reinvestment rate, and the redemption value. (ii) Divide this amount by the initial investment amount ($100). This produces the future value per dollar invested. (iii) Find the interest rate that produces this future value per dollar invested, either from tables or from the formula: RCYTM= $(FVPD)^{1/n}-1$ where RCYTM= realised compound yield to maturity FVPD= future value per dollar invested n= number of periods. Finally, (iv) if the interest payments are not already annualized, take this rate and annualize it.

Bibliography: S. Homer & M. L. Leibowitz. *Inside the Yield Book*. Prentice-Hall, NJ, 1972.
F.J. Fabozzi. Bond Yield Measures and Price Volatility Properties *in* F.J. Fabozzi & I.M. Pollack (eds).*The Fixed Income Securities Handbook*. Dow-Jones Irwin, Homewood, Ill., 1983.

reallowance. US term for that maximum portion of the selling concession that an underwriter may give up or 'reallow' to another NASD member - who need not be a syndicate member. The reallowance is specified at the time of pricing. The term is applied by extension to the EUROBOND market.

receivables. Another word for outstanding debts receivable: the term is usually applied in analysis of a firm's assets and liabilities to describe its claim in respect of payment due for work done or goods sold. Compare PAYABLES.

recourse. The possibility of making a claim on a third party in the event that another party should fail to meet his obligations. For example, if a BILL OF EXCHANGE is dishonoured by its DRAWEE then a holder of the bill

'in due course' (as defined in the UK Bills of Exchange Act of 1882) may demand payment from the drawer: he has recourse to the drawer. The drawer may negative his liability by drawing the bill 'without recourse'. Compare NON-RECOURSE FINANCE.
Bibliography: A. Watson. *Finance of International Trade*. Institute of Bankers, London, 1981.
J. Charlesworth. *Mercantile Law*. 14th edn. Stevens & Sons, London, 1984.

recycling. A term which came into use in the first (1973/4) oil crisis. It refers to the process whereby the balance of payments surpluses of the oil-producing countries were re-lent to the oil-importing countries.
Bibliography: R.C. Bryant. *Notes on the Analysis of Capital Flows to Developing Nations and the 'Recycling' Problem*. World Bank Working Paper no. 476, Washington DC,1981.

red clause. This is a clause, printed in red, on a LETTER OF CREDIT authorizing the negotiating banker to make advances to a beneficiary so he can purchase the goods, and deliver them for shipment. Such credits were devised to assist Australian wool exporters who had to pay large sums to the farmers producing the wool before it could be shipped.
Bibliography: A. Watson. *Finance of International Trade*. Institute of Bankers, London, 1981.

redeemable preference. Term for PREFERENCE STOCKS or shares where there are provisions for the redemption of preference shares at a predetermined time, or times.
Bibliography: T.G. Goff. *Theory and Practice of Investment*. Heinemann, London, 1982.
L.M. Loll & J.G. Buckley. *The Over-the-Counter Securities Markets*. Prentice-Hall, NJ, 1981.

redemption. The cancellation of an outstanding debt -usually a BOND- through cash repayment. (Cancellation by the issue of a new debt is termed REFINANCING or REFUNDING.) In the US it is referred to as CALL. Redemption is normally at PAR but if undertaken before maturity will be at a fixed REDEMPTION PRICE. *See also* PURCHASE FUND; SINKING FUND.

Bibliography: F.G. Fisher. *International Bonds.* Euromoney Publications London, 1982.
F.J. Fabozzi & I.M. Pollack. *The Handbook of Fixed Income Securities.* Dow-Jones Irwin, Homewood, Ill., 1983.

redemption price. The price at which a bond may be redeemed (at the option of the borrower) prior to its maturity date. Redemption prices are determined when the bond is issued and are a function of the original coupon and offering price. The US term is CALL PRICE.

Bibliography: F.G. Fisher. *International Bonds.* Euromoney Publications, London, 1982.
F.J. Fabozzi & I.M. Pollack. *The Handbook of Fixed Income Securities.* Dow-Jones Irwin, Homewood, Ill., 1983.

redemption yield. A UK term for the YIELD on a BOND that is held to REDEMPTION, i.e. till its MATURITY. The US term is generally YIELD TO MATURITY. The redemption yield is that rate of interest at which the total discounted values of future payments of income and capital equate to the current total price. It is *not* a guaranteed compound rate of return to be earned from making an investment at that price, since there is no certainty that future income can be reinvested at the current redemption yield (unless there is no income–i.e. the bond is a ZERO COUPON.) There is no direct formula for calculating redemption yield. It must be found by iteration from the formula for the price of a bond, which is (ignoring ACCRUED INTEREST):

$$P = g a_{\overline{n}|} + R v^n$$

where P = price
R = redemption value (usually 100)
g = coupon per period (e.g. 12% p.a. or 6% per half year)
$a_{\overline{n}|} = (v + v^2 + v^3 + \ldots + v^n)$
n = periods to maturity (in years or half- years)

$$v = \frac{1}{\left(1 + \dfrac{i}{100j}\right)}$$

i = yield to maturity

j = frequency of coupon payment (1 for annual, 2 for semi-annual)

(Care needs to be taken in measuring all items on a consistent basis for annual or semi-annual payment)
This formula needs to be slightly adjusted in the case of accrued interest:

$$P = v^q[g(1 + a_{\overline{n}|}) + R v^n]$$

where q = period from settlement date to next coupon date (measured in years or half years)
Compare NET REDEMPTION YIELD and the entries cited under YIELD.

· Bibliography: P. Phillips. *Inside the Gilt-Edged Market.* Woodhead-Faulkner, Cambridge, UK, 1984.
M. Stigum. *Money Market Calculations.* Dow-Jones, Irvin, Homewood, Ill., 1981.

red herring. US term for a preliminary PROSPECTUS issued to obtain an indication of interest in the issue. It is incomplete because it does not contain the public offering price, the underwriter's discount, or the date of issue. The term is occasionally used also in the UK.

Bibliography: F.J. Fabozzi & I.M. Pollack. *The Handbook of Fixed Income Securities.* Dow-Jones Irwin, Homewood, Ill., 1983.

Rediskontkontingent. German term for the rediscount quota available to German banks at the Bundesbank. Unlike the BANK OF ENGLAND or the FEDERAL RESERVE, the Deutsche Bundesbank establishes limits on the amount of paper it will discount for any one bank, since the rediscount quotas are viewed as permanent sources of reserves : these quotas are reviewed from time to time.

Bibliography: Deutsche Bundesbank. *The Deutsche Bundesbank: its monetary policy instruments and functions.* Deutsche Bundesbank Special Series no. 7, 1982.

réescompte. French term meaning rediscount.

reference bank. The interest rate on a EUROCREDIT will frequently be linked to the interest rate being charged by certain specified 'reference' banks. Compare LIBOR.

reference currency.   In ISSUES denominated in EUROPEAN UNITS OF ACCOUNT the term reference currency denotes a currency used in making payments to the bondholder. For instance, in the 1974 EUA issue by Ireland, the reference currencies were defined as the currencies of the nine EEC members, except for those which had no official PAR VALUE.
Bibliography: H.C. Donnerstag. *The Eurobond Market.* Financial Times Ltd, London, 1975, pp. 35-7.
F.G. Fisher. *International Bonds.* Euromoney Publications, London, 1982.

reference rate.   (1) *See* GREEN CURRENCY.
(2) A term used in discussions of 'correct' foreign exchange intervention policy, meaning the equilibrium rate of exchange.
Bibliography: W. Ethier & A.I. Bloomfield. The reference rate proposal and recent experience. *Banca Nazionale del Lavoro Quarterly Review.* Rome, September 1978.

refinancing.   (1) A financing of a financing (e.g. several countries allow banks to refinance export loans at the central bank.)
(2) A financing arranged to replace an existing financing either because the latter has expired, or because new finance is available on better terms - Compare REFUNDING – or because the borrower is unable to meet the existing repayments in which case it is effectively a RESCHEDULING.
Bibliography: M.S. Mendelsohn. *Commercial Banks and the Restructuring of Cross-Border Debt.* Group of Thirty, New York, 1983.

refund.   US term for 'refinance': the replacement of a financing–particularly a bond–by another financing because it is cheaper. Refunding is disliked by investors and many corporate bonds have included provisions against it.
Bibliography: F.J. Fabozzi & I.M. Pollack. *The Handbook of Fixed Income Securities.* Dow-Jones Irwin, Homewood, Ill,. 1983.

registered.   A security listed on the issuing company's books as held by a named person is said to be registered. Compare BEARER. Although interest on a bond may be collected by presentation of the COUPON, the PRINCIPAL may be transferred only with the endorsement of the registered owner.
Bibliography: L.J. Kemp. *A guide to World Securities Markets.* Euromoney Publications, London, 1984.

registration statement.   US term for documents, including a PROSPECTUS, with exhibits propared by and for an issuing company for filing with the SECURITIES EXCHANGE COMMISSION.
Bibliography: F.J. Fabozzi & I.M. Pollack. *The Handbook of Fixed Income Securities.* Dow-Jones Irwin, Homewood, Ill., 1983.
L.M. Loll & J.G. Buckley. *The Over-the-Counter Markets.* Prentice-Hall, NJ, 1981.

regular delivery (regular way settlement).   (1) In the US government securities market, delivery of a security which is made on the business day following its purchase/sale is called 'regular', as against CASH delivery.
(2) In the US corporate securities market, regular way settlement is on the fifth full business day following the transaction.
Bibliography: F.J. Fabozzi & I.M. Pollack. *The Handbook of Fixed Income Securities.* Dow-Jones Irwin, Homewood, Ill., 1983.
L.M. Loll & J.G. Buckley. *The Over-the-Counter Markets.* Prentice-Hall, NJ, 1981.

Regulation Q.   A regulation imposed by the US Federal Reserve Board which limits the rate of interest that banks may pay on deposits. Its application contributed to the growth of the Eurodollar market because when they needed funds, US banks were able to bid for them in Europe to circumvent Regulation Q. Thus dollar funds were attracted to Europe where higher yields were obtainable. Regulation Q was suspended in 1970 for CDs maturing in 30 to 89 days, and then in 1973 for maturities of over 90 days.
Bibliography: P. Meek. *US Monetary Policy and the Financial Markets.* Federal Reserve Bank of New York, 1982.

reinsurance. The process whereby an insurer passes some of his risk to another insurer. Compare CAPTIVE INSURANCE COMPANY; CEDING COMPANY; EXCESS OF LOSS; FACULTATIVE REINSURANCE; QUOTA SHARE TREATY; SURPLUS TREATY; TREATY REINSURANCE.
Bibliography: R.L. Carter. *Reinsurance.* Kluwer, London, 1984.
C.A. Williams & R.M. Heins. *Risk Management & Insurance.* McGraw-Hill, New York, 1984.

REIT. *See* REAL ESTATE INVESTMENT TRUST.

remitting bank. A term used in COLLECTIONS, denoting the bank which sends, or remits, the documents for collection. Suppose an exporter hands a bill to his bank for collection in another country. The exporter's bank–the remitting bank–will arrange for a bank in the other country–the COLLECTING BANK–to obtain the money owing. It will then transfer it to the remitting bank for payment to the exporter.
Bibliography: A. Watson. *Finance of International Trade.* Institute of Bankers, London, 1981.

Rembrandt. Term sometimes used for a domestic Dutch guilder issue by a foreign borrower. Compare BULLDOG; SAMURAI; YANKEE.
Bibliography: D. Curtin. Deals that made the record book. *Euromoney,* London, September 1983.

réport. French foreign exchange term meaning PREMIUM and also by extension SWAP.
Bibliography: P. Coulbois. *Finance Internationale.1. Le Change.* Editions Cujas. Paris, 1979.

repos. *See* REPURCHASE AGREEMENTS.

repurchase agreements (repos). A US term relating to agreements by a borrower where he sells securities with a commitment to repurchase them at the same price plus a specified interest charge. These agreements (often called repos or RPs) may have a specific period or may be open-ended. They are frequently used by the Federal Reserve as a means of temporarily supplying funds to the market.The repo market developed after 1969, when they were exempted from reserve requirements. By 1982 there were $100 billion in repos outstanding according to official figures, but these cover only part of the market. The market was severely shaken by the collapse of DRYSDALE SECURITIES but after a pause continued to grow. Estimated daily volume is of the order of several hundred billion dollars turnover. Repurchases are also used by the Bank of England, Banque de France, and Bundesbank among others. Compare REVERSE REPURCHASES; GEN-SAKI.
Bibliography: T.Q. Cook & N.J. Summers (eds). *Instruments of the Money Market.* Federal Reserve Bank of Richmond, Virginia, 1981.
M. Stigum. *The Money Market.* Dow-Jones Irwin, Homewood, Ill., 1983.
The Bundesbank's transactions in securities under repurchase agreements. *Deutsche Bundesbank Monthly Report.* May 1983.

rescheduling. This refers to the renegotiation of the terms of existing debt. The term is normally used in the context of government or public sector borrowings by countries which are no longer able to afford repayments. Effectively rescheduling is REFINANCING which is accepted by creditors since the alternative would be DEFAULT. Countries which have rescheduled in recent years include Argentina, Brazil, Zaire and a number of other developing countries.
Bibliography: M.S. Mendelsohn. *Commercial Banks and the Restructuring of Cross-Border Debt.* Group of Thirty, New York, 1983.
D. Suratgar (ed.). *Default and Rescheduling.* Euromoney Publications, London, 1984.

reserve assets. (1) In general, assets which are held as reserves, either as part of foreign exchange reserves, or as reserves of the banking system.
(2) In the UK, the term refers to assets included in the Bank of England's reserve requirements, namely deposits at the Bank, Treasury Bills, GILT-EDGED STOCK with less

than a year to maturity, money at call with the London money market, and certain other assets. Different assets are specified for the DISCOUNT HOUSES. Compare DEFINED ASSETS; RESERVE RATIOS; UNDEFINED ASSETS.

Bibliography: E.R. Shaw. *The London Money Market*. Heinemann, London, 1983.
J.S.G. Wilson. Recent Changes in London's Money Market Arrangements. *Banca Nazionale del Lavoro Quarterly Review*, March, 1983.

reserve clause. A Eurocurrency credit clause permitting the lender to pass on to the borrower any extra costs resulting from the imposition on the lender of new RESERVE REQUIREMENTS.

Bibliography: P. Wood. *Law and Practice of International Finance*. Sweet & Maxwell, London, 1980.

reserve currency. A currency which central banks are prepared to hold on a permanent basis as a store of international liquidity. The classic reserve currencies are the dollar, the pound sterling and (to a lesser extent, for former French colonies) the French franc. Typically, a reserve currency doubles in a number of roles: transactions currency (working balances are held in it); intervention currency (central banks will use it to intervene with); asset currency (private assets are held in it); quotation currency (commodity prices are quoted internationally in it) and peg currency (other currencies' exchange rates will be linked to it.).

Bibliography: C.F. Bergsten. *The Dilemmas of the Dollar*. New York University Press, US, 1975.
J.K. Walmsley. *The Foreign Exchange Handbook*. John Wiley & Sons, New York, 1983.

reserve ratios. Many central banks require commercial banks in their country to hold certain assets in proportion to their liablilities. For example, in the UK, banks used to be required to hold 'reserve assets' of 12% of their 'eligible liabilities'. Similar ratios are enforced in most other countries. Reserve ratios may be varied as a means of controlling the activity of banks (this is normal in Germany, for example) or preference may be

given to stable ratios (as in the UK and US) and manipulation of the supply of reserves assets through OPEN MARKET OPERATIONS or supplementary controls. Compare FREE RESERVES; RESERVES.

Bibliography: J. Welch. *The Regulation of Banks in the Member States of the EEC*. Graham & Tretmen, London, 1981.
P. Meek. *US Monetary Policy and the Financial Markets*. Federal Reserve Bank of New York, 1982.

reserves. Term covering funds held against possible future contingencies. (1) External reserves usually consist of official holdings of CONVERTIBLE foreign currency, gold, SDRS and reserve positions in the IMF.

Bibliography: *How Central Banks Manage Their Reserves*. Group of Thirty, New York, 1982.
J.K. Walmsley. *The Foreign Exchange Handbook*. John Wiley & Sons, New York, 1983.
(2) In the domestic context, the term normally means the assets which banks must hold to comply with their RESERVE RATIOS.

Bibliography: M. Stigum. *The Money Market*. Dow-Jones Irwin, Homewood, Ill., 1983.
D.C. Beek. Excess Reserves and Reserve Targeting. *Federal Reserve Bank of New York Quarterly Review*, Autumn 1981.
E.R. Shaw. *The London Money Market*. Heinemann, London, 1983.

resident. A term of art around which complex legal, tax and EXCHANGE CONTROL definitions have been developed. In the UK, for example, the Inland Revenue has been allowed to call a person resident if, under certain circumstances, he spends one day in the year on UK soil.

Bibliography: F.A. Mann. *Legal Aspects of Money*. Clarendon Press, Oxford, 1983.
Price Waterhouses & Co. *Foreign Nationals in the US*. New York, 1981.

resistance point. A term used by 'chartist' analysts of share prices, commodity prices or exchange rates to suggest that there is inherent market resistance to allowing a price fall or rise through a certain level.

Bibliography: P.J. Kaufman (ed.). *Technical Analysis in Commodities*. John Wiley & Sons, New York, 1983.

retention. US term for the percentage of a syndicate member's underwriting participation which is retained for his own retail sales.

retractable. A BOND which is issued on the basis that the investor is given an option of early redemption a given number of years before the final MATURITY. Such bonds have been common in Canada for many years and have now also been introduced in the EUROBOND market.
Bibliography: R.W. Kopprasch. Early Redemption (Put) Options on Fixed Income Securities *in* F.J. Fabozzi & I.M. Pollack. *The Handbook of Fixed Income Securities.* Dow-Jones Irwin, Homewood, Ill., 1983.

retrocession. A REINSURANCE term. A reinsurer may decide to pass on some of the risk which has been passed on to him by the CEDING COMPANY, i.e. he in turn will cede part of the risk. This second operation is termed retrocession.
Bibliography: R.L. Carter. *Reinsurance.* Kluwer, London, 1984.
C.A. Williams & R.M. Heins. *Risk Management & Insurance.* McGraw-Hill, New York, 1984.

retrocessionaire. A REINSURANCE term. It refers to a reinsurer who buys reinsurance on some of the risks he has agreed to bear.

return on assets (RoA). (1) In general, the earnings achieved on a group of assets, usually in percentage terms.

(2) Specifically, in the EUROMARKETS, the term refers to a method of measuring earnings from EUROCREDITS. In its simplest form, RoA measures the amount of income derived from SPREAD and fees divided by the average outstanding assets employed. For example, a loan participation which generates (i) 40 basis points equivalent in spread income; (ii) 20 basis points equivalent in MANAGEMENT FEES, and (iii) 15 basis points equivalent in commitment and agency fees, is said to have a transaction yield of 75 basis points, relative to average outstanding assets employed.
Bibliography: R.P. McDonald. *International*

Syndicated Loans. Euromoney Publications, London, 1982.

revalorization. A legal term referring to the adjustment of money sums to take account of changes in money's purchasing power: the opposite of NOMINALISM, revalorization resembles INDEX-LINKING.
Bibliography: F.A. Mann. *The Legal Aspect of Money.* Clarendon Press, Oxford, 1983

revaluation. Foreign exchange term. A dollar revaluation of 5% against sterling means that the dollar will buy 5% more sterling than before. Many people use the term to indicate that the change has been formally decided by the authorities concerned rather than being the outcome of market movements. In the latter case the term APPRECIATION would be used. Compare DEPRECIATION; DEVALUATION.
Bibliography: J.K. Walmsley. *The Foreign Exchange Handbook.* John Wiley & Sons, New York, 1983.

revenue bond. US term for a municipal bond supported by a pledge of revenue from a specified income generating facility such as a toll road or power plant. Compare INDUSTRIAL REVENUE BOND.
Bibliography: *Fundamentals of Municipal Bonds.* Public Securities Association, New York, 1981.

reverse conversion. An OPTIONS market trading strategy. A reverse CONVERSION is where one sells the underlying stock or commodity, buys a call on it, and sells a put. A reverse conversion is profitable if the initial sale price of the stock is above the striking price of the options. For example, XYZ stock sells at 55; XYZ January 60 call sells at 2, and XYZ January put at 7.5. Then the trader sells the stock at 55, pays 2 for the call, and sells the put for 7.5, making a net total of 60.5. This locks in a profit of 0.5. To verify this, assume that XYZ is below 60 when the options expire. The call is worthless, and the put is exercised against the trader at 60, i.e. he must buy back the stock at 60, having earned 60.5 from the initial reverse conversion. Equally, if the stock is above 60 at

expiry, the call is exercised (i.e. the trader buys at 60) and the put expires worthless; again, there is a net profit of 0.5 (less any financing costs).
Bibliography: L.G. McMillan. *Options as a Strategic Investment*. New York Institute of Finance, New York, 1980.

reverse repurchases. A US term relating to agreements by a lender whereby he buys securities with a commitment to resell them at the same price plus a specified interest charge. These agreements (often called reverse repos or matched sales) may have a specific period or may be open-ended. They are frequently used by the Federal Reserve to drain funds from the market. Compare OPEN MARKET OPERATIONS; REPURCHASES.
Bibliography: T.Q. Cook & B.J. Summers (eds). *Instruments of the Money Market*. Federal Reserve Bank of Richmond, Virginia, 1981.
M. Stigum. *The Money Market*. Dow-Jones Irwin, Homewood Ill., 1983.

reverse warrant hedge. A technique whereby the investor establishes a SHORT position in WARRANTS on a company's shares and buys the shares to protect himself.
Bibliography: A.E. Young. Options–Warrants *in* M.E. Blume & J.P. Friedman. *Encyclopaedia of Investments*. Warren, Gorham & Lamont, New York, 1982.

reverse yield gap. A situation where fixed-interest securities yield more than industrial shares. Compare YIELD GAP.

revocable letter of credit. A LETTER OF CREDIT which may be cancelled or amended at any time without the prior knowledge of the exporter who is due to receive payment under the letter of credit. Such credits have obvious disadvantages and are seldom used. However, the importer's bank is still obliged to pay under the credit if the documents are in order and payment was made by the exporter's bank before receiving notice of cancellation or amendment. Compare DOCUMENTARY CREDIT.
Bibliography: *Uniform Customs & Practice for Documentary Credits*. International Chamber of Commerce Brochure no. 290, Paris, 1974.
A. Watson. *Finance of International Trade*. Institute of Bankers, London, 1981.

revolver. Another term for REVOLVING CREDIT.

revolving credit. A revolving credit in its simplest form is a credit where it is a condition that any portion used by the borrower and reimbursed to the banker during the period of the credit becomes available again automatically within the term of the credit. Compare EVERGREEN CREDIT.
Bibliography: H.C. Gutteridge & M. Megrah. *The Law of Bankers' Commercial Credits*. Europa Publications, London, 1979.
M. Stigum. *The Money Market*. Dow-Jones Irwin, Homewood Ill., 1983.

revolving underwriting facility. A type of financing where the borrower is given a medium-term facility allowing him to draw at any time during its life. The drawings take the form of short-term PROMISSORY NOTES or – if a bank – CDS. These securities are sold by one or more placing agents to short-term investors. If a placing agent cannot place the securities, a syndicate of banks stands ready to buy the unsold paper. The secret of the RUF is to separate the role of the medium-term risk-taker (the UNDERWRITER) from that of the lender–the buyer of the paper. This allows cost savings in relation to the traditional SYNDICATE technique for EUROCREDITS. Compare PRIME UNDERWRITING FACILITY; TENDER PANEL.
Bibliography: C.R. Dammers. The Internationalization of the World's Money Markets: Some New Products *in* P.H. Darrow & R.A. Mestres (eds). *Creative Financing in the 1980s*. Practising Law Institute, New York, 1983.
C. Grant. The Liquefaction of the Euromarkets. *Euromoney*, London, October 1983.

right-hand side. A currency will be quoted, say, DM2.0755-60. 2.0755 is the rate at which the bank will sell DM against dollars; 2.0760 is the rate at which it will buy DM. Thus from its point of view if a deal is done on the right-hand side it buys DM and sells dollars.

rights issue. Name given to a short-term option granting to a shareholder the right to subscribe at a stated price (which is normally comparatively favourable) to new issues of the company's stock in proportion to present holdings. Also known in the US as stock rights or subscription rights. The formula for establishing the value of rights is normally as follows:-

$$V = \frac{M - S}{N + 1}$$

where V = value
       M = market price of shares
       S = subscription price
       N = numbers of shares held for each new share

Consider a share trading at £5.60. A one for four rights issue is offered at £4.60. Then

$$V = \frac{5.60 - 4.60}{4 + 1} = \frac{1.00}{5} = £0.20.$$

Bibliography: R. Brealey & S. Myers. *Principles of Corporate Finance*. McGraw-Hill, US/UK, 1981. D. O'Shea. *Investing for Beginners*. Financial Times Business Information, London, 1984.

ring. A trading session on the LONDON METAL EXCHANGE.
Bibliography: R. Gibson-Jarvie. *The London Metal Exchange*. Woodhead-Faulkner, Cambridge, UK, 1983.

risk. In the insurance market this term is generally used to refer to an insurance proposition as a whole, rather than to a peril or hazard.

risk arbitrage. US term for taking a position in the stock of a company being acquired, against the stock of the acquiring company.
Bibliography: M.A. Weinstein. Arbitrage *in* M.E. Blume & J.P. Friedman (eds). *Encyclopedia of Investments*. Warren, Gorham & Lamont, New York, 1982.

rolling rate note. A FLOATING RATE NOTE issued on the basis that instead of the floating rate being adjusted at intervals corresponding to the type of REFERENCE RATE (e.g.

every three months if the reference rate were three-month LIBOR), the floating rate is adjusted more frequently in line with a reference rate calculated each month.
Bibliography: G. Ugeux. *Floating Rate Notes*. Euromoney, London, 1981.

rolling yield. A measure of a bond's yield which is determined by the passage of time along the yield curve ('rolling down the yield curve'). The implicit assumption is that interest rates remain constant. Consider a three-year bond with a yield of 6.5%, which is in line with the current level of yields, so that the bond is priced at par. Suppose a 2.5 year bond is priced at 6.3%. The rolling yield over a six months horizon takes into account the expected semi-annual coupon payment of 3.25%, plus the capital gain to be expected from a rise in price of the bond–since in six months' time, if interest rates remain constant, it will yield 6.3%. Such an fall in yield implies a rise in price from 100 to 100.456; so that total yield over the six months will be 3.25+0.456=3.706% or an annualized 7.41%.
Bibliography: M.L. Leibowitz. Analysis of Yield Curves *in* F.J. Fabozzi & I.M. Pollack. *The Handbook of Fixed Income Securities*. Dow-Jones Irwin, Homewood, Ill., 1983.

roll-over. A roll-over credit is one in which banks commit themselves to lend for, say, seven years, and these funds in turn are raised by the banks from the market at more frequent intervals - commonly three or six months. The interest rate payable on the loan is linked to the cost of raising three or six-month money. Elaborate legal clauses have been developed to cover such eventualities as non-availability of the currency of the loan at the time of roll-over, etc. Compare CURRENCY AVAILABILITY CLAUSE; DISASTER CLAUSE; EURODOLLAR; EUROCREDIT.
Bibliography: S.I. Davis. *The Euro-bank*. Macmillan, London/John Wiley, New York, 1981. P. Wood. *Law and Practice of International Finance*. Sweet & Maxwell, London, 1980. L.S. Goodman. Syndicated Eurocurrency Lending: Pricing and Practice *in* A.M. George & I.H.

Giddy. *International Finance Handbook*. John Wiley & Sons, New York, 1983.

roll-over CD (Roly-Poly CD). A roll-over CERTIFICATE OF DEPOSIT is a CD 'package' with a maturity of (say) three years, divided into six-month periods for which CDs are issued. An investor buys the package as a whole but may sell any of the six month CDs on the SECONDARY MARKET. He is nevertheless committed to rolling over the CD by redepositing funds to the amount of the next six-month CD. The device (which is not particularly widely used) was introduced in the US by Morgan Guaranty in 1976 as an attempt to give the bank a longer-maturity CD while overcoming the problem that dealings in CDs of over six months' maturity in the secondary market are not as smooth as for shorter maturities.
Bibliography: T.Q. Cook & B.J. Summers. *Instruments of the Money Market*. Federal Reserve Bank of Virginia, 1981.

roly-poly CD. *See* ROLL-OVER CD.

Roosa bonds. Non-marketable bonds denominated in foreign currency (i.e. not dollars) sold by the US Government to Germany and other countries which found themselves accumulating excess dollar reserves during the early 1960s. The concept was developed by Robert V. Roosa of the US Treasury. The bonds provided special inducements to Germany not to withdraw funds from the US, which would have exacerbated the dollar crises of the period. Compare CARTER BONDS.
Bibliography: F. Hirsch. *Money International*. Penguin Books, London, 1967.

round tripping. UK term for a phenomenon arising from interest rate discrepancies between bank lending rates and rates payable on certificates of deposit. At certain times it has paid companies to borrow money from their bank in order to lend it back to the bank through the medium of a certificate of deposit.
Bibliography: E.R. Shaw. *The London Money Markets*. Heinemann, London, 1983.

A Note on Money Market Arbitrage. *Bank of England Quarterly Bulletin*. June 1982.

RUF. *See* REVOLVING UNDERWRITING FACILITY.

Rule 163(2). A UK Stock Exchange rule allowing deals in the shares of unlisted companies on an occasional basis and subject to the permission of the Stock Exchange for each specific deal. After a period in which dealings in unlisted securities expanded rapidly under Rule 163(2), the Stock Exchange opted for the introduction of the UNLISTED SECURITIES MARKET. If now an active market develops in a company's securities under Rule 163, the Stock Exchange will encourage it to seek entry to the Unlisted Securities Market.
Bibliography: D. Fanning. *Marketing Company Shares*. Gower Publishing, UK, 1982.
Peat Marwick & Co. *Entering the Unlisted Securities Market*. London, 1984.

Rule 415. The rule by which the US SECURITIES AND EXCHANGE COMMISSION permitted SHELF REGISTRATION – a system by which an issuer can file in advance the information that he proposes to make an issue of a certain kind and size, without being committed as to the date of the issue.
Bibliography: B.Mc Goldrick. How Rule 415 put CFOs in the Catbird Seat. *Institutional Investor*. New York, April 1984.

run. A US (and EUROMARKET) term referring to a select group of banks – around ten – whose NAMES are instantly acceptable in the CD and BANKER'S ACCEPTANCE markets. Thus a professional trader will buy a CD from another trader without caring whose CD he buys, so long as it is issued by a bank 'on the run'. At times of serious crisis for an individual bank–such as Continental Illinois – its name will be 'taken off the run'. This is unfortunate for it, since banks whose CD's are 'on the run' issue more cheaply than any one else.
Bibliography: T. Anderson and P. Field. The Tremors that Threaten the Banking System. *Euromoney*. London, October 1982.

running yield. The interest rate on an investment expressed in terms of a percentage of the capital invested, e.g. £100 nominal of 3.5% War Loan bought at £50 gives a 'running yield' of 7%. Also known as 'flat yield', 'current yield' or 'interest yield'. The possibility of any capital gain following redemption is ignored, and the price should be 'clean', i.e. it should exclude any element of accrued interest or dividend.

Bibliography: T.G. Goff. *Theory & Practice of Investment.* Heinemann, London, 1983. L. J. Kemp. *World Money and Securities Markets.* Euromoney Publications, London, 1984.

S

safe harbor lease. US term for a type of lease permitted under the ERTA and TEFRA tax rules, now no longer generally available. Safe harbor leases allowed the LESSEE to buy the equipment for a nominal sum at the end of the lease, thereby making them very attractive.
Bibliography: P.K. Nevitt. *Project Financing*. Euromoney Publications, London, 1983.

Samurai bonds. FOREIGN BONDS denominated in yen and issued in Japan. By 1981 the samurai bond market had become the fourth largest foreign bond market (i.e. as distinct from EUROBONDS) after Switzerland, the US and West Germany, with over 70 issues of a value exceeding ¥ 1 trillion.
Bibliography: L.J. Kemp. *World Money and Securities Markets*. Euromoney Publications, London, 1984.
Compare YANKEE BONDS.

Samurai lease. A subsidized international LEASE by which the Japanese government briefly encouraged an apparent boom in imports as Japanese firms bought assets (which did not necessarily enter Japan) with a view to leasing them overseas. Compare SHOGUN LEASE.
Bibliography: D. Curtin. Japan's Greatest Export Success is Leasing. *Euromoney*, London, June 1982.

sandwich spread. US OPTIONS market term. The sandwich spread is the opposite of a BUTTERFLY SPREAD. While with the butterfly spread the investor hopes to catch the STOCK or commodity price in the wings of the butterfly formed by the spread, with the sandwich spread the investor hopes to sandwich the stock between two prices. To put a sandwich spread on a stock, selling at, say, 50, the investor would buy, say, the 40 and 60 call options, and sell two 50 call options. This strategy is most profitable if the stock continues to remain steady at 50. In that case the investor loses money on the 60 call, which is offset by profit on the 40 call; while the premium earned by selling the 50 calls is pure profit, since the calls expire worthless. The strategy is analogous to the BOX SPREAD except that in the latter the investor holds the stock and buys a put at 40 to protect the downside risk. Compare BOX SPREAD; BUTTERFLY SPREAD; DIAGONAL SPREAD; HORIZONTAL SPREAD; VERTICAL SPREAD.
Bibliography: R.M. Bookstaber. *Option Pricing and Strategies in Investing*. Addison-Wesley, Mass, 1980.

scale. A US term. A bank that offers to pay different rates on CD's of differing maturities is said to 'post a scale'. Commercial paper issuers also post scales.

SCC. *See* STOCK CLEARING CORPORATION.

Schatzwechsel. German term for Treasury bills. At the time of issue the bills are placed by the Bundesbank with the banks on a TAP BASIS. They are normally held to maturity (usually 90 days), but if liquidity is short they are resold to the Bundesbank. They are hardly ever traded between banks.
Bibliography: *The Deutsche Bundesbank: Its Monetary Policy Instruments and Functions*. Deutsche Bundesbank Special Series no. 7, 1982.

Schuldschein (Schuldscheindarlehen). A German financial instrument consisting of a loan made against a borrower's note. No regular statistics are available but it is thought that the private market is about DM100-150bn. in size. Government debt in this market is almost DM 500bn. Perhaps three-quarters of Schuldschein loans are provided by insurance companies. The yield is traditionally higher than on comparable industrial bonds, but because of lower issuing costs the actual burden on the borrower is probably less.

Bibliography: H.A. Lund *et al. Private Placement* Euromoney Publications, London, 1984.

Schuldverschreibung. German term meaning BOND or, occasionally, including also money market instruments, in which case it has the more general meaning of 'debt instruments'. Banks are particularly active issuers of Schuldverschreibungen, with maturities of as short as nine months.

Bibliography: G. Dufey & E. Krishnan. West Germany: Banking, Money and Bond Markets *in* A.M. George & I.H. Giddy (eds). *International Finance Handbook*. John Wiley & Sons, New York, 1983.

SDR. *See* SPECIAL DRAWING RIGHT.

seasoned. US term for corporate securities which have been outstanding for some time (usually a year or more).

Bibliography: R. Bradley & S. Myers. *Principles of Corporate Finance.* McGraw-Hill, New York/London, 1984.

SEC. *See* SECURITIES AND EXCHANGE COMMISSION.

sec. French foreign exchange term meaning OUTRIGHT.

Bibliography: P. Coulbois.*Le Finance International. I. Le Change.* Editions Cujas, Paris 1979.

secondary market. A term describing the market for transactions in existing securities (as distinct from transactions in newly-issued securities, known as the PRIMARY MARKET and the AFTER-MARKET which consists of trading undertaken while the ISSUING SYNDICATE still subsists). The health of the secondary market is important to the success of the primary market, since lenders will be reluctant to invest in new securities if they feel they will be difficult to resell (unless they are confident of being able to hold until maturity).

Bibliography: F.G. Fisher. *International Bonds.* Euromoney Publications, London, October 1982.

secondary offering (secondary distribution). US term for the redistribution (not a new issue) of an outstanding BLOCK of stock by a securities firm(s). It is handled privately off the organized exchanges after the close of the market at a fixed price not exceeding the last sale price on the floor. It may be UNDERWRITTEN as with new offerings of securities.

Bibliography: L.M. Loll & J.G. Buckley. *The Over-the-Counter Markets.* Prentice-Hall, NJ, 1981.

Securities and Exchange Commission. US agency responsible for ensuring that new securities issues comply with certain requirements, and for the proper administering of the securities industry generally.

Bibliography: R.J. Teweles & E.S. Bradley. *The Stock Market.* 4th edn., John Wiley & Sons, New York, 1982.

SEC Annual Reports.

Securities Industry Automation Corporation (SIAC). The processing agent of the US NATIONAL SECURITIES CLEARING CORPORATION. Once a deal is done on an exchange, the comparison data from each broker that is party to the trade are submitted to the SIAC which provides a computerized print-out summarizing the details and noting any discrepancies. The SIAC is a joint subsidiary of the New York and American Stock Exchanges.

Bibliography: A.M. George. The United States Equity Markets *in* A.M. George & I.H. Giddy (eds). *International Finance Handbook*. John Wiley & Sons, New York, 1983.

R.J. Teweles & E.S. Bradley. *The Stock Market.* 4th edn. John Wiley & Sons, New York, 1982.

securitization. US term for the process by which mortgages are transformed into securities by the use of PASS-THROUGH techniques and COLLATERALIZED MORTGAGE OBLIGATIONS. More than 50% of new US mortgages in 1983 were securitized, compared with barely 5% in 1970.

Bibliography: M.A. Smilow. The Move Toward Mortgage Securitization. *Mortgage Banking.* New York, December 1983.

L. Sandler. The mortgage-backed Securities Bonanza. *Institutional Investor*. New York, March 1984.

security dollars.   Another term for INVESTMENT DOLLARS.

seigniorage.   The benefits to a country of appropriating real resources through the issue of 'non-interest bearing debt' (i.e. currency held in the form of working balances etc), through the control of interest rates, or through the exercise of reserve requirements. The term derives from the benefits to the Crown of its privilege in minting coins. The seigniorage issue is a technical and academic one but it also concerns the financial benefit of operating a reserve currency and is therefore relevant in decisions regarding the form any expansion of international reserves should take.
Bibliography: C. F. Bergsten. *The Dilemmas of the Dollar.* University Press, New York, 1975.

self-tender.   A US term for a TENDER by a company for its own shares.

sell-and-write.   An OPTIONS market term for a strategy whereby one sells the underlying instrument and also writes a put. It is essentially a 'covered put', which is appropriate if one is moderately bearish on the instrument. In the stock market it is not a particularly attractive strategy since one is obliged to cover any dividends on the stock sold short, but it is a viable strategy if the underlying instrument is a futures contract such as a gold or Treasury bond future.
Bibliography: L.G. McMillan. *Options as a Strategic Investment.* New York Institute of Finance, New York, 1980.
Comex. *Options on Gold Futures.* New York, n.d.

sell-down.   Where a security or syndicated borrowing is offered to other potential participants outside the SYNDICATE which is underwriting the deal, the proportion which these outsiders take is called the sell-down. A higher sell-down enhances the yield to LEAD MANAGERS. Compare FRONT-END FEES; POOL.

selling concession.   A new issue of securities in the Eurobond or US securities markets is frequently distributed through a SELLING GROUP. The securities are sold by the issuer to this group (via the managers), who in turn re-sell them to other buyers. As an inducement to the selling group, the price charged is reduced (often by 1.5% in the Eurobond market but the amount depends on market conditions). This reduction is the selling concession.
Bibliography: F.G. Fisher. *International Bonds.* Euromoney Publications, London, 1981.
L.M. Loll & J.G. Buckley. *The Over-the-Counter Securities Markets,* Prentice-Hall, NJ, 1981.

selling group.   A term used to denote a group of banks (or securities houses) involved in placing a security (not as UNDERWRITERS but as sellers). Each member will be alloted a certain quantity of the issue and asked to sell it to clients or other institutions.
Bibliography: F.G. Fisher. *International Bonds.* Euromoney Publications, London, 1981.
L.M. Loll & J.G. Buckley. *The Over-the-Counter Securities Markets,* Prentice-Hall, NJ, 1981.

selling group agreement.   An agreement binding together members of the SELLING GROUP in an international bond issue. The agreement lays down the commission paid for sales of bonds, and restrictions (if any) on where, and at what price, bonds can be sold. It may be a separate document or incorporated into one of the other documents distributed in the course of the offering.
Bibliography: F.G. Fisher. *International Bonds.* Euromoney, London, 1981.

selling group pot.   US term analogous to INSTITUTIONAL POT meaning a percentage of an offering which may be set aside for a selling group.

selling period.   The period allotted to a SELLING GROUP of an issue to accomplish its objectives.
Bibliography: F.G. Fisher. *International Bonds.* Euromoney Publications, London, 1981.
L.M. Loll & J.G. Buckley. *The Over-the-Counter Securities Markets,* Prentice-Hall, NJ, 1981.

sell-out. When a buyer of securities fails to accept proper delivery, the seller may, without notice, 'sell-out' the securities and charge the buyer with the costs involved. Compare BUY-IN.

Bibliography: *Rules & Regulations of the Stock Exchange.* The Stock Exchange, London, 1978.
L.M. Loll & J.G. Buckley. *The Over-the-Counter Securities Markets,* Prentice-Hall, New York, 1981.

sender net debit cap. A term used in US money transfer systems. A sender net debit cap is a cap on the net debit, or DAYLIGHT EXPOSURE, allowed to an institution sending payment instructions into the system.

Bibliography: D.B. Humphrey. Reducing Interbank Risk on Large Dollar Payment networks. *Journal of Cash Management.* Atlanta, Ga, September 1984.

senior. US term for debt which ranks ahead of other debts. Compare SUBORDINATED.

Bibliography: P. Wood. *Law & Practice of International Finance.* Sweet & Maxwell, London, 1982.
F.J. Fabozzi & H.C. Sauvain, Corporate Bonds *in* F.J. Fabozzi & I.M. Pollack (eds). *The Handbook of Fixed Income Securities.* Dow-Jones Irwin, Homewood, Ill., 1983.

Sepon. Part of the UK Stock Exchange's TALISMAN settlement process. Sepon stands for Stock Exchange Pooled Nominees. Any seller of a security transfers it into the name of Sepon, while any buyer buys it from Sepon.

Bibliography: J.Dundas Hamilton. *Stockbroking Today.* Macmillan Press, London, 1979.
S. Valentine. The UK Equity Markets *in* A.M. George & I.H. Giddy (eds). *International Finance Handbook.* John Wiley & Sons, New York, 1983.

serial bond. An issue split into a series of maturities, or which was issued as part of a series which matures at stated intervals.

Bibliography: F.J. Babozzi & H.C. Sauvain. Corporate Bonds. *in* F.J. Fabozzi & I.M. Pollack (eds). *The Handbook of Fixed Income Securities.* Dow-Jones Irwin, Homewood, Ill., 1983.

serial floater, FRN. A FLOATING RATE NOTE with a mandatory amortization according to a fixed schedule. Unlike a SINKING FUND where securities to be redeemed are drawn by lot or bought randomly in the SECONDARY MARKET, each note is amortized individually by means of principal repayment COUPONS which are clipped at the same time as the interest coupons.

Bibliography: F.G. Fisher. *International Bonds.* Euromoney Publications, London, 1981.

serial sinking fund. An unusual form of SINKING FUND in which each bond is partially redeemed by the action of the sinking fund. It repays a portion of the principal on each bond's specified coupon dates.

serial zero. A ZERO COUPON bond which is issued in the form of a SERIAL BOND. Thus, for example, in 1983 Chemical Bank of New York issued a serial zero of $450 million, which consisted of a series of 19 annual tranches of $15 million plus $165 million due in 2003.

series. OPTIONS market term for the set of CALL and PUT option contracts on the same underlying security for the same expiration date and STRIKE PRICE.

Bibliography: L.G. McMillan. *Options as a Strategic Investment.* New York Institute of Finance, New York, 1980.

set-off. Legal term relating to the right of a bank to use deposits of a borrower placed with the bank to pay off a defaulted loan. The issue became most publicized in the case of the dispute between the US and Iran, which had placed deposits with US banks which had also lent to it, but is of widespread importance in international banking, especially in the case of PARALLEL or BACK-TO-BACK loans. A common clause to cover the problem might read as follows: 'The Bank may set-off against any obligation of the borrower which is due and payable under this agreement moneys held by the Bank for the account of the Borrower at any branch of the Bank anywhere in the world and in any currency.'

Bibliography: P. Wood. *Law and Practice of*

International Finance. Sweet & Maxwell, London, 1980.

settlement date. The date on which payment for a transaction must be made. (1) In the UK stock exchange settlement is made through fortnightly ACCOUNT periods. In the US, various settlement methods are used; REGULAR WAY, SKIP-DAY SETTLEMENT and CASH DELIVERY.
Bibliography: D. O'Shea. *Investing for Beginners.* Financial Times Business Information, London, 1984.
L.M. Loll & J.G. Buckley. *The Over-the-Counter Securities Market.* Prentice-Hall, NJ, 1981.
(2) In the foreign exchange markets the settlement date for a SPOT deal is two days hence. Compare VALUE DATE.
Bibliography: J.K. Walmsley. *The Foreign Exchange Handbook.* John Wiley & Sons, New York, 1983.

settlement price. The single closing price on a contract on a futures exchange. It is usually determined by each exchange's price committee of directors. It is used primarily by the exchange clearing house to determine the amount of MARGIN capital to be put up by members, and it is also used by some exchanges as the official closing price to determine the price limits for the following day's trading. Compare LIMIT UP.

seven-day put bond. Term sometimes used to refer to a type of US tax-exempt security. A typical seven-day put bond would be a 30-year bond. At any time, subject to seven days' notice, the holder of any bond has the option to demand that the bond be repurchased at par (plus ACCRUED INTEREST). The bond would also be subject to optional redemption at par by the issuer on any interest payment day. Interest on the bonds is paid, and re-fixed, monthly. The net effect of this structure is that although the bond is a 30-year obligation the investor is able to regard it as a seven-day instrument. The firm responsible for repurchasing the bonds from the holder (usually the investment bank organizing the issue) undertakes to remarket the bonds. In the event that the bonds cannot be remarketed, the borrower has the right to draw on a LETTER OF CREDIT to finance himself.
Bibliography: F.J. Fabozzi *et al. The Municipal Bond Handbook.* Dow-Jones Irwin, Homewood, IU. 1983.

shelf registration. US term for arrangements introduced by the SECURITIES AND EXCHANGE COMMISSION in its RULE 415. Under these arrrangements, borrowers have the right to register with the SEC their intention to issue a given quantity of securities of a certain type, without specifiying the date on which they will be issued. That is, the registration is 'left on the shelf'. The benefit to the issuer is that it is possible to market an issue very quickly in response to market conditions, since all necessary SEC formalities have been complied with.
Bibliography: R.C. Ferrara & J.P. Sweeney. Shelf Registration under SEC Temporary Rule 415. *The Corporation Law Review.* Boston, Fall 1982.
B. McGoldrick. How Rule 415 put CFOs in the catbird seat. *Institutional Investor,* New York, April 1984.

Shibosai. Japanese PRIVATE PLACEMENT market.

shipbroker. A person or firm acting as intermediate between a merchant wishing to charter a ship and a shipowner with a ship available. Shipbrokers may also handle the purchase or sale of ships. Compare BALTIC EXHANGE, CHARTERPARTY.
Bibliography: R. Ihre *et al. Shipbroking and Chartering Practice.* Lloyd's of London Press, 1984.

Shogun lease. An international LEASE denominated in Japanese yen. Unlike the SAMURAI LEASE the Shogun lease is an outgrowth of the domestic Japanese leasing industry: its main benefit is very attractive long-term financing. Compare SAMURAI BOND; SAMURAI LEASE; SHIBOSAI.
Bibliography: The Shogun lease takes off in France. *Euromoney,* London September 1982.
D. Curtin. Japan's Greatest Export Success is Leasing. *Euromoney,* London, June 1982.

D. Curtin. Souped-up Shoguns. *Euromoney*, London, February 1984.

short.   To go short of a currency, security or commodity is to incur a net liability in the currency/security/commodity: either to sell more of it than you at present possess, or to borrow it and sell it. Money market dealers also speak of going 'short', either in the sense of shifting their assets into shorter-term instruments, or else of being over-lent in a particular period (i.e. they hope that rates will fall, so that they can fund the position more cheaply later).
Bibliography: J.K. Walmsley. *The Foreign Exchange Handbook*. John Wiley & Sons, New York, 1983.
M. Stigum. *The Money Market*. Dow-Jones Irwin, Homewood, Ill., 1983.
N.H. Rothstein & J.M. Little. *The Handbook of Financial Futures*. McGraw-Hill, New York, 1984.

short covering.   Buying to eliminate a short position.

short date.   In foreign exchange or in money markets the term usually means periods up to one week, but sometimes it is used to refer to periods up to a month.

short interest.   US term for the reported total of all shares sold short and not covered, or bought back, as of a given date on a particular Stock Exchange. These can be sizeable–e.g. in October 1982 the short interest on the New York Stock Exchange was 141 million shares.
Bibliography: New York Stock Exchange. *1983 Fact Book*. New York, 1983.

shorts.   UK term for GILT-EDGED SECURITIES with less than five years to maturity.

short sale.   *See* SHORT.

SIBOR.   *See* SINGAPORE INTER-BANK OFFERED RATE; SAUDI INTER-BANK OFFERED RATE. Compare LIBOR.

SICAV.   *See* SOCIETÉ D'INVESTISSEMENT À CAPITAL VARIABLE.

silent subparticipation.   A SUBPARTICIPATION in which the borrower is not consulted, or told, about the transfer of the loan from the lender.
Bibliography: P. Wood. *Law and Practice of International Finance*. Sweet & Maxwell, London, 1980.
C. Grant. How Banks Revamp Assets. *Euromoney*, London, April, 1984; L. Sandler. The Great Debate over LDC loan swapping. *Institutional Investor*, New York, May 1984.

simple yield to maturity.   A measure sometimes used of the YIELD on a BOND to its MATURITY.It is calculated by adding the capital gain to maturity and the annual coupon income and expressing it as a percentage of the theoretical average price. In other words, it ignores reinvestment income. Compare GROSS REDEMPTION YIELD; REALIZED COMPOUND YIELD TO MATURITY; YIELD TO MATURITY.
Bibliography: M.S. Dobbs- Higginson. *Investment Manual*. Credit Suisse First Boston, London, 1980; F.J. Fabozzi. Bond Yield Measures and Price Volatility Properties *in* F.J. Fabozzi & I.M. Pollack (eds). *The Handbook of Fixed Income Securities*. Dow-Jones Irwin, Homewood, Ill., 1983.

Singapore dollar CDs.   A CD denominated in Singapore dollars. The market was started in May 1975 with issues restricted to a minimum denomination of S$100,000 and a maximum of S$1 million in multiples of S$50,000, with a minimum term of three months and a maximum of three years. Its market growth has been steady if not as spectacular as the ASIAN DOLLAR market.
Bibliography: Y.S. Park. Asian Money Markets [in] A.M. George & I.H. Giddy (eds). *International Finance Handbook*. John Wiley & Sons, New York, 1983.

Singapore Inter-Bank Offered Rate.   The rate of interest at which ASIAN CURRENCY UNITS in Singapore are prepared to lend funds to first-class banks. Compare LIBOR.
Bibliography: Y.S. Park. Asian Money Markets [in] A.M. George & I.H. Giddy (eds). *International Finance Handbook*. John Wiley & Sons, New York, 1983.

Singapore International Monetary Exchange. A FUTURES exchange based in Singapore, set up in 1984, the SIMEX aims to become the futures trading centre for the Far East, particularly in the gold markets.
Bibliography: J. Quek. Will Simex Become the Missing Link? *Euromoney*. London, October 1984.

sinking fund. A fund created by a borrower for the purpose of redeeming bonds. The borrower is obliged to redeem specified amounts of the bond within specified periods (compare PURCHASE FUND). The function is to provide orderly amortization of a debt over the life of the issue. A sinking fund can also be applied to the depreciation of assets in a balance sheet.
Bibliography: F.J. Fabozzi & H.C. Sauvain. Corporate Bonds *in* F.J. Fabozzi & I.M.Pollack (eds). *The Handbook of Fixed Income Securities.* Dow-Jones Irwin, Homewood, Ill., 1983.
F.G. Fisher. *International Bonds.* Euromoney Publications, London, 1982.

SITC, SITC(R). *See* STANDARD INTERNATIONAL TRADE CLASSIFICATION

skip-day settlement. US term for settlement of a securities transaction two business days after the deal is done.

sliding parity. *See* CRAWLING PEG.

slip. An insurance term. Examples of its use include: (1) 'original' slip, which is the abbreviated memorandum prepared by an insurance BROKER containing the information necessary to the marine UNDERWRITER for estimating his risk. Once the 'original slip' is signed by the underwriter, a marine insurance contract (but not a policy) is in existence.
(2) 'Open' slips may be used when insufficient information is available for the preparation of an 'original' slip.
(3) 'Fleet slip' refers to a slip covering all the vessels of a fleet. Compare LINE SLIP.
Bibliography: R.J. Lambeth. *Templeman on Marine Insurance.* Macdonald & Evans, UK, 1981.

Smithsonian. The Smithsonian Institution in Washington was the site of the meeting in December 1971 which fixed new exchange rates after the devaluation of the US dollar in August 1971. EFFECTIVE EXCHANGE RATES are often calculated using the exchange rates fixed at the Smithsonian as a base level.
Bibliography: S. Strange. *International Monetary Relations 1959-71.* Royal Institute of International Affairs, London, 1976.

snake. This term refers to the European system of narrower exchange rate margins which was set up in 1972 and superseded in 1979 by the EUROPEAN MONETARY SYSTEM. The term 'snake' derives from the fact that the original intention was to arrange closer margins between European currencies–forming a 'snake'–within a TUNNEL : the maximum permitted margins of these currencies against the dollar. With the adoption of free floating the tunnel disappeared. Snake members have included at various times all EEC countries, plus Austria, Norway and Sweden as associates.
Bibliography: J.K. Walmsley. *The Foreign Exchange Handbook.* John Wiley & Sons, New York, 1983.

Societé d'Investissement à Capital Variable (SICAV). French equivalent of UNIT TRUSTS or OPEN-ENDED FUNDS. First permitted in 1964, the SICAV movement developed rapidly to the point where in 1975 there were about 90 SICAVs with total assets of around Ff23 billion.
Bibliography: B. Jacquillat. Paris: Equity Markets *in* A. M. George & I. H. Giddy (eds). *International Finance Handbook* John Wiley & Sons, New York, 1983.

Society for Worldwide Interbank Financial Telecommunications (SWIFT). A consortium of just under 500 major international banks based in Brussels, which operates a rapid money transfer system between 15 countries.
Bibliography: *SWIFT:Ten Years.* SWIFT, Brussels, 1983.

soft arbitrage. UK term sometimes em-

ployed for ARBITRAGE between public sector and private paper.
Bibliography: A note on money market arbitrage. *Bank of England Quarterly Bulletin*, June 1982.

solde. French for 'balance': e.g. *solde des mouvements de capitaux* = balance of capital movements; *solde c.a.f/f.o.b.* = payments balance c.i.f./f.o.b.

southbound swap. North American term for a forward foreign exchange SWAP from Canadian into US dollars. Thus 'price in southbound threes' would mean 'price in three-month swap from Canadian to US dollars'. Compare NORTH BOUND SWAP.

sovereign immunity. The doctrine that a state cannot be sued. This is of relevance where a state borrows money on the Euromarkets, and legal steps have been taken in the US and the UK to deal with this problem.
Bibliography: The UK State Immunity Act 1978, and US Foreign Sovereign Immunities Act 1976.
P. Wood. *Law and Practice of International Finance.* Sweet & Maxwell, London, 1980.
C. Lewis. The State Immunity Act. *Lloyd's Commercial and Maritime Law Quarterly,*no.1, 1980.
Sovereign borrowers. Dag Hammarskjöld Foundation/Butterworths, London 1984.

sovereign risk limit. A bank which lends money in the EUROMARKETS will normally place a limit on the amount which it is prepared to lend to one government (and government agencies and/or enterprises which are backed by the full faith and credit of the government). This is referred to as the sovereign risk limit, or sovereign limit. The term sovereign limit may also be applied to the limit which is imposed on the bank's lending to all borrowers in that country, but 'country limit' or COUNTRY RISK is normally preferred for this, broader, limit.
Bibliography: S.I. Davis. *The Euro-Bank.* Macmillan, London/John Wiley New York, 1983.
P. Nagy (ed.). *Country Risk.* Euromoney Publications, London, 1981.

special bracket. Banks or brokers partici-

pating in a loan in the US or Euromarkets are usually listed (on the TOMBSTONE advertising the loan) in BRACKETS according to the amount they have underwritten or provided. The 'special bracket' usually refers to a group of UNDERWRITERS other than the MANAGERS appearing at the head of the list of underwriters.
Bibliography: F.G. Fisher. *International Bonds.* Euromoney Publications, London, 1981.
L.S. Goodman. Syndicated Eurocurrency Lending: Pricing and Practice *in* A.M. George & I.H. Giddy. *International Finance Handbook.* John Wiley & Sons, New York, 1983.

special deposits. A device employed by the Bank of England to regulate the activity of British banks. Special deposits are funds required to be placed with the Bank of England (on which interest payable is linked to the Treasury Bill rate); this reduces the banks' ability to lend.
Bibliography: E.R. Shaw. *The London Money Markets.* Heinemann, London, 1983.

Special Drawing Right (SDR). Introduced in 1970, the SDR represented an attempt by the INTERNATIONAL MONETARY FUND (q.v) to expand INTERNATIONAL LIQUIDITY. A country holding SDRs may use them to acquire foreign currency by transferring them (via the IMF Special Drawing Account) to another country in exchange for foreign currency supplied by that country. SDRs are treated as part of a country's international reserves. The original value of an SDR was 0.88867088 grammes of fine gold, which at the time equalled US\$1. Following the dollar devaluations of 1971 and 1973 this no longer held true and in 1974 a new valuation of the SDR was introduced. Under this system one SDR was set equal to the sum of specified quantities of 16 currencies. A new 'basket' was introduced in 1978, and in January, 1981 a new, simplified SDR was introduced, consisting of US\$0.54+DMK 0.46+ £stg0.071+FFR0.74+Y34. Daily values for the SDR in terms of various currencies are calculated by the IMF and published in newspapers such as the *Financial Times*. The basket of five currencies was chosen so as to simplify the calculations involved, particularly in making private, SDR-linked bank deposits, in which there is a well-established market. There have also been many BOND issues denominated in SDRs. As an example, ENEL of Italy issued a FLOATING-RATE NOTE of SDR100 million for five years in 1981, priced at ¼% over the six month LIBOR rate of the five constituent currencies.

Bibliography: J. Gold. *Special Drawing Rights: Character and Use.* IMF. Washington DC, 1970. J. Gold, SDRs, *Gold and Currencies: Fourth Survey of New Legal Developments.* IMF Pamphlet no. 33, Washington DC, 1980. J.K. Walmsley.*The Foreign Exchange Handbook.* John Wiley & Sons, New York, 1983.

Special Drawing Right Certificates. The US Treasury can MONETIZE its SDR holdings by issuing SDR certificates to Federal Reserve Banks in exchange for a dollar balance at that reserve bank. The process is analogous to the issue of GOLD CERTIFICATES.

Bibliography: *The Federal Reserve System: Purposes & Functions.* Board of Governors, Federal Reserve System, Wasington DC, 1974.

specialist. US Stock Exchange term for a member of the Exchange who engages in the buying and selling of one or more specific issues of stock on the floor of the Exchange. In their capacity as brokers, specialists execute orders for other brokers on a commission. In their capacity as dealers, they act for their own accounts, buying from and selling to the public through other members of the Exchange.

Bibliography: L.M. Loll & J.G. Buckley. *The Over-the-Counter Securities Market.* Prentice-Hall, USA, 1980. R.J. Teweles & E.S. Bradley. *The Stock Market.* John Wiley & Sons, New York, 1982.

specification policies. A marine insurance term referring to insurance policies issued from time to time in respect of batches of shipments under OPEN COVERS. Specifications are normally prepared by insurance brokers to attach to the various policies and they set out the details of each shipment and its insured value.

Bibliography: R.J. Lambeth. *Templeman on Marine Insurance.* Macdonald & Evans, UK, 1981.

specific issue market. A US term for a subsector of the REPURCHASE market. A reverse repurchase agreement is made in respect of a specific security issue whose price is expected by the dealer to fall. (In a normal reverse repurchase the underlying security hardly matters.)

Bibliography: M. Stigum. *The Money Market.* Dow-Jones Irwin, Homewood, Ill., 1983.

split.   The division of the outstanding shares of a corporation into a larger number of shares.

split-level trust.   A UK term for an investment company which was split into two components. Each had a stated life and one part of the capital was entitled to all of the income while the other was entitled to any capital growth. The first split-level trust to complete its life was Acorn Securities Ltd, which was wound up in January 1981. Several other trusts reach their terminal dates over the next few years.

Bibliography: A.A. Arnaud. *Investment Trusts Explained.* Woodhead-Faulkner, Cambridge, UK, 1983.

split spread.   A EUROCREDIT carries a SPREAD over LIBOR; if this spread is fixed at say ⅞% over LIBOR for three years, and 1% over LIBOR for another four, the credit is referred to as a seven-year credit carrying split spread. Split spreads emerged as a response to the squeeze on spreads during 1977-8 and are now common.

Bibliography: L.S. Goodman. Syndicated Eurolending: Pricing and Practice *in* A.M. George & I.H. Giddy (eds). *International Finance Handbook.* John Wiley & Sons, New York, 1983.

spot.   A foreign exchange term. 'Spot' transactions are settled in two working days' time. For example, a purchase of dollars against sterling made on Tuesday will be settled on Thursday. The delay allows completion of the necessary paperwork. The vast majority of tranactions for current requirements will be undertaken on a spot basis, but it is possible to deal for settlement the following working day (*see* TOMORROW/NEXT) or even the same day.

Bibliography: J.K. Walmsley. *The Foreign Exchange Handbook*. John Wiley & Sons, New York, 1983.

spot/next.   In foreign exchange dealing, a purchase of currency on Monday for settlement on Thursday (i.e. the next day after the SPOT DATE) will be transacted at the exchange rate for spot delivery plus an adjustment for the extra day; the adjustment is called 'spot/next'. Thus if spot sterling is \$1.4550/60 and spot/next is 5/4, the OUTRIGHT price for sterling on Thursday would be \$1.4545/56. Analogous terms are 'spot/week' for delivery a week after spot, and 'spot/fortnight' for delivery a fortnight after spot.

Bibliography: J.K. Walmsley. *The Foreign Exchange Handbook*. John Wiley & Sons, New York, 1983.

spread.   (1) In foreign exchange or securities markets, the difference between a dealer's buying and selling price for the currency or security.

(2) In the Euromarkets and certain domestic lending operations the term 'spread' or 'margin' is used to denote the differential between the rate at which a bank borrows money on the inter-bank market and the rate at which it on-lends the funds to its customers.

Bibliography: S.I. Davis. *The Euro-Bank*. Macmillan, London/John Wiley, New York, 1981.

(3) With reference to the EEC SNAKE and the EUROPEAN monetary system, the term spread is used to indicate the gap between the strongest and weakest currencies in the snake: a spread of 1.5% means that the percentage deviation of the strongest currency from its parity, added to the percentage deviation of the weakest from its parity, sum to 1.5%.

Bibliography: J.K. Walmsley. *The Foreign Exchange Handbook*. John Wiley, New York, 1983.

(4) Underwriting spread is the difference between the price to the public and the price

to the issuer of a new security. Compare UNDERWRITER.

(5) In commodity, futures and options markets the term spread is widely used: in many cases it is used interchangeably with STRADDLE. In OPTIONS markets, a spread is the simultaneous purchase of one option and the sale of another, with different terms, on the same security – for example, the purchase of a 45 call and the sale of a 60 call. A straddle would be the simultaneous purchase of a put and a call. In futures and commodity markets, by contrast, a spread is normally considered to refer to a trade in different markets – between, TREASURY BILLS and CD's for example – while a straddle normally refers to trading in the same contract for different maturities. However, this usage is frequently reversed. Compare BEAR SPREAD; BOX SPREAD; BULL SPREAD; BUTTERFLY SPREAD; DIAGONAL SPREAD; HORIZONTAL SPREAD; SANDWICH SPREAD; VERTICAL SPREAD.

Bibliography: L.G. McMillan. *Options as a Strategic Investment*. New York Institute of Finance, New York, 1980.
N.H. Rothstein & J.M. Little (eds). *The Handbook of Financial Futures*. McGraw-Hill, New York, 1984.
C.W.J. Granger. *Trading in Commodities*.

(6) In the LLOYD's insurance market, the term spread is used to mean dispersion of risk: 'there is a wide spread on this' means 'this risk is insured with many UNDERWRITERS'.

spread-lock.   US term for a technique of locking in a spread on a new issue. The borrower is permitted to 'lock in' a spread on his issue over US Treasury securities, but is given the option of fixing the absolute level at some later date. If rates rise, the borrower pays the underwriter a lump sum, while if they fall, the underwriter pays the borrower. The underwriter usually hedges his position by buying Treasury securities, or futures.

Bibliography: Deals of the Year. *Institutional Investor*. New York, December 1983.

spread sheet.   The statistical results of the final pricing meeting for a new issue of a security, which indicate the offering price, the breakdown of the GROSS SPREAD, the terms relating to dividend or interest accrual and the day, date and place of delivery, together with all other pertinent information (e.g. CALL prices or conversion privilege).

square. Refers to a position in a currency, security, or a commodity which is balanced, i.e. neither LONG nor SHORT.

Stabex. A scheme devised by the EEC to stabilize export earnings of developing countries associated with it by the LOMÉ CONVENTION. Essentially the Stabex scheme provides that if a country's export earnings fall below a certain trigger level, financial assistance by grants or loans will be provided by the EEC. Compare COMPENSATORY FINANCING.
Bibliography: *Annual Report of the ACP-EEC Council of Ministers.* Brussels, annually.
A.I. MacBean & P.N. Snowden. *International Institutions in Trade and Finance.* George Allen & Unwin, London, 1981.

stabilizing bid. Eurobond and US securities market term for the bid which the managers of the issue make for the bonds which have been issued. The purpose of the bid is to prevent the price of the security from going below the issue price for a certain period after the issue. This is to prevent an immediate loss to those who have bought the security, which would reduce the borrower's ability to make other issues on favourable terms. Compare GREY MARKET.
Bibliography: F.G. Fisher. *International Bonds.* Euromoney Publications, London, 1981.

stale. (1) A term used to denote a BILL OF EXCHANGE payable on demand, or a cheque which appears on the face of it to have been in circulation for an unreasonable period of time.
(2) A stale BILL OF LADING is one dated subsequent to the expiry date of the DOCUMENTARY CREDIT which covers the shipment, or which shows that the goods involved were shipped on a date later than that authorised by the credit. A bill of lading may also be considered stale if presented so

long after the sailing of the carrying steamer that the goods arrive at the port of destination before the buyer will get the documents, so that he will be unable to obtain possession of the goods on arrival.
Bibliography: Article 41 of *Uniform Customs and Practice on Documentary Credits.* International Chamber of Commerce Brochure no. 290. Paris, 1975.
A. Watson. *Finance of International Trade.* Institute of Bankers, London, 1981.

standard. In money and foreign exchange markets certain amounts and certain maturities are regarded as standard, e.g. in professional inter-bank foreign exchange dealing a standard, amount would be $1 million or a multiple of it and a standard maturity would be 1, 3, 6 or 12 months – in certain currencies 1, 2, 3, 4, 5, 6, 9 and 12. No clear-cut definition is possible since the situation will vary with the level of activity in the market and also in some cases the exchange controls in operation at the time.

Standard and Poor's. A US firm which offers systematic evaluation of the financial condition of a borrower, and ancillary services. Compare AAA, MOODY'S, RATINGS.
Bibliography: *Standard & Poor's Rating Guide.* McGraw-Hill, New York, 1979.

Standard International Trade Classification (SITC). A trade classification system primarily designed for statistical and economic purposes (unlike the CUSTOMS COOPERATION COUNCIL TARRIFF NOMENCLATURE, which is for customs purposes). Revised in 1961 to BTN. The revised classification is denoted by SITC(R).
Bibliography: *Guide to the Classification for Overseas Trade Statistics.* HMSO, London, 1984.
Standard International Trade Classification Revision 2, United Nations, New York 1975.

stand-by commitment. A US term for a commitment by an investor to buy a mortgage from a mortgage banker who pays a commitment fee in return for the right, but not the obligation, to sell such a mortgage to the investor.

stand-by credit.   (l) An arrangment with the INTERNATIONAL MONETARY FUND where a member receives assurance that, during a fixed period of time, requests for drawings on the IMF will be allowed on the member's representation as to need.
Bibliography: J. Gold. *The Stand-by Arrangements of the IMF*. IMF, Washington, D.C., 1970.
J. Williamson (ed.). *IMF Conditionality*. MIT press, Cambridge, Mass., 1983.
(2) A parallel term is applied to an arrangement with a bank or group of banks under which they agree to make a certain amount of funds available to the borrower for a specified period of time.

standby letter of credit   A LETTER OF CREDIT issued to cover against a particular contingency. For example, in the US commercial paper market, it is common for foreign borrowers to obtain a standby letter of credit from a first-class bank. This guarantees that the investors in commercial paper will be repaid, since if the borrower fails to repay the bank will be liable under the letter of credit. Such letters of credit compensate for the fact that US banks may not issue guarantees.
Bibliography: J.A. Nelson. How to Make a Stand-by Credit worth more than the Paper it's Written On. *Euromoney*, London.
Documentary Credits *in* C.M. Chinkin, P.J. Davidson and W.J.M. Ricquier (eds). *Current Problems in International Trade Financing*. National University of Singapore/Butterworths, London, 1983.

stand-by offering.   US term for an offering of RIGHTS by a corporation in which an underwriter offers to 'stand-by' to purchase any of the rights the corporation is unable to sell.

state immunity.   *See* SOVEREIGN IMMUNITY.

step-down spread.   A loan with a SPREAD which falls over time may be described as a step down spread loan. Thus in 1980 Nigeria raised a loan of $35 million with a 1% spread for the first five years, and 7/8% thereafter. Compare SPLIT SPREAD.

stepped-rate bond.   Term for a bond which carries different coupons for different periods of its life (often the bond is an extendible or RETRACTABLE). For example the Canadian government issued a 9% bond in April 1976, due October 1980, but giving holders the option to extend their holdings into 9.5% bonds to be dated October 1980 and due in October 1985.
Bibliography: OECD. *Government Debt Management*. Paris, 1983.

sterilization.   After foreign exchange INTERVENTION there will normally be a change in a country's domestic money supply, which could have inflationary or deflationary consequences. If it wishes to neutralize these, the central bank concerned will 'sterilise' its intervention by undertaking some offsetting operation, usually through OPEN MARKET OPERATIONS but if need be by making some compulsory order freezing the funds involved.
Bibliography: P.B. Kenen. Effects of Intervention and Sterilization in the Short Run and Long Run *in* R.N. Cooper *et al. The International Monetary System Under Flexible Exchange Rates*. Ballinger Publishing Co., Cambridge, Mass., 1982.
J.K. Walmsley. *The Foreign Exchange Handbook*. John Wiley & Sons, New York, 1983.
External Flows and Broad Money. *Bank of England Quarterly Bulletin*. December 1983.

sterling area.   The area within which it was possible freely to transfer sterling, despite UK exchange controls, until June 1972; it consisted of the group of countries which transacted the bulk of their trade in sterling and held most of their external reserves in sterling. It first received formal definition in 1939 with the adoption of wartime exchange controls, and in the absence of UK exchange controls (abolished in 1979) is no longer relevant.
Bibliography: A.R. Conan. *The Sterling Area*. Macmillan, 1952.

sterling balances.   Sums held in sterling by foreign governments and private individuals. The bulk of the build-up in these balances occurred during the Second World War when countries like Egypt and India were made to accumulate sterling credits as a means of financing Britain's war effort. They were a major problem for the UK's external finances until the late 1970s.

Bibliography: F. Hirsch. *Money International.* Penguin Books, London, 1967.
A.R. Conan. *The Sterling Area.* Macmillan, 1952.
Overseas sterling balances 1963-73. *Bank of England Quarterly Bulletin.* June 1974.

Sterling Brokers' Association (SBA). Formed in 1979, the SBA has as its objective the smoothing of trading in the unsecured domestic sterling deposit market, and a code of practice has been set up to facilitate regulation of the market. It maintains close liaison with the Bank of England.

Sterling Eurobonds. A EUROBOND denominated in sterling. Until the abolition of EXCHANGE CONTROL in 1979, sterling Eurobonds were not permitted. They are still relatively scarce but the market has developed to a sizeable scale. For example, in the three months ending mid-February 1984 there were four fixed rate issues raising a total of £175 million, and four FLOATING-RATE NOTES which raised £350 million.

Bibliography: *The Bulldog Market.* De Zoete & Bevan, London, 1983.
Bank of England Quarterly Bulletin, March 1984.

Sterling Foreign Currency Bonds. Until the abolition of UK EXCHANGE CONTROL, the only sterling-denominated issues available to foreign borrowers were sterling bonds with a foreign currency repayment clause. For example, the £25 million issue by Total Oil Marine in 1977 consisted of seven year NOTES for which the principal was payable in sterling or US dollars (at the exchange rate ruling at the time of payment), and interest in dollars.

Bibliography: M.S. Mendelsohn. Those sterling Eurobonds. *The Banker.* London, December 1977.
The Bulldog Market. De Zoete & Bevan, London, 1983.

Sterling Guarantee Scheme. An arrange-ment negotiated in 1968 where the UK agreed to maintain the dollar value of official sterling balances in return for an agreement by the holders that they would keep an agreed proportion of external reserves in sterling. The arrangements were revised in 1973 and 1974, and terminated in December 1974. In January 1977 a new arrangement was made where the UK government offered foreign currency securities to official sterling balance holders as an inducement to the latter to maintain reserves with the UK. Compare BASLE AGREEMENTS.

Bibliography: F. Hirsch. *Money International.* Penguin Books, London, 1967.
International Monetary Cooperation. BIS Annual Reports. *Bank of England Quarterly Bulletin.*
B. Tew *International Monetary Cooperation 1945-70.* Hutchinson, London, 1971.

stipulated loss value (SLV). A LEASING term. It refers to the value placed on the item being leased in the event of its destruction. To protect the lessor of the equipment, the stipulated loss value must be such that, after allowing for any tax implications of the destruction of the asset and payment of the SLV to the lessor, there are enough funds to recover the lessor's outstanding investment.

Bibliography: L.A. Haynes. Stipulated Loss Values and Measuring Lessor Default Exposure. *The Leasing and Financial Services Monitor*, USA, Jan/Feb. 1984.

stock. (1) In the UK, the capital of a company may be held in so much stock or so many shares. Stock may be held and transferred in any amounts (without distinguishing numbers) whereas shares are for fixed amounts and are all numbered; for example, I may hold £150 of stock or 30 £5 shares. Stock, by its nature, is fully paid-up, but shares may be only PARTLY PAID.

Bibliography: J. Dundas Hamilton. *Stockbroking Today.* Macmillan, London 1979.

(2) In the US, stocks – preferred or COMMON STOCKS – are the units into which a company's equity capital is divided, i.e. the equivalent of the UK's shares.

Bibliography: R.J. Teweles & E.S. Bradley. *The*

Stock Market. John Wiley & Sons, New York, 1982.

stockbrokers.   A person or firm who transacts in securities. In the UK the rule has always been that a stockbroker may not act as principal in a stock market deal but acts as a pure agent, or broker, between the buyer and seller. In the US, by contrast, a broker will buy and sell stock. Plans are in hand whereby the UK system will be transformed into one more like the US one.
Bibliography: J. Dundas Hamilton. *Stockbroking Today.* Macmillan Press, London, 1979.
A.M. George. The US Equity Market *in* A.M. George & I.H. Giddy. *International Finance Handbook.* John Wiley & Sons, New York, 1983.

Stock Clearing Corporation.   A corporation formed in 1920 by members of the New York Stock Exchange to provide facilities for clearing transactions in securities. Its functions were taken over in 1977 by the NATIONAL SECURITIES CLEARING CORPORATION.
Bibliography: R.J. Teweles & E.S. Bradley, *The Stock Market.* John Wiley & Sons, New York, 1982.

stop loss reinsurance.   This type of REINSURANCE is also known as Excess of Loss Ratio reinsurance. It differs, however, from EXCESS OF LOSS TREATY REINSURANCE in that Stop Loss treaties are designed to prevent the CEDING COMPANY from losing more than a specified percentage on any one class of business. Thus the reinsurer is not liable for any claim until the ceding company's loss for the year reaches an agreed percentage of its premiums; for example it might be agreed that the reinsurer would be liable if the loss ratio exceeds 80%.
Bibliography: R.P. Bellerose. *Reinsurance for the Beginner.* Witherby & Co., London 1978.

stop order.   An order to buy or sell a stock (or commodity) when a given prices is reached or passed. It becomes a market order as soon (commodity) reaches the specified price. Sometimes known as 'stop-loss' order.
Bibliography: N.H. Rothstein & J.M. Little. *The*

Handbook of Financial Futures. McGraw-Hill, New York, 1984.

stop-out price, stop-out rate.   US term for the lowest accepted price (or, conversely, the highest accepted rate) for TREASURY BILLS at the regular weekly AUCTION. The term is also used in respect of the daily REPURCHASE or GO-AROUND conducted by the FEDERAL RESERVE in the course of its OPEN MARKET OPERATIONS.
Bibliography: F.J. Fabozzi & I.M. Pollack. *The Handbook of Fixed Income Securities.* Dow-Jones Irwin, Homewood., Ill, 1983.

straddle.   Term which is often used interchangeably with SPREAD. In OPTIONS markets, a spread is the simultaneous purchase of one option and the sale of another, with different terms, on the same security – for example, the purchase of a 45 CALL and the sale of a 60 call. A straddle would be the simultaneous purchase of a PUT and a call. In futures and the commodity markets, by contrast, a spread is normally considered to refer to a trade in different markets – between TREASURY BILLS and CD's for example – while a straddle normally refers to trading in the same contract for different maturities. However, this usage is frequently reversed. Compare BEAR STRADDLE; BULL STRADDLE; BUTTERFLY STRADDLE.
Bibliography: L.G. McMillan. *Options as a Strategic Investment.* New York Institute of Finance, New York, 1980.
N.H. Rothstein & J.M. Little (eds). *The Handbook of Financial Futures.* McGraw-Hill, New York, 1984.
C.W.J. Granger *Trading in Commodities.* Woodhead-Faulkner, Cambridge, UK, 1983.

straight.   Term referring to a bond with unquestioned right to repayment of principal at a specified future date, unquestioned right to fixed interest payments on stated dates an no right to any additional interest, principal or conversion privilege.
Bibliography: F.G. Fisher. *International Bonds.* Euromoney Publications, London 1981.
F.J. Fabozzi & I.M. Pollack (eds). *The Handbook of Fixed Income Securities.* Dow-Jones Irwin, Homewood, Ill., 1983.

straight line method. A term used in measuring earnings on a FLOATING RATE NOTE. It measures the investor's return as a margin over LIBOR by adding the quoted margin to the straight line rate of amortization over time of the note's discount/premium to par. The exact calculation is not always clearly defined. A recent formula proposes the following calculation:

Definition 1. The neutral price is the price of the note at the next COUPON date if the simple margin remains unchanged between settlement and coupon date.

Definition 2. The simple margin is the average cash return on the note through its entire life compared with LIBOR, with both returns calculated on a base of par.

Combining these definitions leads to the following formula:

$$SM = \frac{100 - (P + ((L + QM - c) \times d/360))}{Life} + QM$$

where

SM	= simple margin
P	= flat price of note (excluding accrued interest)
L	= Libor to next coupon date
c	= nominal coupon
d	= number of days from settlement to next coupon date
Life	= remaining life to maturity in 360-day years
QM	= quoted margin over Libor paid by the FRN.

Thus consider an FRN which has its coupon fixed at 10.25% – 25 basis points over the LIBOR rate of 10% – at a price of 99. Suppose there are 181 days before the next coupon date and 5.069 years left to maturity. Then the simple margin is:

$$SM =$$

$$\frac{100 - (99 + ((10 + .25 - 10.25) \times 181/360)))}{5.069} + .25$$

$$= .1973 + .25 = 44.7 \text{ basis points.}$$

Bibliography: Credit Suisse First Boston. *Eurodollar FRN Evaluation Techniques.* London, November 1984.

strap. An OPTIONS MARKET term for the purchase of two CALLS and one PUT.

Bibliography: W.B. Riley & A.H. Montgomery. *Guide to Computer-Assisted Investment Analysis.* McGraw Hill, New York, 1982.

streaker. Term occasionally used to refer to a STIPPED bond which has been made into a ZERO COUPON.

street. Generally, 'the market'. For example, 'I can pick up three-month money on the street for six' is the same thing as 'I can borrow three month money in the money market at 6%'.

street name. US term for registering securities in the name of a broker, bank or other third party, instead of the owner, for easy administration. Compare MARKING NAME.

Bibliography: L.M. Loll & J.G. Buckley. *The Over-the Counter Securities Markets.* Prentice-Hall, NJ, 1980.
R.J. Teweles & E.S. Bradley. *The Stock Market.* John Wiley & Sons, New York, 1982.

street practice. US term (1) for any unwritten practice generally in use by the financial community; (2) for the general collection of conventions in used by the financial community for calculating bond yields and prices.

strike, striking price. Term from the OPTIONS market. It is the price at which the option-holder may buy or sell the underlying instrument. Thus, in the US listed stock options market, an option might be described as XYZ July 50 call, meaning a call option on the stock of XYZ Inc. expiring in July, with a striking price of $50 per share. The option is said to have INTRINSIC VALUE depending on the relationhsip of the stock's current price level to the striking price, and hence the latter plays an important part in determining the value of the option.

Bibliography: L.G. McMillan. *Options as a*

*Strategic Investment.*New York Institute of Finance, New York, 1980.

strip. (1) To remove the COUPONS form a BOND in order to sell the coupons and bonds as a series of ZERO-COUPONbonds. The technique generally used is to buy a set of Treasury securities, put them into safekeeping, and then issue receipts against every coupon and principal payment the Treasury is scheduled to make. Compare CATS, TIGERS, FELINES.
Bibliography: J. Laskey. How Stripping Became Respectable. *Euromoney*, December 1982.

(2) A FUTURES market term referring to a succession of contracts. For example, the EURODOLLAR futures contract is for 90-day LIBOR, settling in March, June, September and December. Thus, if one were in January to do an ARBITRAGE between the INTEREST RATE SWAP market and the Eurodollar futures contract, one might do a swap involving receipt of the one-year rate and payment of three-month LIBOR, settled quarterly. To hedge the obligation to make LIBOR payments every three months, one would 'buy the strip' – i.e. buy contracts for March, June, September and December.
Bibliography: N.H. Rothstein & J.M. Little. *The Handbook of Financial Futures.* McGraw Hill, New York, 1984.

(3) An OPTIONS MARKET term for the purchase of two PUTS and one CALL Compare STRAP.
Bibliography: W.B. Riley & A.H. Montgomery. *Guide to Computer-Assisted Investment Analysis.*McGraw-Hill, New York, 1982

strip yield curve. Term for the YIELD CURVE generated by a STRIP of futures contracts. The strip yield curve is worked out by realizing that the rates on the futures contracts are implicit FORWARD RATES: to derive the underlying CASH yields implied one has to work back from the near end of the cash market and the next futures contract; having worked out this cash yield one proceeds to the next contract, etc. The formula used is:

$$R2 = \frac{360}{T2}\left[\left(f\left[\frac{T_2 - T_1}{360}\right] + 1\right)\left(1 + \frac{R_1 T_1}{360}\right) - 1\right]$$

where
R1 = rate on short cash insturment, already known
R2 = the longer cash rate to be found
T1 = maturity of short cash instrument
T2 = maturity of long cash instrument
f = rate on futures instrument, already known.

As an example, suppose in the cash market a 90-day CD yields 14.4% on March 15. The IMM June CD is priced at 84.88, so yields 15.12% – a 180-day rate. We want to know that the implied cash 180-day CD rate is, so we write

$$R2 = \frac{360}{180}\left[\left(.1512\left[\frac{180 - 90}{360}\right] + 1\right)\right.$$
$$\left.\left(1 + \frac{.1440 \times 90}{360}\right) - 1\right] = 15.03\%$$

Hence we know that on the strip yield curve the 180 day rate is 15.03%, and we can now compare this rate with the actual cash market rate to see if it can be arbitraged.
Bibliography: N.H. Rothstein & J.M. Little. *The Handbook of Financial Futures.* Dow-Jones, Irwin, Homewood., Ill., 1984.
J.K. Walmsley. *The Foreign Exchange Handbook.* John Wiley & Sons, New York, 1983.

stub period. BOND market term for a period which is shorter than the rest. Unless a bond is bought on a COUPON settlement date, there will normally be a 'stub' period until the next coupon payment which is shorter than the later coupon payment periods; e.g. if a semi-annual bond is bought 30 days after the last coupon date, there will be a stub period of around 152 days.

subject. Subject to confirmation. In US usage, (1) a price quotation that is not firm.
(2) In new issue terminology, a word indicating to would-be buyers that all securities have provisionally been sold but that depending on subsequent availability the buyer's order may be filled.

subject premium. The insurance premium of the CEDING COMPANY to which the REINSURANCE premium rate is applied in order to produce the reinsurance premium.
Bibliography: R.P. Bellerose. *Reinsurance for the Beginner.* Witherby & Co., London 1978.

sub-major bracket, underwriter. *See* BRACKET.

subordinated. Term which refers to a promise to pay which cannot legally be fulfilled until payments on certain other obligations have been made and any other conditions, defined in the INDENTURE have been met. These other obligations are said to be senior to the subordinated obligation. For example, in the case of an unsecured bond issued by a bank, repayment may be guaranteed on a subordinated basis, as far as any claim to repayment is subordinated to the claims of the bank's depositors and its secured creditors, but ranks PARI PASSU with other unsecured claims. Compare SENIOR.
Bibliography: F.G. Fisher, *International Bonds.* Euromoney Publications, London, 1981.
F.J. Fabozzi & I.M. Pollack (eds). *The Handbook of Fixed Income Securities.* Dow-Jones Irwin, Homewood, Ill., 1983.

subparticipation. A technique of lending under which a bank or group of banks makes a loan to a borrower and then arranges for other banks to take on part of the loan. The usual method is that the bank granting the participation agrees with the participant that (a) the granting bank grants a certain percentage of the toal loan; (b) the participant agrees to provide funds to the lead bank which the lead bank uses to make that proportion of the loan; (c) the granting bank agrees to pay the participant a pro rata share of the receipts from the borrower. The technique can be controversial in that it can be viewed as the granting bank 'walking away' from a problem loan; on the other hand, it can allow the granting bank to lend more to the borrower.
Bibliography: P. Wood. *Law and Practice of International Finance.* Sweet & Maxwell, London, 1980.

C. Grant. How Banks Revamp Assets. *Euromoney*, London, April, 1984.
L. Sandler. The great debate over LDC loan swapping. *Institutional Investor.* New York, May 1984.

subscription agreement. Part of the issue process in the international BOND market. The agreement is signed by the MANAGER and the issuer binds the managers (as principals, not as agents for the UNDERWRITERS) to their commitments to purchas the bonds issued. It is not usually executed until a sufficient number of underwriters have agreed to buy bonds.
Bibliography: F.G. Fisher. *International Bonds.* Euromoney Publications, London 1981.

supplementary financing facility. A special supplementary facility arranged by the INTERNATIONAL MONETARY FUND in 1979. SFF resources are combined with the ordinary resources of the IMF made available through credit tranches and the EXTENDED FINANCING FACILITY (EFF) according to prescribed mixing ratios. For example, under an extended financing arrangement, a member borrows in equal proportions up to the limit of 140% of quota available under the EFF (i.e. up to 140% of quota in ordinary resources matched by 140% in SFF resources). Above this, all borrowings are SFF borrowings.
Bibliography: The Financial Structure and Operations of the IMF. *Bank of England Quarterly Bulletin*, December 1983 & March 1984.

supplementary special deposits. *See* CORSET.

supplier credit. Export finance made available to the supplier of the goods (as distinct from credits to the overseas buyer under BUYER CREDITS. A typical supplier credit would involve the exporter supplying goods to an overseas customer on a credit basis, receiving from the buyer a cash sum amounting to perhaps 20% of the value of the contract, and bills of exchange or promissory notes payable over a period representing the balance. The supplier then sells these instruments to a bank or group of banks, who are often given a guarantee by the supplier's national export credit organization.

Bibliography: *The Export Credit Financing Systems in OECD Member Countries.* Organization for Economic Cooperation & Development, Paris, 1982.
A. Dunn & M. Knight. *Export Finance* Euromoney Publications, London, 1982; *ECGD Services.* ECGD, London, 1983.

support point. (1) In foreign exchange, the point at which a central bank is obliged to intervene in order to support its currency. Such a point is only clearly defined in a regime of fixed exchange rates or a joint float arrangement such as the EUROPEAN MONETARY SYSTEM. It is often referred to as an 'intervention point'. Compare PARITY GRID.

(2) A term from TECHNICAL ANALYSIS. A support point is said to exist when a stock or commodity has repeatedly fallen to a particular price, only to bounce back upwards; or if it is less on the lower side of a CHANNEL.

Bibliography: P.J. Kaufman (ed.). *Technical Analysis in Commodities.* John Wiley & Sons, New York, 1980.
E.W. Schwartz. *How to Use Interest Rate Futures Contracts.* Dow-Jones Irwin, Homewood, Ill., 1979.

surety. This term can mean either (1) a promise made by a person to become obligated to a second person for the debt, obligation or conduct of a third person – as, for example, in a SURETY BOND.

(2) the person making the promise. A surety may be a private individual, or a corporation. So far as concerns international trade and finance, sureties are normally banks (though in the US, owing to restrictions on guarantees, this is normally done by STAND-BY LETTERS OF CREDIT), insurance companies, or specialist surety companies. A surety plays an important part in ADVANCE PAYMENT BONDS, BID BONDS, PERFORMANCE BONDS, and TENDER BONDS. *See also* BOND.

Bibliography: Confederation of British Industry. *Performance Bonds and Guarantees.* London, 1978.
D. Sassoon (ed.). *Bidding for Projects Financed by International Lending Agencies.* Gower Press, UK, 1982.

surety bond. A PERFORMANCE BOND given by a surety company (normally) guaranteeing to a buyer that the seller will perform his duties. Unlike an 'on-demand' bond, it can be called (i.e. payment demanded under it) only when the seller's default is declared by an agreed process. The surety bond technique has been used to guarantee the repayment of a borrowing. For example, 1984 the Rockefeller Group issued a $100 million EUROBOND with the backing of a surety bond issued by Aetna Casualty & Surety Co. The technique was used in this instance because the borrower, being a private corporation, was reluctant to disclose financial details.

surplus line. (1) The amount of REINSURANCE required after the maximum LINE has been set on a reinsurance TREATY.

(2) US term for a RISK which a BROKER is unable to place in this own state and must therefore place outside the state.

surplus treaty. A reinsurance term. The surplus treaty allows the ceding company to reinsure under the treaty any part of the risk, i.e. the surplus, which it is not retaining for its own account.

Bibliography: F.L. Carter. *Reinsurance.* Kluwer, London, 1979.
C.A. Williams & R.M. Heins. *Risk Management & Insurance.* McGraw-Hill, New York, 1984.

surveillance. The INTERNATIONAL MONETARY FUND maintains a regular supervision, or surveillance, over the appropriateness of its members' exchange rate policies 'in an attempt to ascertain whether these policies are consistent with the countries' broad obligations under Article IV (of the IMF Articles of Agreement) and the principles for the guidance of members' exchange rate policies adopted by the Fund in April 1977.'

Bibliography: Annual Reports of the IMF.
A.W. Hooke. *The International Monetary Fund: Its Evolution, Organization, and Activities.* IMF Pamphlet no. 37, Washington DC, 1981.

Svensk Exportkredit. A Swedish company half owned by the state, half by a consortium of commercial banks. It was founded in 1962 for the provision of export finance at commercial rates.

Bibliography: *The Export Credit Financing Systems in OECD Member Countries*. Organization for Economic Cooperation & Development, Paris, 1982.

Sveriges Investeringsbank. Swedish bank (state-owned) which provides, *inter alia*, finance for exports on commercial terms.

Bibliography: *The Export Credit Financing Systems in OECD Member Countries*. Organization for Economic Cooperation & Development, Paris, 1982.

swap. (l) In foreign exchange, the term refers to the purchase/sale of a currency in the spot market combined with a simultaneous sale/purchase in the forward market. Such swaps are sometimes used as an instrument of monetary control, e.g. in Switzerland, the Netherlands and Canada. Compare CURRENCY SWAP.

Bibliography: J.K. Walmsley. *The Foreign Exchange Handbook*. John Wiley & Sons, New York, 1983.

(2) In central banking terms 'swap' refers to the bilateral stand-by credit agreements ('swap lines') which have been made between a number of central banks under which temporary payments imbalances may be financed by swaps of currencies (purchases with a commitment to reverse within three months).

Bibliography: F. Hirsch. *Money International*. Penguin Books, London, 1967.
J.K. Walmsley. *The Foreign Exchange Handbook*. John Wiley & Sons, New York, 1983.

(3) In the US bond market the term refers to the sale of one security for the purchase of another. Such swaps fall into three basic categories. (a) *Substitution:* swaps done in order to improve on one or more characteristics of the original bonds; (b) *inter-market spread swaps:* swaps done in anticipation of a change in the yield spread between two issued from different market sectors; (c) *rate anticipation swap:* swaps done in anticipation of a change in the overall level of interest rates (i.e. going long or going into lower coupon stocks when expecting a fall in rates, and vice versa).

Bibliography: S. Homer & M.L. Leibowitz. *Inside the Yield Book*. Prentice-Hall, US, 1972.
F.J. Fabozzi & I.M. Pollack (eds). *The Handbook of Fixed Income Securities*. Dow-Jones Irwin, Homewood, Ill., 1983.

(4) The term can be used to apply to an exchange of loans or SUBPARTICIPATIONS by banks.

Bibliography: L. Sandler. the Great Debate over LDC Loan Swapping. *Institutional Investor*. New York, May 1984.

(5) Compare CURRENCY SWAP, INTEREST RATE SWAP.

SWIFT. See WORLDWIDE INTER-BANK FINANCIAL TELECOMMUNCIATIONS.

swing credit. A system used by Comecon countries for yearly borrowing and lending to finance trade with each other.

Bibliography: P. Verzariu, *Countertrade, Barter and Offsets*. McGraw-Hill, New York, 1984.

switch. (l) A term referring to the sale of a security in order to reinvest in another because the security bought is considered to be undervalued against the security sold. Compare ARBITRAGE, SWAP.

Bibliography: P.Phillips. *Inside the Gilt-Edged Market*. Woodhead-Faulkner, Cambridge, UK, 1984.

(2) A term used in the analysis of the effects of exchange rate movements on the BALANCE OF PAYMENTS. A switching policy is one which switches the pattern of ABSORPTION toward the home market from overseas or *vice versa*.

Bibliography: W. M. Corden. *Inflation, Exchange Rates and the World Economy*. Oxford University Press, UK, 1977.

(3) A department in a bank concerned with ensuring the NOSTRO ACCOUNTS of a bank are kept at the correct level may be referred to as the Switches Department.

(4) On the LONDON METAL EXCHANGE the term refers to exchanging metal in one warehouse for that in another. For example, if I am long of L00 worth of cocoa for May delivery I may sell it and buy L100 for June delivery. Compare STRADDLE.

switch trading. A form of trade finance

used where restrictions exist on the availability of foreign currency. A typical switch deal might be as follows. A French company sells electrical instruments to Rumania against payment in CLEARING DOLLARS to India. The French company contacts an Austrian switch house, which then finds an importer of Indian jute to Germany who is willing to pay US$95 per 100 clearing dollars. The switch house pays the French company US$94 per 100 clearing dollars and sells them to the German importer. The need for switch transactions and their cost varies widely from country to country and according to circumstances.
Bibliography: P. Verzariu. *Countertrade, Barter & Offsets*. McGraw-Hill, New York, 1984.

syndicate.   (1) A group of reinsurance UNDERWRITERS at LLOYD'S.
Bibliography: H.L. Cockerell. *Lloyd's of London: a portrait*. Woodhead-Faulkner, Cambridge, UK/ Dow-Jones Irwin, Homewood, Ill., 1984.
   (2) A group of bankers and/or brokers who underwrite and distribute a new issue of securities or a large block of an outstanding issue.
Bibliography: S.I. Davis. *The Euro-Bank*. Macmillan, London, 1983.
F.G. Fisher. *International Bonds*. Euromoney Publications, London 1981.

A.W. van Agtmael. Issuance of Eurobonds: Syndication & Underwriting Techniques & Costs *in* A.M. George & I.H. Giddy (eds). *International Finance Handbook*. John Wiley & Sons, New York, 1983.

syndicate agreement.   An agreement binding a group of banks or brokers into a SYNDICATE for the purpose of managing, underwriting or selling a bond or credit.
Bibliography: F.G. Fisher. *International Bonds*. Euromoney Publications, London 1981.
A.W. van Agtmael. Issuance of Eurobonds: Syndication & Underwriting Techniques & Costs *in* A.M. George & I.H. Giddy (eds). *International Finance Handbook*. John Wiley & Sons, New York, 1983.

syndicated guarantee facility.   A facility provided by banks to a firm which has to guarantee completion of its project; the guarantee facility often has to be syndicated because of the large scale of modern projects.

syndicate restrictions.   The contractual obligations placed on the underwriting group for a security relating to distribution, price limitations and market transactions.
Bibliography: A.W. van Agtmael. Issuance of Eurobonds: Syndication & Underwriting Techni-

UK/EUROPEAN AND EUROMARKETS (THREE TIER)

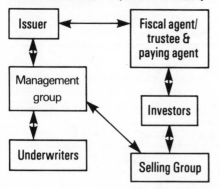

US (TWO-TIER) SYSTEM

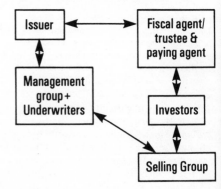

After: F.G. Fisher *International Bonds* Euromoney Publications, London, 1982.

SYNDICATION

ques & Costs *in* A.M. George & I.H. Giddy (eds). *International Finance Handbook*. John Wiley & Sons, New York, 1983.

syndicate termination (or release). The point at which sydicate restrictions are terminated. In the US this occurs when the security involved is trading or expected to trade at or over its initial offering price, but this does not necessarily apply in the Euro-bond market.

Bibliography: F.G. Fisher. *International Bonds*. Euromoney Publications, London 1981.
A.W. van Agtmael. Issuance of Eurobonds: Syndication & Underwriting Techniques & Costs *in* A.M. George & I.H. Giddy (eds). *International Finance Handbook*. John Wiley & Sons, New York, 1983.

T

Tagesgeld. German term for money lent until the following day and automatically repaid on that day.
Bibliography: J.K. Walmsley. *The Foreign Exchange Handbook.* John Wiley & Sons, New York, 1983.
H.D. Deppe. Geldmarkt und Geldmarktkonzepte. *Kredit und Kapital.* Dunckler und Humblot, Berlin 1980.

Tagesgeld bis auf weiteres. German term for money lent on the basis that it will be repaid on demand. Normally it is repaid on the same day if notice is given by (approximately) 11 a.m.
Bibliography: J.K. Walmsley. *The Foreign Exchange Handbook.* John Wiley & Sons, New York, 1983.
H. D. Deppe. Geldmarkt und Geldmarktkonzepte. *Kredit und Kapital.* Dunckler und Humblot, Berlin 1980.

Tagliches geld. German term for money lent until the following day and automatically rolled over to the next day until repayment is demanded. Such repayment is made the following day in contrast to TAGESGELD BIS AUF WEITERES where repayment is made the same day.
Bibliography: J.K. Walmsley. *The Foreign Exchange Handbook.* John Wiley & Sons, New York, 1983.
H.D. Deppe. Geldmarkt und Geldmarktkonzepte. *Kredit und Kapital.* Dunckler und Humblot, Berlin 1980.

tail. In the US (1) in Treasury cash auctions, refers to the difference between the average ISSUING PRICE and the STOP-OUT PRICE.

(2) in the REPURCHASE AGREEMENT (RP) market, a dealer may obtain funds by an RP agreement and on-lend them by means of a reverse RP. A 'tail' is established when he deliberately makes the reverse RP for longer than the RP, in the hope that in the interim interest rates will have fallen and he can make a new RP to finance at lower cost the remaining period of the reverse RP.
Bibliography: M. Stigum. *The Money Market.* Dow-Jones Irwin, Homewood, Ill., 1983.
M. Stigum. *Money Market Calculations.* Dow-Jones Irwin, Homewood, Ill., 1982.

'take-and-pay' contract. A term used in PROJECT FINANCE meaning a guarantee to buy an agreed amount of a product or service, provided it is delivered. Also known as 'take-if-delivered' contract. Since there is not an unconditional obligation to buy the product –the commitment is only to buy if delivered – take-and-pay contracts are not regarded as being such good security as TAKE-OR-PAY CONTRACTS.
Bibliography: P.K. Nevitt. *Project Financing.* Euromoney Publications, London, 1983.

take back. The recapture of shares or bonds, by the SYNDICATE manager of a new issue, that have been allotted for the retention of the SELLING GROUP or the UNDERWRITERS. The syndicate manager has the contractual right to take back bonds or shares which have not been CIRCLED.

take down. The number of shares or bonds allotted to underwriters or any allotment to members of the SELLING GROUP of a new issue of a security.

'take-or-pay' contract. A term used in PROJECT FINANCE meaning an unconditional guarantee to buy an agreed amount of a product or service whether or not it is delivered. The advantage is that the contract provides a 'bankable' asset and can assist in raising finance for the project (see diagram). The obligation may take a variety of forms. Minimum payments sufficient to service debt

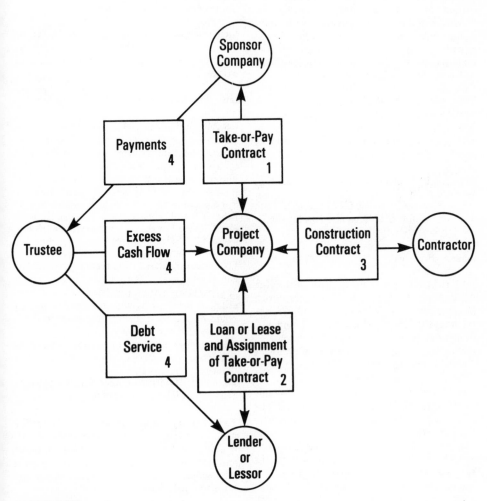

SUMMARY

1. A sponsor company enters into a take-or-pay contract with a project.
2. A project company arranges a loan or lease with a lender or lessor and assigns the take-or-pay contract as security to the lender or lessor or to a security trustee acting for them.
3. Proceeds of the loan or lease are used to finance the construction of the property.
4. Take-or-pay contract payments are made to the trustee which, in turn, pays debt service to the lender(s) or lessor(s); any excess cash flow is paid to the project company.

Source: P. K. Nevitt, Project Financing, Euromoney Publications, London, 1983.

PROJECT FINANCING SUPPORTED BY A TAKE-OR-PAY CONTRACT

plus payments for product or service as delivered or performed are one method. Another method provides for payment for certain minimum amounts of service or product whether or not delivered, with credit against future obligations to pay where larger payments than required are made.

Bibliography: *Standard & Poor's Ratings Guide*. McGraw-Hill, New York, 1979.
P.K. Nevitt. *Project Financing*. Euromoney Publications, London, 1983.

take-out. (1) US term for the increase in cash resulting from the sale of one block of bonds and the purchase of another block at a lower cost.

Bibliography: S. Homer & M. L. Leibowitz. *Inside the Yield Book*. Prentice-Hall, NJ, 1972.

(2) Also refers to ECGD 'taking a bank out' of a loan if problems arise under the its foreign currency facility.

taker. Borrower.

TALISMAN. Acronym for Transfer Accounting. Lodgment for Investors, Stock Management for Jobbers. The UK Stock Exchange's computerized delivery and settlement system for stocks and shares.

Bibliography: J. Dundas Hamilton. *Stockbroking Today*.Macmillan, London, 1979.

tap. Term for a security available for sale on an 'as required' basis at a stated price. The price can be varied to keep in line with market prices. Most commonly found in Government stock issues, e.g. the UK GILT-EDGED market, but also common in the EUROBOND market. Compare TENDER.

Bibliography: OECD. *Government Debt Management: Debt Instruments and Selling Techniques*. Paris, 1983.
F.G. Fisher. *International Bonds*. Euromoney Publications, London, 1983.

tap CD. A CD issued by a bank on an 'as required' basis. Such CD's are generally issued in large denominations ($1m. or more) and are placed directly by the bank, in contrast to TRANCHE CD's which are usually

in smaller amounts and are often placed by an AGENT BANK.

Bibliography: H.A. Lund *et al. Private Placements*. Euromoney Publications, London, 1984.

tarif douanier commun. French for 'common customs tariff'–the EEC has a common customs tariff between itself and the outside world.

taux d'intérêt. French for 'interest rate'.

taxable equivalent yield. US term for the yield on a BOND producing taxable income which would be required to match the yield on a tax-exempt bond. The formula is given under CORPORATE TAX EQUIVALENT.

Bibliography: M.L. Leibowitz. Total Aftertax Bond Performance and Yield Measures *in* F.J. Fabozzi & I.M. Pollack (eds). *The Handbook of Fixed Income Securities*. Dow-Jones Irwin, Homewood, Ill., 1983.

tax benefit transfer. US term for a mechanism briefly available in 1981-2 under which appropriately structured LEASE transactions enabled those firms with tax credits, which could not be used, to transfer them to firms that needed tax credits.

Bibliography: P.K. Nevitt. *Project Financing*. Euromoney Publications, London 1983.

Taxe (pl.: taxieren). German for QUOTATION of an interest or exchange rate.

Tax Equity and Fiscal Responsibility Act. The 1982 US tax act which substantially eliminated TAX BENEFIT TRANSFER leases and introduced FINANCE LEASES.

Bibliography: P.K. Nevitt. *Project Financing*. Euromoney, London, 1983.

tax sparing. Euromarket term for a loan which benefits from a double exemption of WITHHOLDING TAX – in the borrowing country and the lender's country – so that it is possible to lend at very narrow margins over LIBOR and even, in some cases, negative SPREADS over Libor – i.e. below Libor – yet still make a profit for the lending banks. Many tax authorities have recently restricted these loans, but they are still possible for some countries, such as Malaysia–$200 million was raised on a tax-spared basis in 1984. The arithmetic is as follows -assuming Malaysian withholding tax of 15%, UK corporation tax of 52%, loan interest income of $100 and the bank's cost of funds is $90:

Interest (grossed up by Malaysian	
withholding tax):	$115
less cost of funds	90
Taxable balance	$ 25
Tax at 52%	$ 13
Credit for withholding tax	15
Net benefit	$ 2

Thus the bank actually earns a tax credit from its loan. Compare GROSS LOANS.

Bibliography: P. Clarke. How the British taxpayer gives London banks a helping hand. *The Banker.* London, August 1979.

R. White & W. Diehl. International bank lending: the thorny issue of taxation. *The Banker,* London September 1984.

T bill.   *See* TREASURY BILL.

T-bond.   *See* TREASURY BOND.

TEFRA.   *See* TAX EQUITY AND FISCAL RESPONSIBILITY ACT.

telegraphic transfer.   A cable message to effect the transfer of funds from one bank to another. The basic means by which foreign currency payments are now made by banks. Compare SWIFT.

tender.   (1) In general, the term refers to any formal offer to supply or to purchase goods and services or securities. Compare TENDER OFFER.

(2) By extension, the term is used in the UK for the weekly issue of Treasury bills by the Bank of England. (The tender method has also been used for the issue of GILT-EDGED stock.) Under current practice tenders are made for 91-day bills on the last business day of the week, stating the amount tendered for and the price offered. The price is expressed as a net amount per cent, e.g.

£98.86 for every £100. Tenders are accepted in descending order of price until the total accepted equals the total to be allotted; then the Bank of England announces the average rate of discount for bills allotted (the TREASURY BILL rate,. Compare AUCTION.

Bibliography: E.R. Shaw. *The London Money Markets.* Heinemann, London, 1983.

(3) In commodity markets, to tender means to deliver into the PHYSICAL MARKET. A commodity to be tendered must be graded as up to the market quality standard and delivered into one of the market's approved warehouses. The seller may tender during a set period, normally but not always the named delivery month.

tender bond.   A BOND entered into by a company which is quoting (tendering) for a contract. It provides security that the company will fulfil its obligations under the tender. A typical tender bond involves the company tendering (the tenderer), a bank (which acts as SURETY for the tenderer) and the purchaser. The surety and the tenderer are liable to pay the purchaser the amount of the tender bond if the tenderer fails to comply with its obligations. It is not uncommon for these bonds to be in the form of 'first demand' bonds, in which case the bank must pay the purchaser as soon as asked to do so, no matter whether the tenderer has failed to perform or not. There are obvious risks in this procedure but sometimes it is necessary, especially in the Middle East.

Bibliography: Confederation of British Industry. *Performance Bonds and Guarantees.* London, 1978.

D. Sassoon (ed.). *Bidding for Projects Financed by International Lending Agencies.* Gower Press, UK, 1982.

tender offer.   US term for a cash offer to the public (usually at a premium over current market price) for a specific aggregate amount of securities. They are normally in cash but may include a share exchange.

Bibliography: D.V. Austin. Tender Offer Update. *Mergers and Acquisitions.* Philadelphia, Summer 1983.

R.J. Teweles & E.S. Bradley. *The Stock Market.* John Wiley & Sons, New York, 1982.

tender to contract cover. A UK export credit term for ECGD insurance to bridge the gap between the exchange rate when an exporter makes a tender, and the rate when the contract is signed. It ensures the exporter knows when tendering what his sterling revenue will be if he gets the contract. Increasingly, such cover is also now provided by commercial banks who will write a CURRENCY OPTION for the exporter.

tender panel. A form of REVOLVING UNDERWRITING FACILITY where a group of banks, who need not be UNDERWRITERS agree at the syndication stage to act as PLACING agents on a BEST EFFORTS basis for the PROMISSORY NOTES. On each TRANCHE they are requested to place a certain amount of PAPER. A tender panel has the advantage of increasing competition among the placing agents, but also increases the risk of a disorderly market in the paper.
Bibliography: C.R. Dammers. The Internationalization of the World's Money Markets: Some New Products *in* P.H. Darrow & R.A. Mestres (eds). *Creative Financing in the 1980s.* Practising Law Institute, New York, 1983.

10-K, 10-Q A US SECURITIES EXCHANGE COMMISSION reporting form. The 10-K supplements the annual report, in considerable detail. The 10-Q is its quarterly equivalent.

tenor. The period of time, as stated or indicated on a bill of exchange, for which the bill is drawn to run before it matures. or example, 'at sight' or 'three months after date' or 'on 30 June fixed.' Compare USANCE.
Bibliography: A. Watson. *Finance of International Trade.* Institute of Bankers, London,1981.

termaillage. French term for LEADS AND LAGS – modification of payment terms in anticipation of the REVALUATION or DEVALUATION of a currency.
Bibliography: P. Coulbois. *Finance Internationale. I. Le Change.* Editions Cujas, Paris, 1979.

terme. French for 'period'. Thus, *changes à terme* means forward foreign exchange; *effets a moyen terme* are medium-term paper.
Bibliography: P. Coulbois. *Finance Internationale. I. Le Change.* Editions Cujas, Paris, 1979.

termes de l'echange. French term meaning TERMS OF TRADE –the ratio between export and import prices.

terme sec. French term meaning OUTRIGHT transaction in forward foreign exchange.
Bibliography: P. Coulbois. *Le Finance Internationale. I. Le Change.* Editions Cujas, Paris, 1979.

Termingeld. German term for money market operations of over one month's maturity.
Bibliography: J.K. Walmsley. *The Foreign Exchange Handbook.* John Wiley & Sons, New York, 1983.
H.D. Deppe. Geldmarkt und Geldmarktkonzepte. *Kredit und Kapital.* Dunckler und Humblot, Berlin 1980.

Terminiertes Tagesgeld. German term for fixed-term money market operations of less than one month's maturity.
Bibliography: J.K. Walmsley. *The Foreign Exchange Handbook.* John Wiley & Sons, New York, 1983.
H.D. Deppe. Geldmarkt und Geldmarktkonzepte. *Kredit and Kapital.* Dunckler und Humblot, Berlin 1980.

terms of trade. The ratio of export prices to import prices. An 'improvement' in terms of trade occurs when export prices rise faster than import prices, thus enabling a country to import more for a given volume of exports. However, such an 'improvement' may be the result of excess domestic inflation which may produce offsetting effects on export and import volumes.
Bibliography: R.A. Allen & R.N. Brown. *The Terms of Trade.* Bank of England Quarterly Bulletin. September 1978. .
J.S. Hodgson & M.G. Herander *International Economic Relations* Prentice-Hall, NJ, 1984.

third market. US term for trading of large BLOCKS OVER-THE-COUNTER although the shares are LISTED. Owing to the abolition of

fixed commissions, the third market by 1978 had shrunk to under 3% of New York Stock Exchange turnover. Compare BLOCK; BLOCK AUTOMATION SYSTEM; BLOCK POSITIONER.
Bibliography: L.M. Loll & J.G. Buckley. *The Over-the-Counter Securities Markets*. Prentice-Hall, NJ, 1980.

through. US term: 'We were able to issue through Treasuries' means 'we were able to issue at a rate below the rate paid by the US Treasury for that maturity'. Compare THROUGH THE MARKET.

through Bill of Lading. A BILL OF LADING issued to cover shipment by a number of modes of transport or by a number of carriers.
Bibliography: A. Watson. *Finance of International Trade*. Institute of Bankers, London, 1981.

throughput agreement. An agreement to put a specified amount of product through a production facility in an agreed time period, or, if not, to pay for the availability of the facility. Used mainly in the context of pipeline projects.
Bibliography: P.K. Nevitt. *Project Financing*. Euromoney Publications, London, 1983.

through the market. US term for a situation when a new bond offering has come to market and the yield to maturity is lower than comparable bonds outstanding; the new bond is said to be offered through the market.

Thursday/Friday dollars. A foreign exchange technicality which owed its existence to the fact that the New York Clearing House, until 1981, took an extra day to clear funds. It no longer exists.
Bibliography: J. Heywood. *Foreign Exchange and the Corporate Treasurer*. Adam & Charles Black, London, 1978.

tiering. *See* MULTI-TIER LIBOR.

TIGR. *See* FELINE, STRIP.

time charter. A form of CHARTERPARTY issued when the vessel is chartered for an agreed period of time. It places the vessel in the possession of the charterer. It may, however, provide that the owner shall man and provision the vessel. From the banker's point of view, a time charter is a desirable use of the vessel, since it generally provides a more predictable revenue stream than the VOYAGE CHARTER.
Bibliography: M. Wilford *et al. Time Charters*. Lloyd's of London Press Ltd. London, 1978.

time policy. An insurance policy valid for a specified period of time.
Bibliography: R.J. Lambeth. *Templeman on Marine Insurance*. Macdonald & Evans, UK, 1981.

time value. An OPTION commonly sells at a price, or PREMIUM. The time value of the option is defined as the premium less the INTRINSIC VALUE of the option. Thus for a call option on XYZ July 45, when XYZ is trading at 48, the intrinsic value of the option is 3 points; if the option itself sells for 5 points, then the time value is said to be two points. The time value of the option decays as the expiration date of the option comes closer.
Bibliography: L.G. McMillan. *Options as a Strategic Investment*. New York Institute of Finance. New York, 1980.

Tokyo Round. A set of international trade negotiations begun in Tokyo in 1973 under the auspices of the GATT. The Tokyo Round was not completed until 1979, and the length of the negotiations reflected the difficult international trading climate of the 1970s. As a result, the Round did not achieve the large cuts in tariffs hoped for by its organisers, but it did achieve some significant progress, particularly as regards NON-TARIFF BARRIERS and certain other areas.
Bibliography: Director-General of GATT. *The Tokyo Round of Multilateral Negotiations*. GATT, April 1979.
A.I. MacBean & P.N. Snowden. *International Institutions in Trade and Finance*. George Allen & Unwin, London, 1981

tom/next. Foreign exchange and money market term meaning 'from tomorrow to the next business day'. SPOT foreign exchange deals are for VALUE two days hence. A company may require value tomorrow. In this case the tom/next rate will have to be used to adjust the spot rate. Suppose the selling DM/£ rate is 4.1072 for spot delivery and the tom/next is 4 points premium, then the DM/£ rate for value tomorrow is 4.1076.
Bibliography: J.K. Walmsley. *The Foreign Exchange Handbook*. John Wiley, New York, 1983.

tombstone. Slang for the advertisements which announce that a credit has been arranged or a bond issue made. The term is called 'tombstone' because the advertisements are usually outlined in black. The tombstone lists the participants in BRACKETS according to the amount they subscribed. Compare SPECIAL BRACKET.

total currency flow. UK term used in balance of payments analysis during 1970-5. It was replaced by the 'balance for official financing'.
Bibliography: P. Allin. Drawing the line in the balance of payments accounts. *Statistical News*. UK Central Statistical Office, no. 36, 1977.

total return. The return on a bond including interest, plus interest on reinvested interest proceeds, plus any capital gain/loss on the bond over the period.
Bibliography: S. Homer & M.L. Leibowitz. *Inside the Yield Book*. Prentice-Hall, NJ, 1972.
M.L. Leibowitz. Total Aftertax Bond Performance and Yield Measures for Taxable Bonds held in Taxable Portfolios *in* F.J. Fabozzi & I.M. Pollack (eds). *The Handbook of Fixed Income Securities*. Dow-Jones Irwin, Homewood Ill., 1983.
P. Phillips. *Inside the Gilt-Edged Market*. Woodhead-Faulkner, Cambridge, UK, 1984.

trade balance. *See* BALANCE OF TRADE.

trade bill. UK term for a bill of exchange drawn by one trader on another. Such bills can normally be discounted with the trader's bankers or with the London discount market in certain circumstances.

Bibliography: A. Watson. *Finance of International Trade*. Institute of Bankers, London, 1981.

traded option. An OPTION which can be sold to someone else. For example, in the stock market, if I have a normal option to buy say 3,200 shares of XYZ Co. at 125p in three months' time, I cannot sell the option to a third party. However, a traded option, wich is an option expiring at a standard date, and for multiples of 1,000 shares, can be resold–it is FUNGIBLE. A traded options market has existed in Chicago since 1973 (the CHICAGO BOARD OPTIONS EXCHANGE) and since 1978 in London and Amsterdam.
Bibliography: L.G. McMillan. *Options as a Strategic Investment*. New York Institute of Finance, 1980.
M.D. Fitzgerald. Listed Options – a Successful Introduction. *The Banker*, London, June 1983.

trading profits. In general, profits made in the course of trade. Specifically, a US term for the profits made by a securities dealer from buying and selling securities; distinguished from CARRY INCOME which is his net interest earnings on the securities.
Bibliography: M. Stigum. *The Money Market*. Dow-Jones Irwin, Homewood Ill., 1983.

tranche. French word meaning 'slice' and thus applied to activities undertaken in 'chunks' such as the issue of securities or the drawing down of a borrowing. Borrowings from the IMF are taken in tranches. *See* INTERNATIONAL MONETARY FUND.
Bibliography: A.W. Hooker.*The International Monetary Fund: Its Evolution, Organization, and Activities*. International Monetary Fund, Washington DC, 1981.

tranche CD. A CERTIFICATE OF DEPOSIT offered in the form of a tranche. Such an offer is in fact a form of 'managed' issue on the lines of a public offer for sale. Tranche CD's differ from TAP CD's in that they are usually offered for a single maturity in a single block, often placed by a managing bank, and divided into relatively small denominations. Tap CD's are issued normally without a predetermined limit by the issuing bank directly in large blocks. The first tranche issue of fixed rate CD's was launched in 1967. Deals are typically for $5.50 million for 3-5 years. Denominations range from $25,000 to $1 million.

Bibliography: H.A. Lund *et al. Private Placements* Euromoney Publications, London, 1984.

transactions exposure. Term relating to the foreign exchange exposure of a company deriving from its current transactions. The concept was popularized by the US Financial Accounting Standards Board. Consider a Swiss corporation with a German subsidiary. Say the German subsidiary has an account receivable of US$100. At the start of period 1, exchange rates are US$1= DM2= SF2, but the dollar then depreciates to US$1= DM 1.7778= SF1.60 at the start of period 2. In this case, the subsidiary has a transactions loss, because it was LONG of a US$ asset while the dollar was falling, of DM22.22. But the Swiss parent has a TRANSLATION EXPOSURE, since the German subsidiary's account receivable will be recorded as an asset in the Swiss balance sheet; the translation loss will amount to SF40.

Bibliography: J.K. Walmsley. *The Foreign Exchange Handbook.* John Wiley & Sons, New York, 1983.
Financial Accounting Standards Board. *Statement of Financial Accounting Standards no. 52.* Stamford, Conn., 1981.

transferable letter of credit. A DOCUMENTARY CREDIT under which the beneficiary has the right to give instructions to the paying or accepting bank or to any bank entitled to effect NEGOTIATION to make the credit available to one or more third parties (the 'second' beneficiaries).

Bibliography: A. Watson. *Finance of International Trade.* Institute of Bankers, London, 1981.
Uniform Customs and Practice for Documentary Credits. International Chamber of Commerce Brochure no. 400, Paris, 1983.

Transferable Loan Instrument (TLI). Introduced in July 1984 in a £25 million loan for Irish Telecommunications Investments Ltd., TLI is a variation of the REVOLVING UNDER-WRITING FACILITY. The AGENT BANK arranges the SYNDICATION of a medium-term loan in the normal way. But the loan agreement gives the syndicate bank the option of converting its participation into a transferable loan instrument which it can sell on to another bank. A standard sales agreement form evidences commitment under the medium-term loan and entitles the holder to receive the interest and benefits on that part of the loan which has been converted to TLI.

transferable rouble. An accounting device used by Communist countries associated with the INTERNATIONAL BANK FOR ECONOMIC COOPERATION or IBEC. Essentially it is a device for clearing bilateral trade balances between member countries. Payments to settle the balance are made through the books of IBEC. The precise functions of the transferable rouble are complex — it is neither CONVERTIBLE nor the national currency of the USSR. It is not automatically transferable between countries and its value is not unambiguously determined, since it depends on export and import prices of member countries.

Bibliography: M. Kaser. Exchange rate policy in member countries of the IBEC. *Papers in East European Economics* no. 58. St. Antony's College, Oxford, 1978.
D. Fairlamb. No Love for the Transferable Rouble. *The Banker*, October 1983.

transfer pricing. Term for the pricing of transfers of goods or services within component parts of an organization. In the international context, transfer pricing is surveyed very carefully by the relevant tax authorities to ensure that it is not used to shift profits from one country to another.

Bibliography: J.S. Arpan. *Intracorporate Pricing: Non-American Systems and Views.* Praeger, New York, 1972.
L.H. Radebaugh. International Accounting *in* A.M. George & I.H. Giddy (eds). *International Finance Handbook.* John Wiley & Sons, New York, 1983.

transfer risk. The risk that a country will, by the use of EXCHANGE CONTROLS , prevent the transfer of funds out of the country. This risk is particularly relevant to international banks, who must take it into account in lending to borrowers in other countries.

Bibliography: P. Wood. *Law & Practice of International Finance*. Sweet & Maxwell, London, 1980.

translation exposure. The EXPOSURE faced by a firm which has foreign-currency denominated items in its balance sheet (as distinct from its TRANSACTIONS EXPOSURE which affects its income statements). Consider a Swiss corporation with a German subsidiary. Say the German subsidiary has an account receivable of US$100. At the start of period 1, exchange rates are US$1= DM2= SF2, but the dollar then depreciates to US$1= DM 1.7778= SF1.60 at the start of period 2. In this case, the subsidiary has a transactions loss, because it was LONG of a US$ asset while the dollar was falling, of DM22.22. But the Swiss parent has a translation exposure, since the German subsidiary's account receivable will be recorded as an asset in the Swiss balance sheet; the translation loss will amount to SF40.

Bibliography: J.K. Walmsley. *The Foreign Exchange Handbook*. John Wiley & Sons, New York, 1983.
Financial Accounting Standards Board. *Statement of Financial Accounting Standards no. 52*. Stamford, Conn., 1981.

Treasury bill. (1) In the UK, a bearer security in the form of a BILL OF EXCHANGE entitling the holder to a payment of a fixed amount out of the Consolidated Fund of the UK at a fixed date — normally 91 days after issue. They ensure the financing of the Government's cash requirements. The bills are issued at a weekly TENDER and constitute perhaps the single most important short-term financial instrument in the UK. Compare DISCOUNT HOUSE; GILT-EDGED.

Bibliography: E.R. Shaw. *The London Money Market*. Heinemann, London, 1983.
(2) In the US, the Treasury bill takes a similar form. Offerings are also made weekly at the AUCTION. Many countries have similar instruments. Compare UNVERZINSLICHE SCHATZANWEISUNGEN, BON DU TRESOR.

Bibliography: T.Q. Cook & B.J. Summers (eds). *Instruments of the Money Market*. Federal Reserve Bank of Richmond, Virginia, 1981

Treasury bond. A COUPON security of the US Treasury which generally carries a maturity of more than 10 years. There is a statutory limit of 4.25 % on the coupon rate of Treasury bonds, though issues are regularly made at higher coupons under an exemption procedure.

Bibliography: M. Stigum & F.J. Fabozzi. US Treasury Obligations *in* F.J. Fabozzi & I.M.Pollack (eds). *The Fixed Income Handbook*. Dow-Jones Irwin, Homewood Ill., 1983.

Treasury note. A coupon security issued by the US Treasury with a maturity of not less than one year nor more than 10 years (i.e. filling the maturity range between TREASURY BILLS and TREASURY BONDS). These notes are available in minimum denominations of $1,000 in either bearer or registered form.

Bibliography: M. Stigum & F.J. Fabozzi. US Treasury Obligations *in* F.J. Fabozzi & I.M.Pollack (eds). *The Fixed Income Handbook*. Dow-Jones Irwin, Homewood Ill., 1983.

Treasury stock. (1) A US term for stock issued by a company but later reacquired by it. It may be held in the company's treasury, reissued, or retired. It receives no dividends and has no vote while held by the company.

Bibliography: L.M. Loll & J.G. Buckley. *The Over-the-Counter Securities Markets*. Prentice-Hall, NJ, 1981
R.A. Anderson *et al. Business Law*. South Western Publishing Co., Cinnicuati, Ohio 1984.
(2) General UK term for GILT-EDGED stocks.

Treasury tax and loan account. US term for an account held by the Treasury with a commercial bank. Funds built up in the account are transferred to the FEDERAL RESERVE on a regular basis. Frequency of the transfer depends on the size of the banks, which are graded A, B or C. Group A banks are the smallest and least frequently 'called' on to transfer funds.

Bibliography: P. Meek. *US Monetary Policy and*

Financial Markets. Federal Reserve Bank of New York, 1982.

treaty. A contract providing for REINSURANCE over a period of time.

treaty reinsurance. A method of REINSURANCE where the insurer who is reinsuring his risks exercises little or no selection in regard to the risks reinsured, in contrast to FACULTATIVE REINSURANCE. A reinsurance treaty is an obligatory contract on both sides. It is a binding agreement during its life where the ceding insurer is bound to declare and the reinsurer to accept, in the proportions or amounts provided for in the treaty, all risks accepted by the origianl insurer which come within the terms of the treaty. Compare QUOTA SHARE TREATY; SURPLUS TREATY.
Bibliography: R.L. Carter. *Reinsurance.* Kluwer, London, 1983.
C.A. Williamson & R.M. Heins. *Risk Management & Insurance.* McGraw-Hill, New York 1984.

Trendtex. *See* SOVEREIGN IMMUNITY.

Treuarbeit. A private West German company which runs, jointly with HERMES, the country's official export credit insurance.
Bibliography: *The Export Credit Financing Systems in OECD Member Countries.* Organization for Economic Cooperation and Development, Paris, 1982.

triangular trade. Trade between three countries: an example would be when a US firm sells to Eastern Europe, which sells to Egypt, which sells to the US firm. It is a form of BARTER or COUNTERTRADE.
Bibliography: P.D. Ehrenhaft (ed.). *Countertrade: International Trade Without Cash.* Law & Business/Harcourt Brace, New York, 1983.
R. Birley. Can't Pay? Will Pay, But in Sultanas. *Euromoney,* London, May 1983.

Troc, troquer. French foreign exchange term meaning SWAP.
Bibliography: P. Coulbois. *Finance Internationale. I. Le Change.* Editions Cujas, Paris, 1979.

trust receipt A form of receipt given by a borrower to a bank when he asks the banks to release documents of title to gods which have been pledged to the bank as security for credit facilities, without repaying the credit or giving other security. This may occur if the borrower has to get hold of the goods (by means of the documents of title) in order to warehouse them, but is not yet in a position to repay the credit which is financing the purchase of the goods. This is also known as 'trust letter' or 'letter of hypothecation'.
Bibliography: Gillett Brothers Discount Company. *The Bill on London.* Methuen & Co., London, 1976.
L. C. Mather. *Securities Acceptable to the Lending Banker.* Waterlows, London, 1973.
A. Watson. *Finance of International Trade.* Institute of Bankers, London, 1981.

trustee. In international (or domestic) bond issues it is common to appoint a trustee who represents the interests of the bond-holders. Under the terms of a trust deed, the borrower will enter into COVENANTS which will often include a NEGATIVE PLEDGE and other restrictions. These covenants, and the timely payment of principal and interest, are monitored by the trustee, which has the power to take action to recover the investors' money if a covenant is broken or a DEFAULT occurs.
Bibliography: P.Wood. *Law and Practice of International Finance.* Sweet & Maxwell, London, 1980.
F.G. Fisher. *International Bonds.* Euromoney Publications, London, 1981.

trustee status. UK term designating investments permitted to trustees of estates etc. under the Trustee Investments Act 1961.
Bibliography: *Stock Exchange Official Yearbook* Macmillan, London, annually.

T/T. *See* TELEGRAPHIC TRANSFER.

TT & L. *See* TREASURY TAX & LOAN ACCOUNT.

tunnel. Part of the original 'snake in the tunnel' concept, relating to the European system of narrower exchange rate margins, the 'tunnel' was the band in which the SNAKE could fluctuate against the dollar. With the advent of generalized floating in 1973 the 'tunnel' concept was discarded.

Bibliography: *The European System of Narrower Exchange Rate Margins*. Deutsche Bundesbank Monthly Report, Frankfurt, January 1976.

two-tier gold price. During 1968-76 gold was traded at a fixed official price (see OFFICIAL GOLD PRICE), between monetary authorities. Private individuals traded in the free market. Compare BULLION; JAMAICA AGREEMENT.

Bibliography: S. Strange. *International Monetary Relations of 1959-71*. Royal Institute of International Affairs, London, 1976.

two-tier markets. An exchange rate regime which normally insulates a country from the balance of payments effects of capital flows while it maintains a stable exchange rate for current account transactions. Capital transactions are normally required to pass through a 'financial' market, while current transactions go through an 'official' or 'convertible' market. However the precise differentiation can be varied. The best-known example of a two-tier market is Belgium, which has operated such a system since 1958, but France and Italy also experimented with such systems during the early 1970s, and the UK INVESTMENT CURRENCY market was a similar system. Compare FINANCIAL RAND.

Bibliography: J.K. Walmsley. *The Foreign Exchange Handbook*. John Wiley & Sons, New York, 1983.

two-way price, quotation. In foreign exchange and Eurocurrency deposit dealing it is normal for a bank, when asked by another bank to quote an exchange rate or deposit rate, to quote its buying and selling price or bid and offer interest rate. It is said to make a two-way price in the currency or deposit.

U

UFINEX. *see* Union pour le Financement et l'Expansion du Commerce International.

ULCC. *See* ULTRA-LARGE CRUDE CARRIER.

Ultimo. Continental (especially Swiss, German) term for the end of a month or a year.

Ultra-Large Crude Carrier (ULCC). A tanker capable of carrying large amounts of crude oil. No definite limits are fixed but a ULCC would probably be of the order of 450-400,000 dead-weight tons.
Bibliography: L.D. Anderson. Tanker & Shipping Loans *in* W.H. Baughn & D.R. Mandich (eds). *the International Banking Handbook* Dow-Jones Irwin, Homewood, Ill., 1983.

uncalled capital. *See* PAID-UP CAPITAL.

UNCITRAL. *See* UNITED NATIONS COMMISSION ON INTERNATIONAL TRADE LAW.

unconditional call money. Japanese money market term for funds which are lent for an initial period of two days and which may then be called for repayment upon one day's notice. Unconditional call money constitutes almost the whole of the Japanese CALL MONEY market, the balance being in overnight transactions. Compare CALL MONEY; GEN-SAKI; TAGLICHES GELD.
Bibliography: D.L. Allen. Japan: Banking, Money and Bond Markets *in* A.M. George & I.H. Giddy(eds).*International Finance Handbook*. John Wiley & Sons, New York, 1983.

unconfirmed documentary credit. A DOCUMENTARY CREDIT where the ADVISING BANK merely informs the beneficiary of the terms and conditions of the credit without adding its undertaking (or 'confirmation') that it will honour drawings on the credit.

Bibliography: *Uniform Customs & Practice for Documentary Credits*. International Chamber of Commerce Brochure no. 400, Paris, 1983.
A. Watson. *Finance of International Trade*. Institute of Bankers, London, 1981.

uncovered. Another term for an 'open' foreign exchange position, i.e. one where a liability or asset denominated in a foreign currency exists and where no corresponding forward purchase/sale of foreign currency has been made. Compare COVER; EXPOSURE.

uncovered interest arbitrage. Term denoting a situation where an investment is made in a foreign currency asset to benefit from a more attractive rate of interest, without simultaneously taking out forward exchange cover to protect the investor against the risk of intervening exchange rate changes. Compare ARBITRAGE; COVERED MARGIN.

UNCTAD. *See* UNITED NATIONS CONFERENCE ON TRADE & DEVELOPMENT.

underwriter. (1) In insurance the employee of a company or the member of a LLOYD'S SYNDICATE who is authorized to bind the company (or syndicate) in respect of an insurance risk.
Bibliography: R.J. Lambeth. *Templeman on Marine Insurance*. Macdonald & Evans, UK, 1981.
(2) A person who, when an issue of securities is being made, agrees with the issuer to buy or find buyers for those securities which are not taken up by the public. Alternatively, he may agree to buy the entire issue in the first instance. It is normal in Switzerland, for example, for certain underwriters to act together in a SYNDICATE whose membership may be stable over time or which may vary according to the type of issue involved.

Bibliography: *The Underwriting Business in Switzerland*. Union Bank of Switzerland, Zurich, 1979.
F.G. Fisher. *International Bonds*. Euromoney Publications, London, 1981.
L.M. Loll & J.G. Buckley.*The Over-the-Counter Securities Markets*. Prentice-Hall, NJ, 1981.

underwriters' agreement. *See* agreement among underwriters.

underwriting fee. A fee payable to the members of the underwriting syndicate of a particular security issue. In the US, it is often a percentage of the spread (between the price at which the syndicate buy the securities and the price at which they are resold to the public) which accrues only to members of the syndicate in proportion to the amount of the issue they have underwritten. In the EURO-MARKET, the fee tends to be a sum allocated to each syndicate member. Compare MANAGEMENT FEE; PARTICIPATION FEE.

Bibliography: The Underwriting Business in Switzerland. Union Bank of Switzerland, Zurich, 1979.
F.G. Fisher. *International Bonds*. Euromoney Publications, London, 1981.

undo. Colloquial term meaning to reverse a transaction. A foreign exchange dealer may undo a spot purchase by means of a forward sale, or if the original transaction was done in error it is undone by a spot sale.

unfranked income. *See* FRANKED INCOME.

uniform customs and practice. Standardized code of practice issued by the International Chamber of Commerce in Paris covering Documentary Credits.

Bibliography: *Uniform Customs and Practice for Documentary Credits*. International Chamber of Commerce Brochure no. 400 (1983 revision).

uniform price auction *See* DUTCH AUCTION.

uniform rules. Standardized rules issued by the International Chamber of Commerce in Paris covering Collections (ICC Brochure No. 322) and Combined Transport Documents (ICC Brochure No. 298) and Contract Guarantees (ICC Brochure no. 325).

Union d'Assurance des Crédits Internationaux. *See* BERNE UNION.

Union pour le Financement et l'Expansion du Commerce International. French body formed by the banks to assist in the financing of overseas investments, typically of a minimum Ff500,000 up to 15 years.

Bibliography: M. Schlogel. *Les Relations Economiques et Financières Internationales*. Masson et Cie, Paris, 1972.

unissued capital (stock). If a company's issued CAPITAL STOCK is less than its authorized capital (stock) the balance is available to be issued in future and is referred to as unissued.

Bibliography: J. Dundas Hamilton. *Stockbroking Today*. Macmillan, London, 1979.

unit of account. (1) An artificial concept designed to provide a consistent reference value against varying exchange rates. Various units have been devised. *See* ARCRU; ASIAN CURRENCY UNIT; B-UNIT; EEC UNIT OF ACCOUNT; EURCO; EUROPEAN CURRENCY UNIT; EUROPEAN UNIT OF ACCOUNT; EUROPEAN MONETARY UNIT OF ACCOUNT; GOLD FRANCS; INTERNATIONAL FINANCIAL UNIT; SPECIAL DRAWING RIGHTS.

(2) Money is said to act as a unit of account in calculating the value of different goods in relation to each other.

United Nations Commission on International Trade Law. A commission set up by the United Nations to work for the improvement of international trade law.

Bibliography: J.D.M. Law & C. Stanbrook (eds). *International Trade Law & Practice*. Euromoney Publications, London, 1984.
UNCITRAL: Model Law on Commercial Arbitration. *Journal of World Trade Law*. UK, November/December 1983.

United Nations Conference on Trade, Aid and Development (UNCTAD). The first UNCTAD met in 1964, and it was subse-

quently formed into a permanent organ of the United Nations. Since then UNCTAD has met in New Delhi (1968), Santiago (1972), Nairobi (1976), and Manila (1979). Its achievements have generally been small, but the introduction of the GENERALISED SCHEME OF PREFERENCES was initially the work of UNCTAD.
Bibliography: L.N. Rangajaran. *Commodity Conflict*. Croom Helm, London, 1978.
A.I. MacBean & P.N. Snowden. *International Institutions in Trade and Finance*. George Allen & Unwin, London, 1981.

United Terminal Sugar Market Association. The LONDON TERMINAL SUGAR MARKET is administered by this association. It has 30 full members together with numerous associate and overseas affiliated members. It provides standard contracts and clearing facilities for the market via its association with the INTERNATIONAL COMMODITIES CLEARING HOUSE and the LONDON COMMODITY EXCHANGE of which it forms a part. Since the switch of the main sugar contract from sterling to US dollars, trading volume in the market has declined, with business being switched to New York.
Bibliography: C.W.J. Granger. *Trading in Commodities*. Woodhead-Faulkner, Cambridge, UK, 1983.

unit trust. British equivalent of OPEN-END MUTUAL FUND. Unit trusts have a variable capital, unlike INVESTMENT TRUSTS. Units can be created or cancelled by the management in line with demand. The price of units varies with the asset value of the trust but also with pressure of demand.
Bibliography: C. Gilchrist. *Unit Trusts: What Every Investor Should Know*. Woodhead-Faulkner Cambridge, UK, 1976.
The Unit Trust Yearbook. Fundex, London, 1978.

universal bond. The advent of SHELF REGISTRATION has made it technically feasible for a BOND to be issued simultaneously in the US and in the Eurobond markets. Such a bond is called a 'universal bond'. To date its use has been relatively rare, however.
Bibliography: D. Magraw. Legal Aspects of International Bonds *in* A.M. George & I.H. Giddy. *International Finance Handbook*. John Wiley & Sons, New York, 1983.

Unlisted Securities Market. A UK Stock Exchange term. It refers to the second-tier market in the securities of companies which have not yet applied for a full LISTING on the Stock Exchange. In essence it is a market where smaller companies' stocks can be traded in a more flexible manner than in the main market. Securities traded are not officially listed, and transactions can be matched either in-house by a stockbroker, negotiated with another stockbroker, or with a JOBBER. A company must normally have been trading for at least three years before it may be brought to the USM. Compare OVER-THE-COUNTER.
Bibliography: D. Fanning. *Marketing Company Shares*. Gower Publishing UK, 1982.
Peat Marwick & Co. *Entering the Unlisted Securities Market*. London, 1984.

Unverzinsliche Schatzanweisungen. Obligations of the German government and its agencies, issued usually for 6–24 months' maturities. They yield interest by virtue of being issued at a discount on their face value.
Bibliography: Economists Advisory Group.*The British and German Banking Systems*. London, 1981.
H.D. Deppe. Geldmarkt und Geldmarktkonzepte. *Kredit und Kapital*. Duncker und Humblot, Berlin, vol. 3 1980.

upstreaming. A loan, or other transfer of funds, from a subsidiary to its parent.

up-tick. US term used to designate a transaction made at a price higher than the preceding transaction in the same security.
Bibliography: L.M. Loll & J.G. Buckley. *The Over-the-Counter Markets*. Prentice-Hall, NJ, 1981.
R.J. Teweles & E.S. Bradley. *The Stock Market*. John Wiley & Sons, New York, 1982.

usance. Strictly, this means the time allowed by custom for the period of bills of exchange in trade between two particular countries. Today, the term is also frequently used to mean the period of time for which any bill is drawn, i.e. its TENOR.

Bibliography: A. Watson. *Finance of International Trade*. Institute of Bankers, London, 1981.

U-Schatze. Abbreviation for UNVERZINS-LICHE SCHATZANWEISUNGEN.

usury laws. Different states of the USA (and other countries) have laws limiting the maximum rate of interest chargeable on a loan. When US prime rates were over 20% in 1980/81 this became a problem in certain cases, though it has now generally been overcome by modifications of the relevant laws.

Bibliography: P. Wood. *Law and Practice of International Finance*. Sweet & Maxwell, London, 1980.

utilization fee. A fee sometimes charged on EUROCREDITS, perhaps in lieu of a COMMITMENT FEE. Thus in 1984 Electricite de France borrowed $500 million, with a utilization fee structure linked to the average utilization over a six-month period: 0.15% of the total if average utilisation was less than 33%, 0.20% if less than 50%, 0.275% if less than 75% and 0.35% if less than 100%.

V

value date. The date on which payment is made to settle a transaction. For example, a SPOT foreign exchange transaction on Tuesday will be settled on Thursday: one could refer to the deal as being value Thursday. The value date for a Eurobond deal under the rules of the AIBD is the seventh calendar day following, regardless of holidays. Compare REGULAR WAY DELIVERY; SETTLEMENT DATE.
Bibliography: Rules and Recommendations of the AIBD.
J.K. Walmsley. *The Foreign Exchange Handbook.* John Wiley & Sons, New York, 1983.

variable-rate bonds. BONDS on which the COUPON is allowed to vary according to some predetermined formula. For example, Italy, Sweden and the UK have all issued government bonds which have their coupon linked to the TREASURY BILL rate or the central bank discount rate.
Bibliography: *Government Debt Management: Vol. II. Debt Instruments and Selling Techniques.* OECD, Paris, 1983.

variable-rate CDs. Introduced in the US in 1975, this is a CERTIFICATE OF DEPOSIT with a normal minimum maturity of 360 days. Its interest rate is pegged by the issuing bank at a specified spread over the bank's current rate on 90-day CDs and is adjusted every 90 days. The device is an attempt to raise longer-term funds for the bank while partially protecting the investor against swings in interest rates. Compare FLOATING-RATE CDS; ROLL-OVER CDS.

variable-rate gilts. British GILT-EDGED stocks on which the interest rate payable varies. The stock has generally had a maturity of 4-5 years, with interest calculated as ½% over the daily average TREASURY BILL RATE

for the previous six months. Variable rate gilts were introduced to provide the authorities with a means of borrowing at a time when interest rates were expected to rise (because the variable-rate provision means that the capital value of the stock should be less sensitive to rising interest rates).
Bibliography: *Government Debt Management: Vol. II. Debt Instruments and Selling Techniques.* OECD, Paris, 1983.

variation margin. A FUTURES market term. A trader in futures need not pay the full purchase price of his CONTRACTS when he trades, but only the INITIAL MARGIN. But if the market then moves against him, he must pay a variation margin. Suppose he buys a Treasury bond contract and deposits a $2000 initial margin. Suppose the market price of the contract falls by ¾ of a point, causing him to lose $750, then he must generally pay a variation margin of $750 to bring his total margin back to $2000.
Bibliography: N.H. Rothstein & J.M. Little. *The Handbook of Financial Futures.* McGraw-Hill, New York, 1984.

velocity of money. The speed with which a unit of money circulates in an economy. For practical purposes it is often calculated as the ratio of annual national income to the average money stock in that year. A stable velocity of money (or, putting it the other way round, a stable demand for money function) is crucial to the so-called MONETARIST approach.
Bibliography: M. Friedman (ed.). *Studies in the Quantity Theory of Money.* University of Chicago Press, 1956.
R. T. Coghlan. A transactions demand for money. *Bank of England Quarterly Bulletin,* March 1978.
P. Meek. (ed.). *Central Bank Views on Monetary Targeting* Federal Reserve Bank of New York, 1983.

213

vertical spread. OPTIONS market term for a SPREAD in which the CALLS or PUTS involved have the same expiration date but different STRIKE PRICES.
Bibliography: L.G. McMillan. *Options as a Strategic Investment.* New York Institute of Finance, New York, 1983.

Very Large Crude Carrier (VLCC). A tanker capable of carrying large amounts of crude oil. No definite limits are fixed but a VLCC would probably be of the order of 100,000 to 450,000 dead-weight tons. *See also* ULTRA-LARGE CRUDE CARRIER.
Bibliography: L.D. Anderson. Tanker & Shipping Loans *in* W.H. Baughn & D.R. Mandich (eds.). *The International Banking Handbook.* Dow-Jones Irwin, Homewood, Ill., 1983.

Visby Rules. *See* HAGUE RULES.

visible supply. Commodities market term for the amount of a commodity that can be accurately accounted for, usually because it is kept in known warehouses or storage places. The visible supply is an important determinant of price, since a large visible supply in relation to normal suggests that there is an overhang of stocks which will tend to depress prices.

visibles. A term referring to international trade in 'visible' items (i.e. merchandise imports and exports) as opposed to INVISIBLES–trade in services, remittances from abroad etc.

VLCC. *See* VERY LARGE CRUDE CARRIER.

volatility. (1) In general, the degree of instability of an exchange rate or commodity or stock price.
(2) Specifically in OPTIONS markets, volatility is an important component of pricing models such as the BLACK-SCHOLES model; it is generally measured by the annual standard deviation of the daily price changes of the security, commodity or currency. It is not the same as the BETA, since the latter measures volatility in relation to the market as a whole.
Bibliography: L.G. McMillan. *Options as a Strategic Investment.* New York Institute of Finance, New York, 1980.

vostro account. An account held by a bank on behalf of a correspondent bank; from Italian for 'yours'. It is the counterpart of NOSTRO: my nostro account with you is your vostro account for me.
Bibliography: A. Watson. *Finance of International Trade.* Institute of Bankers, London, 1981.

voyage charter. In a voyage charter the shipowner agrees to carry cargo in his vessel between designated ports or areas for a single voyage, or he agrees to a number of voyages in succession–'consecutive voyage charter'.
Bibliography: C.T. Grammenos. *Bank Finance for Ship Purchase.* University of Wales Press, 1971. L.D. Anderson. Tanker & shipping Loans. *in* W.H. Baughn & D.R. Mandich (eds). *The International Banking Handbook.* Dow-Jones Irwin, Homewood, Ill., 1983.

voyage policy. An insurance policy whose subject matter is insured 'at and from, or from one place to another or others'. Compare TIME POLICY.
Bibliography: R.J. Lambeth. *Templeman on Marine Insurance.* Macdonald and Evans, UK, 1981.

W

WA. *See* WITH AVERAGE.

WACH. *See* WEST AFRICAN CLEARING HOUSE.

warehousing. (1)Term sometimes used for temporary holding of a foreign exchange, money market, securities or other position—either for tax reasons, or else because the position is in the nature of things intended to be temporary.

(2) US term for the borrowing of funds by a mortgage banker on a short-term basis from a commercial bank using mortgage loans as a security.

(3) UK term for the accumulation of shareholdings in the name of nominees with the intention of mounting a subsequent takeover bid.

warehouse keeper's warrant. *See* DOCK WARRANT.

warrant. (1) A certificate giving the holder the right to purchase a security at a stipulated price, either for a specified period of time or perpetually. Warrants giving conversion rights into a company's equity capital may be issued in conjunction with a bond in which case they normally can be traded separately from the bond which then carries no right of conversion (as distinct from the CONVERTI-BLE where the right of conversion is integral to the convertible bond). A major attraction of a warrant is its GEARING or LEVERAGE. Suppose a US company's shares trade at $40 and a warrant is exerciseable at $30. Then the warrant will trade for $10. If the shares now rise to $50–a rise of 25%–the warrant will rise to $20–a rise of 100%. Warrants have also been attached to CD's. For example, the HK$100 million floating rate Hong Kong dollar CD's issued by Citicorp in July

1981.Or they can be issued separately, as in the case of Citicorp's 1982 raising of $100 million by the issue of 100,000 warrants to buy 11% bonds due 1989.
Bibliography: P. Welham. *Investing in Share Options, Warrants & Convertibles.* Woodhead-Faulkner, Cambridge, UK, 1975.
J.C. Ritchie. Convertible Bonds and Warrants *in* F.J. Fabozzi & I.M. Pollack. *The Handbook of Fixed Income Securities.* Dow-Jones Irwin, Homewood, Ill., 1983.
T. Anderson. Warrants: the Swing from Distaste to Appetite. *Euromoney*, July 1982.

(2) The document of title to metal stored in a LONDON METAL EXCHANGE warehouse. It is a bearer instrument.
Bibliography: R. Gibson-Jarvie. *The London Metal Exchange.* Woodhead-Faulkner, Cambridge, UK/Nichols Publishing, New York, 1983.

warrant hedging. A technique whereby the investor buys the WARRANTS on a company's shares and hedges it by a SHORT position in the underlying shares.
Bibliography: A.E. Young. Warrants–Options *in* M.E. Blume & J.A. Friedman. *Encyclopaedia of Investments.* Warren, Gorham & Lamont, New York, 1982.

warranty insurance. An insurance policy written on the warranty that some other insurance company, in whose judgment the insurer has confidence, has accepted and is carrying a policy on the same subject matter and on the same general terms.
Bibliography: B.J. Daenzer. *Excess and Surplus Lines Manual.* Merritt Co., California, 1976.

wash sale. US term for the sale of a security, coupled with the purchase of a substantially identical security within the 61 day period beginning 30 days before the sale and ending 30 days after the sale. Any loss incurred on a wash sale is not deductible for tax purposes; a CALL option is regarded as substantially

215

identical to the underlying security. Compare BED AND BREAKFAST.

Bibliography: R.M. Bookstaber. *Option Strategies and Pricing in Investing.* Addison-Wesley, Mass, 1980.

weighted hedge. A FINANCIAL FUTURES market term. It often happens that a trader must HEDGE a CASH market position with a futures position which is not an exact match of the underlying instrument. For example he might seek to hedge holdings of a position in 30-day CD's, but the only available futures contract is a 90-day CD contract. In that event, he would need to sell one-third of the value of his position in the futures market to hedge his full cash position (since a given rate change has three times the impact on profits for a 90-day contract compared to a 30-day one). Such a hedge, where the size of the position must be adjusted by a weighting factor, is called a weighted hedge.

Bibliography: J.K. Walmsley. *The Foreign Exchange Handbook.* John Wiley & Sons, 1983.
N.H. Rothstein & J.M. Little. *The Handbook of Financial Futures.* Dow-Jones Irwin, Homewood Ill., 1984.

Wertpapiersammelbank. Term for a German security depositary performing a similar function to a KASSENVEREIN.

West African Clearing House (WACH). The WACH began operations in 1976, with the objective of facilitating the clearing of international payment between its members, who are identical to those of the Economic Community of West African States, with the exception of Guinea, Guinea-Bissau and Mauritania.

Bibliography: *Annual Report on Exchange Restrictions.* International Monetary Fund, Washington DC, annually.

West African Development Bank (WADB). Founded in 1973, and first operational in 1976, the WADB has its headquarters in Lome, Togo. Its membership consists of the governments of Benin, Ivory Coast, Niger, Senegal, Togo and the Upper Volta, plus the Central Bank of the West African States. Its

objectives are to promote the economic development and integration of West Africa.

Bibliography: United Nations Industrial Development Organization. *Financial Resources for Industrial Projects in Developing Countries.* United Nations, New York, 1976.

wet lease. An OPERATING LEASE of an asset such as an aircraft or contract drilling vessel where personnel supplied by the owner rather than the user operate the equipment.

white knight. A more desirable bidder for a target company in a hostile take-over battle. The white knight is generally chosen by the target company as a means of thwarting the hostile bidder.

wholesale money. A term to describe money borrowed in large amounts from banks, large companies or financial institutions, in contrast to 'retail money' which is acquired by attracting small deposits from private individuals and small firms.

wi. US abbreviation for 'when issued'. Typically there is a lag between the time a new Treasury bill or bond is auctioned, and the time it is actually issued–usually ten days or so. During this interval, the security trades 'wi' or 'when, as, and if issued'. Compare WIWI

Bibliography: M. Stigum. *The Money Market.* Dow-Jones Irwin, Homewood, Ill., 1983.

window. A short period of availability of funds in a market which is otherwise difficult to issue in. The phenomenon is particularly noticeable in the EUROBOND market, which is much given to cycles of famine or feast, but is now increasingly noticeable in domestic US and UK markets also, given the unstable interest rate environment of recent years.

window-dressing. The practice where banks, financial institutions and companies raise funds for particular dates (year-end or end-of-financial-year) to give the appearance of high liquidity. In general, the term refers to special adjustments in a firm's financial position undertaken with a view to complying with reporting requirements or to present a particular appearance.

with average. A marine insurance term which means that the insurance covers not only total loss but also partial loss. The expression really refers to PARTICULAR AVERAGE. The normal marine insurance 'with average' clause is that laid down in the INSTITUTE OF LONDON UNDERWRITERS' Institute Cargo Clauses (with average) or ICC (WA).
Bibliography: R.J. Lambeth. *Templeman on Marine Insurance.* Macdonald and Evans, UK, 1981.

withholding tax. A tax levied by a country on, for example, interest payments or dividends paid on securities issued in that country. This tends to discourage foreign investors because even if they are not liable to the tax because of double-taxation agreements, they will be required to undergo certain formalities in order to benefit from such exemption. In the case where no such exemption exists, e.g. the investor is operating from a tax-free zone and has no tax to offset under the double-taxation system, the after-tax return to him is significantly reduced. Therefore, the existence or otherwise of withholding tax is an important determinant of the competiveness of a financial centre. Compare TAX SPARING.
Bibliography: P. Wood. *Law and Practice of International Finance.* Sweet and Maxwell, London, 1980.
R. White & W. Diehl. International bank lending: the thorny issue of taxation. *The Banker* . London, September 1984.

with particular average. A marine insurance term which means that the insurance covers not only total loss but also partial loss. The opposite of FREE OF PARTICULAR AVERAGE and often shortened to WITH AVERAGE.
Bibliography: R.J. Lambeth. *Templeman on Marine Insurance.* Macdonald and Evans, UK, 1981.

without. MONEY BROKER'S or FOREIGN EX-

CHANGE BROKER'S term sometimes used to mean 'I do not have a price on that side'. For example, 'I am 50 bid without the offer' is sometimes shortened to '50 bid without'.

wiwi. US Treasury bills trade on a WI basis between the day they are auctioned and the day they are issued. Bills traded before they are even auctioned are said to be traded wiwi. Wiwi trading is essentially a form of short-term Treasury bill FINANCIAL FUTURES trading, but outside the usual financial futures markets.
Bibliography: M. Stigum. *The Money Market.* Dow-Jones Irwin, Homewood, Ill., 1983.

working capital acceptance. US term for a BANKERS' ACCEPTANCE which does not finance a specific trading transaction but finances a company's general working capital requirements. As such it is not eligible for rediscount at the Federal Reserve. Compare ACCOMMODATION PAPER.
Bibliography: M. Stigum. *The Money Market* Dow-Jones Irwin, Homewood, Ill., 1983.

Working Party Three. A working party of the OECD whose job it is to monitor balance of payments developments and the general economic situation in member countries' economies; as such it has at times played an important part in international economic policy making. Members are normally drawn from the OECD Secretariat and the Treasury or Ministry of Finance of member countries (with central bank representatives where appropriate).
Bibliography: S. Strange. *International Monetary Relations 1959-71.* Royal Institute of International Affairs, London, 1976.

World Bank. Formerly known as the International Bank for Reconstruction and Develpment, the World Bank was founded at BRETTON WOODS. Initially it was concerned with post-war reconstruction in Europe. Since then its aim has been to assist the development of member nations by making loans when private capital is not available on reasonable terms to finance productive investment. Membership of the INTERNA-TIONAL MONETARY FUND is a precondition of Bank membership. The Bank's capital is provided by members' subscriptions and by borrowing in world markets. Its extremely high reputation has enabled it to borrow at the best terms. In addition to loans at relatively low interest rates, it provides substantial technical assistance to borrowers. As of 31 December 1983, a total of 146 countries were World Bank members.

Bibliography: World Bank. *The World Bank and the International Finance Corporation.* Washington, 1983.
Annual Reports of the World Bank.

WPA. *See* WITH PARTICULAR AVERAGE.

WP3. *See* WORKING PARTY THREE.

wrap lease. A LEASE structure in which one lease is 'wrapped' around another. In the ordinary lease, the leasing company is the lessor and owner of the equipment, and it receives the tax benefits of the transaction. If, however, it has limited taxable capacity, it may arrange for another company to buy the asset. It then leases the asset from this company in order to on-lease it to the lessee.

Bibliography: A.F. Gargiulo & R.J. Kenard. *Leveraged Leasing.* American Management Association, New York, 1981.
P.K. Nevitt. *Project Financing.* Euromoney Publications, London, 1983.

Y

Yankee bond. A BOND issue made in the US by a foreign borrower payable in US dollars and registered with the SECURITIES AND EXCHANGE COMMISION. Technically, the term Yankee refers to bonds that would have been subject to the INTEREST EQUALIZATION TAX and so does not include Canadian or supranational bonds. From 1974, the year of IET's removal, the volume of Yankee issues rose from $1 billion to $10 billion in 1976, falling back in 1980 to $3.5 billion. Yankee bonds pay interest semi-annually, unlike their EUROBOND counterparts which pay annually. Compare FOREIGN BOND, SAMURAI BOND.
Bibliography: M.D. Hadzima & C.M. Small. *Perspectives on International Bond Investing in* F.J. Fabozzi & I.M. Pollack. *The Handbook of Fixed Income Securities*. Dow-Jones Irwin, Homewood, Ill., 1983.

Yaounde Convention. Convention between the EEC and its Associate Members regarding aid and development finance; subsequently replaced by the LOMÉ CONVENTION
Bibliography: C.C. Twitchett. Lomé II: a new ACP-EEC Agreement. *The World Today*. Royal Institute of International Affairs, London, March 1980.

yard. Slang for 1,000 million (from 'milliard').

yearling. UK stocks issued by local authorities for a period of a year or more and quoted either on the Stock Exchange or the discount market. A 'yearling' may have a maturity of up to four years. Issues are normally made in amounts of £200,000–£1 million.
Bibliography: E.R. Shaw. *The London Money Market*. Heinemann, London, 1983.

Yellow Book. The requirements for a London stock market quotation are laid down in this, the UK Stock Exchange's *Admission of Securities to Listing,* published by the Quotations/Department, Stock Exchange, London, 1984.

yield. The annual rate of return on a security or an investment expressed in percentage terms. There are many definitions of yield, but they fall essentially into three classes: calculations on a discount basis (compare DISCOUNT-TO-YIELD, BOND EQUIVALENT YIELD), calculations allowing only for current income (referred to as CURRENT YIELD FLAT YIELD, INCOME YIELD, INTEREST YIELD or RUNNING YIELD) and calculations allowing for capital gains over some specified life: the full maturity of the bond, or some shorter period such as the first call or put date. *See* GROSS REDEMPTION YIELD; NET REDEMPTION YIELD; YIELD TO ADJUSTED MINIMUM MATURITY; YIELD TO AVERAGE LIFE; YIELD TO CALL; YIELD TO MATURITY; YIELD TO PUT. Further refinements include adjustments for taxation (CORPORATE TAX EQUIVALENT, NET REDEMPTION YIELD) or for reinvestment income (REALIZED COMPOUND YIELD TO MATURITY; TOTAL RETURN). Finally, it should be noted that Japanese yield calculations differ from those generally used elsewhere. Compare also CORPORATE BOND EQUIVALENT; MINIMUM YIELD; YIELD CURVE; YIELD MARGIN; YIELD PRICING.
YIELD PRICING.

yield auction. *See* AUCTION.

yield curve. A diagram showing the relationship between yields and maturities on a set of comparable securities (or deposits). A normal ('positively-sloping') yield curve rises to the right (i.e. longer maturities are associated with higher interest rates). A reverse yield curve ('negatively-sloping') slopes down to the right: this would indicate that longer-term interest rates are below short-term rates (i.e. rates are expected to fall). A flat, or horizontal, curve indicates that investors are indifferent whether they invest short or long. Rates are probably expected to fall slightly, offsetting the normal requirement for a slightly higher yield on longer maturities because of the greater risk in investing long-term. A 'humped' yield curve may occasionally be seen usually indicates that at some interim maturity special strains are foreseen (e.g. an expected tax payment date).

Bibliography: Yield curves for gilt-edged stocks: An improved model. *Bank of England Quarterly Bulletin*, June 1982.
M.L. Leibowitz. Analysis of Yield Curves *in* F.J. Fabozzi & I.M. Pollack (eds). *The Handbook of Fixed Income Securities*. Dow-Jones Irwin, Homewood, Ill., 1983.

yield gap.   UK term for the difference between the average yield on stocks making up the Financial Times Industrial Ordinary share index, and that on 2 Consols. In general between ordinary shares and fixed interest securities. Compare REVERSE YIELD GAP.

Bibliography: D. O'Shea. *Investing for Beginners* Financial Times Business Information, London 1984.

yield maintenance.   US term referring to the adjustment upon delivery of the price of a GNMA or other mortgage security bought under a futures contract or STANDBY COMMITMENT, to provide the same yield to the buyer that was specified in the original agreement. Yield maintenance becomes necessary when the coupon on the GINNIE MAE that is delivered is different from the coupon that had been expected at the time the agreement was made.

yield margin.   Term used in, amongst others, the BULLDOG BOND market. In that market, the main method of pricing an issue is by setting a yield margin over some INDICATOR in the gilt-edged market.

Bibliography: de Zoete & Bevan. *The Bulldog Market*. London, 1983.

yield margin tender.   A technique which has been used in the BULLDOG BOND market. Issues for Finland and Sweden were on the basis of a tender on the yield margin to be added to the INDICATOR yield. An underwritten margin of 0.75% was set and investors were asked to tender at this yield or lower.

Bibliography: de Zoete & Bevan. *The Bulldog Market*. London, 1983.

yield pricing.   A technique whereby a new BOND is issued on a yield basis in line with current SECONDARY MARKET yields. Unlike the normal EUROBOND technique whereby the COUPON is generally indicated in advance, leaving the ISSUE PRICE as the only variable to be fixed at the time of issue, yield pricing allows greater flexibility since both coupon and price can be adjusted.

Bibliography: F.G. Fisher. *International Bonds*. Euromoney Publications, London, 1981.

yield to adjusted minimum maturity.   US term for a measure designed to give the yield to the shortest possible life of a bond. It is based on the assumption of maximum sinking fund operation and a call on the bond as early as possible.

Bibliography: S. Homer & M.L. Liebowitz. *Inside the Yield Book*. Prentice-Hall, NJ, 1972.

yield to average life.   The yield derived when the average maturity of the bond is substituted for the final maturity date of the issue.

yield to call.   When a BOND is redeemable prior to MATURITY at the issuer's option, the cash flow implicit in the yield-to-maturity figure is subject to possible alteration. The 'yield to call' is therefore calculated on the assumption that the bond is called on the first permissible date, and redemed at the price laid down in the indenture for the first call date. Compare MINIMUM YIELD.

Bibliography: S. Homer & M.L. Liebowitz. *Inside the Yield Book*. Prentice-Hall, NJ, 1972.

yield to crash. *See* YIELD TO ADJUSTED MINIMUM MATURITY.

yield to maturity. Originally US term for the return a bond earns on the price at which it was bought if it is held to MATURITY, assuming that COUPON payments are reinvested at the yield to maturity. The exact formula is given under REDEMPTION YIELD, the UK term.

Bibliography: M. Stigum *Money Market Calculation.* Dow-Jones Irwin, Homewood, Ill., 1982.
F.J. Fabozzi & I.M. Pollack (eds). *The Handbook of Fixed Income Securities,* Dow-Jones Irwin, Homewood, Ill., 1983.

yield to put. US term for the return a bond earns assuming that it is held until a certain date and put (sold) to the issuing company at a specific price (the put price).

yield to worst. *See* YIELD TO ADJUSTED MINIMUM MATURITY.

York-Antwerp Rules. Laid down in 1890, and most recently revised in 1974, these marine insurance rules define GENERAL AVERAGE the basis on which general average expenses are borne and what losses are included.

Bibliography: *Lloyd's Calendar.* Lloyd's of London Press, London, annually.
R.J. Lambeth. *Templeman on Marine Insurance .* Macdonald & Evans, UK, 1981.

Z

Z Certificate. Certificate issued by the Bank of England to DISCOUNT HOUSES in lieu of stock certificates to facilitate their dealings in short-dated GILT-EDGED securities.
Bibliography: *This is Bill-Broking*. Allen, Harvey & Ross, London, 1975.

ZEBRA. Acronym for ZERO COUPON EUROSTERLING BEARER or REGISTERED accruing securities. This is the UK equivalent of the US CATS and TIGERS, i.e. a GILT-EDGED BOND from which the coupons are STRIPPED.

zero coupon. A BOND issued on the basis that it pays no interest–its COUPON is zero. Such bonds were introduced on the US market in 1981 and were initially popular because of a tax advantage. They are now only attractive to those (such as pension funds) that are not taxed on interest income, since otherwise the investor must pay tax on imputed interest which he will not receive until the maturity of the bond. On the other hand, the tax-free investor benefits from the key advantage of the zero coupon, namely, total freedom from reinvestment risk on coupon payments. From a theoretical point of view zero coupon bonds have a number of interesting features: in particular, for any given maturity, zero coupon bonds have more volatility than any other bond. Compare COUPON STRIPPING.
Bibliography: S. Homer & M.L. Leibowitz. *Inside the Yield Book*. Prentice Hall, New Jersey, 1972.
F.J. Fabozzi & H.C. Sauvain. Corporate Bonds *in* F.J. Fabozzi & I.M. Pollack. *The Handbook of Fixed Income Securities*. Dow-Jones Irwin, Homewood, Ill., 1983.
T.E. Klaffky & R. W. Kopprasch. *Understanding the Volatility of CATS and Other Zero-Coupon Bonds*. Salomon Brothers, New York, 1983.